THE
BOND
BOOK

THE BOND BOOK

Everything Investors Need to Know
about Treasuries, Municipals, GNMAs,
Corporates, Zeros, Bond Funds,
Money Market Funds, and More

Third Edition

Annette Thau

New York   Chicago   San Francisco   Lisbon   London
Madrid   Mexico City   Milan   New Delhi   San Juan
Seoul   Singapore   Sydney   Toronto

This publication is designed to provide accurate and authoritative information in regard to the subject matter covered. It is sold with the understanding that neither the author nor the publisher is engaged in rendering legal, accounting, securities trading, or other professional service. If legal advice or other expert assistance is required, the services of a competent professional person should be sought.

—*From a Declaration of Principles Jointly Adopted by a Committee of the American Bar Association and a Committee of Publishers*

Exhibits 7.3, 7.4, 8.4, 8.5, and 10.2: The bond content is presented by BondDesk Group LLC. © Copyright 2010 Moody's Investors Service. Copyright © 2010 Standard & Poor's Financial Services LLC, a subsidiary of The McGraw-Hill Companies, Inc. All rights reserved.

McGraw-Hill books are available at special quantity discounts to use as premiums and sales promotions, or for use in corporate training programs. To contact a representative, please e-mail us at bulksales@mcgraw-hill.com.

This book is printed on acid-free paper.

TO FRED

CONTENTS

Chapter 4

How Much Will I Earn, or Basic Bond Math 51

Chapter 5

What You Need to Know before Buying Bonds 73

PART TWO INDIVIDUAL SECURITIES 97

Chapter 6

Treasuries, Savings Bonds, and Federal Agency Paper 99

Chapter 7

Municipal Bonds 129

Chapter 8

Corporate Bonds   173

Chapter 9

Mortgage-Backed Securities   205

Chapter 10

International Bonds   243

PART THREE INVESTING THROUGH FUNDS   263

Chapter 11

Bond Mutual Funds: An Overview   265

Chapter 12

Money Market Funds and Tax-Exempt Bond Funds   301

Chapter 13

Taxable Bond Funds   327

PREFACE

This is the third edition of a book that was initially published in December of 1991. After working for a number of years as a credit analyst, I had started personally investing in bonds. At the time, I looked for a book that would explain in clear English some of the basic concepts used by professionals to manage bond portfolios; and that would contain detailed information about the various types of bond investments available to individual investors. None of the books I found fit that description. Most books that dealt seriously with bonds were not comprehensible to anyone who was not a finance professional. Years later, I decided to write the kind of book I would have liked to have read. Evidently, it would fill a need. Little did I imagine when the first edition was published that I would be revising this book again, for the third time, almost 20 years later.

Over the past 20 years, both the bond market and the stock market have had dramatic ups and downs. Investor psychology toward the bond market has also had its ups and downs. For example, the second edition of this book was written around the year 2000. In retrospect, that was almost the last year of the great bull market in stocks that had started in 1982. At that time, pundits were proclaiming that we were in a "new era." "Experts" were recommending that individuals invest 100% of their portfolios in equities (or perhaps keep a small percentage, say 10%, in cash), and nothing at all in bonds. The decade between 2000 and 2010 proved the "experts" wrong. Between 2000 and 2010, the stock market suffered two devastating bear markets: in 2002 and in 2008. Even though many sectors of the bond market suffered significant declines during the financial panic of 2008, for that decade, investments in many sectors of the bond market had positive returns and enabled investors to ride out a lost decade in the stock market.

Investor psychology seems to have changed once more: for the past year, more money has been flowing into bond funds than into stock funds. But if these flows reflect the search for a safe harbor, then some investors may be in for an unpleasant surprise. Investors need to be aware that all sectors of the bond market are not equally safe and predictable. Many bonds and bond funds are as volatile and unpredictable as stock funds, posting equity like returns one year, and dismal losses the next. Indeed, some steep losses have occurred in bond funds that had been initially marketed as very low risk investments.

This book, like prior editions, is intended to be a complete introduction to the bond market and to the different types of investments in bonds: individual bonds, as well as different types of bond funds.

There is virtually no section of this book that has not been heavily or totally rewritten. My emphasis has been on changes that have occurred since the 2000 edition. One of the more important changes is that investors can now access a great deal of information, such as pricing data, that in the past was available only through brokers. That information is available on the Internet, and it is free. In addition, all chapters on individual securities include new information. The chapters on bond funds have been totally rewritten. They include a detailed analysis of the performance of all types of bond funds, during and since the financial panic of 2008, as well as ten-year returns through December 2009. There is also a new section on bond exchange-traded funds (ETFs) as well as an expanded section on closed-end bond funds.

This book is divided into four parts. The first part is introductory, and it is basic to understanding everything that follows. It explains the fundamentals of bond investing, including the basic vocabulary of bond investments; how bonds are brought to market and sold; bond pricing and markups; how to research the price history of bonds; why the price of bonds (and bond funds) goes up and down; key concepts used to measure bond returns; and much more. That part of the book should be read first, in entirety.

The second part of the book discusses individual securities: Treasuries, munici¬pal bonds, corporate bonds, GNMAs and other mortgage-backed securities, and international bonds. One chapter is devoted to each security. The third part of the book analyzes the major types of bond funds: open end mutual funds; as well as closed-end bond funds and the newest kids on the block, ETFs. The fourth part of the book deals in a more general way with the management of bond portfolios. Parts 2, 3, and 4 may be read in any order desired.

While much of the material in the book is new, my initial orientation remains the same. This book assumes little or no knowledge of any bond investment, but it explains the critical information required to buy any security, be it a Treasury bond, a municipal bond, or a bond fund.

Several basic themes run through the book. First, I explain in detail the risks that underlie the purchase of any security. The main reason for this is that it is patently silly to lose money because you are buying a security thought to be riskless only because the risk factors are unknown. After you read this book, this will no longer happen. Equally important, while it is not possible to forecast where interest rates are going, if you understand the risks of specific bond investments, then you can control the amount of risk you take. If you want to be sure that you are investing in the safest corners of the bond market, then this book will clearly explain what those are. If you want to speculate in the riskier corners of the bond market, this book will point what those are.

Second, this book will define areas of opportunity. Just as you can lose money because you don't realize that an investment is risky, you can also earn less because you are restricting yourself unnecessarily. There may be areas of opportunity that you just don't know are out there.

Third, at minimum, any investor needs to understand enough technical information to be able to discriminate between sound analysis and hot air. You will learn a lot of technical terms and concepts so that, in the future, no one can intimidate you. If you sound like an informed investor, the next time you talk to a bond salesman, he will be much more likely to be honest with you and less likely to try to sell you a bill of goods.

Fourth, another theme is how to obtain information. Many chapters contain sample tables and graphs along with explanations on how to interpret them. The most useful information is now found on the Internet. References for additional research are listed at the end of many chapters. If you wish to pursue any topic in greater depth, you will know where to look.

I kept in mind that investors differ both in the amount of time they have to devote to investing and the amount of personal interest. Throughout the book, I have pointed out techniques that minimize risk for safety-minded investors who have limited time to devote to investing.

Above all, this book is intended to be practical and to answer fundamental questions such as: Should I invest in individual bonds or in bond funds? How do open-end funds differ from closed-end funds, or from ETFs? Should I invest in taxable or in tax-exempt bonds? If I am right about a particular investment in bonds, how much can I earn? And if things go wrong, how much can I lose? For all types of bond investments, it will address what is perhaps the most fundamental question in the bond market: What risks am I taking in order to earn a higher yield? Ultimately, this book should enable you to select fixed-income investments that match your tolerance for risk and your overall investment goals and strategies.

Some vocabulary notes are in order. First, a word about the term "bond": the term designates any debt instrument or fixed-income security available on the market. No single term exists to cover this type of instrument. For the sake of variety, the terms bond, fixed-income security, or debt instrument are used interchangeably throughout the book. Second, it was necessary to decide how to deal with gender to refer to men and women as investors, or as salespeople. I considered using "he/she" but rejected it as too clumsy. Instead, I decided to use either "he" or "she" in random fashion. This should introduce some variety in the text.

Finally, I have no ax to grind. This is not a book for bonds or against bonds. Bond investments are more complex and less predictable than is generally realized. This book will explain how and why. You may, after reading it, decide to allocate more of your portfolio, or less, to bonds. My objective in writing this book is to enable you to navigate the bond market—whatever its future shape turns out to be—in a more informed manner.

So, many happy returns!

ACKNOWLEDGMENTS

I have been fortunate when writing each edition of this book to be able to benefit from the many insights, suggestions, and knowledge of many people within the industry who were kind enough to take time out from busy working lives in order to help me put this book together. Once again, I would like to acknowledge and thank those individuals whose help made this book possible.

I would like to thank, first of all, those individuals who read portions of the manuscript and who made valuable suggestions for changes. They include Maria Crawford Scott, former editor of the AAII Journal; Cecilia Gondor, Executive V.P., Thomas Herzfeld Advisors; Matt Tucker, Managing Director in BlackRock's Fixed Income Portfolio Management Group; and Chris Shayne, CFA, Manager of Marketing Communications, BondDesk Group, LLC.

I would also like to acknowledge and thank the many individuals who not only provided data but who spent time answering innumerable questions and discussing fine points of certain securities. They include Cecilia Gondor, Executive V.P., Thomas Herzfeld Advisors; Chris Shayne, CFA, Manager of Marketing Communications, BondDesk Group, LLC; Dominic Maister, Executive Director at Morgan Stanley; Christine Pollak, Vice President, Morgan Stanley; Professor Edward Altman, Professor, New York University Salomon Center; Christine Hudacko, Director, BlackRock Corporate Communications; Kathryn Edmundson, Team Leader, Investinginbonds.com; and Justin Pica, Director, Uniform Practices Group, at EMMA.msrb.org.

I would like to single out for particular thanks Jeff Ttornejoh, Research Manager for the United States and Canada of the Lipper organization (now Thomson Reuters) not only for generously supplying data on bond funds but also for being particularly unstinting with his time both for this book and for prior writing projects.

Finally, there are a number of individuals whose help I cannot acknowledge due to policies of the firms that employ them. They know who they are, and that their help was greatly appreciated; and they also know that I regret I cannot thank them by name.

To one and all who made this book possible: Thank you! The opinions expressed in this book are my own. Any omissions or errors are, of course, entirely my own responsibility.

PART ONE

The Basic Basics

This part of the book is introductory and basic to understanding all that follows. Its purpose is to explain the fundamentals of bond investing. The idea behind these introductory chapters is to familiarize you, the reader, with concepts that will enable you to understand potential returns of different types of investments in the bond market, as well as the risks you are taking with those investments.

- Chapter 1 defines bonds and explains how they are originated and sold.
- Chapter 2 is an overview of the bond market. It also introduces key terms used in discussing bonds and the bond market.
- Chapter 3 is at the heart of the book. It explains why bond prices go up and down through a detailed discussion of the two major risks in the bond market: namely, interest rate risk and credit risk. It also includes a brief history of interest rates as well as a brief discussion of the role of the Federal Reserve in determining interest rates.
- Chapter 4 is an introduction to basic bond mathematics. It defines the key concepts used to measure return (that is, what you will actually earn) from investments in bonds, as well as bond cash flows. The chapter also introduces duration, which can help you evaluate the riskiness of investments in bonds.
- Chapter 5 discusses topics and data commonly used in the press and on the Internet to analyze what is happening in the bond market. It also introduces three Web sites which have been developed by several regulatory and trade agencies: FINRA.org/marketdata, Investinginbonds.com, and

EMMA.msrb.org. These Web sites make information available to investors that in the past was available only to brokers, including, for example, trade data about bonds within 15 minutes of a trade. Finally, Chapter 5 introduces some guidelines to shopping for individual bonds.

CHAPTER 1

The Life of a Bond

This chapter

- ◆ Defines a bond
- ◆ Explains how bonds are issued and traded
- ◆ Defines some key terms used in buying and selling bonds

FIRST, WHAT IS A BOND?

Basically, a bond is a loan or an IOU. When you buy a bond, you lend your money to a large borrower such as a corporation or a governmental body. These borrowers routinely raise needed capital by selling (or, using Wall Street vocabulary, by "issuing") bonds for periods as brief as a few days to as long as 30 or 40 years. The distinguishing characteristic of a bond is that the borrower (the issuer) enters into a legal agreement to compensate the lender (you, the bondholder) through periodic interest payments in the form of coupons; and to repay the original sum (the principal) in full on a stipulated date, which is known as the bond's "maturity date."

HOW BONDS ARE ISSUED AND TRADED

The process of issuing bonds is complex. Because the sums involved are so large, issuers do not sell bonds directly to the public. Instead, bonds are brought to market by an investment bank (the underwriter). The investment bank acts as an intermediary between the issuer and the investing public. Lawyers are hired by both parties (that is, the issuer and the underwriter) to draw up the formal terms of the sale and to see to it that the sale conforms to the regulations of the Securities and Exchange Commission (the SEC).

To illustrate the process, let us say that the State of New Jersey needs to borrow $500 million in order to finance a major project. New Jersey announces its intention through trade journals and asks for bids. Underwriters (major broker-dealer firms such as Merrill Lynch, Goldman Sachs, Morgan Stanley, etc.) or smaller, less well-known firms (there are dozens of them) compete with each other by submitting bids to New Jersey. A firm may bid for the business by itself in its own name. More often, firms form a group called a syndicate, which submits a joint bid. The State awards the sale to the firm or syndicate which submits the bid which results in the lowest interest cost to the state. The underwriters then get busy selling the bonds.

The underwriter (or the syndicate) handles all aspects of the bond sale, in effect buying the bonds from the issuer (New Jersey) and selling them to the investing public. The investing public is made up of large institutions such as banks, pension funds, and insurance companies as well as individual investors and bond funds. The large institutional investors are by far the biggest players in the bond market.

Once the bonds have been sold, the underwriter retains no connection to the bonds. Payment of interest and redemption (repayment) of principal are—and will remain—the responsibility of the issuer (New Jersey). After the sale, the actual physical payment of interest, record-keeping chores, and so forth are handled for the issuer by still another party, a fiduciary agent, which is generally a bank that acts as the trustee for the bonds.

KEY TERMS FOR BONDS

The exact terms of the loan agreement between the issuer (the State of New Jersey) and anyone who buys the bonds (you or an institution) are described fully in a legal document known as the *indenture,* which is legally binding on the issuer for the entire period that the bond remains outstanding.

First, the indenture stipulates the dates when coupons are paid, as well as the date for repayment of the principal in full; that is, the bond's maturity date.

The indenture then discusses a great many other matters of importance to the bondholder. It describes how the issuer intends to cover debt payments; that is, where the money to pay debt service will come from. In our example concerning the State of New Jersey, the indenture would specify that the State intends to raise the monies through taxes; and in order to further document its ability to service the loan, there would be a discussion of the State's economy. The indenture also describes a set of conditions that would enable either the issuer or the bondholder to redeem bonds at full value before their stipulated maturity date. These topics are discussed in greater detail in the sections dealing with "call" features and credit quality.

All of the major terms of the indenture, including the payment dates for coupons, the bond's maturity date, call provisions, sources of revenue backing the bonds, and so on, are summarized in a document called a *prospectus*. It is a good idea to read the prospectus. Until recently, a prospectus was available only for new issues. Bond dealers were allowed to destroy a prospectus six months after a bond was issued. The prospectus of all new municipal bonds, as well as many older issues, is now archived and available online (see Chapter 5).

When the prospectus is printed before the sale, it is known as a "preliminary prospectus," or a "red herring"—that term derives from the printing of certain legal terms on the cover of the prospectus in red ink. After the sale, it is sometimes called an *official statement*, or OS.

The most elementary distinction between bonds is based on who issued the bonds. Bonds issued directly by the U.S. government are classified as *Treasury* bonds; those issued by corporations are known as *corporate* bonds; and those issued by local and state governmental units, which are generally exempt from federal taxes, are called *municipals* or "munis" for short. The actual process of selling the bonds differs somewhat from sale to sale but generally conforms to the same process.

Many bonds are issued in very large amounts, typically between $100 million and $500 million for corporates and munis; and many billions for Treasuries. To sell the bonds to the public, the investment bank divides them into smaller batches. By custom, the smallest bond unit is one bond, which can be redeemed at maturity for $1,000. The terms *par* and *principal value* both refer to the $1,000 value of the bond at maturity. In practice, however, bonds are traded in larger batches, usually in minimum amounts of $5,000 (par value).

Anyone interested in the New Jersey bonds may buy them during the few days when the underwriter initially sells the bonds to the investing public (this is known as buying "at issue") or subsequently from an investor who has decided to sell. Bonds purchased at the time of issue are said to have been purchased in the "primary market." Bonds may be held to maturity, or resold anytime between the original issue date and the maturity date. Typically, a bondholder who wishes to sell his bonds will use the services of a broker, who pockets a fee for this service.

There is a market in older issues, called the "secondary market." Some bonds (for example, 30-year Treasuries) enjoy a very active market. For many bonds, however, the market becomes moribund and inactive once the bonds have "gone away" (that is an expression used by traders) to investors. It is almost always possible to sell an older bond; but if the bond is not actively traded, then commission costs for selling may be very high. Pricing, buying, and selling bonds, as well as bond returns, are discussed in greater detail in Chapters 2 and 4.

During the time that they trade in the secondary market, bond prices go up and down continually. Bonds seldom, if ever, trade at par. In fact, bonds are likely to be priced at par only twice during their life: first, when they are brought to market (at issue), and second, when they are redeemed, at maturity. But, and this is an important but, regardless of the purchase price for the bonds, they are always redeemed at par.

But, you may well ask, if the issue price of a bond is almost always $1,000, and the maturity value is always $1,000, why and how do bond prices change? That is where the story gets interesting, so read on.

CHAPTER 2

The Bond Market:
An Overview

This chapter discusses

- ◆ The bond market: an overview
- ◆ Bond pricing: markups and commissions
- ◆ How bonds are sold: dealers, brokers, and electronic platforms
- ◆ Terms used in buying, selling, and discussing bonds

THE BOND MARKET: AN OVERVIEW

While people speak of the bond market as if it were one market, in reality there is not one central place or exchange where bonds are bought and sold. In fact, unlike stocks, bonds do not trade on an exchange. Consequently, there is also no equivalent to a running tape, where prices are posted as soon as trades occur. Rather, the bond market is a gigantic over-the-counter market, consisting of networks of independent dealers, organized by type of security, with some overlaps.

The core of this market consists of several dozen extremely large bond dealers who sell only to institutional buyers such as banks, pension funds, or other large bond dealers. Among these dealers, there is a network of "primary dealers." These are the elite dealers: They buy Treasuries directly from the Federal Reserve in order to then sell them to the largest banks and to large broker-dealer firms. The broker-dealer firms, in turn, resell bonds to smaller institutional investors and to the investing public. Whereas stocks sell ultimately on one of three independent exchanges (the New York Stock Exchange, the American Stock Exchange, or the Nasdaq), many bonds continue to be sold dealer to dealer. Surprising as it may seem, many bond trades, even those involving sums in the millions, are still concluded by phone, person to person. (One exception to this is a small—and dwindling—number of corporate bonds, which are listed and sold on the New York Stock Exchange.)

This market is so vast that its size is difficult to imagine. Although the financial media report mainly on the stock market, the bond market is actually several times larger (estimates of its actual size vary). Overwhelmingly, this is an institutional market. It raises debt capital for the largest issuers of debt, such as the U.S. government, state and local governments, and the largest corporations. The buyers of that debt are primarily large institutional investors such as pension funds, insurance companies, banks, corporations, and, increasingly, mutual funds. These buyers and sellers routinely trade sums that appear almost unreal to an individual investor. U.S. government bonds trade in blocks of $1 million, and $100 million trades are routine. The smallest blocks are traded in the municipal market, where a round lot is $100,000. Another way of characterizing this market is to call it a wholesale market.

Enter the individual investor. In the bond market, individual investors, even those with considerable wealth, are all little guys, who are trying to navigate a market dominated by far larger traders. Indeed, many of the fixed-income securities created over the last two decades were structured to suit the needs of pension funds and insurance companies. Their structure makes them unsuitable to meet the needs of individual investors.

In the bond market, the individual investor faces many disadvantages when compared to institutions. Commission costs are higher. In addition, institutions have developed a vast amount of information concerning bonds, as well as mathematical models and sophisticated trading strategies for buying and selling bonds, which are simply not available to individual investors.

BOND PRICING: MARKUPS AND COMMISSIONS

Buying bonds differs in many respects from buying stocks. One of the main differences concerns the cost of actually buying and selling bonds, in other words, markups and commissions.

"Bid," "Ask," and "Spread"

Markups and commission costs for buying or selling bonds are hidden much of the time. The price is quoted net.

In the bond market, among traders, bond prices are quoted in pairs: the "bid" and the "ask," also known as the "offer." The difference between the "bid" and the "ask" is known as the "spread." The spread is a markup: it is the difference between what a dealer pays to buy a bond, and the price at which he wants to sell it. (Let us note, in passing, that the term "spread" is used a lot in the bond market. We will encounter many other meanings of the same word.)

Technically, the bid is what you sell for; the ask, the price at which you buy. It is not difficult to remember which is the "bid" and which is the "ask." Just remember this: If you want to buy, you always pay the *higher* price. If you want to sell, you receive the *lower*. For example, a bond may be quoted at "98 bid/100 ask." If you are buying the bond, you will pay 100; if you are selling, you will receive 98.

When you are quoted a price for a bond, however, the spread is hidden. The price of the bond is quoted net. The markup is not broken out. That has been the case since time began and, perhaps surprisingly, much of the time, it continues to be the case.

Spreads vary widely. One of the chief factors in determining the spread is the demand for a particular bond, that is, how easy it is to sell. If you are selling an inactively traded bond (and that description applies to many bonds), then the broker makes sure that she buys it from you cheaply enough so that she will not lose money when she resells.

For an individual investor, the spread typically ranges from 1/4 of 1% (or even less) for actively traded Treasury issues to as much as 4% on inactively traded bonds. The spread varies for many reasons

- The price the dealer pays and his customary markup
- The type of bond being sold (Treasury, muni, mortgage-backed, or corporate)
- The number of bonds being traded (that is, the size of the lot)
- The bond's maturity
- Its credit quality
- The overall direction of interest rates
- Demand for a specific bond
- Demand for a particular bond sector

As a rule, bonds that are desirable or low risk, or higher quality, sell at narrower (that is, lower) spreads. Bonds that are perceived as being riskier, or lower quality, sell at wider spreads. Typically, the wider the spread, the higher the yield. But one important rule to remember is that, in the world of bonds, higher yield means higher risk.

The size of the spread reflects what is known as a bond's *liquidity*; that is, the ease and cost of trading a particular bond. A narrow spread indicates high demand and low risk. Conversely, a wide spread indicates an unwillingness on the part of a dealer to own a bond without a substantial price cushion. Any characteristic that makes a bond less desirable, such as lower credit quality, or longer maturity, increases the size of the spread.

Spreads and liquidity vary widely. They vary first of all, based on the sector of the bond market in which bonds trade. Treasuries are considered the most "liquid" of all bonds. Consequently, they sell at the narrowest spreads. For any maturity, Treasury yields are lower than those of any other bonds. Municipals and corporates are considered far less liquid. They sell at much wider spreads than Treasuries. Consequently, for any maturity, they have higher yields than Treasuries. Note that liquidity also varies within each sector, again based on credit quality and maturity length.

Let's illustrate with some concrete examples. Treasury bonds sell at the narrowest spreads (as low as between $1/4$% and $1/2$% for Treasuries with short maturities) no matter how many bonds, or the direction of interest rates. High-quality intermediate munis (AA or AAA, maturing between three and seven years) sell at spreads of between 1% to perhaps 2%. Thirty-year munis sell at spreads of between 2% and 4%. The more strikes against a bond, the more difficult it is to sell. Trying to sell a long maturity, low credit quality bond in a weak market is a worst-case scenario because you may have to shop extensively just to get a bid. Similarly, an unusually wide spread (4% or more) constitutes a red flag. It warns you that at best, a particular bond may be expensive to resell and, at worst, headed for difficult times. The dealer community, which earns its living buying and selling bonds, has a very active information and rumor network that is sometimes quicker to spot potential trouble than the credit rating agencies.

Spreads and liquidity also vary over time. In strong markets, spreads tend to narrow; in weak markets, they widen. During the financial panic of 2008, spreads widened so far beyond the norm that many bonds could not be sold at any price. In fact, for a short period of time, only bonds with the highest credit quality found buyers, and those found bids only at fire sale prices.

Note, in passing, that when you buy a bond at issue, even though the spread is built into the deal, the spread is usually closer to what a dealer would pay for the bond, at that point in time, than when bonds trade in the secondary market. Hence, the individual investor may receive a fairer shake by buying at issue than by buying in the secondary market.

HOW BONDS ARE SOLD: DEALERS, BROKERS, AND ELECTRONIC PLATFORMS

Dealers and Brokers

The process of actually identifying, selecting, and buying bonds is also very different from that of buying stocks. To begin with, when you buy a stock, you have probably identified a specific stock that you want to buy, say Apple. You can then look up the ticker symbol and the most recent price at which Apple stock sold; it is displayed on a "tape" in real time. If you decide to buy the stock, whether you purchase it from a full-service broker, a discount broker, or online, whether you are buying 10 shares or 1,000 shares, the price per share will be the market price.

When you buy bonds, on the other hand, chances are that you will not be shopping for a specific bond. Rather, you will put together a bunch of criteria; and then shop for a bond that satisfies those criteria. Suppose, for example, that you decide to invest in tax exempt municipal bonds. Your criteria may include: the state in which the bond was issued (to avoid state taxes); the approximate maturity of the bond; the bond's credit rating; a target yield and perhaps, whether or not the bond is callable. But chances are that at the outset, you do not have a specific bond in mind. Instead, you will search a variety of sources to find bonds that satisfy the criteria you have established.

It is now possible to buy bonds from many of the same sources as stocks including full service brokers, discount brokers, and financial advisers. And in fact, it is now possible to buy and sell many types of bonds completely online, without having to call a broker to complete the trade. But similarities with buying stocks end there.

When you are shopping for bonds, you will find that the availability of bonds varies widely from dealer to dealer, particularly in the less liquid sectors of the market such as corporates and municipals. You cannot just assume that any firm you approach will have or can get specific bonds. In fact, there may be times when you cannot find bonds that match your criteria. Moreover, if you approach a number of firms in all likelihood, you will be offered not only different bonds, but also bonds differing in price, in maturity, in coupons, and in yields, all nonetheless apparently matching your criteria.

One reason for this state of affairs is the structure of what, for want of a better term, I will call the "dealer community." Although often the terms "dealer" and "broker" are used virtually interchangeably, in the bond market, the word "dealer" has a very specific meaning. A dealer is someone who puts his own money at risk to buy and sell bonds. This is also known as "taking a position" in certain bonds, or being a "principal." Maintaining an inventory is risky. The dealer does not know how long he will have to hold the bond before finding a buyer; and the future price of the bond is uncertain. As we will see in Chapter 3, bond prices go up and down. Among dealers, the "bid/ask" spread, or markup, is viewed in part as compensation for the risks taken to buy and maintain an inventory. Dealers mark up their bonds indepently: the same bond may be sold by different dealers at different prices.

A "broker," on the other hand, is someone who executes a trade (whether a buy or a sell) for a customer, and in doing so, earns a commission. The broker is not required to own the bond that is being traded. And many brokers do not own the bonds they sell. Both discount brokers and financial advisers rely primarily on "electronic platforms" to sell bonds. (Platforms are discussed at greater length in the section entitled "electronic platforms," later in the chapter). The broker, in legal terms, merely acts as an *agent* for the customer. In other words, unlike a dealer, a broker does not put principal at risk.

This is not merely an academic distinction. Rather, it is one of the reasons that differences exist in the availability and pricing of bonds. Firms that sell bonds vary enormously. Dealer firms, whether large or small, maintain inventories of bonds. But many firms that sell bonds (for example, discount brokers and financial advisers) do not maintain inventories. If you buy a bond from a discount broker, or from a financial adviser, that firm has to locate the bond in order to sell it to you. Increasingly, this is done through the use of "electronic platforms."

Electronic Platforms

"Electronic platforms" (also called "e platforms") have been a growing presence in the bond market over the past decade. You may not be aware of their existence. But if you have searched for bonds online, or if you have purchased any fixed income security online, then you have been doing so through an "electronic platform."

How Electronic Platforms Work

Electronic platforms are businesses that supply data: they gather lists of bonds that dealers want to sell, and transmit that information to brokerage firms. In the dark ages prior to computers, that function was performed by inter-dealer brokers, who would call hundreds of firms daily to find out what bonds they owned, and wanted to sell. They would then compile and fax master lists that would be circulated among dealers and brokers. In effect, these lists became central databases. With the advent of computers, and the development of software, these master lists became searchable databases. The next step was to make them available to online brokers. When you are searching for bonds on the Web site of an online broker, most often, what you are searching is the database supplied by an electronic platform.

At their inception, electronic platforms enabled investors only to search for bonds online. But with very few exceptions, online brokers required investors who wanted to purchase a bond to place the order with a broker. This is no longer the case. Many online brokers now allow investors to complete the purchase entirely online. What investors may not realize is that when they complete the purchase entirely online, they are in effect trading entirely through the electronic platform. Unless you actually consult a broker prior to completing a trade, the online firm whose Web site you are consulting is acting almost entirely as an intermediary. And since that firm does not buy or otherwise hold the bonds in inventory, that brokerage firm is essentially engaged in a riskless transaction.

At its most basic level, an electronic platform can be described as an electronic bulletin board where hundreds of sellers (dealers, banks, pension funds, etc.) list bonds for sale and the price at which they are offering them. But electronic platforms supply a great deal of additional information and software. That includes disclosure information, analytic details about specific bonds, yield and price information; as well as sophisticated software that enables investors to conduct targeted searches for bonds meeting specific criteria.

Electronic platforms list fixed income securities from virtually every corner of the bond market: Treasuries, Agencies, corporate bonds, municipal bonds, CDs, and more. The listings of many of the major online discount brokers such as E Trade, Schwab, or Fidelity consist primarily or perhaps almost entirely of feeds from one or more electronic platforms. But dealer firms also may augment their own inventories with feeds from one or more electronic platform.

The mechanics of these listings are not obvious. First, the listed dealer price includes at least one, and sometimes several markups. That is because that price is marked up based on the instructions of the listing dealer. It is also marked up based on the instructions of the listing broker. Both dealer and broker markups vary. What this means is that you may see the same bond listed by one broker Web site at a price of 100; on another at 102; and on still another at 103. And oh yes, of course, the platform also gets a cut (I am told a small cut).

One reason you may not be aware that you are consulting an electronic platform is that all online brokers have distinctive formats. In addition, many firms apply proprietary screens to "filter" the offerings of electronic platforms. As a result, different brokers, even those using the same electronic platforms, may wind up with totally different lists of bonds. Some firms filter out bonds whose price is deemed to be too high: for example, 3% above the most recent inter-dealer price. But some brokers exclude the bonds of certain dealers just because they don't like those dealers, or for other idiosyncratic reasons. In any case, these screens are one of the reasons availability of bonds differs so widely from broker to broker.

Buying bonds online is relatively straightforward. You see a bond you like, click on the bond, and a ticket is created. But note that electronic platforms are dynamic: the price can change throughout the day, as the market moves. Some online Web sites acknowledge this with a disclaimer that "Prices, yields and availability are subject to change with the market."

When you submit a bid for a bond, a "ticket" is created. If the price has changed compared to the original posting, you are not obligated to go through with the purchase. You are only obligated if you click on "submit". A small percentage of buy orders (perhaps about 5%) are "fails": Occasionally, brokers may decide not to fill the order as submitted. Most dealers, however, are committed to filling an order, once a customer clicks on "submit." Note also that some listings, particularly those for corporate bonds include both a "bid" and an "ask" price. That indicates the listing dealer is willing to pay an investor selling the bond the price listed as the "bid ". When no bid is listed, an investor wishing to sell a bond can fill out a "bids wanted" request: dealers can then submit "bids" for the bond which will be transmitted to the brokerage site you are consulting.

Between 2000 and 2002, electronic platforms generated a great deal of enthusiasm. Dozens of firms entered the business, but few of these survived. At the moment, there are four dominant electronic platforms which service brokers and individual investors. The four are (in no particular order): Bond Desk, MuniCenter, Knight Bond Point, and Trade Web. Each is attempting to develop a unique niche in order to compete with the other three. No doubt, this will result in changes in their business model. For example, MuniCenter,as its name implies, is endeavoring to establish itself as a powerhouse for the municipal bond market. It has its own inventory of municipal bonds, and it lists municipal bonds not available on other electronic platforms. Moreover, the bonds listed on its platform are available in real time, at the price quoted. Bond Desk, is focusing on developing sophisticated supporting software for managing the portfolios of individual investors.

Among institutions, electronic platforms have become even more sophisticated and widely used than at the retail (that is, the individual investor) level. At the institutional level, electronic platforms also known as "Alternative Trading Systems," (or "ATS," for short) serve large institutional investors or other dealers. ATS include systems that allow various forms of trading to take place, including auction systems, cross-matching systems, inter-dealer systems, and single dealer systems. Hundreds of securities are bought and sold virtually instantaneously on some of these ATS. These dealer systems operate largely outside the view of individual investors. But they are responsible for the development of new forms of extremely rapid trading, as well as for the development of "Exchange"-Traded Funds (ETFs).

Benefits And Costs of Electronic Platforms

To what extent has the use of electronic platforms changed the way bonds are brought to market and sold? This is still unclear It is not clear, for example, what percentage of bonds in any one sector of the bond market are purchased after being listed on electronic platforms, as opposed to being purchased directly from a dealer. People I consulted came up with widely different numbers: anywhere from 30% to 50%. But these numbers are not based on any empirical evidence.

The current dynamic is moving in the direction of increasing use of electronic systems. For brokerage firms, of course, the benefit of electronic platforms is huge. These platforms enable brokers to offer a wide selection of bonds to their customers at a very low cost. This is "inventory" they can offer without putting their own capital at risk.

Investors benefit by being able to consult a large database—and they can do so, moreover, anonymously, online. Another advantage is that many platforms now include software that allows investors to search for

bonds that meet specific criteria such as maturity, credit quality, desired
yield, etc. (Examples of such searches are included in later chapters). And
finally, electronic platforms provide a good source of information about
availability and pricing of bonds in different sectors of the bond market.
Moreover, platforms have excellent disclosure: they list all the features of
a bond required by the SEC and that an investor needs to understand.

But have electronic platforms resulted in lower markups? In some
cases, the answer is yes. For actively traded bonds, if several dealers list
the same bond for sale, then only the lowest price will be listed on the
platform. That competitive aspect is a clear benefit. But in the less liquid
sectors of the bond market, such as municipals, for example, bonds are
typically listed in smaller lots, by one dealer. Therefore, that competitive
aspect does not apply.

But there are also several costs to investors that they may not be
aware of. Most importantly, an investor completing the purchase of a
bond without consulting a broker takes on all of the risks of the trade.
Even though disclosure may be excellent, if an investor does not fully
understand all of the risks inherent in the purchase of a specific bond, he
has no recourse.

Also, if you buy a bond entirely online, you forfeit the ability to
"bargain" on price. In most instances, if you discuss the purchase with a
broker, at any firm including that of a discount broker, that broker is usually willing to contact the dealer selling the bond, and ask if the dealer
will accept a lower price. Bear in mind that the price of a bond on an electronic platform includes the full dealer markup. Depending on what is
happening in the market on any one day, dealers may be willing to shave
prices both for an investor who wants to sell a bond; and for an investor
who wants to buy a bond.

Can you tell when you are consulting the online Web site of a broker
whether you are looking at dealer inventory or at an electronic platform?
You can assume that all of the large online discount brokers rely primarily
on electronic platforms. For other firms, it is less clear. Sometimes you
can. Somewhere on the screen, the name of one or more electronic platform is posted as the source of the data, typically in a disclaimer. But not
always. Some brokers also commingle their own inventory and that of an
electronic platform. If a firm holds some bonds in inventory, it will clearly
be anxious to sell those first.

The use of electronic platforms raises a number of issues. One is
whether it pays to buy bonds entirely online, without discussing the trade

with a broker. Many brokerage firms, and particularly those of discount brokers, focus their ads on commission costs per bond. Those are usually quite low: anywhere between $2.00 to $5.00 fee per bond to buy a bond. This creates the impression that you are buying bonds "for less." But that commission cost per bond is merely the fee charged by the brokerage firm for executing the trade. Even though it is the only part of the cost of buying the bond that is disclosed, it is technically not part of the markup. In fact, it is only the tip of the iceberg. The dealer markup, as well as the broker markup, remains undisclosed. You are paying list price, and you are paying the full dealer and broker markups.

But the other side of that coin is that if you are dealing with a full service broker, the price of the bond is also quoted net: the commission (that is, the fee charged by the broker for completing the trade) is not disclosed. And those commission costs may be extremely high.

So is there any advantage in buying bonds from a discount broker? Here, the answer is also, it depends. The disclosed commission of discount brokers is quite low. But the dealer markup is not disclosed. So unless you are well informed, and compare prices, it is difficult to tell whether the bond is fairly priced or not.

How can you determine whether a price listed for a bond online is a fair price? The good news is that help is now available. Several regulatory and trade associations have developed Web sites: FINRA.org/marketdata; EMMA.msrb.org; and Investinginbonds.com whose goal is to bring a greater degree of "transparency" to the bond market. (Many online brokers now have direct links to one or more of these Web sites). These Web sites enable individual investors to access pricing information, including markups, within fifteen minutes of a trade. They also enable you to search for comparables. This information is free and available to anyone. These three Web sites are described in more detail at the end of Chapter 5. Chapters 7 through 10, dealing with individual securities also include examples that illustrate the type of information that is available, and how it can be used to shop for bonds in different sectors of the bond market.

TERMS USED IN BUYING, SELLING, AND DISCUSSING BONDS

The bond market has its own vocabulary. This section will introduce some key terms used in buying, selling, and discussing bonds.

Par, Premium, and Discount Bonds

The "par" value of a bond is its value at maturity; that is, $1,000. When a bond begins to trade, it normally ceases to sell at par. If it sells at less than par (less than $1,000), it is said to be selling at a "discount." If it sells at more than par (above $1,000), it is called a "premium" bond.

CUSIP Numbers

The CUSIP numbering system was established in 1967 in order to provide a uniform method for identifying bonds. (CUSIP stands for Committee on Uniform Security Identification Procedures.)

   This is a nine-digit number that identifies individual bonds. It is equivalent to a ticker symbol for a stock, and it identifies each bond issue precisely. Suppose, for example, you own a State of New Jersey bond. That bond is only one of perhaps hundreds of State of New Jersey bonds that are outstanding at any given time. Each one of these bonds has very precise and individual provisions: coupon, issue date, maturity, and call provisions. These bonds are not interchangeable. If you want to buy or sell a bond, the CUSIP number identifies the precise issue you are dealing with.

   CUSIP numbers are assigned to municipal, corporate, and pass-through securities. International issues are identified by a CINS number. (CINS stands for CUSIP International Numbering System.)

Bond Pricing Conventions

When the broker "shows" you a bond (that is the term generally used), she will say something like "I want to show you this great bond we just got in. It is the State of Bliss 5¼ of 15, and it is priced at 96 bid and 97 ask." Well, what did she say?

   Actually, that statement is easily decoded. Bonds are always identified by several pieces of information; namely, the issuer (State of Bliss); the coupon (5¼); the maturity date, of "15"; and the price, quoted as 97.

   Let us examine each of these details more closely. First, the coupon. Coupons are always quoted in percentages. That percentage is set at issue and is therefore a percentage of par. The percentage value, however, is immediately translated into a fixed dollar amount, and that amount remains the same throughout the life of the bond no matter what happens to the price of the bond. In the previous example, the 5¼ coupon represents 5¼% of $1,000, that is, $52.50. (That is also the interest income you would receive if you bought the bond.) Unless stipulated otherwise, coupons are paid semiannually. You will receive half of that amount, that is, $26.25, twice a year, for as long as the bond remains outstanding. (Floating-rate bonds vary from this pattern. For floating-rate bonds, coupon rates are reset at predetermined intervals.)

The maturity date is designated by the last two digits, in this instance, 15. This has to be 2015. Note that with few exceptions, bonds are not issued with maturities above 30 years.

Finally, the price was quoted as 97. Bond prices are quoted in percentages, and again, percentages of par. So the quote of 97 should be interpreted as 97% (or 0.97) times $1,000, which equals $970. To compute price, add a zero to the percentage quote.

You can now translate what the bond broker is telling you. She would like to sell you a State of Bliss bond, maturing in 2015, with a coupon of $52.50, at a price of $970.

Accrued Interest

Let us suppose you decide to buy the State of Bliss bonds. When you receive your confirmation notice, it is probable that the price will turn out to be somewhat higher than the $970 that you were quoted. No, the broker is not ripping you off. The difference between the price that you pay and the $970 that you were quoted is "accrued interest." Let's explain.

You will remember that interest payments are made twice a year. But actually, bonds earn (the Wall Street word is "accrue") interest every single day. The owner of a bond earns or accrues interest for the exact number of days that he owns the bond.

Now suppose you are buying the State of Bliss bonds three months after the last coupon payment was made (and therefore, three months before the next interest payment occurs). In three months, you will receive an interest payment for the past six months; but you will have earned that interest for only three months. The gentlemanly thing to do is to turn over three months' worth of interest to the previous owner.

In fact, that is what you do when you buy the bond—only you do not have any choice in the matter. The three months of interest due to the previous owner are automatically added on to the purchase price. The buyer pays the seller the accrued interest. When you (the buyer) receive the next coupon payment, the interest you receive will cover the three months' worth of interest you earned and the three months of interest that you paid the previous owner.

Accrued interest is paid on par, premium, and discount bonds. The amount of accrued interest depends entirely on the coupons, divided by the number of days interest is owed. It has nothing to do with the price.

Accrued interest is calculated based on a standardized formula. For bond pricing purposes, for many bonds (but not for notes), the year has 360 days. To compute accrued interest, divide the annual coupon by 360 days and multiply the result by the number of days accrued interest is owed. Add accrued interest to the purchase price. The day count varies somewhat, depending on the type of bond.

Calculating accrued interest has now become infinitely easier: Web sites listed below, such as FINRA.org/marketdata and Investinginbonds.com, include calculators that enable you to determine accrued interest.

Call Risk

"Call risk" is the risk that bonds will be redeemed ("called") by the issuer before they mature. Municipal and corporate bonds are subject to call; Treasuries generally are not. Some older 30-year Treasuries may be callable five years before they mature, but the Treasury no longer issues any callable bonds.

The ability to call bonds protects issuers by enabling them to retire bonds with high coupons and refinance at lower interest rates. But calls are usually bad news for bondholders. A call reduces total return because typically, bonds are called when interest rates are lower than the coupon interest of the bond that is being called. A call lowers total return in two ways: a high interest rate, thought to be "locked in," disappears; and the bondholder is forced to reinvest at lower rates.

The prospectus spells out call provisions by stipulating the earliest date when a bond may be subject to call; as well as a price at which it may be called, typically a bit above par. By law, any listing or any quote for a bond that is subject to call, must include those call provisions.

Call provisions differ, depending on the type of bond you are buying. Call provisions for corporates can be obscure. Mortgage-backed securities do not have stipulated call dates, but prepayments constitute a type of call risk. Call features of municipal and corporate bonds will be discussed in greater detail in the chapters dealing with these securities. But bear in mind that call provisions affect both the price you pay when you buy a bond, and potentially, how much you will earn by buying a particular bond.

You need to be particularly careful about call provisions if you are buying premium bonds. If a bond is purchased at par, or at a discount, a call does not result in a loss of principal. But when a bond is purchased at a premium (say for $1,100), an unexpected early call at par would translate into a loss of principal for each bond (in this example, a $100 loss per bond).

Note further that if you buy a premium bond whose coupon rate is a lot higher than current interest rates, it is prudent to assume that the bond will be called. If, for example, you buy a premium bond issued with a 6% coupon, and bonds with the same maturities yield 4% at the time of purchase, it is prudent to assume the bond will be called and evaluate the bond based on its quoted yield-to-call rather than its quoted yield-to-maturity. (These terms are defined in Chapter 3.)

Form of a Bond: Certificate, Registered, and Book-Entry

If you bought a bond before 1980, you received as proof of ownership an ornate document with coupons attached at the side. This document was known as a "certificate." The certificate did not have your name on it. To collect interest, it was necessary to physically clip the coupons and to send them to the trustee, who would then mail you the interest payment. (That is the origin of the term "coupon.") The certificate functioned like a dollar bill. It was presumed to be owned by the bearer. Those bonds were also known as "bearer bonds."

In the early 1980s, certificates began to be issued with the name of the owner imprinted on the certificate. Those were called "registered" bonds. Interest payments are sent automatically to the owner of record.

With the spread of computerization, the process has become almost entirely automated. All bonds are now issued in "book-entry" form. No certificates are issued. Instead, when you buy a bond, you receive a confirmation statement with a number on it. That number is stored in a computer data bank and is the only proof of ownership. Coupon payments are wired automatically to the checking or bank account that the owner designates. Notification of calls is automatic. A very few older bonds may still be available in bearer form, but bearer bonds are bound to disappear as older issues mature.

You may hold certificates in your own possession or leave them in your account with a broker. Brokers always prefer holding the certificates. There are two good reasons for letting them do so. First, if the firm is covered by the Securities Insurance Protection Corporation (SIPC), and most are, the bond is protected against loss—that is, against physical loss of the certificate—not against a decline in price due to market conditions. Second, the firm is more likely than you to be immediately aware of calls. If a bond is called, the firm should immediately redeem the bonds. That should protect you against loss of interest.

Leaving a bond in a brokerage account does not prevent you from selling the bond through a different broker. To transfer a book-entry bond, you need only to notify your broker to transfer it by wire to any other firm.

If your bond is in certificate form, however, the matter becomes more complicated because you need to deliver the certificate within three days after the sale. (A recommendation has been made that trades should settle one day after the sale, but that is not yet the rule except for Treasuries.) And six weeks or more may be needed to obtain the document because it is usually not stored in the branch office. Selling through the firm holding your bond eliminates actually having to get your hands on the document, and it permits you to sell at any time. If you want to sell through a different broker, then you must allow enough time to obtain the certificate.

Basis Points

Interest rates rise from 6% to 7%. How much have they gone up?

No, they have not gone up 1%. On a percentage basis, that increase represents a percentage difference of 16.67%. This may seem like nitpicking. But suppose, for example, that interest rates rise from 6% to 6.12%? How would you label that increase, using percentages?

The answer to that question would be either imprecise or confusing. Since institutional investors make or lose thousands of dollars on seemingly minute percentage changes, they have divided each percentage point into 100 points, each of which is called a "basis point" (abbreviated as bp). The difference between an interest rate of 6% and one of 7% is 100 basis points; between 5% and 6%, it is still 100 basis points. An increase in interest rate yield from 6% to 6.12% represents an increase in yield of 12 basis points (which would be recorded as 12 bp).

The term "basis point" is used to compare both price and yield. If, for example, you are comparing two different bonds, you might note that the three-year bond yields 6.58%, whereas the two-year bond yields 6.50%. In this instance, the three-year bond yields 8 basis points more than the two-year bond. Changes in interest rates from one day to the next, or from one year to the next are denoted in basis points.

Under normal circumstances, yields of most bonds vary from day to day by no more than a few basis points. But occasional moves are higher. A rise or a decline in yield from one day to the next of more than 10 basis points constitutes a major price move and therefore a major change in the direction of interest rates. Remember that changes in yield translate into changes in price and vice versa. Experienced investors and salespeople think in basis points. It is far easier and more precise than using percentages. Using the term will immediately mark you as a knowledgeable investor. It will be used through the rest of the book.

CHAPTER 3

Volatility: Why Bond Prices Go Up and Down

This chapter discusses

- ◆ Interest rate risk
- ◆ Credit ratings before and after the financial panic of 2008
- ◆ A short history of interest rates
- ◆ The role of the Federal Reserve in setting interest rates

Bond prices go up and down primarily in response to two factors: changes in interest rates and changes in credit quality. Individual investors who purchase bonds tend to worry a lot about the safety of their money. Generally, however, they tie safety to credit considerations. Many individual investors do not fully understand how changes in interest rates affect the price of bonds. Since the late 1970s, changes in the interest rate environment have become the greatest single determinant of bond returns. Managing interest rate risk has become the most critical variable in the management of bond portfolios. In this chapter we'll see why.

INTEREST RATE RISK, OR A TALE OF PRINCIPAL RISK

"Interest rate risk," also known as "market risk," refers to the propensity bonds have of fluctuating in price as a result of changes in interest rates.

All bonds are subject to interest rate risk.

All bonds are subject to interest rate risk.

All bonds are subject to interest rate risk.

Why am I repeating this statement so many times?

Because if nothing else makes an impression, but you learn that all bonds are subject to interest rate risk, regardless of the issuer or the credit rating or whether the bond is "insured" or "guaranteed," then this book will have served a useful purpose.

The principle behind this fact is easy to explain.

Let us suppose you bought a 30-year bond when 30-year Treasuries were yielding 4%. Further suppose that you wish to sell that same bond at a later date when interest rates for the current maturity of your bond have risen to 10%? How can you convince someone to purchase your bond, yielding 4%, when he can buy new issues yielding 10%?

Well, there is only one thing you can do: you mark down your bond. In fact, the price at which a buyer would buy your bond as readily as a new issue is that price at which your bond would now yield 10%. That would be approximately 30 cents on the dollar, or about $300 per bond.

But, you will object, if I sell my $1,000 bond for $300, I have lost $700 per bond! That is precisely the point.

Obviously, I used a whopping increase in yield in order to make a point. An increase of this magnitude does not take place, as in this example, instantaneously. It occurs over a period of years. But changes of this magnitude, in fact larger ones, have occurred within the last 30 years. Between 1980 and 2009, the yield of the 30-year Treasury bond has been as high as 16% in 1982 (no, that is not a misprint) and as low as 3% in 2008. Swings of 1% (100 basis points) sometimes occur over periods of a few weeks or a few months. In the early 1980s, swings of 5% (500 basis points) occurred within the space of a few years, in seemingly random fashion.

The fundamental principle is that interest rates and prices move in an inverse relationship. If interest rates rise, then the price of a bond declines. On the other hand, when interest rates decline, then the price of the bond goes up.

The following questions and answers discuss management of interest rate risk.

Is There Anything You Can Do to Protect Your Money against Interest Rate Fluctuations?

Yes. You can buy bonds with maturities that are either short (under one year) or short-intermediate (between two and seven years).

Again, the reason for that is easy to explain. While all bonds are subject to interest rate risk, *that risk is correlated to maturity length*. As maturity length increases, so do potential price fluctuations. Conversely, the

shorter the maturity of the bond you buy, the lower the risk of price fluctuations as a result of changes in interest rate levels. For the moment, let
us leave aside the question of exactly how much the price of a bond will
go up and down in response to changes in interest rates. The main point
to remember is that price fluctuations for bonds are correlated directly to
maturity length. If interest rates rise, the value of bonds with very short
maturities (under a year) changes only a little. That is why such bonds are
considered cash equivalents. Each additional year in maturity length adds
some degree of volatility. A very rough rule of thumb is that a 100-basis-
point rise in yield (say, from 5% to 6%) will result in a loss of value of
about 10% of principal (a loss of $100 per $1,000 par value bond) for bonds
with 30-year maturities. Steeper rises in interest levels result in even
steeper losses.

To illustrate, let's look at Exhibit 3.1. This table shows what would
happen to the price of a bond selling at par ($1,000), with a 7% coupon,
for several different maturities, under three different scenarios: if interest
rates were to go up modestly by 50 basis points, to 7.5%; or by 100 basis
points, to 8%; or, more steeply, by 200 basis points, to 9%.

Exhibit 3.1 shows that if interest rates rise very modestly, by 50 basis
points, the price of the two-year bond changes very little. But even that
modest rise results in a decline of 3.5% ($35) for the 10-year bond and
5.9% ($59) for the 30-year bond. For the 30-year bond, the decline of 5.9%
wipes out almost the total amount of interest income for the entire year. If
a much sharper rise in interest rates occurs, from 7% to 9%, declines
become correspondingly larger: from 3.6% ($36) for the two-year bond,

EXHIBIT 3.1

What Would Happen to the Price of a $1,000 Par Value Bond with a 7% Coupon if Interest Rates Rise by 50 Basis Points, to 7.5%? By 100 Basis Points, to 8%? And by 200 Basis Points, to 9%?

Maturity	to 7.5%	to 8%	to 9%
2 years	−0.9%	−1.1%	−3.6%
5 years	−2.1%	−3.5%	−4.7%
10 years	−3.5%	−6.8%	−13.0%
30 years	−5.9%	−11.3%	−20.6%

Source: Merrill Lynch. Material supplied to the author.

through 13% ($130) for the 10-year, and 20.6% ($206) for the 30-year bond. (All numbers are rounded.) Clearly, if interest rates go up, the holder of bonds with shorter maturities would be less unhappy than the holder of bonds with long maturities.

This phenomenon, happily, operates in reverse. As interest rates decline, bond prices rise. This is shown in Exhibit 3.2.

Exhibit 3.2 shows changes in price for various maturities under three different scenarios: first, if interest rates decline by a small amount, 50 basis points, to 6.5%; or by 100 basis points, to 6%; or more steeply, by 200 basis points, to 5%. Once again, the change in price is much smaller for the two-year maturity. But it rises gradually through the maturity spectrum. If interest rates decline by 50 basis points, the price of the two-year increases by a minor amount, 0.9% ($9). But the value of the 30-year rises by 6.6% ($66). A decline in rates of 200 basis points would result in more significant price increases for all maturities, ranging from 3.8% ($38) for the two-year to 30.9% ($31) for the 30-year. (Again, all numbers are rounded.) In this instance, the holder of a bond would benefit from holding the longest maturities because the longer the maturity, the higher the gain. That is the reason that investors anticipating a decline in interest rates position themselves at the long end, in order to realize the largest capital gains.

Several qualifications need to be made concerning both of the preceding tables. First, the exact price changes illustrated are assumed to have occurred as a result of instantaneous changes in yield. In practice, such changes may take weeks, months, or even years. Changes occurring

EXHIBIT 3.2

What Would Happen to the Price of a $1,000 Par Value Bond with a 7% Coupon if Interest Rates Decline by 50 Basis Points, to 6.5%? By 100 Basis Points, to 6%? And by 200 Basis Points, to 5%?

Maturity	to 6.5%	to 6%	to 5%
2 years	+0.9%	+1.9%	+3.8%
5 years	+2.1%	+4.3%	+8.7%
10 years	+3.6%	+7.4%	+15.6%
30 years	+6.6%	+13.8%	+30.9%

Source: Merrill Lynch. Material supplied to the author.

over longer time periods would result in somewhat different numbers because, as noted earlier, the price of a bond moves towards par as it gets closer to maturity, and those price changes occur regardless of what happens to interest rates.

Second, the exact price changes illustrated in Exhibits 3.1 and 3.2 apply only to bonds selling at par, with a 7% coupon. The numbers would be different for bonds with coupons that are either higher or lower than 7%. Price changes would be somewhat *larger*, in both directions, if the coupons are *lower* than 7%, and the price changes would be *lower* if the coupons are somewhat *higher* than 7%.

Third, if you look at the price changes that occur in both directions, you will note that these changes are not linear. If interest rates rise, the price of a bond declines as maturity length increases, but those increases occur at a declining rate. That decline in the rate of increase begins to be noticeable approximately after the 10-year mark. Similarly, if interest rates decline, the price of bonds increases as maturity length increases, but again, at a declining rate that begins to be noticeable at the approximate 10-year mark. Nonetheless, it remains the case that price changes are greatest at the highest maturity length.

Finally, note that the price changes that occur if interest rates move up or down are somewhat larger if interest rates decline than if they go up. For example, for the 30-year bond, if interest rates go up by 100 basis points, the price of the bond declines by 11.3%. But if interest rates decline by 100 basis points, the price of the same bond goes up by 13.8%. Similarly, if interest rates go up by 200 basis points, the price of the 30-year bond declines by 20.6%. But if interest rates decline, the price of the same bond goes up by 30.9%. That distinction is obviously a desirable characteristic: your bond appreciates more in value if interest rates decline than it loses if interest rates rise. This characteristic has a somewhat formidable name: it is known as *convexity*.

In summary, while the numbers vary somewhat for different bonds, both Exhibit 3.1 and Exhibit 3.2 show two basic principles. First, the price of bonds and interest rates move in opposite directions. If interest rates decline, the price of a bond goes up, and if interest rates rise, the price of a bond declines. Second, bonds with longer maturities incur significantly higher interest rate risk than those with shorter maturities. That is a disadvantage if interest rates rise, but an advantage if interest rates decline.

So now we have the two faces of interest rate fluctuations, both up and down: risk and opportunity. It may sound paradoxical, but a rising or

strong bond market is one in which interest rates are declining because
that causes bond prices to rise. You can sell a bond for more than you paid
for it and make a profit. A weak bond market is one in which interest rates
are rising and, as a result, prices are falling. If you have to sell your bonds,
you have to do so at a loss. In either case, the changes in price are correlated to maturity length.

For more on the relationship between interest rates and bond prices,
see the section on duration in Chapter 4.

If Long-term Bonds Are So Risky, Why Would Anyone Purchase Them?

Mainly because many investors believe that long-term bonds provide the
highest yields (or maximum income). That, however, should be qualified.
If all other factors are equal, long-term bonds have higher coupons than
shorter-term bonds of the same credit quality. But, intermediate bonds in
the A to AA range often sport yields close to those of AAA bonds with far
longer maturities, but with far less volatility. (Note that this relationship
assumes a normal, that is, an upward sloping yield curve. Occasionally,
interest rates on short maturities are higher than interest rates on longer
maturities. When this happens, the yield curve is said to be inverted. This
is discussed in the section on yield curves in Chapter 5.)

You might, of course, want to purchase long-term bonds for other
reasons. One would be to "lock in" an attractive interest rate for as long
as possible, if you think you are not going to sell the bonds before they
mature. Also, if you think interest rates are about to decline, buying bonds
at the long end positions you for maximum capital gains. That would
imply that you consider potential capital gains as important (or more so)
than interest yield, and in all likelihood that you intend to resell the bonds
before they mature.

How Do Interest Rate Fluctuations Affect the Price of a Bond if I Hold It to Maturity?

If you hold bonds to maturity, you recover your principal in full (assuming there has not been a default). No matter what kind of roller coaster ride
interest rates take during the life of a bond, its value will always be par
when the bond is redeemed. Bonds purchased either above par (premium
bonds) or below par (discount bonds) are also redeemed at par. The price
of discounts gradually rises to par; the price of premiums falls to par.
These changes occur very gradually, in minute annual increments and are
reflected in the current price of any bond.

I Own Bonds Issued Years Ago, When Coupon Rates Were 4%. Rates Are Now Much Higher. Can't I Sell My Old Bonds and Buy New Ones with Higher Coupons in Order to Earn More Income?

The swap by itself will not result in higher yields: if you buy a bond that is comparable in maturity length and credit quality, the transaction will be a wash. This is because you would sell at that price at which the buyer of your old bonds would be "indifferent" (using a word from economics) to buying your bond, or one carrying a higher coupon, meaning at the exact price which would result in the prevailing yield. Therefore, your income from the bonds would not change.

For example, let us assume you own bonds with a par value of $10,000 and a coupon rate of 4%. That means that annually you receive interest (coupon) income of $400. Assume further that over a period of several years, interest rates have risen to 8%. You sell your bonds for approximately $500 per bond, for a total of $5,000, which you now reinvest. You now own $5,000 (par value) bonds, and you will now receive annual interest of 8%; that is, $400. Therefore, even though you are now earning a coupon rate of 8%, you will be earning the same dollar amount as before the swap. Moreover, you would be out the transaction costs (commissions) incurred in selling the old bonds and buying the new bonds.

This does not mean that you should never consider swaps. There are other valid reasons for swapping. On the preceding transaction, you would generate a capital loss of approximately $5,000 and that might be used for tax purposes to offset capital gains on other transactions. Or you might swap to upgrade credit quality. You might increase yield by buying lower-quality bonds, or by buying different bonds.

Please note two caveats. In the preceding example, you would have taken an enormous hit to principal. Also, costing out a swap accurately is complex. For more on swaps, see Chapter 15.

CREDIT RATINGS: HOW CREDIT QUALITY AFFECTS THE VALUE OF YOUR BONDS

Since the financial crisis of 2008, the role of the major credit rating agencies, and credit ratings themselves, have come under fire. The attacks on the credit rating agencies stem primarily from the virtual collapse in value of mortgage-backed bonds derived from subprime mortgages. These bonds had been rated AAA despite the fact that the underlying mortgages had been issued without the usual stringent credit checks. Beginning in

2007, subprime mortgages began to default; and as defaults multiplied, hundreds of billions of mortgage-backed bonds collapsed in value. This collapse resulted in major losses to some of the largest financial institutions in the country, including multi-national banks, and insurance companies, including the major bond insurance firms, investment banks, and broker-dealer firms. The losses eventually threatened the entire financial system of the United States (and abroad). Blame was heaped on the credit rating agencies for ratings that turned out to have grossly understated risk.

During 2009 and 2010, proposals have been under consideration to enact regulations intended to prevent another major financial crisis. Some of these proposals affect credit ratings as well as regulations tied to credit ratings. A few of these proposals have already been adopted, notably changes to the credit rating scales of municipal bonds (described later on in this chapter, and also in greater detail in Chapter 7, on municipal bonds); as well as changes in minimum credit quality requirements for money market funds (described in Chapter 12). In addition, as this book is going to press, a major bill is being signed into law that enacts a number of sweeping changes to the regulatory environment of the financial system. This bill includes provisions to set up commissions that will study credit rating firms, as well as the entire process of issuing credit ratings. But this defers additional changes for several years. Nonetheless, with the exceptions noted above, bonds continue to be issued and rated pretty much the way they were prior to the crisis of 2008.

This section will first discuss the ratings process as it continues to exist: how ratings are assigned; what the rating symbols mean; and how ratings affect returns from bonds. This part of the rating system will probably change less than some of the regulations tied to ratings. This section will then briefly discuss some of the proposed changes.

Credit Risk and Credit Ratings: Interpreting Credit Ratings

Most individual investors (and many institutional investors as well) do not perform extensive credit analyses. Instead, they rely on bond ratings to evaluate the credit quality of specific bonds. Credit ratings are intended to indicate on a scale of high to low the probability of default: that is, the probability that debt will not be repaid on time in full. Failure to redeem principal at maturity constitutes a default. Failure to make interest payments on time (that is, to pay coupons to bondholders) also constitutes a default. In plain English, ratings answer two questions: How likely am I to get my money back when the bond matures? And how likely am I to get my interest payments on time?

Any security issued *directly* by the U.S. government is considered free of default risk. This includes all Treasury securities, as well as savings bonds and GNMAs, which are guaranteed directly by the government. Although these bonds are not rated, they are considered the safest and highest-quality securities that you can buy because a default by the U.S. government is deemed impossible.

All bonds other than those issued or guaranteed by the U.S. government are considered to have some degree of default (or credit) risk. The amount of risk is evaluated by firms that specialize in evaluating credit quality. The best-known rating firms are Moody's, Standard & Poor's (S&P), and Fitch (now Fitch IBCA). Bonds are rated when issuers initially come to market, and subsequently, as issuers bring additional issues to market. Issuers pay the agencies for the rating.

On a scale from the best credit quality to the lowest, Exhibit 3.3 lists the symbols used by each of the major credit rating agencies. These symbols are on the left-hand side. The right-hand side of Exhibit 3.3 is a translation into plain English of what the ratings mean. Standard & Poor's adds plus (+) and minus (−) signs to its ratings. A plus signifies higher quality; a minus signifies somewhat lower quality. For instance, a rating of B⁺ is slightly higher than a rating of B. A rating of B⁻ is slightly lower than a B

EXHIBIT 3.3

Credit Quality Ratings and What They Mean

Moody's	Standard & Poor's	Fitch	
Aaa	AAA	AAA	Gilt edged. If everything that can go wrong, goes wrong, they can still service debt.
Aa	AA	AA	Very high quality by all standards.
A	A	A	Investment grade; good quality.
Baa	BBB	BBB	Lowest investment grade rating; satisfactory; but needs to be monitored.
Ba	BB	BB	Somewhat speculative; low grade.
B	B	B	Very speculative.
Caa	CCC	CCC	Even more speculative. Substantial risk.
Ca	CC	CC	Wildly speculative. May be in default.
C	C	C	In default. Junk.

rating. Moody's adds a "1" to indicate slightly higher credit quality; for instance, a rating of A1 is a higher quality credit rating than an A rating.

The lowest rating that is considered "investment grade" corresponds to BBB (Standard & Poor's) and Baa (Moody's). The term "investment grade" stems from the fact that fiduciary institutions, such as banks, are permitted by law to invest only in securities rated at the minimum "investment grade." Note in passing that this rating denotes a "fair" margin of safety, meaning that it is not gilt-edged. Bonds rated just investment grade need to be monitored for potential changes in the financial strength of the issuer.

How Ratings Are Assigned

The process of rating bonds involves both economic analysis of the current financial strength of the issuer; and forecasts of its future economic strength.

While the approach differs somewhat based on what sector of the bond market is being rated, the basic process for arriving at a rating follows the same pattern. The rating agencies assign a team and meet with the issuer. They conduct a basic analysis of the issuer's finances, with particular focus on the specific revenues that will be dedicated to paying interest on the bond being rated. Those revenues are estimated over the entire life of the bond. These estimates are then compared with costs of debt service. Remember that costs are known. They are the interest payments on the bonds, and interest costs are fixed when the bonds are issued. Revenues, on the other hand, must be forecast based on models of future economic activity.

The more money that is predicted to be available for debt service, over the entire life of the bond, compared with costs of debt service, the higher the rating. As an example, an issuer whose revenues are estimated to equal 10 times costs of debt service would be assigned a very high rating. At the other extreme, if revenues are forecast to be less than the costs of debt service, and therefore insufficient to cover debt service, the rating will fall to somewhere below investment grade; how low will depend on the estimated shortage of funds. Most ratings fall on a graduated scale, somewhere between these two extremes.

... and Why They Are Subject to Change

When forecasting economic conditions for the next six months or for perhaps one year, experts stand on reasonably secure ground. But the further

they predict into the future, the more imprecise and unreliable their forecasts become. Any prediction of economic conditions that goes out more
than five years becomes guesswork. Bear in mind, however, that the rating extends over the entire life of the bond, even if that is 30 years.

As a result, when ratings are reviewed, they often change. As the economic fortunes of the issuer vary, so do the ratings. Over time, changes in
ratings can be major and sometimes sudden. Prior to the crisis of 2008,
many of the most dramatic changes in ratings took place in the corporate
sector. This happened, for example, if a company bought another company
using debt to pay for the acquisition. The purchase increased the amount
of debt of the acquiring firm virtually overnight. And that increase caused
the rating of the acquiring firm to plummet virtually overnight as well.

Credit Ratings and Bond Returns: How Credit Ratings Affect Interest Income

Credit ratings matter because they affect the cost of borrowing; that is, the
interest rate that will have to be paid by the issuer to attract buyers.
The interest cost to the issuer, you will remember, is the coupon; that is,
the interests income that you will earn.

The principle for this is easy to explain. Think of a bond as a loan
(which, you will recall, is what it is) and imagine that you are a bank that
is lending to a borrower. You would ask a lot of questions relating to the
probability of repayment. To whom would you rather lend money: to a
struggling businessman with no collateral who wants to start a business,
or to IBM? To someone who has one million dollars in the bank and wants
to borrow money for a yacht, or to John Doe, who has barely enough earnings to cover his mortgage payments and who wants to borrow money for
home improvements? The answer is obvious. Now suppose you are the
struggling businessman or John Doe. Chances are that if your banker
turns you down, you will find a different banker, who will charge you
higher interest costs. You may even go to your neighborhood loan shark
(or equivalent), who will lend you the money, but charge you a much
higher interest rate than the bank.

This is also true for bonds. The most creditworthy issuers—say,
large states with diverse economies, blue chip corporations with very little debt, or the U.S. government—borrow at a lower cost. Less creditworthy clients have to pay higher interest. Consequently, bonds with the
highest quality credit ratings always carry the lowest yields; bonds with
lower credit ratings yield more. The yield, in a very real sense, provides a

scale of creditworthiness: higher yields indicate higher risk—the higher the yield, the higher the risk.

Note that issuers pay the rating agencies for a rating. That fee is the reason that some issuers, particularly small issuers, only have only one rating; they do not want to pay for two or three ratings. Theoretically, ratings are monitored periodically. In practice, ratings are reviewed when an issuer issues new bonds and pays for a rating.

Clearly, paying issuers for a rating creates a conflict of interest. For the rating agencies, ratings are big business. Moreover, the role of the rating agencies was increased significantly in 2006, when the SEC won authority to oversee credit rating firms by recognizing certain major firms as "Nationally Recognized Statistical Rating Organizations" (NSROs). Concurrently, institutions such as pension funds, banks, and insurance companies were required to invest only in securities rated by NSROs, with ratings set above designated minimum credit ratings. Similar regulations also tied to ratings also govern investments in money market funds.

How Changes in Ratings Affect the Price of Bonds

If bonds are downgraded (that is, if the credit rating is lowered), the price of the bond declines. If the rating is upgraded, the price goes up. In fact, bond prices sometimes change if there is even a strong possibility of an upgrade or a downgrade. This is because anxious investors sell bonds whose credit quality is declining and buy bonds whose credit quality is improving.

Unless there is a genuine risk of default, however, price changes in response to upgrades or downgrades are far less major than those occurring due to changes in interest rate levels. If ratings go up one notch or down one notch in the rating scale, prices go up or down by a small percentage. The change in price corresponds to the amount necessary to bring the yield of a bond (and therefore its price) in line with other bonds rated at the same level. For bonds rated AA, for example, a downgrade to A^+ may not make a noticeable difference in the price.

This point needs to be emphasized because many individual investors are needlessly worried about relatively minor downgrades and this fear is sometimes exacerbated by the financial media. For bonds that have very high ratings (AA or AAA), a downgrade of one or even two notches is not a major cause for concern. It would not result in a serious deterioration in the price of the bond. Distinctions between ratings are often based on nuances. Any bond-rated investment grade or higher continues to have good margins of safety, even after a downgrade.

However, certain downgrades are more significant than others and should be viewed as red flags. Those would include any downgrade that drops a bond rating to below investment grade; a downgrade of more than one notch (say from AA to A⁻); or a series of downgrades in close succession. If any of these occurs, you might want to review whether you wish to continue owning that security.

My Bonds Are Insured, or AAA, or Government Guaranteed. Won't that Guarantee that Principal Won't Decline in Value?

No. What is guaranteed is that interest payments will be made on time and that principal will be redeemed in full at the bond's maturity. There is no connection between that guarantee and what happens to the price (or value) of bonds due to fluctuations in interest rates. If interest rates rise, the value of your bonds will decline. If interest rates decline, the value of your bonds will rise. Period. No exceptions.

I am repeating this point because this is one of the most widely misunderstood aspects of investing in bonds. Many investors assume that if bonds are insured, or obligations of the U.S. government, then somehow the bonds never go down in price. That is a major and costly mistake. Changes in interest rates affect *all* bonds, whether they are those of Fly-by-Night airlines or obligations of the U.S. government. The major variant in the size of the decline (or appreciation) will be the maturity length of the bonds.

The panic of 2008 provided an example of this type of investor behavior. Investors poured money into Treasuries of all maturities including 10-year and 30-year Treasuries whose yields had sunk to record lows (about 2% for the 10-year bond and 3% for the 30-year bond). At these levels, any experienced investor knows that a rise in interest rates of 100 basis points, to 3% for the 10-year and 4% for the 30-year, would result in a decline in the price of the bond of around 25%. Clearly, in 2008, panicked investors were ignoring interest rate risk. (With the wisdom of hindsight, let us note that an ETF investing in long-term Treasuries [ticker symbol, TLT] did decline about 25% based on the highest price it reached in 2008, about $120, to its lowest price in 2009, which was around $87.)

How Frequently Do Defaults Occur?

There is a gradation in risk of default. Any bond that is a direct obligation of the U.S. government is deemed to have zero possibility of default.

Bonds issued by federal agencies are deemed to have almost equally high credit quality. Municipal bonds come in a wide variety of ratings, but in the aggregate they have low default rates. Corporate bonds are far less predictable. Default rates for junk bonds, which by definition are rated below investment grade, have been much higher. Debt of so-called emerging markets is highly unpredictable and speculative.

Note, however, that even when defaults occur, bond investors seldom lose 100% of the principal value of the bond. Defaulted bonds usually have some salvage value. There is a good deal of speculation in the bonds of defaulted or bankrupt issuers. That is because such bonds may be purchased very cheaply, sometimes for as little as 10 to 30 cents on the dollar. Also many defaults have taken the form of a suspension of coupon payments. Such bonds are said to be trading flat. If coupon payments are resumed, the price of the bonds can soar. Bondholders may also benefit from the sale of assets of issuers under bankruptcy proceedings. Finally, some bankrupt companies emerge successfully from bankruptcy proceedings, leading to a bonanza for anyone who purchased the bonds while the company was in default.

The issue of defaults will be revisited in later chapters dealing with individual securities.

Credit Quality Spreads

I am singling out this concept for comment because the term has come into widespread use.

Differences in yield due to differences in credit ratings show up directly in what are known as "credit quality spreads." Those are simply differences in yield between bonds of the same maturity, but with different credit ratings. The principle behind this is once again, that bonds with lower credit ratings have higher yields than bonds with higher credit ratings. For example, a one-year corporate A-rated bond will have a higher yield than a one-year corporate bond rated AA. A 30-year corporate bond rated BBB (the lowest investment grade rating of Standard & Poor's) will have a higher yield than an A-rated bond.

Credit quality spreads change over time. They tend to be narrower (that is, lower) when the economy is booming (risk is perceived to be lower); and wider (that is, higher) during times of recession (risk is perceived to be higher).

Prior to the financial crisis of 2008, credit quality spreads between bonds of the same maturity, with different ratings, tended to be modest.

For example, credit quality spreads might be approximately 10 or 20 basis points between steps on the rating scale, say between a rating of A and AA, or AA and AAA, for bonds with maturities under five years. Credit quality spreads widen as riskiness is perceived to increase, either as maturities become longer; or credit quality lower. When either of these things happens, the yield of the riskier bond rises; and its price declines. Hence, as spreads widen, this results in losses to holders of the riskier bond. The reverse is also true: narrowing spreads result in price appreciation of riskier bonds.

These patterns are so widely known and followed that many professional traders base trading strategies on the extent to which the spreads vary from what is considered "normal."

Credit Quality Spreads and the Panic of 2008

Prior to the financial panic of 2008, sudden changes in credit ratings and major defaults resulted in panics primarily in two sectors of the bond market: emerging market bonds and junk bonds. (These panics are discussed in chapters of the book dealing with those securities.)

What happened in 2007 and 2008, however, was of a different order of magnitude. As housing prices started to decline, the rate of defaults on subprime home mortgages began spiraling upward. As a result, a sector of the mortgage-backed bond market, whose bonds had been rated AAA, suddenly collapsed. Unfortunately, this sector of the bond market had a value in the hundreds of billions of dollars. These bonds were owned (and are still on the balance sheets) of many of the largest financial institutions in this country (indeed, throughout the world): multinational banks and insurance companies. The eventual amount of the losses caused by the meltdown of this sector of the bond market is still unknown.

The panic, however, spread well beyond mortgage-backed securities, to the stock market and to every sector of the bond market other than Treasuries. As panic gripped the bond market, credit quality spreads widened beyond any previous norms. Any bond with any whiff of risk was priced as if it was junk. But genuinely risky bonds could not find a buyer, at any price. For example, in the municipal bond market, spreads between AAA- and A-rated bonds, with short maturities, which normally would be somewhere between 50 and 70 basis points, widened to well over 300 basis points. Spreads widened even more among bonds with longer maturities. These widening credit quality spreads were the chief reason for the declines that took place in the bond market. These declines were most clearly visible in the enormous price declines that occurred in bond funds. (These are discussed in Chapter 12.)

For much of 2009, it appeared as if the panic that gripped all sectors of the bond market other than Treasuries would permanently change both spreads to Treasuries and credit quality spreads within individual sectors of the bond market. But the second half of 2009 saw massive rallies take place in both the corporate and municipal bond sectors. As I write this, credit quality spreads have narrowed significantly. In both of these sectors, credit quality spreads are close to where they were prior to the financial panic of 2008.

Nonetheless, some sectors of the bond market continue to show significant levels of fear. The clearest evidence remains the extraordinarily low level of Treasury yields for maturities below the five-year mark (below 1% for five-year bonds; around 10 basis points for one-month and three-month Treasury bills). Another is that the market for mortgage-backed securities (other than GNMAs, which are guaranteed by the U.S. government) still remains partially frozen. What the new "normal" will be remains unclear.

Sell-Off Risk

The enormous declines in price that took place in the bond market during the financial panic of 2008, as well as the more localized declines that occasionally occur in sectors such as junk bonds and emerging market bonds, are two faces of a risk that is sometimes called "sell-off" risk. At some point, what happens during any panic is that there is a tremendous imbalance between buyers and sellers. This is what Wall Street wags sometimes call a "to whom" market; in other words, to whom can I sell? This is a market where buyers disappear and sellers all try to exit the market at the same time.

The declines that took place in the bond market in 2008 may constitute possibly the most extreme example of that risk the bond market has ever seen, primarily because it encompassed every sector of the bond market not specifically guaranteed by the Treasury; and also because the sell-off lasted well over one year.

It is worth noting, however, that even during that sell-off, bonds with maturities in the short to intermediate range, and high credit quality ratings, emerged virtually unscathed. For evidence, see Chapter 12, on bond fund performance.

Proposed Changes to the Credit Rating Process

As noted at the beginning of this chapter, the major credit rating firms were widely blamed for the financial crisis caused by defaults of mortgage-backed securities tied to subprime mortgages. The crisis has caused a reexamination of the entire credit rating process, starting with the conflict of interest created by the issuer pay model. The rating agencies have been accused of rating securities (particularly bonds deriving from subprime mortgages and their derivatives) that were so complex that the ratings of those securities were, at best, guesswork, and at worst, totally misleading; and furthermore, that the rating firms rated these incomprehensibly complex securities primarily because it was too lucrative a business to turn down. Even supporters of the credit rating firms have had to agree that their judgment proved extremely poor. But criticism extends well beyond the ratings of securities tied to subprime mortgages. Basically, the credit ratings firms have been accused of doing a poor job of doing due diligence to monitor credit quality of most bonds.

Beginning in 2008, the SEC and a number of congressional committees have been holding hearings to examine the credit rating agencies, the rating process, and regulatory issues tied to ratings. Wide-ranging proposals have been made which would potentially affect banks, pension funds, and insurance companies whose investments in bonds are regulated partly based on credit ratings. The idea behind many of these proposals is to decrease the role of credit ratings in regulating investments in bonds. One possibility would be to develop other criteria for evaluating risk. Some proposals would subject rating firms to greater regulation. Another proposal would allow litigation against credit rating firms for ratings that turn out to have been grossly inaccurate. To date, no proposal has emerged which would deal satisfactorily with the conflict of interest created by the issuer pay model. But one solution proposed by a number of firms petitioning to be recognized as NSROs is to have users, rather than issuers, pay for ratings.

One of the more sweeping proposals to emerge from the hearings deals with the rating scales themselves. Traditionally, rating scales for each sector of the bond market have evaluated the financial strength of an issuer by comparing that issuer to others within the same sector. For example, ratings of corporate bonds are based on comparisons of the finances of one corporation to those of other corporations.

According to many observers, this type of analysis is misleading because it understates default risks in some sectors of the bond market; and overstates risk in other sectors. Instead of comparing the financial strength of one issuer to that of another issuer within the same sector, the rating agencies are being asked to adopt a so-called "global" rating scale, which would base credit quality ratings on actual default experience.

The adoption of a "global" scale would be of benefit primarily to municipal bonds which have lower default rates than corporate bonds. Adopting a "global" rating scale would result in higher ratings for most municipal bonds.

The proposal to move to a "global" rating scale for municipal bonds was adopted by both Fitch and Moody's. Both agencies announced changes to the rating scales of municipal bonds during April 2010. (Details of these changes are discussed in Chapter 7, which deals with municipal bonds.)

There is also some evidence that one permanent result of the crisis is that credit ratings are encountering a good deal more skepticism than was the case prior to 2008. In October 2009, for example, the *Wall Street Journal* reported that a number of prominent European corporations had successfully issued debt without any ratings. But while the rating process has come under enormous criticism, for the moment, no viable alternative has taken its place. Many, if not most, investors, continue to rely on ratings to evaluate the credit quality of bonds.

Until there is more clarity, following is a summary of what you will want to remember concerning ratings:

- Most of the time, bond ratings for a specific bond by the different rating agencies are close. If they are not, then to be safe, assume the lowest rating is accurate.
- Buy bonds rated investment grade (or higher), depending on your risk tolerance. For maximum safety, stick to bonds rated at least A^+ or higher.
- Be sure that you understand the main reasons for the rating. What sources of revenue will pay debt? What is the credit history of the issuer? Has it been upgraded or downgraded? Why?
- When you own a bond, monitor its rating.
- Note also that occasionally the price of some bonds drops in advance of a rating change. The market is sometimes ahead of the rating agencies in sniffing out that a particular security may face potential problems.
- Diversify. Don't put all your assets in one bond. If you have a total of $50,000 to invest, it is more prudent to buy five $10,000 lots than one $50,000 lot. Buy bonds of different issuers to diversify credit risk. And buy bonds with different maturities to diversify interest rate risk.

Finally, bear in mind that the rating agencies do not have any connection to actual debt service payments, which are made by the issuer. Nor should ratings be interpreted as recommendations either to buy or to sell a particular security. A low rating does not mean that a default will occur; and a high rating does not guarantee safety. If you are not comfortable buying securities whose rating you do not fully understand, then by all means, buy only securities whose credit quality you consider impeccable.

A SHORT HISTORY OF INTEREST RATES

We read all kinds of discussions concerning interest rate levels. Pundits expound on whether they are high or low, and above all, where they are headed. These discussions make little sense, however, unless you have some sense of the history of interest rates and the kinds of changes in these levels that have occurred in the past, and that may well occur again. Exhibit 3.4 presents a simplified history of interest rates between 1953 and 2009.

EXHIBIT 3.4

A History of Interest Rates between 1953 and 2009

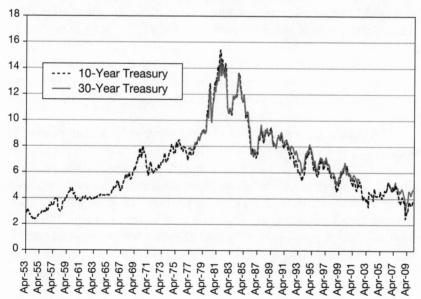

Source: the Federal Reserve Bank.

The interest rates shown are for the longest maturities issued by the U.S. government from 1953 to 2009. Prior to the early 1970s, the longest maturity issued by the Treasury was the 10-year bond. The Treasury began issuing 30-year bonds in 1977. Between 1977 and 2000, the 30-year Treasury bond (also called the "long bond") was the most widely traded security in the world. During that period, the long bond was issued four times a year. Because it was such a key security, the 30-year bond was considered the bellwether bond. In 2000, the Treasury announced that it would issue 30-year bonds only once a year (ironically, due to the fact that the government at the time was running surpluses, and anticipating surpluses "as far as the eye can see"). As a result, the 10-year bond became the new bellwether. At the current time, when people in the financial world refer to interest rates, they are usually discussing the 10-year bond and the interest rate level of that maturity.

If we went back further than the period shown in Exhibit 3.4, to between 1930 and 1940, we would see that during the Great Depression, the yield on bonds with the longest maturities (at the time, the 10-year bond) fell to a low of around 2%. Between 1940 and 1950, interest rates barely budged. But in 1950, as shown in Exhibit 3.4, rates began a long and almost uninterrupted rise. Rates rose first slowly, then more steeply, from 2% in 1950 to 4% in 1960. (Some of you may remember that in those days bank passbook accounts paid 2% to $2^{1}/_{2}$% interest.) By the late 1960s, yields began to rise, reaching 6% in 1970 and then after 1979, climbing sharply and steeply upwards. In 1981, the long bond briefly yielded above 15%. The actual peak was 15.2% in October 1981. Since all interest rates key off the bellwether bond, during the early 1980s, yields on tax-exempt bonds with 30-year maturities reached numbers that seem almost unbelievable at the current time: 12% to 14%, depending on credit quality.

The period between 1950 and 1982 represents a bear market in bonds that lasted well over 30 years. During many of those years, bonds were said not to "have earned their coupon," meaning that the principal value of bonds declined by more than the interest income received. During the disastrous 1970s, the worst of those three decades, satirists described long-term bonds as "fixed rate instrument(s) designed to fall in price" and "certificates of confiscation." Bondholders suffered staggering losses as bonds purchased in the 1960s and 1970s with coupons of 4% to 6% declined by 50% or more ($500 per $1,000 bond) as interest rates approached 15% on the long bond.

Note further that these bondholders suffered a double whammy. Not only was the value of their bonds sharply down, but to add insult to injury, they were earning meager returns of 4% to 6% while interest rates went into the double digits even on short-term and tax-exempt securities. The final blow was that during that period double-digit inflation was eroding the purchasing power of every dollar.

In 1982, however, bond yields began a very sharp decline. Bond prices soared! For most of the 1990s, the yield on the long bond fluctuated somewhere between 8% at the high end and 5% at the low end (the exact low for that decade was 4.78%, in 1998). Yields continued to decline in irregular fashion after 2000: between 2000 and 2009, the yield of the 10-year bond reached a high slightly above 5% (in 2006 and 2007) and a low of close to 2% in December of 2008. During the same period, the yield on the long bond fluctuated between 6% in 2006 and 3% in 2008.

The roughly three decades between 1981 and 2009 saw the biggest bull market in bonds in the history of the United States. The returns earned on long-term bonds between 1982 and 2009 are unprecedented and unlikely to repeat. The high total returns were due to two factors. The first was the historically high yields of the late 1970s and early 1980s. Any investor who purchased Treasuries with coupon rates between 11% and 15% (and correspondingly high rates in other sectors of the bond market), earned unprecedented rates of interest. The second factor in the high returns was the significant capital gain component reaped by anyone who sold high coupon bonds. During the late 1980s, for example, U.S. Treasury bonds with coupons of 14% to 15% sold for as much as $1,700 per bond, for a capital gain of 70%. Beginning in the 1990s, and up to the present, returns were lower than during the 1980s, but still high by historical standards. Treasury yields remained relatively high in the 1990s (above 6% for much of that period) and consequently, bonds with high coupons continued to realize lower but still significant capital gains.

Hard as it may be to believe, in spite of the enormous bull market in stocks that took place between 1982 and 2001, anyone who was either clever enough or lucky enough to have purchased 30-year Treasury bonds in 1982 or 1983 enjoyed returns on those bonds that exceeded those of the stock market. Perhaps even more startling, returns on many sectors of the bond market have exceeded those of stocks for the decade between 1999 and 2009.

Since interest rates in all sectors of the bond market key off Treasuries, interest rate levels in other sectors of the bond market (corporates, munis, mortgage backed, etc.) followed the general patterns seen in the Treasury market. Keep this history of interest rates in mind as you read the book. We will refer to it again and again. You cannot understand bond returns for any of the past three decades unless you factor in the level of interest rates prevailing at the time, and the capital gains component of that return. Keep that in mind when you evaluate potential investments in the bond market, with 10-year Treasury yields currently in the 3% to 4% range.

Finally, you probably noticed the startling symmetry in Exhibit 3.4. In 2008, interest rates on Treasuries with maturities between 10 and 30 years fell back to levels prevailing around 1940, in the depths of the Great Depression. Even more dramatic, yields on T-Bills remain (as noted above) around 10 basis points (that is, one-tenth of 1%), annualized. And money market yields as well as passbook accounts yield less than they did during the Great Depression.

Is it possible that from their current level, Treasury rates could once again retrace the path taken in the late 1970s? Indeed, some economists are warning that the unprecedented stimulus package passed by the Obama administration is bound to result in inflation and higher interest rates some time in the future. But it should be noted that interest rates move in very long cycles. The spikes that took place in the 1970s and early 1980s took over a decade to develop. The decline in rates that began in 1982 has lasted well over 30 years. While inflation and higher interest rates are a possibility somewhere down the line, an equally plausible scenario is a Japan style very low-growth economy for a number of years, with interest rates even at the longer end not rising significantly from current levels.

"Real" and "Nominal" Rates of Return

The terms "real" rate and "nominal" rate are sometimes used to refer to rates of return on bonds. These terms represent a method of adjusting bond yields for the rate of inflation. The nominal rate measures the actual dollars earned, based on interest rate yields. To obtain the real rate, subtract the inflation rate from the nominal rate. For example, at the time this is being written, the coupon rate on the long bond is currently approximately 4.5%. That is the nominal rate. Subtracting the current rate of inflation, which is around 2.5%, results in a real rate of return of about 2.0%.

The relationship between the real rate of return and the nominal rate has varied during the century. So has the level of interest rates. Interest rate levels are governed, first, by what is happening to prices (that is, inflation or deflation) and, second, by expectations of what will happen to prices. Until 1950, even though interest rates were low, bonds earned a real rate of return because inflation was low. As inflation began to rise, the real rate of return began to decline, despite a rise in nominal rates. The real rate of return throughout the 1960s and 1970s was negative even though rates were high and rising. Moreover, inflation eroded the purchasing power of older issues. That was the main reason interest rates rose to such high levels: few investors were willing to purchase long-term bonds because the nominal rate did not appear high enough to compensate for anticipated increases in yield as a result of continuing high inflation.

Historically, the real rate of return on long bonds has averaged about 3% above the inflation rate. Since that is an average, it has sometimes been higher and sometimes lower. During the 1990s inflation averaged under 3% a year, and that rate is considered benign. For the first time since the Great Depression, the financial crisis of 2008 resulted in several months of actual deflation and the continuing deep recession threatened further deflation. It is partly to combat this threat that the Federal Reserve lowered short-term rates to virtually zero. Whether these policies will eventually result in a continuing period of very low inflation or in higher inflation down the road is still uncertain.

While inflation rates between 2% and 3% have been considered relatively "benign" over the last couple of decades, it is worth noting that low rates of inflation do not equate to no inflation. Over a 30-year period, if inflation were to remain as low as a constant 2% a year, an item costing $100 at year one would cost $181 at year 30. If inflation rates were to rise to 3% over that same 30-year period, an item costing $100 at year one would cost $243 at year 30. Unless there is an extended period of actual deflation, nominal rates will probably continue to remain 2% to 3% above the inflation rate. But none of this is predictable. No one knows whether the next 30 years will see deflation or whether higher inflation rates will return. The one point no one disputes is that crystal balls have been notoriously unreliable in predicting future interest rates. More to the point, no one has ever consistently predicted interest rates correctly over a period of 30 years; that is, over the life of the long bond.

The strategies described in this book are predicated on the assumption that interest rates cannot be predicted. You can, however, control the amount of risk you take so that no matter what happens to interest rates, your portfolio will be protected.

Note also that beginning in 2000, the US Treasury has been issuing a new type of bond that is indexed to inflation and is therefore guaranteed a "real" rate of return. These bonds are Treasury Inflation Protected Securities (TIPS) and also I Bonds. Both of these will be discussed in Chapter 6.

THE FEDERAL RESERVE AND INTEREST RATES

The Federal Reserve Bank (the Fed, for short) plays a major and critical role in determining the level and changes in interest rate levels. That function, in turn, in part determines how the economy performs. Critical as the Fed's role has been in the past, it has become even more significant because of the role it played during the financial crisis of 2008. Discussing the role of the Fed in influencing interest rates, as well as its role in the overall economy, would require an entire book. But I just want to touch on a number of recent activities which will be critical in determining both the level and the direction of interest rates on Treasuries in the United States.

Despite its enormous importance, the Federal Reserve actually controls only two interest rates directly: the Fed Funds rate and the discount rate. Both of these are the shortest interest rates in the bond market. They are, in fact, overnight rates: The Fed Funds rate is the rate the Fed charges banks that need to borrow overnight money to bring their capital reserves up to required levels. The discount rate is the rate banks charge each other for overnight loans. When the Fed raises these overnight rates, interest rates on other securities with very short maturities typically rise as well. In practice, these increases generally extend to maturities of two to five years. But longer term rates may or may not follow. The Fed may hope or intend to influence rates on longer maturities; but it is not always successful in doing that.

The Fed has many other functions that affect the level of economic activity and, indirectly, interest rates. For example, it increases or decreases the money supply by purchasing or selling Treasuries through primary dealers. When it buys Treasury securities, it pays the primary dealers and this increases the money supply. This promotes economic activity. When the Fed sells Treasury securities, again, it does this through primary dealers who then have to pay the Federal Reserve Bank. This decreases the supply of money in circulation. And that slows economic activity.

During the panic of 2008, the Fed undertook a number of unprecedented steps. It opened a lot of new facilities whose purpose was to keep the financial system from collapsing by buying distressed securities and thereby increasing the amount of money in circulation. In particular, the Federal Reserve bought an enormous amount of mortgage backed securities, worth well over $1 trillion. (During this period, the Fed became the largest purchaser and owner of mortgage-backed bonds in the country.) This was done to promote "liquidity" in a market that had seized up; and also, to keep interest rates on mortgages low. Those purchases stopped at the end of March 2010.

All of these actions have created a lot of uncertainty concerning the future course of interest rates. At some point, the Fed will have to raise the shortest rates. The Fed's current target rate of 0 to 25 basis points for the shortest rates would appear to be unsustainable on a long-term basis. What will happen to longer interest rates (that is, to rates between 5 and 30 years) when the Fed raises short-term rates, is not predictable. It does not follow that longer term rates will necessarily rise. There have been periods when the Fed raised the Fed Fund rates over a long and sustained period of time, and when longer rates actually declined. The most recent example occurred between 2004 and 2006, when the Fed raised the discount rate 17 times and yet longer interest rates actually declined. Note also that there is a great deal of uncertainty about the timing of an increase in short term rates, and also about the levels of such increases. It is worth noting that in Japan, for example, rates on long-term and short-term bonds have been exceptionally low (lower than 2% for the 10-year bond) for well over 15 years.

Another major uncertainty is due to the fact that at some point, the Fed in all likelihood will want to sell the securities that were purchased in 2008 and 2009. This includes the trillion plus amount of mortgages and many other billions worth of distressed securities. Note that the Federal Reserve does not have to sell these securities: it may hold them until they mature or are retired. Nonetheless, a number of programs are underway to begin this unwinding. Some mutual fund firms have signaled that they want to create funds that will invest in some distressed securities. But the major uncertainty is related to the Fed's holdings of mortgages. Mortgage rates are a critical factor in the housing market, and housing activity constitutes a major sector of the economy. How the Fed's sale of mortgages will affect future mortgage rates is a big question mark.

As a result of all of these programs, the Fed has enormously expanded its role in influencing the future both of interest rates and of the economy. But whether the unwinding of the Fed initiatives will result in inflation or deflation, that is, in higher rates down the line or continuing deflation, is still unclear.

SUMMARY

This chapter has briefly reviewed the major sources of risk in the bond market; namely, interest rate risk and credit risk. If interest rates go up, bond prices decline. If interest rates decline, bond prices rise. How much they go up or down is directly related to the maturity length of bonds. Over the last 30 years, changes in the level of interest rates have been the major factor in determining returns earned by investment in bonds, as interest rates on long term Treasuries have declined from a peak of about 15% in 1982, to between 3% and 4% in 2010. That decline has been the most significant factor behind the almost 30-year bull market in bonds.

For bonds that are at least investment grade, credit risk is a second, but less significant risk factor. Prior to 2008, most investors relied on the credit ratings of the major rating firms to evaluate the credit quality. During the financial panic of 2008, bonds initially rated AAA (that is the highest rating) plummeted in value as a result of multiple defaults of bonds derived from "subprime" mortgages. As a result, the credit rating firms have come under closer scrutiny; as have the credit rating scales. One result has been a total "recalibration" of the credit rating scale of municipal bonds. But most bonds continue to be issued and rated as before. This chapter discussed rating scales and explained how and to what extent they impact the cost of borrowing as well as bond returns.

Finally, this chapter briefly touched on the role played by the Federal Reserve in determining both the level and the direction of interest rates.

CHAPTER 4

How Much Will I Earn, or Basic Bond Math

This chapter discusses basic bond math. This includes

◆ Bond cash flows and the magic of compounding
◆ The many meanings of yield
◆ Total return
◆ Duration and volatility

Discussions of bond returns begin and end with numbers. If your eyes glaze over when numbers and formulae appear, you may be tempted to skip this chapter. But that would be a mistake because it is impossible to evaluate bonds without an understanding of basic bond math. But fear not. I, too, am a charter member of the math anxiety crowd. The mathematics in this section is at the level of arithmetic, or at most, elementary algebra. More importantly, the emphasis is on concepts that help you to understand and evaluate how much you will actually earn when you buy or sell bonds, and not on mathematical formulae.

BOND CASH FLOWS

When you buy a bond, you earn money from three sources. We have mentioned the first source a number of times. It is the simple interest derived from coupons, usually paid twice a year. The second source arises from the difference between the purchase price of a bond and its sale or redemption price. If you sell (or redeem) a bond for more than your purchase price, then you realize a capital gain. If you sell (or redeem it) for less than you paid, then you realize a capital loss. The third source is earned when coupons are reinvested: at that point, you earn interest on your interest income. This creates still another source of revenue, appropriately called "interest-on-interest." On Wall Street, each of these sources of income is called a "cash flow." Let's look at each in turn.

Simple Interest

Let's start with simple interest (that is, the coupon payments).

Let us say you invest $10,000 in 30-year bonds, paying 7% a year, semiannually. Every six months, you will receive a coupon paying $350. At the end of year one, you will have received $700. If you hold the bonds until they mature, you will receive a total of 60 coupons which all together total $21,000. Those coupons represent coupon income, also called interest income.

Interest-on-Interest, or the Magic of Compounding

If you are investing primarily to receive income, and if you spend the coupons, then the coupon interest is all you will earn. But if the coupons are reinvested, those produce additional interest. Subsequently, if those earnings are reinvested, you earn interest on that interest, and so on. That entire income stream is called, logically enough, "interest-on-interest," or "compound interest."

This illustrates the basic way in which compounding works. But it does not make clear how significantly interest-on-interest increases the total amount that can be earned on the original investment. The simplest way to explain the process is with some examples.

Let us assume that you reinvest each $350 coupon. After six months, you will have the following amounts:

Principal originally invested:	$10,000.00
Interest income (1/2 of 7%):	$350.00
Total amount:	$10,350.00

You can choose to spend the coupon or to reinvest it. Let's assume you decide to reinvest the entire amount, and furthermore, that you reinvest it at the same 7% rate. At the end of the year, you would have not $10,700, but rather, $10,712.25. The $12.25 difference results from reinvesting your first interest payment. Compared with your original investment, this is how you get to the final number at the end of year one:

Principal originally invested: $10,000.00

First coupon payment: $350.00

Second coupon payment: $350.00

Interest on first coupon payment: $12.25

Total at the end of year one: $12,712.25

That may not sound like a major difference, and indeed, after one year and two coupon payments, interest-on-interest amounts to a trivial amount of money. But that is only the beginning of the story. Exhibit 4.1 shows how coupon payments and interest-on-interest would continue to grow if you held the bonds for 30 years and if you continue to reinvest the coupons at 7%.

A look at Exhibit 4.1 shows that over a period of 30 years, the income generated by coupon payments (that is, $21,000) constitutes only a limited portion of the total income you earn from your $10,000 investment. A much larger amount ($47,780) is generated by interest-on-interest.

Furthermore, the longer you hold the bonds, the higher the percentage of total income is generated by interest-on-interest. After five years, you would have received 10 semiannual coupon payments, for a total of $3,500. Interest-on-interest would amount to $606.

After 20 years, on the other hand, interest-on-interest actually exceeds the amount of income generated by the coupon payments: as shown in Exhibit 4.1, the 40 coupon payments total $14,000, but interest-on-interest amounts to almost $15,593.

EXHIBIT 4.1

Interest and Interest-on-Interest on 30-year, $10,000 Par Value Bond with a 7% Coupon. Coupons Reinvested at 7%, Semiannually

Time	Number of Coupons	Coupon Interest A	Interest-on-Interest (Cumulative) B	Total Interest A + B	Total Value of Investment
Year 1	2	$700	$12.25	$712.25	
Year 5	10	$3,500	$605.99	$14,105.99	
Year 10	20	$7,000	$2,897.89	$19,897.89	
Year 20	40	$14,000	$15,592.60	$39,592.60	
Year 30	60	$21,000	$47,780.91	$68,780.91	$78,780.91*

*Year 30: redeem the bonds at par ($10,000).

After 30 years, the amount of income generated by interest-on-interest ($47,781) is more than double the amount generated by the 60 coupon payments (which add up to a total of $21,000). At the 30-year mark, interest-on-interest constitutes approximately 69% of the total amount of earnings generated by the bond.

As Exhibit 4.1 shows, the amount of interest-on-interest earned is directly related to the time allowed for compounding: the longer the time frame, the larger the percentage produced by interest-on-interest.

For truly long-term holdings (30 years or more), interest-on-interest may comprise up to 80% of the total amount earned. In fact, even apparently minor percentage differences, compounded over long periods of time, result in significantly higher returns. For example, over a 10-year period, increasing the annual return to 7.5% from 7% would increase total earnings by almost 5%; after 20 years, by somewhat over 10%; and after 40 years (for the investor with a long-term perspective), by an astonishing 20%.

Compounded interest has been called the eighth wonder of the world. And yet it works for everyone. It requires no special aptitude and is totally automatic. In fact, only two ingredients are required: reinvesting and time.

The rate at which assets compound is critical to the total actually earned. Money reinvested (tax-free) at 4%, semiannually, will double every 17.5 years; at 6%, every 11.7 years; at 8%, every 8.8 years; and at 10%, every 7 years. Over very long periods, compounding achieves extraordinary results. Over a period of 50 years, $1,000, compounded semiannually at a rate of 8%, would grow to $50,504. For the investor with a truly long-term view, over a period of 100 years, $1,000 compounded semiannually would grow to $2,550,749.[1]

Compounding has been heavily advertised for zero coupon bonds, but it applies equally to all financial investments, whether stocks, bonds, or savings accounts. Wherever you consult information concerning an investment (a mutual fund, stocks, or bonds), the merits of that investment are usually illustrated with graphs showing that if you had invested in that particular vehicle, you would now be (or you will become) very rich. All those graphs basically illustrate the magic of compounding. The differences in the final result are not due to the particular vehicle that is being advertised. Rather, those differences are the result of two variables, namely, the actual rates at which that instrument compounds (that is, the actual reinvestment rates) and the amount of time.

The long explanation that accompanies Exhibit 4.1 is intended to give a basic understanding of how compounding works. It may appear to

---

1. Sidney Homer and Martin Leibowitz, *Inside the Yield Book* (Englewood Cliffs, NJ: Prentice Hall, 1973), p. 32.

be overly detailed, but that is intentional. A genuine understanding of how compounding works over time is the beginning of investment wisdom. Compounding puts time on your side. Compounding at even modest levels over years of investing is startlingly effective in building a significant nest egg.

Understanding how compounding works over long periods of time is particularly relevant to anyone using tax-deferred plans such as IRAs and 401Ks. Typically, someone beginning to invest through such a plan may begin investing when she is in her twenties, and continue investing through her sixties, a period lasting well over 40 years. Furthermore, it would not be unusual for such an investor, when retired, to withdraw some annual amounts over the next 20 to 30 years, through her eighties or even nineties. And note finally that during the withdrawal period, sums remaining in the tax-deferred plan continue to compound. Therefore, investments in the plan may compound for a period lasting well over 70 years.

The opposite of compounding is what can be called the "arithmetic of loss." Again, let's start with a $10,000 investment. Suppose you have a sudden large loss, say 50% (the approximate loss of the major stock market indices between 2007 and 2008). Your $10,000 investment has now shrunk to $5,000.

What percentage gain is required to bring your investment back to even? (The answer is 100%—a 50% gain brings your $5,000 back up only to $7,500.) Moreover, even if you earn 10% a year every year for the next few years, it will take eight years to earn back that 100% (it takes eight years—and not ten—because of compounding). But the last straw is that after you have earned back 100%, you still have not made any money: you are back to square one.

This cruel arithmetic is the reason many wise investors maintain that the first rule of investing is not to lose money. And that the second rule of investing is not to forget the first.

THE MANY MEANINGS OF YIELD

Bonds are marketed on the basis of yield. It is a logical assumption that the higher the quoted yield, the more you will earn from your bond investment. So it may come as a surprise to learn that this does not necessarily work out to be the case.

The term "yield" actually has several different meanings. The yield that is quoted most often is the yield-to-maturity (usually abbreviated as YTM). In reality, however, the quoted YTM is not a prediction of what you will earn. Rather, it is an estimate of what you may earn if certain conditions are realized.

At the time you purchase an individual bond, you can be sure of three price quotes: the purchase price, the coupon interest, and the redemption value of the bond at maturity. But in order to understand how much you will actually earn from your bond investments, you need to understand what the yield quotes actually measure. This is discussed in the section below on the different meanings of yield. In addition, however, you also have to understand other potential sources of gain or loss. That will be discussed later on in the chapter, in the section entitled Total Return.

The term "yield" appears in a number of phrases: "coupon yield," "current yield," and "yield-to-maturity." Each has a very precise meaning. Let's look at each in turn.

Coupon Yield

This is the simplest meaning of yield. Coupon yield is set when a bond is issued. It is the interest rate paid by a bond, listed as a percentage of par (for example, $5^1/_2\%$ or $7^1/_4\%$). It designates a fixed-dollar amount that never changes through the life of the bond. If you buy a bond with a 7% coupon, you will receive $70 a year, usually paid out in two semiannual increments of $35. You will receive that exact amount in dollars, no matter what happens to the price of the bond, until the bond is redeemed on its maturity date. The only exception to this are floating-rate bonds, whose interest rate is reset at predetermined intervals, based on a stipulated benchmark interest rate.

Current Yield

Almost as soon as a bond starts trading in the secondary market, it ceases to trade at par. Current yield is simply coupon divided by price.

Let us assume you purchase three bonds: the first at par ($1,000), the second at a premium ($1,200), and the third at a discount ($800), each paying out $100 (two coupons, each $50, paid twice a year). Dividing the coupon ($100) by the price results in a current yield of 10% for the par bond, ($100 divided by $1,000); 8.33% for the premium bond ($100 divided by $1,200); and 12.5% for the discount bond ($100 divided by $800). Current yield is equal to coupon yield for the par bond, lower than coupon yield for the premium bond, and higher than coupon yield for the discount.

Current yield is quoted for bonds of any maturity, whether short or long. In none of the preceding examples was the bond's maturity specified. That is because current yield is based only on coupon and price. Current yield, therefore, fails to measure two important cash flows earned from bonds: interest-on-interest and appreciation or decline in the price of the bond when you sell or redeem it at maturity.

Yield-to-Maturity

Yield-to-maturity is a far more comprehensive measure of return than current yield. It estimates the total amount that you will earn over the entire life of a bond, from all possible cash flows. Therefore, in addition to coupon income, it includes interest-on-interest, and gains or losses due to the difference between the price you pay when you purchase the bond, and par (the redemption price).

Calculating YTM with paper and pencil involves a tedious trial-and-error algebraic procedure. In practice, almost no one uses the formula any more. Before the advent of calculators, the investor (or his broker) used bond yield tables to come up with an approximate YTM. Nowadays the process has been enormously simplified (and made more accurate) through the use of financial calculators such as the Hewlett-Packard HP 12C.[2]

For example, let's use a financial calculator to compute the YTM of a 10-year discount bond purchased for $800 and redeemed for $1,000, with one $50 coupon payment annually. Feed all of those numbers into the calculator as follows:

◆ Plug in the price of $800 as PV (present value), using the *PV* key, with a minus sign: -$800.

◆ Plug in the par price of $1,000 (the redemption value) as FV (future value), using the *FV* key.

---

2. The HP 12C has been around since the 1980s. It continues to be sold although several somewhat improved versions are on the market. This financial calculator enables you to calculate almost any aspect of bond math that you choose, but it has many additional applications, such as calculating future value, annuity payments, compounding, etc. The advantage of a financial calculator (compared with just plugging in numbers using a program on the Internet) is that it helps you to understand the principles behind the actual calculations; and, in turn, this can guide some of your investment decisions.

- Enter the dollar amount of the coupon payment ($50), using the *PMT* (payment) key.
- Finally, enter the number of years to maturity, using the *n* key (10 years).
- Solve for YTM by hitting *i*, the interest key.

Result: the YTM is 7.98%. That is higher than the coupon rate, (5%), because you purchased this bond at a discount, for $800. When the bond is redeemed at par, you earn an additional $200, which represents the difference between the price you paid ($800) and the redemption price at par ($1,000).[3]

Why YTM Is Only an Estimate

So, you may ask, since YTM includes all potential cash flows, why is it only an estimate?

The answer is that the actual return is likely to differ from the YTM, perhaps considerably, because the YTM will only be realized under certain conditions. Those conditions are:

- That you hold the bond to maturity
- That the coupons are reinvested (rather than spent)
- That the coupons are reinvested at the YTM rate

Let's briefly look at each assumption.

That You Hold the Bond to Maturity
The YTM quote is based on the assumption that the bond will be redeemed at par at maturity. If you sell a bond before it matures at a price other than par, then you will realize either a capital gain or a capital loss. Either will change what you actually earn. If, for example, you purchase a bond at par

---

3. The steps used in this calculation represent a quick way of calculating YTM.
   In this example, as well as the others in this chapter, I did not plug in the
   date of purchase and the date the bond matures. The better financial calculators
   enable you to compute YTM, prices, and total return with great precision, by
   plugging in the specific dates from date of purchase to date of maturity.
   They are inexpensive. Specifically request one that is set up for calculating
   bond yields.

and sell it at a premium, say, $1,200, the $200 difference represents a gain of approximately 20% compared with the purchase price of the bond. That boosts actual return by a very significant amount. But if you buy a bond at par and sell it at a loss, say, $800, you lose about 20%. Clearly, that will mean that you would earn far less than the YTM initially quoted.

That You Reinvest Coupons and Also Reinvest Them at the YTM Rate

YTM calculations are based on the assumption that coupons are never spent; they are always reinvested.

Clearly, if you spend coupons, then the interest-on-interest goes out the window. You will then earn less than the anticipated YTM. How much less depends both on how many coupons you spend and on the maturity of the bonds.

In addition, and this is probably the most confusing aspect of the YTM quote, the assumption is made that the coupons are reinvested at the quoted YTM rate. This may sound like double-talk. However, what this means is that if a broker quotes a YTM of 7% for a bond, then that yield will be earned *only if each and every coupon is reinvested at a rate of 7%*, that is, at the same rate as the quoted YTM. Clearly, particularly with longer-term bonds, that is highly unlikely to happen. Some coupons will be reinvested at more than 7%; others, at less than 7%. If you reinvest coupons at a higher rate, you will actually earn more than the bond's stated YTM. If you reinvest coupons at lower rates, you will earn less.

Reinvestment Rates and Actual Returns

Both of these factors alter what you actually earn, compared to the anticipated YTM. Exhibit 4.2 shows what the actual yield would be for a 25-year par bond, with a 7.5% coupon, under a variety of reinvestment assumptions. The YTM quoted at the time of purchase is 7.5%.

As Exhibit 4.2 shows, the anticipated 7.5% YTM is realized only if all coupons are reinvested at 7.5% (line 4). If no coupons are reinvested (line 1), the anticipated 7.5% YTM is cut to 4.27%. On the other hand, if coupons are reinvested at a higher rate than 7.5%, the actual yield rises: to 7.77% if coupons are reinvested at 8%, but more significantly, to 8.91% if coupons are reinvested at 10%. The higher the reinvestment rate, the higher the actual return.

The amount of total earnings due to interest-on-interest varies both with the maturity of a bond and with the reinvestment rate. It is less significant for shorter than for longer bonds. This was actually illustrated by

E X H I B I T   4.2

How the Reinvestment Rate Affects Actual Yield over the Life of a 25-year, 7.5% Par Bond

	Dollars per $1,000 Bond for the Life of the Bond				
Assumed Reinvestment Rate (Semiannual Basis)	Coupon Income (A)	Interest-on- Interest (B)	Total Interest (A + B)	Interest-on- Interest as Percent of Total Interest	Actual Yield
0.0%	$1,875	$ 0	$1,875	0%	4.27%
5.0%	$1,875	$1,781	$3,656	49%	6.25%
6.0%	$1,875	$2,355	$4,230	56%	6.73%
7.5%	$1,875	$3,426	$5,301	65%	7.50%
8.0%	$1,875	$3,850	$5,725	67%	7.77%
10.0%	$1,875	$5,976	$7,851	76%	8.91%

Source: Frank Fabozzi, et al., *The Handbook of Fixed-Income Securities*, 2nd ed. (Homewood, Ill.: Dow Jones Irwin), p. 596. Adapted with permission.

Exhibit 4.1, in the section concerning compounding. As we saw, interest-on-interest constituted only a minor portion of the total amount of income generated by a bond at the two-year mark. For the same bond, however, interest-on-interest represented 15% of total income at the five-year mark, 53% at the 20-year mark, and almost 70% at the 30-year mark. Particularly if you are investing over the long term, for periods of over 20 or 30 years (as you would, for example, in a retirement plan), the importance of reinvestment rates cannot be stressed enough. Because interest-on-interest constitutes the major part of returns for long-term holdings, you need to be as aware of reinvestment rates as about initial YTM, or perhaps even more so.

Reinvestment Risk

When the YTM is quoted to you, reinvestment rates are assumed to be both constant and known: They are set at the YTM rate. In real life, of course, you cannot know at the time of purchase the rate at which future coupons will be reinvested, since you don't know where interest rates will be in the future. Consequently, you cannot know at the time of purchase exactly how much you will earn either in actual dollars or as a percentage value. That uncertainty is known as the *"reinvestment risk."*

Calling this uncertainty a "risk" is somewhat confusing in that there is no risk of an actual loss, either of principal or interest. But, as noted earlier, if you reinvest coupons at a lower rate than the YTM, actual return will then be lower than the YTM quoted to you when you bought the bond. Reinvestment risk may work in your favor if coupons are reinvested at a higher rate: you would then earn a higher amount than the YTM initially quoted to you.

How to Intepret and Use "Yield-to-Maturity" Quotes

Two factors affect the reliability of the YTM quote. The first is the maturity of the bond: as maturities become longer, since the amount represented by the interest-on-interest becomes greater on a percentage basis, the YTM becomes increasingly less accurate and less reliable as a forecast of what you will actually earn. If you buy 30-year bonds, for example, and hold them for the entire period, the total return is likely to be very different from the YTM quoted at the time of purchase. Remember that for 30-year bonds, interest-on-interest may provide up to 80% of the total return. If you hold 30-year bonds until they mature, and you reinvest coupons at lower rates, then you will earn far less than the YTM you were initially quoted. But if interest rates go up and you are able to reinvest coupons at higher interest rates, then you will earn an amount higher than the YTM initially quoted.

The second factor that affects the reliability of the YTM quote is the size of the coupon. If interest rates are particularly high at the time you buy your bonds, or if you buy a bond that has a particularly high coupon (for example, a premium bond), again, it becomes more likely that you will earn less than the YTM quoted to you. The larger the size of the coupons, the more likely it is that you will be able to reinvest coupons only at rates lower than either the coupon interest or the YTM quote.

If YTM does not predict actual return, what does it tell you? The chief usefulness of YTM quotes is that they permit direct comparison between different securities, with dissimilar coupons and prices (par, premium, and discount). Suppose, for example, that you are considering three different securities for purchase, the first an A-rated bond, selling at a discount, and maturing in five years; the second a AAA bond selling at a premium and maturing in five years; and the third an A-rated bond selling at par and maturing in 30 years. The YTM enables you to evaluate, for instance, how much yield you might be giving up for higher credit quality; or how much yield you are picking up as you lengthen maturities.

Overall, there is too much emphasis on yield. YTM should not be the main criterion for selecting bonds. More appropriate criteria would depend on your objective when you purchase bonds. If, for example, you do not intend to reinvest coupons, then you might look for bonds with high current yield. If you are primarily interested in stability of principal, that would dictate selecting bonds with intermediate (two-to-seven-year) maturities. Such criteria are discussed at greater length in other sections of the book.

One final note: you can eliminate reinvestment risk by purchasing zero coupon bonds. That may be an attractive option under certain conditions.

"Yield-to-Call" and "Yield-to-Worst"

When a bond is callable, investors can compute the yield-to-call using the same formula as for YTM. Typically, the price at which the bond can be called on the first call date is somewhat above par; it may decline to par on subsequent call dates.

Typical calculations are made to the first call date; or to the first par call date. Since the formula for calculating the "yield-to-call" is the same as that for calculating the YTM, it suffers from the same shortcoming, namely, the assumption that all coupons will be reinvested at the yield-to-call rate.

For a bond that is selling at a premium, many investors calculate both the yield-to-call and the YTM, and select the lower of the two to evaluate the attractiveness of the bond. But that is not necessarily warranted because there is no guarantee the bond will be called.

Finally, some investors calculate the yield to all possible call dates, as well as the YTM. The "yield-to-worst" is the lowest possible yield that could be earned by purchasing this bond. But again, there is no guarantee that this is the most accurate measure of the bond's eventual total return.

TOTAL RETURN

Investors in bonds sometimes make the mistake of equating interest income or YTM with return without taking into consideration what is happening to principal. A more useful way of measuring return includes the changing value of principal. It is called "total return." Total return consists of whatever you earn in interest income, plus or minus changes in the value of principal. To be 100% accurate, you would also subtract taxes and commission expenses from return.

Put differently, YTM is quoted to you at the time you purchase a bond. It is an estimate of what you will earn from your investment in the bond. Total return, on the other hand, measures what you have actually earned. But it is calculated after you have redeemed or sold the bond, or after you have held it for a while.

For example, let's assume that you purchase ten bonds maturing in 15 years at par. The YTM is 5% and so is the coupon. The quoted YTM is therefore 5%. But suppose that three years later, interest rates rise and bonds with similar maturity and credit quality yield 6%. Suppose further that you decide to sell the bonds at that time. Because interest rates have risen, the value of your bonds has declined. So you sell your bonds for approximately $850 each. What have you earned on that investment? And how do your returns compare with the yield-to-maturity quoted when you purchased the bonds?

One answer is that you have earned simple interest income (based on the dividend distributions) of 5% or $500 each year. You may also have earned some interest-on-interest—say 5% on that 5%, about $176. But let us calculate the total return based on your purchase price, interest income and sale price. To calculate total return, you have:

Coupon income (3 years):	$1,500
Interest-on-interest (estimate):	$176
Proceeds from sale of bonds:	$8,500
Purchase price:	$10,000 (minus)

If you add the total interest earned to the proceeds of the sale of your bonds, that amounts to $10,176. Subtract from that total your initial investment in the bonds, $10,000. Your total earnings from that investment amount to $176 over the three years. In percentage terms, the total earned, cumulatively, is 1.6%.

That amount is called the total return. The total can be averaged for the three years you have held the bonds. If you average that amount over the three years, that number is the average earnings for each year you owned the bonds. The average annual return is approximately one half of 1%. Clearly, however you figure it, you have not earned the 5% YTM quoted when you bought the bond.

In the preceding example, the total return calculation is the same even if you continue to hold the bonds. Many investors calculate total return for their investments on an ongoing basis. If you sell the bonds, you are said to have realized the loss. If you still own the bonds, but they have gone down in value, the loss is said to be unrealized. Whether you actually realize the loss, or keep the bonds, the total return is the same.

In the trade, among professionals, this kind of calculation is done daily and is known as "marking-to-market." It describes to each trader exactly what his holdings are worth at the end of the day if he had to or wanted to sell them.

The important point to remember is that when you are evaluating fixed-income securities, you must assess potential fluctuations in the value of the principal and not just rely on yield, whether coupon yield, or YTM. This is why, when you buy a bond (or a bond fund), you need to take into consideration how long you plan to hold it. If you need to sell a bond, or a bond fund, before it matures, and if interest rates have moved against you, you may take a real hit to principal. Even if you decide not sell your bonds (or your bond fund) and do not realize the loss in principal value, you may experience another loss: you are unable to take advantage of the currently higher yields (that is called an "opportunity cost"), and you have lost liquidity because you may be unwilling to sell a bond if it has declined significantly in value.

If you look only at the yield side, bond investments look very predictable. But if you include potential changes in a bond's principal value, and you look at bonds as total return vehicles, the picture changes vastly.

But, you may be thinking, "I just want to invest in bonds for income."

Unfortunately, whether you like it or not, like Molière's character who found out that he had been speaking in prose all his life without realizing it, if you are buying bonds with 30-year maturities, you are making a bet on interest rates, whether you know it or not.

Investors intent on boosting yield sometimes place their principal at risk for very little gain. When purchasing bonds, the first question to ask, always, is, "How much more am I really earning?" The second is, "What kinds of risk am I assuming in order to earn that extra amount?"

One final note: Total return is calculated in the same way for any bond investment, whether a bond fund or an individual bond. But that is not true of YTM. Most bond funds do not have a maturity date, and consequently, cannot quote a YTM. Also, if you hold an individual bond until it matures, as noted earlier, its price returns to par. Again, that is not true of bond funds. Since most bond funds maintain a constant maturity, the future price of a bond fund is not predictable. This will be discussed in greater detail in the section dealing with bond funds.

No one can quote total return to you ahead of time. Total return is actual return to you, based on your own investment experience. For any investment, you start out with a given sum. For a chosen period of time (say, one year), add all the income streams that have accrued (whether from dividends, interest-on-interest, or capital gains), subtract all transaction costs, and be sure to add or subtract any changes in principal value. You can also subtract taxes to obtain total return on a net-after-tax basis. For the year, calculate how much (as a percentage) your investment has grown or declined. That is your total return.

There is one further virtue to "total return": the concept is easy to understand. If you like precision, the exact formula for calculating total return is:

(Ending Figure + Dividends + Distributions) – Beginning Figure

The same formula can be used to calculate total return on any investment, whether it's stocks, gold bullion, baseball cards, or real estate. Calculating total return keeps you honest; it helps you to evaluate what your investments are really doing for you. It is, therefore, a very useful concept.

DURATION AND BOND PRICE VOLATILITY

The concept of "duration" originated in 1938. It has come into widespread use over the past two decades. Duration is not a measure of return. It is used primarily as a gauge of the sensitivity of a bond to interest rate changes; that is, it is used to predict how much specific bonds will go up (or down) in price if interest rates change. Duration is used by professionals for the management of institutional portfolios. The term is also cropping up increasingly in analysis of bonds, or of bond funds. Even if you do not know how to actually derive duration, you can easily look it up. And knowing the duration of a bond (or of a bond fund) enables you to evaluate how much interest rate risk you are taking.

Duration is based on the same cash flows as YTM; that is, coupon payments, interest-on-interest, and the sale or redemption value of a bond. But duration adds in as important elements the timing (exactly when you receive the cash flows) and the size of all the cash flows. It takes into account not only how many dollars will be received as coupons but also when those cash flows occur. That is because the timing and the size of the cash flows affect interest-on-interest. If, for example, you buy premium bonds, which have high coupons, that gives you more money to reinvest each time you receive a coupon payment. If you buy discount bonds, which typically have lower coupons, you will then have less money to reinvest. Therefore, two bonds with the same YTM, but one a discount bond and the other a premium bond, will have different durations.

The Time Value of Money

The formula for calculating duration involves the use of the concept of "the time value of money," either future value or present value. Future value tells you how much a dollar today will be worth at some future date, based on assumed annual percentage increases. Present value tells you how much a dollar received at some future date is worth today, again based on an assumed annual percentage rate of return.

Both concepts can be illustrated with a financial calculator. Suppose you want to know how much $50,000 invested today will be worth in 20 years if you earn 7% per year: that would be the future value of the $50,000. Take out your financial calculator and plug in the following numbers:

- Plug in $50,000 as PV, using the *PV* (present value) key (you need to use a minus sign in front of the -$50,000 number).
- Plug in 7, using the *i* (interest) key.
- Plug in 20, using the *n* key (for the number of years).
- Solve for FV (future value), using the *FV* key.
- The answer is $193,484.22.

If you want to test how much more you would earn if you earned 10% a year, simply plug in 10 using the *i* (interest) key. The answer is $336,375.00. (Incidentally, this provides another example of the magic of compounding.)

Present value is the reverse. Suppose you know that you will need $100,000 in 20 years. How much money would you need to put away today (assuming you are putting away a lump sum)? The answer to that question would be the present value of the $100,000. Well, once again, you have to assume a rate at which the money would compound; let's say 7%. Again, take out your financial calculator. You would plug in the following numbers:

- Plug in $100,000 as FV, using the *FV* key.
- Plug in 20, using the *n* key (for the number of years).

♦ Plug in 7, using the *i* (interest) key.

♦ Solve for present value (PV), using the *PV* key.

The answer is $25,842. That number is the present value of $100,000 compounding at an annual rate of 7% for 20 years.

When you work from future value back to present value, the annual percentage rate at which money is assumed to compound is known as the *"discount"* rate. Both present value and future value are based on compounded numbers, that is, they assume interest-on-interest if you are calculating dollar amounts.

Now that we have illustrated the time value of money, let's apply it to the concept of duration. The definition of duration is "a weighted average term-to-maturity of a security's cash flows."[4] Solving for duration is a tedious process, involving several different steps. You first need to calculate the present value of all of a bond's known cash flows: coupon payments, redeemed principal, and capital gains (or losses), if you did not purchase the bond at par. (You calculate the present value of these known cash flows by discounting them—for interest-on-interest—at the assumed reinvestment rate.) The present values of all the bond's cash flows are then adjusted, by weight, for the exact time when they are received.

The resulting number is the bond's duration, in years. In effect, the number you have obtained readjusts the maturity date to account for the size of the coupons, as well as potential interest-on-interest. Duration is correlated to maturity length. But it is readjusted for the size and timing of the bond's cash flows. The reason for this, again, is interest-on-interest. If you own a premium bond with high coupons, you receive larger sums earlier, which can be reinvested to earn interest-on-interest. On the other hand, if you own a discount bond, with low coupons, you have less money to reinvest to earn interest-on-interest. Also, one of the bond's cash flows—the capital gain you receive when you redeem a discount bond at par—is received when the bond matures. Therefore, throughout its life, the discount bond throws off lower cash flows than the premium bond.

As a result, bonds with lower coupons have longer durations than bonds with higher coupons. With the exception of zero coupon bonds, the duration of a bond is always shorter than its term-to-maturity. Because all of a zero coupon bond's cash flows are received on a single

---

4. Frank Fabozzi, ed., *The Handbook of Fixed Income Securities*, 5th ed. (New York: McGraw-Hill, 1997), p. 85.

date, its maturity date, zero coupon bonds have the longest durations. In fact, the duration of zero coupon bonds equals their term-to-maturity.

How Duration Enables You to Evaluate Risk

When you buy a bond or a bond fund, you should find out its duration. If all other factors are equal, a bond (or a bond fund) with a longer duration is always more volatile than one with a shorter duration. In fact, duration can be used to calculate approximately how much the price of a bond will go up or down if interest rates move up or down; that is, how much interest rate risk you are taking on. The general guideline is that for every 100 basis points (1%) that interest rates go up or down, the price of a bond will go up or down by the duration number. For example, suppose you own two different bonds with a 6% coupon: the first has a maturity of five years and an approximate duration of 4.4 years, and the second has a 20-year maturity and a duration of almost 12 years. If interest rates were to go up to 7%, the price of the five-year bond would decline by approximately $4\frac{1}{2}\%$ (or close to its duration of 4.4 years). That of the bond with the 20-year maturity would decline by approximately 12% (close to its duration of almost 12 years).

Bonds with the same maturity, but with larger coupons than the two preceding examples would have somewhat lower durations, and therefore, somewhat lower volatility. Suppose, for example, you own two other bonds with 9% coupons: one with a five-year maturity and one with a 20-year maturity. The respective durations of these two bonds would be approximately 4.2 years and 11 years. If interest rates were to go up by 100 basis points (1%), these two bonds would decline by approximately 4.2% and 11%, respectively, somewhat less than the two bonds in the previous example.

Duration can be calculated both for individual bonds and for bond funds. For bond funds, the duration of the fund is the weighted-average duration of all the bonds in the portfolio. The same guidelines for calculating price changes hold both for declines in price if interest rates go up and for increases in price if interest rates are declining.

If you are considering purchase of three bonds with the same YTM quotes, one a discount, one a premium, or one a zero, then the premium bond would be the least volatile, the discount would be more volatile, and the zero the most volatile. The same principle would apply to bond funds quoting the same yield but with different durations.

The concept of duration has some limits. For calculating how much the price of a bond will go up or down if interest rates change, duration works more accurately for smaller changes in interest rates than for larger changes. Also, as the term-to-maturity becomes longer, duration becomes somewhat less precise. Finally, the guidelines suggested above are somewhat approximate. But they are precise enough for the purposes of most individual investors. (There are actually two different definitions of duration and different formulas for calculating duration. But these would be of concern primarily to institutional investors for whom a difference to the fourth decimal point can translate into several thousand dollars.)

Let's summarize a number of features of duration:

- With the exception of zero coupon bonds, the duration of a bond is always shorter than its term-to-maturity.
- The longer the duration of a bond, the higher its volatility.
- Bonds with lower coupons have longer durations than bonds with larger coupons. That is the reason that bonds with higher coupons are less volatile than bonds with lower coupons.
- For zero coupon bonds, duration and maturity are the same. That is why zero coupon bonds are the most volatile of all bonds.
- Duration is more accurate for small changes in interest rate levels than for larger changes in interest rate levels.

We shall use the concept of duration in several chapters of this book: when bond funds are discussed, and also in the discussion of portfolio management.

Future Value and Future Expenses

Finally, let's turn briefly back to the concepts of future value. An entire industry seems to have grown up to tell you how much money you need to save periodically in order to have a certain amount of money in your retirement years. Brokerage firms and mutual fund groups are eager to supply this type of information, usually based on a questionnaire. This is actually a simple illustration of the concept of future value. These firms are using software programs which calculate the future value of whatever sums they start with, based on two assumptions: an assumed rate of inflation (to calculate how much money you will need to maintain an assumed level of purchasing power); and an assumed rate of return (to estimate how much you will need to save periodically). Both of those assumptions, of course, are absolutely critical. Particularly over long time periods, a difference of even $1/2\%$ in the assumptions makes a significant difference in their conclusions. If you know how to use a financial calculator (or a spreadsheet) you can easily do the arithmetic yourself. But in any case, it is critical to be aware of the assumptions. If the assumptions are totally unrealistic (for example, assuming you will earn 10% a year for the next 20 years), then the scenario may be just a fantasy. Different firms come up with different numbers simply because they are using different assumptions for both inflation and annual percentage returns.

Note, finally, that FINRA.org/marketdata has a "calculator" that allows you to simulate a variety of scenarios to determine how much you need to put aside for a variety of purposes such as retirement, a child's college education or any other future known expense.

Convexity

This is one more concept which is used to measure the sensitivity of bonds to changes in interest rates; and therefore, to estimate volatility.

Convexity is a concept used to correct some of the limitations of duration. As noted above, duration is an approximate measure. It is also much more accurate for small changes in yield than for larger changes in yield. The concept of convexity is intended to correct inaccuracies in the measure of duration. But convexity adjustments are generally extremely small: somewhere between 1% and 3%.

This mathematical concept is used by managers of extremely large portfolios to quantify how specific bonds would react to hypothetical interest rate scenarios; and the impact of these changes on the total portfolio. For individual investors, this is not a particularly useful measurement.

To complicate this concept further, let us note that there are different formulas used to estimate convexity; and that unless you know which formula has been used, the concept becomes meaningless.

Finally, note that the same term, "convexity," is used to describe a totally unrelated concept: It defines the curvature of the price/yield relationship of bonds on a graph.

I mention convexity only because some Web sites now list a number for convexity among the characteristics of a bond, without any further explanation of which formula or meaning of the word is being used. Used in this manner, it is just jargon and not very useful. Just ignore it.

An Easy Way to Calculate Bond Cash Flows

Two Web sites described at the end of Chapter 5, namely, Investinginbonds.com and FINRA.org/marketdata have software, which enables you to calculate almost every mathematical concept discussed in this chapter. Click on "tools," type in some numbers, and you can calculate anything from accrued interest to YTM to duration. The reason for the preceding discussion is that my emphasis is on what the numbers actually mean and the information they convey, rather than just trying to come up with a number.

SUMMARY

This chapter discussed a number of ways of evaluating bond returns. It first showed how bond cash flows interact to compound over time and pointed out the importance of compounding (the eighth wonder of the world) in building assets. The different concepts of yield were then defined. Current yield is based on coupon and price only. It ignores all other cash flows. Yield-to-maturity takes into account all of the bond's known cash flows. It is only a projection, however. Your actual realized return (that is, your actual total return) is likely to differ significantly from the YTM because neither the price at which you sell (if you sell before the bond matures) nor the rates at which you reinvest coupons can be predicted at the time you buy the bond. The YTM should be used primarily to compare different bonds to each other before you purchase a bond.

The only way to measure what you have earned in a bond accurately is to measure its total return. Total return includes changes in the value of your bond, commission costs, interest income, and interest-on-interest. A brief example illustrated the various steps involved in pricing and calculating total return for a bond purchase. This example illustrates how changes in the price of bonds due to interest rate fluctuations affect returns from fixed-income securities. It is important to consider them when you buy bonds, and not just buy on the basis of the quoted YTM.

Finally, the concept of duration was also introduced. Duration can be used to predict potential changes in the value of a bond (or of a bond fund) if interest rates go up or if they go down. If you know the duration of a bond, you can anticipate how much interest rate risk you are taking on before purchasing the bond.

CHAPTER 5

What You Need to Know before Buying Bonds

This chapter discusses

- ◆ The bond market in the financial press and on the Internet
- ◆ The Treasury market and the yield curve
- ◆ "Yield spreads" to Treasuries and benchmarks
- ◆ Investinginbonds.com, FINRA.org/marketdata, and EMMA.msrb.org
- ◆ Shopping for bonds: some guidelines

THE BOND MARKET IN THE FINANCIAL PRESS AND ON THE INTERNET

Coverage of the bond market has always taken a back seat to coverage of the stock market in the daily financial pages of most newspapers. But since the last edition of this book, in 2001, coverage of the bond market in newspapers has become even more limited. It seems that newspaper editors have concluded that most readers are going to get most of their facts about the bond market from the Internet and the newspaper coverage keeps on getting skimpier.

On the other hand, the good news is that financial Web sites have multiplied. Many of these, for example Yahoo Finance and Bloomberg.com, now include a lot of information about the bond market. Major newspapers also maintain Web sites with financial data. A number of those (including, for example, the *Wall Street Journal* and the *New York Times*) include features not found in their printed pages. Another advantage of these Web sites, compared with the printed pages of the newspaper, is that much of the coverage on the Web sites occurs close to real-time during the day, and not the next day, as it does in a printed newspaper.

It would be pointless to try to identify the "best" general Web sites. There are many good ones, depending on what is of most interest to you. Also, this is a constantly changing picture. Instead, I will identify some of the basic information that you need to focus on, wherever you get your information on the bond market.

However, the most significant development concerning information available on the Internet about the bond market is that several trade and regulatory organizations have developed Web sites intended for individual investors. Their goal is to promote "transparency" by disseminating information. The Web sites in question are: Investinginbonds.com, EMMA.msrb.org, and FINRA.org/marketdata. All of these Web sites include trade data on specific sectors of the bond market, but the information they contain extends far beyond the data. These Web sites are described in detail at the end of this chapter. As we will see, the data and information they contain is so useful that no one should shop for any type of bond (other than Treasuries) without first consulting the pertinent Web sites.

In this chapter, I will first describe some of the information available in the financial pages of your newspaper, as well as on general Web sites, which you need to follow if you invest in bonds. I will then turn to Investinginbonds.com, EMMA, and FINRA. Finally, I will include some guidelines on shopping for bonds.

THE TREASURY MARKET

If you want to be informed about the bond market, you need to first find out what is happening in the bond market for U.S. Treasuries. All other sectors of the bond market (and to some extent, the stock market as well) key off Treasuries. It bears repeating that the market in U.S. Treasuries is the key bond market not only for the United States, but worldwide. The shortest maturities—one- to three-month bills—are used as a proxies for risk-free returns by professionals. Similarly, the most recently issued 10-year bond, referred to as the bellwether bond, is the most widely traded bond worldwide. If you want to find out what is going on in the bond market anywhere, you must begin with U.S. Treasuries.

Any other type of bond is deemed to be riskier than a Treasury, even if the risk is minor. Therefore, all other securities will have a higher yield than a Treasury of the same maturity. The difference in yield between that security and a Treasury security is known as the spread. (Yes, this is still another meaning of the term.)

Unfortunately, what used to be the centerpiece of coverage about the bond market, the "Table of Treasury Bills, Bonds, and Notes," is no longer published in either of the two major financial dailies, namely the *New York Times* or the *Wall Street Journal*. To my knowledge, only *Barron's* now publishes this table, but since it appears only on the weekend, it is far less useful. What made this table unique is that it listed the exact price, the yield, and the changes in price in the Treasury market on the previous day, for a broad range of issues ranging from the shortest maturities (from one month T-bills to the longest maturity (namely, 30 year Treasury bonds). It provided a virtually instant picture of the entire Treasury market. Therefore, it constituted a perfect starting point for assessing the bond market.

One peculiarity of Treasury pricing should be noted. Unlike other bonds, the price of Treasuries is not quoted entirely as a percentage of par. The price of Treasuries is quoted at par plus fractions in 32nds of a point. One point represents $10.00 per $1,000 par value bond. The notation "minus .01" ($-.01$) does not mean minus one cent. It means minus one 32nd ($-1/32$) of a point. Therefore, 1/32nd of a point is $10.00 divided by 32, that is, 32.25 cents. As an example of Treasury bond pricing, suppose you see the price of a Treasury bond listed as 99.29. That should be read as 99 (i.e., 99% of par) and 29/32nds of a point. Translated, 99 becomes $990; 29/32nds is $10.00 multiplied by 29/32nds, which equals $9.06. The two together add up to $999.06.

One thirty-second (1/32) of one point is also called a "tick." Reporters on Treasuries may say something like, "Today, the 10-year moved up two ticks" or "today, the two-year moved down eight ticks" and it is understood that each tick represents 1/32nd of a point.

The Yield Curve and What It Can Tell You

The closest equivalent to the Table of Bills, Bonds, and Notes is a graph that looks like Exhibit 5.1 This graph is called a "yield curve." It plots yields (the yield-to-maturity) of Treasuries at key maturities. The exact points along the graph may vary, but the graph typically includes short, intermediate, and longer maturities; for example, interest rates for the three-month, six-month, one-year, two-year, five-year, seven-year, 10-year, and 30-year Treasury maturities. The yield curve is usually accompanied by a summary table listing "key rates," which shows the precise yields of Treasuries at those key points along the curve. Exhibit 5.1 shows both the yield curve "graph" and the accompanying "key rates" table that was published on August 14, 2009.

E X H I B I T   5.1

Yield Curve for Treasuries, August 14, 2009, and Key Rates for the Same Date

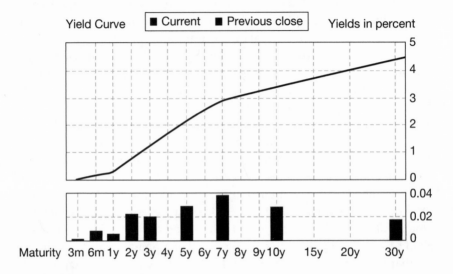

U.S. Treasuries	Coupon	Maturity Date	Current Price Yield	Time
3-Month	0.000	02/18/2010	0 / .01	11/20
6-Month	0.000	05/20/2010	0.13 / .13	11/20
12-Month	0.000	11/18/2010	0.26 / .26	11/20
2-Year	1.000	10/31/2011	11-16+ / .72	11/20
3-Year	1.375	11/15/2012	100-12 / 1.25	11/20
5-Year	2.375	10/31/2014	100-29½ / 2.18	11/20
7-Year	3.125	10/31/2016	101-12½ / 2.90	11/20
10-Year	3.375	11/15/2019	101-02+ / 3.37	11/20
30-Year	4.375	11/15/2039	101-11 / 4.29	11/20

Source: Bloomberg Finance L.P.

Note that this particular Web site displays the exact time of the quote; yields of Treasury securities typically change continually throughout the day. Posting the time for the quote makes it more accurate.

At its most basic level, the yield curve, together with the accompanying key rates table, provides a quick picture of interest rates prevailing in the Treasury market at key maturities. Consulting the yield curve on the Internet, moreover, shows these yields close to real-time.

The Shape of the Yield Curve

To bond market watchers, the yield curve itself is a valuable source of information. To these observers, the most important aspect of the curve is its shape. The word "shape" actually refers to numbers, that is, the difference in yields of different maturities. The yield curve is considered upward sloping or "normal" when yields of longer maturities are higher than those of shorter maturities. Of equal importance is whether the slope of the yield curve is steep or relatively flat. The curve is said to be steep if yields of longer term bonds differ from those of shorter maturities by well over 200 basis points (2%). It is said to be flat when yields of longer maturities differ from those of shorter maturities by 100 basis points (1%) or less. Occasionally, yields of shorter maturities are actually higher than those of longer maturities. When that happens, the yield curve is said to be downward sloping, or inverted.

For purposes of comparison, let's look at Exhibit 5.2, which shows three yield curves that differ significantly from each other and from the 2009 yield curve shown in Exhibit 5.1. Pay particular attention both to the interest rate levels and to the shape of the curve.

EXHIBIT 5.2

Three Different Treasury Yield Curves

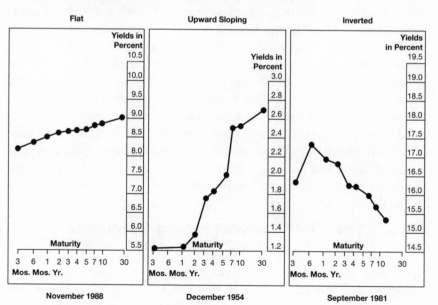

The first graph, dated November 16, 1988, shows three-month bill rates at about $8^1/_4$% and 30-year rates at 9%. Even though rates were high historically, the difference in yield between the three-month rate and the 30-year rate is about 80 basis points (less than 1%). That is considered very narrow. As a result, this would be considered a relatively flat yield curve.

The December 1954 graph shows bill rates at about 1.2% and 30-year bonds at about 2.7%. The spread between the shortest three-month paper and the 30-year maturity is about 150 basis points ($1^1/_2$%). That is considered a normal, that is, an upward-sloping, yield curve, with long bonds yielding considerably more than short maturities. The 150-basis point spread is somewhat narrow for an upward sloping curve, perhaps due to the overall low interest rate level.

Finally, look at the last graph, dated September 1981. Three-month rates are close to 16%; six-month rates are 17%; 30-year rates are actually below six-month rates, at 15%. That is an example of an inverted yield curve, with long rates actually lower than short rates.

I have purposely used the December 1954 and September 1981 yield curves for shock value. The interest rate levels are so different from those prevailing during most of the past two decades that they appear to be mistakes. These levels demonstrate "graphically" that current conditions may be no more normal, or permanent, than those that prevailed during earlier periods.

Let's return briefly to Exhibit 5.1, the yield curve shown for August 14, 2009. It turns out that this yield curve, in some ways, is the most unusual of all. Even though interest rates along the entire curve are low compared to those prevailing a few years earlier, this curve is the steepest of all the yield curves shown: the three-month yield is 0.16% (no, that is not a misprint); and the 30-year is 4.43%, so that the difference in yield between the shortest and the longest rates is over 427 basis points. Astonishingly, short rates are actually lower than they were in 1954. The yield curve is steeply upward sloping not because rates on long-term bonds are so high (they are actually much lower than those that prevailed for most of the last decade). Rather, the yield curve is so steep because short rates are among the lowest in history.

The Yield Curve: Trading Strategies and a Crystal Ball

The shape of the yield curve changes over time because interest rate expectations of the major users of credit (that is, large corporations and institutional investors) change constantly. If buyers expect an increase in inflation and a concurrent rise in interest rates, they seek the safety of short-term paper. As a result, short rates decline. If, on the other hand, they anticipate lower economic growth, recessionary times, and lower interest rates, they try to "lock in" high yields, which results in declines of long-term interest rates. Expectations also vary depending on whether traders anticipate that the Fed will lower the rates it controls (Fed funds and the discount rate) in order to encourage economic activity; or whether traders anticipate that the Fed is about to raise rates in order to prevent inflation. In a sense, it is true that the yield curve both reflects consensus expectations about future interest rates; but also, that it helps shape the direction of future interest rates.

As a result, the shape of the yield curve at any one time, and its future shape, are topics of endless discussion. Professional traders have developed trading strategies grounded on the steepness of the curve, and predictions of its future shape. One strategy, for example, is called "riding the yield curve." It is used to boost return on debt instruments held for short periods. For example, a trader who wants to hold T-bills for three months will buy six month T-bills, which he intends to sell in three months. His objective is to generate incrementally higher returns based on two sources of gains. One is that he will earn a slightly higher yield on the six month bills than he would have earned on the three month. And assuming interest rates have not changed, or have declined, at the time of the sale, the price of the bill will have appreciated by a minute amount simply because it is three months closer to its maturity date; and therefore, its price has risen slightly towards par. This strategy works best if the yield curve is steep and if interest rates decline. But if interest rates rise, it may backfire. This and other similar "curve" strategies, however, are designed for traders who routinely trade sums in the millions. An individual investor trading much smaller sums would incur much higher transaction costs, and would be unable to generate any meaningful boost in earnings.

Some professional economists argue that the shape of the yield curve contains an implicit consensus forecast of the future of the economy as well as of future interest rates. A steeply upward sloping yield curve is considered bullish for the economy and, therefore, for stocks. Such a curve typically follows a series of aggressive rate cuts by the Federal Reserve, intended to stimulate economic growth. The same steeply upward sloping curve is also thought to forecast rising long-term rates. An inverted yield curve, on the other hand, is thought to predict a recession. Typically, an inverted yield curve follows a series of increases in the Fed Funds rate by the Federal Reserve, intended to slow economic growth. Inverted yield curves occur less often than upward sloping curves. In the year 2000, for example, three-month bill rates reached 6.3% while 30-year rates were at

5.6%. This inverted curve was followed by a recession. It should be noted, however, that an inverted yield curve does not precede all recessions.

Overall, however, predictions of future economic activity based on the steepness of the yield curve are too vague to be really useful to the average individual investor. Anyone who follows interest rates soon learns that at any given time there are some "experts" who believe longer term interest rates will go up and can make a good case for that, while other "experts" can make an equally strong case explaining why the same interest rates must go down.

A perfect example of this dilemma is the shape of the yield curve at the time this is being written. This yield curve is similar to the one shown in Exhibit 5.1. Even though overall interest rates, particularly at the short end, remain at record lows, the yield curve remains steeply upward sloping, with interest rates on the 30-year bond at about 4.8%. The shape of this yield curve has a very clear explanation. Short-term rates are as low as they are because the Federal Reserve, in order to cope with the ongoing financial crisis, has kept the shortest interest rates, i.e., those it controls (Fed funds), between 0 and 25 basis points. As I am writing this more than one year after the financial crisis began, at the beginning of 2010, it is clear that these extraordinarily low rates cannot be permanent. At some point, the Federal Reserve will have to raise short-term rates. The more interesting question, however, is what will then happen to longer-term rates?

You can look to historical precedent to find an answer, but history does not provide a clear answer. Short-term rates and long-term rates do not always move in sync. For example, between 2004 and 2006, the Federal Reserve, under Chairman Alan Greenspan, raised short-term rates one-quarter of 1 point 17 times. During that period, the Fed funds rate climbed from 1.00% to 4.25%. Nonetheless, long-term rates actually declined, against the expectations of most of the advice published by gurus and pundits. In fact, even chairman Greenspan called it a "conundrum."

The Yield Curve and the Individual Investor

Whatever its shortcomings, however, the yield curve can be used by the individual investor in a number of ways.

- ◆ As a quick summary of current interest rate levels at key points along the maturity spectrum.
- ◆ To pinpoint advantageous buy points as far as maturity length is concerned.

♦ To provide, specifically, a very precise answer to the question, for the additional risk to principal incurred in going out further along the yield curve: How much more am I earning?

At the time this is being written, for example, the 10-year bond is yielding around 3.8% and the 30-year bond is yielding around 4.8%. Clearly, because the yield curve is extremely steep, by investing further out along the yield curve, an investor picks up a much higher yield. On the other hand, potential volatility of the 30-year bond is significantly higher than that of the 10-year bond. Therefore, the risk to principal is also significantly higher.

Whether yields are attractive at any point along the curve depends on the shape of the curve. For example, if the yield curve is relatively flat, two-to-seven year maturities sometimes yield perhaps only 30 to 50 basis points less than the 30-year bond, but interest rate risk, and therefore, risk to principal, is dramatically lower. You have to ask yourself, if you can capture perhaps 90% of the yield of the 30-year bond with lower risk to principal, are you getting compensated for the additional risk?

It bears repeating that investors intent on boosting yield sometimes place principal at risk for very little extra gain. When purchasing bonds, always ask yourself, "How much more am I really earning?" and "What kinds of risk am I assuming in order to earn that extra amount?"

Finally, note that while I have discussed the yield curve for Treasuries only, a yield curve can be constructed for any other security as well. Yield curves for any sector are useful to evaluate buy points for those securities.

Note finally that yield curves in the municipal bond market tend to be more steeply upward sloping than those in the Treasury market, so that typically, to capture 85 to 90% of the yield of 30-year bonds, you may need to go out further along the yield curve than you would for Treasuries. Typically, for municipals, the best tradeoffs between risk and yield are found between the seven-year and the 15-year maturities.

"YIELD SPREADS" AND BENCHMARKS

Coverage of the bond market has expanded to include regular features about sectors of the bond market that were hardly mentioned in the past. This includes, for example, high-yield corporate (also known as junk) bonds and international bonds. These sectors are receiving increasing attention because of two developments: one is the proliferation of exchange-traded funds (ETFs), which invest in highly specialized sectors of the bond market, and the other is the growing importance for U.S. investors of foreign markets.

This type of coverage only occasionally takes the form of regular columns or articles. Most often, it is found in tables listing "spreads" to Treasuries, and tables of "benchmark" yields. We will briefly touch on both of these.

"Spread Products"

Let's first discuss "yield spreads." As noted above, bonds in every sector of the bond market key off Treasuries of the same maturity. The difference in yield between Treasuries and other bonds is known as "the spread." In fact, taxable bonds such as corporate and international bonds are sometimes called "spread products."

Spreads of bonds in these sectors of the bond market, compared with Treasuries, are highly variable. There is, moreover, a wide range of credit qualities and ratings at every maturity in these sectors and as a result, a very wide range of yields. Nonetheless, spreads to Treasuries of an entire sector tend to widen or narrow as economic conditions change. So, for example, at any one time, you might hear "experts" or analysts tell you that corporate bonds are particularly cheap, and therefore, attractive buys; or that they are expensive and should be sold.

Note also that yields of Treasuries, and those of bonds in other sectors may move in different and opposite directions. Suppose, for example, that the economy is slowing. That may result in declining yields for longer-term Treasuries. But a slowing economy may raise concerns about credit quality of junk bonds, which would result in a rise in yields for junk bonds. In turn, this type of scenario would translate into a widening spread between Treasuries and junk: the price of Treasuries would rise at the same time that the price of junk bonds declines.

Buy or sell recommendations for specific sectors of the bond market are typically based on yield data showing how wide or how narrow spreads happen to be, compared with Treasuries. Professional traders have used spread data for years in order to decide whether sectors of the bond market are cheap or expensive. This type of data is now being published, but in fragmented form, usually in tables.

Exhibit 5.3 is an example of a table showing spreads of various types of bonds compared with those of Treasuries. Formats of tables showing these data are not standardized, and vary from newspaper to newspaper and from Web site to Web site. Some tables show spreads of specific bonds compared to Treasuries; others use benchmarks. Exhibit 5.3 is a highly simplified table showing the type of presentation you are likely to find.

EXHIBIT 5.3

Tracking Yield Spreads to Treasuries

Bond Sector	Maturity In Years	April 2010 Spread Over/Under Treasuries In Basis Points	April 2009 Spread Over/Under Treasuries In Basis Points	Change From A Year Ago
U.S. Corporate Index	5	+100 bp	+400 bp	−300 bp
U.S. High Yield Corporate Index (Junk)	5	+600 bp	+2000 bp	−1400 bp
Emerging Market Bond Index	5	+350 bp	+900 bp	−550 bp
Canadian Bonds	5	+50 bp	+50 bp	0

It shows the spread to Treasuries (in basis points) of various bond market sectors. (In this table, the benchmarks are simply names of bond sectors, not actual benchmarks.) All numbers are approximate. But the numbers reflect both the general level of yields and the direction of interest rates you would have seen in April 2010.

Reading from left to right, Exhibit 5.3 shows

- The sector of the bond market
- The maturity in years
- The spread in basis points compared with Treasuries at two different dates: the most recent date (April 2010); and a year earlier
- The change in the spread compared to a year earlier

In Exhibit 5.3, spreads of almost all bond sectors compared with those prevailing a year earlier indicate that the spread to Treasuries narrowed significantly, and prices rose. The largest change occurred in the U.S. high yield (junk) sector, narrowing by about 1,400 basis points (14%). As will be seen in Chapter 9, on U.S. corporate bonds, this change was the reason for the enormous gains the junk bond sector experienced in 2009. Similar, but smaller, changes occurred in other sectors. Little change in the spread occurred in high quality sovereign bonds (such as Canada, for example) compared with Treasuries.

Tables published either on financial Web sites or in the financial pages of your newspaper will be far more detailed and precise. But these tables are typically somewhat confusing. The purpose of Exhibit 5.3 is to point you to what you should be focusing on.

Why look at changing spreads? For several reasons. One is that bond market professionals are sometimes quicker to sniff out changes in the economic climate than stock market investors. If, for example, spreads of corporate bonds to Treasuries are widening (yields of corporate bonds rising compared with those of Treasuries), that may be a clue that the economy is weakening. This can be an important clue for stock market investors as well.

Another reason for tracking the size of spreads is that this is sometimes the best indicator (typically a contrarian indicator) that suggests whether bonds in that sector are attractive buys or not. In 2006 and 2007, for example, spreads to Treasuries of corporate bonds (both investment grade and junk) narrowed to record levels. That was a period of rising stock prices and general euphoria about the economy. But to some investors, the record "narrowness" of the spreads constituted a red flag. These investors realized that they were not being compensated for the risks they were incurring. In times of panic, such as 2008, spreads widen considerably as fear grips certain sectors. Wide spreads may eventually result in opportunities for speculation—but panic can last for years, and losses can become very steep.

Data on spreads to Treasuries will be discussed in greater detail in chapters dealing with corporate bonds and with international bonds.

Benchmarks

Broader coverage is also being devoted to benchmarks or benchmark indices for bonds.

Benchmark indices have become increasingly prominent for two reasons. One is that managers of bond funds are sometimes compared to, and remunerated, based on how their performance compares with a benchmark index. Another is the increasing number of newly created bond exchange-traded funds, many of which track benchmark bond indices. Creating indices has become big business. As a result, numerous benchmark indices have been constructed for every sector of the bond market.

Constructing benchmark indices for the bond market, however, is much more complicated than constructing benchmark indices for the stock market. The main reason is that the universe of bonds is much larger than the universe of stocks. Any one sector can include thousands of different bonds. Moreover, all sectors change constantly as more bonds are issued, each one with its own coupon, credit rating, maturity, and so on. Also, benchmarks can be sliced and diced in many different ways: by sector (corporate bonds, mortgage-backed bonds, municipal bonds, for example); by maturity (short-term bonds, intermediate bonds, etc.); by credit quality (high grade, junk, etc.); by country (Japanese bonds, etc.); by grouping sectors (emerging market bonds, etc.); and so on.

By comparison, stock indices are much simpler: the S&P 500 index is a weighted index of 500 stocks—all indices on the S&P 500 will list the same 500 stocks. Typically, given the nature of the bond market, however, bond indices are constructed using sampling techniques that attempt to replicate the risk profile of a much larger number of bonds in whatever sector of the bond universe they track.

Benchmark indices have been proliferating. Many track increasingly narrow and specialized segments of the bond market. There are now hundreds of benchmarks covering every aspect of the bond market. But, one unfortunate aspect of this trend is that the names of benchmark indices sometimes fail to describe the universe of bonds they are tracking. They may be identified simply under the name of the institution developing the benchmark, and a cryptic phrase ("John Doe high-yield index") without much information about the portfolio makeup of the benchmark.

Moreover, because pricing of bonds varies from dealer to dealer, and also because many bonds in a benchmark index do not trade daily, the pricing of a bond benchmark, even though it looks precise, may actually be an estimate rather than an actual price. As a result, it would not be unusual for bond funds tracking similar benchmark indices to be priced differently.

Benchmarks will be revisited, particularly in the section dealing with ETFs, in Chapter 14.

INVESTINGINBONDS.com, FINRA.org/ marketdata AND EMMA.msrb.org

By far the most useful information on the bond market is to be found in these three Web sites. They are described below in no particular order.

Investinginbonds.com

The oldest of these three Web sites is Investinginbonds.com. This Web site was initially developed by the Bond Market Association, at the time the trade association for the municipal bond market. In 2006, the Bond Market

Association merged with the Securities Industry Association to form the Securities Industry Financial Markets Association, SIFMA.

Investinginbonds.com has expanded significantly since its inception in the 1990s. Initially, it was devoted almost entirely to the municipal bond market. It listed the price at which a number of actively traded municipal bonds traded, but only if they traded at least four times in one day. These listings, moreover, were available one day after the trades took place.

Over time, however, listings expanded. Since 2005, *all* municipal bond trades are reported on the day of the trade: 15 minutes after each trade (that is, close to real-time). More recently, corporate bond trades have been added, via a feed from TRACE (see below). And beginning in March 2010, trades for actively traded government agency bonds (known as Agencies) have also been added, although trade data for Agencies is not as detailed as it is for both munis and corporates.

You may wonder why trades are not available as soon as a trade occurs. Bear in mind that the bond market remains an over-the-counter market. Unlike stocks, which trade on an exchange, there is no "tape" displaying prices. Dealers are required to report trade prices under rules developed by the SEC. That process takes a few minutes. Compliance, however, seems to be the rule.

Price data is extensive. It starts with price data for all bonds that trade on any particular day. But Investinginbonds.com also includes a complete trade history of all municipal bonds, going back to 2005. To find out the trade history of any bond, type in its CUSIP number. (Bear in mind that many municipal bonds trade only a few times a year.)

Information is not limited to price data, however. Investinginbonds.com has an enormous amount of information available about the bond market in general, and about each sector in particular. It groups its data and general information into four categories entitled

- ◆ "The municipal market at a glance"
- ◆ "The corporate bond market at a glance"
- ◆ "The agency market at a glance"
- ◆ Investinginbondseurope.org (a sister Web site)

There is also a section on mortgage-backed securities, but that section does not report trade data.

Information to be found in each sector and about each sector is extensive. In addition to trade data, information provided includes an overview of yields currently available in each sector, through daily yield curve graphs and tables of representative yields. Helpful question marks guide you to definitions and general descriptions of each sector. There is also historical information and commentary about the sector.

Finally, this is a very user friendly Web site. It is clear and easy to navigate.

EMMA.msrb.org

EMMA.msrb.org is the acronym for Electronic Municipal Market Access. This Web site was launched in July 2009. It is being developed by the Municipal Securities Rulemaking Board, which is the federal regulator of brokerage firms that underwrite and trade municipal bonds. EMMA is intended to become the primary source of data and information for the municipal bond market. EMMA bills itself as "The Official Source for Municipal Disclosure and Market Data." I quote its objectives: "EMMA's market activity pages provide a window for viewing market-wide information about municipal securities. Click on the tabs below to view recent trade data, official statements, continuing disclosures, advance refunding documents, daily market statistics[.]"

To some extent, data found on EMMA overlaps some of the data found in Investinginbonds.com. This includes trade data, for example, which is virtually identical on both Web sites. But EMMA includes many features not found on Investinginbonds.com.

First of all, EMMA will now be the official (and the only) repository for the official statements (OS) of municipal bonds when they are issued. Any investor who wishes to consult the official statement when a bond is issued will be directed to EMMA. But in addition, EMMA has archived official statements going as far back as the 1990s. (Be warned, however: downloading a prospectus requires fast Internet delivery. Don't try it with dial-up.)

In addition, EMMA has become the sole repository of information falling under the heading of "continuing disclosure." All issuers of municipal bonds are required to file at least one statement annually, reporting their finances. In addition, however, all issuers are also required to file information disclosing any changes that would "materially" affect the price of a bond. This is what is called "continuing disclosure." This rubric is somewhat vague; the issuer needs to decide what would constitute "material" information. It would, for example, include any change in the credit rating of a bond. But it might also include details such as late

payments of interest due on a bond, or a decline in the reserve fund dedicated to paying debt service on the bond; and generally speaking, any development that would potentially cause a decline in the price of a bond.
Continuing disclosure could, of course, also include information that
would cause the price of the bond to rise.

Given the newness of the site at the time this is being written, it is
still too early to tell how well compliance of continuing disclosure
requirements will work, and how useful all of the features of this site
will turn out to be for individual investors. It will take at least one year,
for example, for all issuers to file at least one statement of their finances.
But conversations with an official suggest that compliance is widespread.
EMMA lists trade data for approximately 1.5 million CUSIPs. Eight
months after its launch, one million issuers had filed at least one continuing disclosure document. And the site also reports an enormous number of viewer "hits."

One additional unique feature of EMMA is particularly noteworthy.
It is an interactive feature called: "Alert me." Any investor logged on to
EMMA can type in her e-mail address, as well as CUSIP numbers, and
ask to receive the OS and any continuing disclosure information filed
about the CUSIP number. By all means, if you own individual municipal
bonds, try this feature.

One more note about EMMA: it too is easy to navigate and is user
friendly.

FINRA.org/marketdata

Last but not least is FINRA.org/marketdata (FINRA is acronym for Financial
Industry Regulatory Authority). This Web site is being developed jointly by
the National Association of Securities Dealers and Dow Jones Market Watch.
It incorporates the TRACE search engine (Trade Reporting and Compliance
Engine), which reports real-time trade data on corporate bonds. In March
2010, TRACE also began reporting trade data on government Agency bonds.
Brokers and dealers are required to report trade data 15 minutes after each
trade, as they are for municipal bonds. TRACE feeds trade data on both
corporate and Agency bonds to Investinginbonds.com.

One unique feature of FINRA is a screen called "company information." This screen includes the current stock price of corporations
(in real-time), as well as some background information about the company. It also includes a list of bonds outstanding for the firm, as well as

their current credit rating. (An illustration of this screen is included in Chapter 8 on corporate bonds.)

The FINRA Web site is extraordinarily comprehensive. It includes data for almost any security that trades, including not only bonds, but also stocks, options, mutual funds, etc. It also includes documents filed with the SEC and software that enables investors to conduct targeted searches for bonds. It also incorporates municipal bond trade data via a feed from the MSRB.

Beginning some time in 2011, FINRA will undertake a pilot project to track trade data on mortgage-backed securities. At least initially, the data will not be disseminated to the public. It has not yet been decided when or whether these data will be listed on the Web site.

FINRA.org/marketdata has two separate menus: one for individual investors and one for professionals. That hints at the degree of detail and information that is available on the site. Because it is extremely content rich, it is somewhat less user friendly than either EMMA or Investinginbonds.com. It does have a tutorial, however, which is well worth watching.

Note, finally, that FINRA regulates all brokers and dealers who work in the securities industry. Two of its features are related to regulatory enforcement of trade practices among brokers and brokerage firms. The first, called "BrokerCheck," allows you to get background information on both individual brokers and brokerage firms. FINRA also has an extensive mediation and arbitration function. (Both of these features are described below.)

All three of the Web sites described above incorporate a variety of tools such as calculators of various kinds. All three enable investors to conduct a variety of searches, such as searches for data about specific bonds or targeted searches to find bonds matching certain criteria. Illustrations of searches are included in chapters dealing with individual securities. They include examples from all three Web sites that show how to utilize the data on the Web sites when shopping for bonds. Needless to say, all three Web sites are constantly adding new features and changing. But these illustrations should provide a good introduction.

Shopping for Individual Bonds: Some Guidelines

Now that we have established sources of information about the bond market, let's summarize some steps you can go through when shopping for bonds.

First, you need to decide whether you want to buy taxable or tax exempt bonds. For assets in a retirement account, taxables are the way to go. For assets not in retirement accounts, munis make sense if you are in a high tax bracket. If you are not sure whether munis make economic sense for you, check the taxable equivalent yield of municipal bonds. (You can look it up on Investinginbonds.com.)

Browse through the pertinent Web site (Investinginbonds.com, FINRA.org/marketdata, or EMMA.msrb.org) to get an overview of yields available in the sector of the bond market that interests you. Establish some parameters to guide your browsing. Parameters should include

* Maturity
* Credit quality
* Yield

Note that I place yield last. In the bond market, there is always a trade-off between yield and safety. Higher yield means higher risk. The highest yields available at any time, for any bond, are the riskiest at that time. You need to decide how much risk you are willing to take.

Also browse your favorite online broker Web sites to try to zero in on availability of bonds in the sector that you have identified. That varies tremendously. Sometimes, the choice is vast. At other times, it is quite limited.

When you have identified bonds that appear to be attractively priced, look up their trading history, again on the pertinent Web site. Are the bonds actively traded? Are spreads wide or narrow? (That will vary, of course, by sector.) Also, zero in on comparable bonds for pricing and yield.

Should You Buy Bonds Entirely Online?

It has been possible to buy Treasury bonds entirely online for well over 10 years through Treasury Direct (discussed in Chapter 6). And if you want to buy individual Treasuries of any maturity, that remains the cheapest and most efficient way to buy them.

Virtually all brokers now have online Web sites. Nonetheless, some brokers still require individual investors to place the order with a broker, in order to complete a purchase or a sell. Many individual investors seem to feel that if they can buy bonds entirely online, that is the way to go.

But while it is now possible to buy municipals and corporates entirely online as well, that may not be the best way to proceed. Of course, that would depend partly on your degree of familiarity and comfort with the bond sector you are investing in. But knowledgeable industry sources caution against it.

Why? The most obvious reason is that the bond market is complex: any broker who is in the market daily is bound to acquire a level of expertise that most individual investors do not have. A broker may be able to point out features of particular bonds that may not be immediately obvious.

Even more important, however, is the fact that when you buy a bond online without discussing it with a broker, you are assuming all the risks. If there is a feature of the bond that you misunderstand, or fail to notice, you have no recourse.

Note also that the price listed on a dealer Web site is often negotiable. Most brokers expect informed customers to research bonds online and many are ready to negotiate on price. Most brokers, even at discount firms, are willing contact a listing dealer to find out whether that dealer will accept a lower price. But you need to ask. Note also that if you call a broker about a specific bond you may have seen on his Web site, that broker may have bonds in his inventory that are better buys. Obviously, any broker will be anxious to sell bonds out of his inventory first. Moreover, in most cases, it costs you nothing to consult a broker. But that is something you will want to check. Some brokers have instituted a sliding scale of fees, and consulting a broker may raise the cost of commissions.

Bear in mind finally that discount brokers typically do not maintain inventories of bonds. Their displays are those of electronic platforms (described in Chapter 2). There may be good values among them, but the only way to know is to shop around and become informed.

How Do You Find a Knowledgeable Broker?

Particularly if you are new to investing in bonds, a first-rate broker can be an invaluable resource etc. But finding a really good broker requires some effort.

To find a knowledgeable broker, try to locate either a firm that specializes in bonds; or within a bank or brokerage firm, an individual who specializes in selling particular types of bonds to individual investors. Take the trouble to interview brokers and discuss your needs with them. This book will suggest a number questions that you can ask. In order to protect your own interests, if you want to buy individual bonds, you need to become an informed investor, and you need to stick to bonds whose characteristics and risks you understand. But be aware that at a full-service firm commission costs may be quite high. Whether the costs are worth it to you depends partly on how high those costs turn out to be; and also on the quality of the service provided.

You can also locate a good broker at discount firms. One strategy that works is to ask good questions and keep asking until you find someone who can give you really good answers. Or ask to speak to a senior trader or to a senior broker.

You can judge the quality of a firm (or of a broker) partly by what that firm tries to sell you. If you tell a broker that your first priority is to protect principal, and you are consistently offered only high-yielding—and therefore risky—securities, go elsewhere. Certain firms, referred to unceremoniously as "bucket shops," are known for their high-pressure tactics. Such firms sometimes rely on cold-calling, that is, telephoning strangers in order to find buyers who will buy without investigating carefully. Typically, the cold-caller will tell you that he is offering you a unique opportunity to buy a terrific bond, but that if you do not purchase this bond immediately, the opportunity will disappear. Years ago, checking out information might have required calling a number of dealers. Pricing information now readily available on any of the Web sites described earlier should enable you to quickly check out whether you are being offered a good deal. In fact, after you buy a bond, your trade will be listed on any of the three Web sites named in this chapter. You will be able to compare the price you paid to the price paid by others. That will enable you to determine whether the price you paid was fair.

Even if you have always done business with a particular firm (or a particular broker), it pays to shop around and be as well informed as possible about market conditions. You are more likely to negotiate a better price if your broker realizes that you are shopping around.

Also, if you have located a bond online that you think you might want to buy, by all means, call your broker. She may actually be able to buy that bond for less than you could buy it yourself. And you will get a second opinion on the bond.

"BrokerCheck"

While I suggest you discuss potential bond purchases with a broker, you want to deal with a knowledgeable and honest source.

First, you want to avoid the rip-off artists. FINRA now has two features to assist individual investors. There is extensive information on the FINRA Web site on both of these functions. So I will summarize only the basic information concerning these two features.

The first is called "BrokerCheck." BrokerCheck functions as a kind of Better Business Bureau that enables you to obtain background information both for individual brokers and for brokerage firms. FINRA suggests consulting the Web site and taking a number of steps before dealing with a firm or individual new to you. By consulting BrokerCheck, you can find out first of all whether the broker is duly registered with FINRA as well as whether she is licensed in the state in which you reside. You can also find out whether there have been any complaints lodged against the broker.

To what extent is the information on BrokerCheck reliable? BrokerCheck information is based on questionnaires and voluntary disclosure. But there are some checks on the truthfulness of the broker. All brokers are fingerprinted, and those fingerprints are sent to the FBI. This should uncover any broker guilty of criminal activity. Also, regulators are required to report complaints either against brokers or against brokerage firms, so that information would also show up on BrokerCheck.

BrokerCheck has professional background information on approximately 850,000 current and former FINRA–registered brokers and 17,000 current and former FINRA–registered brokerage firms. This includes information on financial adviser firms as well. Finally, BrokerCheck has a toll-free number (800) 289–9999.

Suppose you have been dealing with a broker and, suddenly, you find there have been complaints lodged against that broker? All complaints are not necessarily legitimate. One suggestion would be that you call the broker and ask to hear her side of the story.

FINRA: Arbitration and Mediation

FINRA operates the largest forum for arbitration and mediation in the industry.

If you have been dealing with a broker, or a brokerage firm, and you feel you have been dealt with unfairly, your first recourse is to call the broker and see if the two of you can negotiate a satisfactory solution to whatever your problem may be.

In the event you are unable to negotiate a satisfactory settlement, FINRA offers two venues to settle the dispute which may be less costly, and less time consuming, than suing in court.

The more formal procedure is the use of arbitration. Arbitration involves filing a complaint and holding hearings in front of designated arbitrators. Arbitration involves a number of fees. First, there is a filing fee ranging from $50 to $1,800, depending on the amount of damages you are seeking. FINRA also charges hearing session fees ranging from $50 to $1,200. (These amounts are current as this is being written.) The amount varies both based on the number of arbitrators involved, as well as the amount of damages you are seeking. The decision of the arbitrators determines who is responsible for paying the hearing fees. Finally, because disputes going to arbitration may involve complex legal issues, you may decide to hire a lawyer, which would involve additional legal fees.

Note that the decision of the arbitrators is final and binding. You should be aware that when you open an account with a brokerage firm that firm may require you to sign an arbitration agreement. If you sign such an agreement, you agree that any dispute with a broker must be settled through arbitration.

The second venue for settling a dispute is mediation. Mediation is less formal and less costly than arbitration. Typically, mediators do not impose a solution to a dispute. They attempt to get the parties in the dispute to come to a mutually satisfactory solution. Fees for mediation are modest, ranging from $50 for disputes involving less than $25,000 up to $250 for disputes for amounts over $100,000.

Decisions reached through mediation are typically non-binding.

Both BrokerCheck, and mediation and arbitration procedures are discussed in detail in a 30-page PDF document on the FINRA Web site entitled, "The Investor's Guide to Securities Industry Disputes: How to Prevent and Resolve Disputes with Your Broker."

SUMMARY

This chapter reviewed a number of concepts regularly reported in the media which are key to understanding the interest rate environment: namely, key data on the Treasury market, chiefly the level of interest rates at different maturity levels. Those levels are reported primarily through a graph known as a yield curve. Two related concepts were also discussed: namely, how the yield curve is interpreted and used; as well as the construction and increasing use of bond benchmarks.

The most valuable information for bond investors, however, is to be found on the Internet, on three Web sites which are free and available to anyone. The oldest of these is Investinginbonds.com, which was initially developed to provide data on the municipal bond market; but which has expanded significantly to include data on other sectors of the bond market. The second, which went live on the Internet in 2007, is FINRA.org/marketdata. That Web site provides data on equities, bonds and mutual funds. The newest entrant is EMMA.msrb.org. EMMA will become the official repository for disclosure information and documentation for the municipal bond market. These three Web sites provide invaluable information including price data within 15 minutes after bond trades (that is, close to real time); as well as software enabling investors to conduct targeted searches for bonds. They also include in-depth information about specific bonds; as well as general information about various sectors of the bond market. These three sectors were described in some detail in this chapter. But Chapters 7 through 10 include detailed illustrations on how to use these Web sites in researching bonds.

Finally, some general guidelines regarding shopping for bonds were included in this chapter.

PART TWO

Individual Securities

If you have at least $50,000 to invest (less for Treasuries, since you can buy individual Treasury bonds with complete safety for as little as $1,000), you might consider purchasing individual bonds.

I chose the sum of $50,000 because the first rule of investing, in bonds or anything else, is to diversify. If you do not have at least $50,000, you will be unable to buy a diversified portfolio. Also, your transaction costs, namely commission costs incurred in buying and selling, would be too high.

This section discusses five different types of bonds:

- Treasury bills
- Municipal bonds
- Mortgage-backed securities
- Corporate bonds
- International bonds

These securities are discussed in order of their appeal for individual investors.

Treasuries are the benchmark against which all other debt instruments must be compared. They have the highest degree of safety. They are inexpensive to buy and sell. And they are easy to understand. Anyone looking for safety who does not have a great deal of time or interest in finance could very well limit himself to Treasuries alone, or for an investor in higher income brackets, to a combination of high-grade municipals and Treasuries.

Municipal bonds may be the bonds most widely held by individual investors. Their appeal is twofold. They are sound investments, and because of the exemptions from federal and some state and local taxes, they are among the safest and highest-yielding bonds that an individual investor can buy. But a number of significant changes have come to this market. One of them is the demise of bond insurance. In addition, pricing and disclosure information now available on the Internet is transforming shopping for these bonds.

Mortgage-backed securities and corporates both have higher yields than Treasuries, but they are more complex than either Treasuries or munis. Each requires owner involvement. They should not be purchased unless the investor has both the time and the interest to analyze specific securities in some depth before purchase and to monitor them after purchase.

Chapter 10, on international bonds, has been almost totally rewritten. This is an area which has grown in importance, given the enormous capital needs of the developing world and the increasing globalization of the more developed economies. Chapter 10 describes the basic types of international bonds currently available in the U.S. market.

CHAPTER 6

Treasuries, Savings Bonds, and Federal Agency Paper

This chapter discusses

- ◆ Treasury bills, notes, and bonds
- ◆ Treasury Inflation Protected Securities (TIPS)
- ◆ TreasuryDirect: How to buy Treasuries directly at auction, without paying commissions
- ◆ Zero coupon bonds
- ◆ Series EE and Series I savings bonds
- ◆ Federal agency debt

This chapter will discuss the main types of debt securities that are direct obligations of the U.S. government. There are four distinct types of instruments.

The first, and perhaps the most familiar, are the securities issued by the Treasury, and sold at auction by the Federal Reserve Bank, popularly known as "Treasuries." They come in three different flavors, based on maturity length. The shortest instruments, called bills, mature in one year or less. Notes mature in two to 10 years. Bonds mature in 10 to 30 years. In 1997, the Federal Reserve Bank (the "Fed") brought out a new type of Treasury security: inflation-linked securities. These are also sold at auction, like other Treasuries. There is a very active secondary market in all Treasuries, which is the largest, most active, and most liquid debt market in the world.

The second type of Treasury is not sold directly by the Fed. It was actually created by investment bankers out of Treasury bonds and continues to be generated and sold by investment bankers. Those are zero coupon bonds ("zeros").

The third type of instrument are the familiar savings bonds, sold by the government directly to individuals through banks, and now, directly on the Internet. Savings bonds do not trade in the secondary market. As a result, the face value of savings bonds does not vary with changes in interest rates. That is a major difference between savings bonds and Treasuries. You may remember savings bonds mainly as those certificates given to you as presents by your least favorite aunt when you were a kid, to be cashed in at some far off future date. If so, you will be overlooking attractive opportunities. The government now sells two types of savings bonds: Series EE and Series I. Interest rates on EE bonds are now more competitive. And I bonds are particularly attractive because their total return is indexed to inflation.

Finally, we will turn to a fourth type of security. These are the bonds issued by the various Federal Agencies. They are not direct obligations of the Federal government. But they have implicit government backing. These are collectively called Federal Agencies.

Each of these instruments will be discussed in turn.

WHAT IS UNIQUE ABOUT TREASURIES?

I want to buy a security that is completely safe, easy to buy, easy to sell, easy to understand, and high yielding. Is there such an instrument?

Surprisingly, the answer is yes. Treasuries are that rare paradox: common and high quality. While they are not formally "insured," since Treasuries are a direct obligation of the U.S. government, itself the ultimate insurer, Treasuries are (if one can rate safety among issues backed by the U.S. government) safer than insured accounts. In addition, since 1985, long-dated Treasuries have not been callable before maturity—far more generous call protection than is afforded by any other debt instrument. Finally, Treasuries are the most liquid securities you can buy; they trade with lower markups than any other debt instrument.

Before buying any other fixed-income security, you should check out the yield of a Treasury with a comparable maturity. Professionals do. Every single debt instrument is priced by professionals off Treasuries. Never buy a security with a maturity comparable to a Treasury unless the additional yield (the spread to the Treasury yield) is large enough to compensate for the additional credit risk of the other security. The greater the risk, the wider the spread should be.

If you are risk averse and/or don't have much time to devote to the management of your finances, then Treasuries are for you. Even if you have a lot of time, Treasuries may still be your best option.

The only real decision that has to be made when buying a Treasury is how much interest rate risk you want to assume; that is, where on the yield curve you will find the best trade-off between return and interest rate risk. If this were a perfect world, there would be no interest rate risk. But as we know, the price of long Treasury bonds is as volatile as the price of any other long-dated instrument. However, if you limit your purchases to maturities of five years or less and hold securities until maturity, you can put together a portfolio that has complete safety of principal and predictable returns.

What is surprising is that in spite of their high quality, on a total return basis, Treasuries often outperform other debt instruments. There are two main reasons for this. First, whenever any financial market becomes turbulent, investors sell other financial assets—stocks, for example—and put their money in Treasuries. This is referred to as a "flight to quality buying." The financial panic of 2008 could have been invented as an advertisement for Treasuries. That year, all other securities, both stocks and bonds, went into a tailspin. But Treasuries soared in value. And second, the significant call protection Treasuries enjoy, compared with other debt instruments, boosts the return of long-dated Treasuries whenever interest rates decline significantly.

Treasury bonds are issued periodically by the Treasury and sold through auctions run by the Federal Reserve Bank. Most Treasuries are sold to large dealers, called "primary dealers," who in turn sell to everyone else, e.g., banks, brokerage firms, large and small institutions, money market funds, or individual investors. Individuals can purchase Treasuries from banks or from brokerage firms. But you can also purchase Treasuries directly at auction in amounts ranging from $100 to $5 million.

Treasuries are taxable at the federal level, but exempt from state and local taxes. As a rule, in states with high income taxes, this feature adds about 50 to 60 basis points (approximately $1/2$ of 1%) to the yield of a Treasury. As a result, net-after-tax yield of Treasuries (particularly those with maturities under five years) may occasionally be competitive with tax-exempt paper.

TREASURY BILLS, NOTES, AND BONDS
Treasury Bills

Treasury bills (T-Bill for short) are short-dated instruments, maturing in one year or less. T-Bills are currently issued in three-month, six-month, and one-year maturities. They are offered in minimum denominations of $10,000, with multiples of $5,000 thereafter.

A Treasury bill is technically a non-interest-bearing instrument. When you purchase a T-Bill, you do not receive interest in the form of a coupon. Instead, the T-Bill is sold at a discount from par. When it matures, the Treasury redeems the T-Bill at par. The difference between the discounted price paid and the face value of the bill when it is redeemed is its yield.

Individuals can purchase bills directly at the Fed's weekly auctions. They can also purchase T-Bills trading in the secondary market for any desired maturity—from a few days to one year—from banks or from brokerage firms, for a small fee. T-Bills may be resold any time; they are the most liquid of all instruments. T-Bills are issued in book-entry form only.

Most newspapers and financial Web sites list T-Bill yields for the one-month, three-months, and six-months maturity. T-Bill yields may be quoted in either of two ways: at the discount at which a T-Bill sells from par; and on a so-called "bond-equivalent yield basis." The two are not identical. A simplified explanation is that the discount is quoted on the basis of the one-time premium earned when a T-Bill is redeemed, which is equivalent to simple interest. But when a three-month or six-month bill is redeemed, the investor has the opportunity to reinvest that money and earn interest-on-interest. Therefore, the actual rate of return (annualized) is higher than the discounted rate. The bond-equivalent yield of T-Bills is always slightly higher (by between 10 and 20 basis points) than the discount rate. In effect, the bond equivalent yield of a T-Bill, as its name implies, enables you to compare its yield to that of a coupon bearing security. The formula for converting discount rate to bond-equivalent yield is complicated, but anyone selling a T-Bill has tables quoting both rates.[1]

---

1. Several other factors go into the calculation of bond-equivalent yields. For one thing, the Treasury calculates the price of T-Bills as if a year had 360 days. When the yield is annualized (to a 365-day year), the actual yield turns out to be slightly higher than the discount. Also, the bond-equivalent yield is computed on the assumption that the interest-on-interest will compound at the issue rate and for a 364-day year. (One-year bills are actually outstanding for 52 weeks, exactly 364 days.)

Without a doubt, T-Bills are the safest instruments that you can buy. They have zero-credit risk. And they are so short that interest rate risk may be ignored. In fact, the yield on the shortest bills is used by investment professionals as a proxy for a risk-free rate of return, and institutions use them as cash equivalents.

Note, however, that while T-Bills are perfect as a parking place for cash, they are not appropriate as long-term investments. Over long holding periods, total return is lower than for riskier investments; and reinvestment risk is very high.

Why Treasury Notes Should Be in Your Portfolio

Treasury notes mature in two to 10 years. Currently, the Treasury is selling the following maturities:

- Two-year
- Three-year
- Five-year
- Seven-year
- Ten-year

The price of notes fluctuates more than the price of T-Bills in response to interest rate changes, as you would expect given their longer maturities. Consequently, if you need to resell a note before it matures, its price may be higher than you paid or lower than you paid. Price changes, you will remember, are directly tied to maturity length. The smallest price changes would occur for two-year notes and increase gradually as maturity lengthens. Interest rate risk remains relatively modest under the five-year mark. But it rises gradually and becomes increasingly significant after that mark.

Treasury notes are extremely attractive securities. They yield more than T-Bills, typically 50 to 150 basis points, depending on the shape of the yield curve. If you buy and hold to maturity, you are guaranteed to get back 100% of principal. In addition, on a net-after-tax basis, there are times when Treasury notes may actually yield more than tax-exempt paper. This can occur, for example, in states that have high state taxes because Treasury notes are exempt from state and local taxes. Also, whenever the yield curve is inverted (that is, when yields on shorter securities are higher than those on long-dated instruments), Treasury notes maturing in two to five years may yield more than municipal bonds, on an after-tax basis, by a significant amount. Yield curve inversions occurred in 1987 and 1988, as well as in 2000.

Are you giving up return by purchasing notes rather than longer-term Treasuries? There have been long stretches of time when, based on authoritative studies, notes have actually done as well, or slightly better, than long-dated Treasuries. For example, one study, by Ibbotson Associates, showed that between 1926 and 1997, average annual total return of Treasury notes was 5.3%, compared with 5.2% for longer dated Treasuries.[2] The higher return of notes compared with longer-dated paper is due to the lower price volatility of the notes in response to changes in interest rates.

Data for more recent periods is less conclusive. Moreover, given the extremely steep yield curve as this is being written, and the very low yields of Treasuries with five-year maturities (about 60% of the yield of the 10-year bond; and 40% of the yield of the 30-year bond), this is not an obvious choice. There is no way to predict, as this is being written, whether the total return of the five-year note will in the long run prove to have been the better choice, compared with longer dated Treasuries. That will depend entirely on the direction of interest rates (whether they rise over the next few years, stay the same, or decline); and the future shape of the yield curve.

What can be said with certainty is that notes continue to have a significantly higher yield than T-bills; and that if you hold the notes until they mature, you will recover invested principal, in full. But given the uncertainties about the future direction of interest rates, this would be a good time to "ladder". (See Chapter 14 on how to build a ladder).

Treasury Bonds

Treasury bonds are the longest-dated instruments issued by the Treasury, maturing in 10 to 30 years. Currently, the Treasury sells a 10-year and a 30-year bond at auction. (It no longer sells either 15- or 20-year bonds.) But because the market in Treasuries is extremely active, any other maturity may be purchased in the secondary market.

A further advantage of long-dated Treasuries is that they enjoy far more generous call protection than either corporates or munis. They are not callable for 25 years.

But unlike shorter maturities, longer-dated Treasuries expose you to significant interest rate risk. This is particularly relevant given the interest rates prevailing as this is being written; a range of approximately 3% to 4% for the 10-year, and 4% to 5% for the 30-year. There is, of course, no way to predict whether interest rate levels will rise or decline from

2. *Stocks, Bonds, Bills and Inflation: 1998 Yearbook* (Chicago: Ibbotson Associates, 1998), pp. 10–30.

current levels. But it bears repeating that you can earn perhaps 80% to 85% of the 30-year yield, and reduce interest rate risk significantly by staying at or under the 10-year maturity.

INFLATION-INDEXED SECURITIES

In 1997, the U.S. Treasury introduced a new type of bond—Treasury Inflation-Indexed Securities, also known as Treasury Inflation-Protected Securities, or TIPS for short. As their name suggests, these bonds were intended to assure a real rate of return even if there is inflation, and also to protect the purchasing power of monies invested in these securities.

Why TIPS Are Unique

TIPS share a number of characteristics with other Treasury bonds:

♦ They are backed by the full faith and credit of the U.S. government and, therefore, have the highest credit quality.

♦ They are sold at Treasury auctions on a quarterly basis. Like other Treasuries, TIPS are issued with a fixed rate coupon, which is paid twice a year. Since the time TIPS were introduced, the fixed-rate coupon of the 10-year bond has varied from a high of 4.25% at one of the first auctions to a low of 1.375% at the most recent auction in January 2010.

♦ TIPS are issued at the regular quarterly auctions by the Treasury like any other Treasury bond. They are currently issued in five-year, 10-year, and 30-year maturities.

♦ The distinguishing characteristic of TIPS, however, is that their face value is adjusted periodically based on the Consumer Price Index for All Urban Consumers (CPI-U) published by the Bureau of Labor Statistics. Since the CPI-U is announced monthly, there is a lag in the price adjustment of somewhat over one month. Except for this lag, however, over time, the inflation adjustment results in a rise in the face value of the bond at the rate of inflation.

This inflation adjustment also applies to the coupon interest thrown off by TIPS. As noted above, the interest rate of TIPS is set when the bonds are sold at auction. That rate never changes. But because the face amount of the TIPS is adjusted at the rate of inflation, interest income rises as the value of the TIPS rises. Interest rates set at auction for the 10-year TIP have varied from a high of 4.25% at one of the first auctions to a low of 1.375%

EXHIBIT 6.1

How TIPS Work: An Illustration

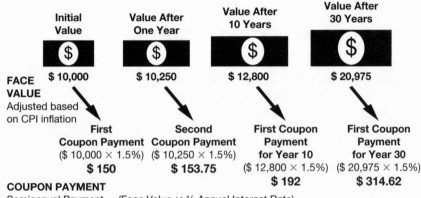

COUPON PAYMENT
Semiannual Payment = (Face Value × ½ Annual Interest Rate)

Source: Annette Thau, "An Investor's Guide to Inflation-Protected Securities," *The AAII Journal*, Vol. XXIX, No. 4, p. 6.
Drawing reprinted with permission.

at the January 2010 auction. Interest rates for the 30-year TIP are somewhat higher: 2.125% at the January 2010 auction. The inflation adjustment, however, is the same for all TIPS: whether 5-year, 10-year, or 30-year.

Exhibit 6.1 shows how TIPS work.

Let us illustrate how TIPS work with the hypothetical TIP illustrated in Exhibit 6.1. Assume you invest $10,000 in this particular TIP. It has a face value of $10,000, it matures in 30 years, and the interest rate is set at auction at 3%. Further assume that the inflation rate averages 2.5% a year over the life of the TIP. Finally, assume that as is normally the case, the 3% annual interest is distributed in two annual coupons, averaging 1.5% each.

+ The first interest payment will be ½ of 3% multiplied by $10,000, or $150.
+ At the end of year one, the value of the bond will rise by 2.5% (the assumed rate of inflation for the entire year), to $10,250.
+ Therefore, the second coupon payment will be based on the increased value of the bond. So it will be ½ of 3% multiplied by $10,250, or $153.75.

You may be looking at these numbers and thinking something like: "Big deal. A 3% interest rate, and minute adjustments in the amount of the coupon don't amount to very much." But actually, if you estimate the numbers, after 10 years, the numbers begin to look a lot more attractive.

Remember that interest income is calculated on a rising base. If, as in our example, inflation averages out to 2.5% a year: over that 10-year period, the value of the principal would rise to approximately $12,800. And the coupon payment would increase to about $192 twice a year (or $384 annually). After 30 years, the redemption value of the TIP would have risen to approximately $20,975 and the coupon payment to $314.62 twice a year, or $$629.24 annually.

All of these numbers are hypothetical, of course, since interest rates for TIPS vary at each auction; and since inflation is not likely to remain constant over the life of the bond. Nonetheless, even if, as in our example, you assume a fairly modest rate of inflation (2.5%) and a fairly modest interest rate (3%), the nominal rate of return would be equivalent to somewhere between 6% and 7% over a 30-year period.

In effect, what this accomplishes is that you are guaranteed a real rate of return. Historically, the real rate of return of Treasuries has averaged about 3% above the rate of inflation. The structure of inflation-linked bonds guarantees a return equivalent to the real rate of return. Moreover, the structure of these bonds guarantees that the purchasing power of the principal will not erode due to inflation. Finally, as an additional layer of protection, the Treasury guarantees that in the unlikely event deflation occurs, the final value of the bond will not be less than par, or the initial price of the bond at issue.

In the event of deflation, the inflation adjustment would result in a decline in the face value of the TIP. This would also result in a corresponding decline in the interest payment. For the first time in many decades, during 2009, for a few months, the CPI-U actually went negative (at −2.78%). While continued deflation does not appear likely, it is no longer totally improbable. Note, on the other hand, that if there was a period of sustained deflation, anyone who holds a TIP until it matures has some protection. When the TIP matures, it will be redeemed at the adjusted value of principal or its initial face value, whichever is higher.

TIPS: Volatility

In theory, TIPS sound like very simple and predictable instruments. It was assumed, for example, that because of the inflation adjustment, TIPS would be less volatile than conventional bonds. It was also assumed that TIPS would perform better during periods of rising interest rates than during periods of declining interest rates.

In the real world, however, TIPS have proved to be complex and in fact, highly unpredictable. Like all bonds, once they trade in the secondary market, the price of TIPS changes daily. Changes in the price of TIPS result from two different factors. First, there is a daily change in the inflation factor, which translates to a very minute change in price. But equally important, the price of TIPS is also affected by daily changes in the level and direction of interest rates. Over periods of weeks, months, or even a year, changes in price due to fluctuations in interest rates have been the dominant factor affecting the price of TIPS. They have swamped the inflation adjustment.

Contrary to initial expectations, moreover, TIPS have proved to be extremely volatile, more volatile in fact than conventionally structured bonds of the same maturity. A number of explanations have been offered for the higher volatility: One is that the lower coupon of TIPS bonds, relative to conventional bonds of the same maturity, results in a longer duration, and therefore, higher volatility. Other explanations revolve around inflation expectations. Surprisingly, the price of TIPS sometimes goes up, based not on actual inflation experience, but rather, on expectations of inflation.

Whatever the cause of the volatility, the fact remains that when interest rates rise, TIPS often decline in price more than conventionally structured bonds; and when interest rates decline, TIPS rise in price more than conventional bonds with the same maturity. To complicate matters further, interest rates of TIPS and those of conventional bonds with the same maturity occasionally move in totally opposite directions, as they did, for example, at the beginning of 2004. During that time, the yield of the 10-year TIPS bond declined by about 40 basis points; whereas the yield of the conventional 10-year bond went up by about 30 basis points. (In both cases, the coupon rate did not change; the yield changed as a result of the change in price of the underlying bond.)

To sum up TIPS cash flows: if you buy a TIP at auction, and hold it until it matures, it will mature at a value which will reflect the inflation adjustments throughout the life of the bond. But if you buy a TIP in the secondary market, or if you sell it before it matures, the price may be lower than your initial purchase price, or it may be higher, based on daily fluctuations in the price of TIPS.

TIPS: "Phantom Income" and Taxes

In addition to their volatility, TIPS have a second major drawback, namely, the way they are taxed. For that, we need to look more closely at the inflation adjustment.

The inflation adjustment of TIPS, as noted above, is reflected in the daily market value of these bonds. But the IRS does not actually pay out the inflation adjustment on the face value of the TIPS until TIPS are redeemed, at maturity. For that reason, the inflation adjustment is sometimes referred to as "phantom income." Nevertheless, the inflation adjustment is taxed annually, even though that income may not be received for many years.

Note, also, that if you have a modest amount invested in TIPS, reinvesting interest income can be difficult because interest income from TIPS is low.

TIPS versus "Coupon Treasuries"

Suppose you are wondering whether to buy the 10-year TIPS or the 10-year Treasury note. Which will have higher returns, TIPS or conventional Treasuries with coupons? The answer to that question is: Nobody knows.

Generally, the interest yield of the TIPS is a good deal lower than that of the conventional Treasury. Over the past few years that difference has amounted to about 200 basis points, sometimes a bit more, sometimes a bit less. But remember that the two yields are not equivalent.

The conventional Treasury coupon yield actually includes two different components: an implicit inflation rate and an interest rate payment. If you subtract the inflation rate from the nominal rate, the resulting number is what is called the real rate of return of the bond, that is, the rate of return after accounting for inflation.

Let us assume that you buy a TIP whose coupon is 2% at a time when the 10-year Treasury coupon is 4%. Can you determine, based on these numbers, which is the better buy?

The answer to that is: You don't know and you can't know at the time you purchase the bond. That's because the yield of the TIPS does not include the inflation adjustment that will be applied monthly to the price of the TIPS. It may be higher than 2% or lower, depending on the future inflation rate.

In order to compare potential returns of TIPS to those of conventional bonds under different inflation scenarios, analysts have introduced a concept known as the "breakeven rate." The breakeven rate is defined as the rate that would result in equivalent total returns for both types of bonds. In our hypothetical example, if inflation turns out to equal exactly 2%, then the total return of each bond will be equal.

If the rate of inflation turns out to be higher than 2%, then due to the inflation adjustment, the TIPS will turn out to have been the better buy. But if the rate of inflation is lower than 2%, then because of higher interest payments during the life of the conventional T-Note, that will turn out to have been the better buy.

Of course, at the time you purchase a bond, you cannot predict the future rate of inflation.

So to get back to the original question: Which is the better buy, the 10-year TIPS or the conventional 10-year T-note? The only statement that can be made with certainty is that ultimately, over very long holding periods (10 or more years) the total return of TIPS will parallel the inflation rate. But TIPS will outperform conventional bonds only if inflation is higher than the breakeven rate over these holding periods. Over short periods of time (say one or two years), there is no way to predict which will have a higher total return.

Buying TIPS

The simplest and cheapest way for individuals to buy TIPS is to purchase them directly at the Treasury's regular quarterly auctions, through the TreasuryDirect program via what is called a "noncompetitive tender," whereby you agree to accept the yield of the auction. (Treasury Direct is described below.) The minimum purchase is $1,000; the maximum that can be purchased by an individual at one auction is $5 million. (Note that if you purchased TIPS any time since their inception up to January 2007, these are now called Legacy TIPS.) Older TIPS, can of course be purchased in the secondary market.

To sum up, because of their high volatility, TIPS are poor investments for the short term (anything less than a few years). For inflation protection, you buy them and put them away and don't trade them. Moreover, the tax features of TIPS virtually dictate that TIPS should be purchased only in tax-sheltered accounts, such as IRAs destined for retirement. That eliminates having to pay a tax annually on phantom income.

BUYING TREASURIES: TREASURYDIRECT

The simplest option for purchasing any security issued by the U.S. Treasury is to open an account with TreasuryDirect, through its TreasuryDirect program. TreasuryDirect allows accounts both for individuals and for "entities" such as trust funds, estates and the like. You can buy securities for as little as $1,000, with additional increments of $1,000. This is a very attractive option:

- ◆ It eliminates all transaction costs.
- ◆ Individuals receive the same yield as institutional investors.
- ◆ All of your Treasury securities can be consolidated in one account.
- ◆ When you open an account through TreasuryDirect, you are banking directly with the Fed. The Web site of TreasuryDirect is TreasuryDirect,gov.

TreasuryDirect now functions entirely online. All aspects of the program, from opening an account to buying securities, are managed online. To open an account, go to TreasuryDirect.gov. You need to provide some data including your taxpayer ID number, your email address; and choose a password. You also need to provide the number of an account that you hold with either a commercial bank or a major brokerage firm. When you place an order for a bond, the Fed will automatically debit that account for any securities you purchase at auction on the day of the auction. The Fed will also wire interest payments and matured principal directly to that account. In short, the Fed will be your friendly banker. Moreover, the Fed will not charge you for any of this unless your account has over $100,000 in securities. If you have more than that amount, you will be charged an annual fee of $25.00.

Once you have opened an account, you can participate in any auction held by the Fed. To purchase a security, you submit a very brief form called a "noncompetitive tender," whereby you agree to purchase the maturity you select at the average yield of the auction—that is, the average of all the competitive tenders submitted by dealers purchasing billions of dollars worth of securities. Tenders are submitted online. All securities are sold in book-entry form only.

TreasuryDirect is a highly efficient operation. Interest payments are automatically wired to the account that you designate, as is matured principal. You can choose to automatically reinvest or to withdraw cash periodically. No matter how many different securities are in your account, in whatever combination of maturities you desire, all are held in one central account with one account number. You may access information about your account via the Web site or through the Buy Direct toll-free telephone number.

The TreasuryDirect program is primarily intended for individuals who intend to buy securities and hold them to maturity. But the Fed has now added a feature called *Sell Direct*, which enables you to sell Treasuries before they mature. If you direct the Fed to sell securities, the

Fed will obtain quotes from several brokers and sell at the highest quote obtained. Proceeds from the sale will be deposited automatically into the bank account you have designated. The Fed charges a modest fee for this service (currently $45.00).

Purchasing individual Treasury bills, notes, and bonds directly is actually safer than purchasing them through a mutual fund. This is because by buying individual securities and holding them to maturity, you can be certain that you will redeem your principal in entirety. As you will see in Chapter 12, on bond funds if you buy the same securities through a mutual fund, you may not.

The most accurate information about upcoming auctions is available on the Treasury Direct Web site. Tentative three-month calendars are published in February, May, August, and November. Minimum amounts required for purchase are $100 for any security, with additional increments of $1,000, up to $5,000,000.

Would you like to estimate the probable yield before you purchase a Treasury of any maturity at an auction? You can come fairly close by checking the most recent Treasury yield curve on Investinginbonds.com for the maturity that interests you.

If you do not have online access, Treasury bills, bonds, and notes can be purchased through banks and brokerage firms, but not through TreasuryDirect. Fees are modest, no higher than $25 or $50 per transaction, regardless of the amount purchased. Note that many brokers have eliminated fees for purchasing Treasuries, particularly if they are purchased at an auction. But note also that Treasury Direct only sells new issues. If you want to buy older, outstanding issues; or if you want to buy zeros, you need to do so through a broker.

One final note. The Web site maintained by TreasuryDirect, is in a class by itself. This Web site is detailed, updated continually, and easy to use. It is your best source of information about any debt instrument issued by the U.S. government.

ZERO COUPON BONDS

Zero coupon bonds (zeros for short) are also colloquially known as "strips." This is not a humorous nickname. The word "strips" actually describes the process of creating zeros.

Behind every zero stands an ordinary so-called plain vanilla U.S. Treasury bond. In 1982, investment banks got the brilliant idea of separating the different revenue streams of government bonds (the coupons-only and the principal-only) and repackaging each separate stream as a distinct security. The zero was born.

Whether the zero is based on the interest-only or principal-only strip is unimportant to the buyer. In either case, the buyer of a zero (like that of a T-Bill), does not receive any interest coupons. Instead, the zero is sold at a very deep discount from par, but it matures at par. The difference between the discounted price paid and par represents the interest earned. You will recall that when you invest in ordinary bonds, return on the bond includes interest-on-interest earned by reinvesting the coupons. For long-term maturities, the interest-on-interest is the major source of return. Since zeros have no coupons, you might think that you lose that source of income. Quite the contrary. The final lump sum payment is calculated so that it includes the interest-on-interest that would have been received if the coupons had been reinvested periodically *at the yield-to-maturity rate.* That is why zeros seem to multiply like magic. Invest $197 in a zero with a coupon rate of 8.3%; in 20 years you will receive $1,000.

Advertising for zeros makes them look like a unique method of creating wealth. You invest a small sum. In a number of years, say 10, you realize a huge profit—guaranteed. It looks magical. Actually, this is just another manifestation of the magic of compounding. The main difference between a zero and another Treasury of the same maturity is that the zero has no reinvestment risk. The actual return in dollars is known and guaranteed. Furthermore, reinvesting is automatic and efficient: it is built into the structure of the bond. If you buy a Treasury of comparable maturity, the actual return will vary depending on the rates at which you reinvest coupons. Realized return may be higher or may be lower than for the zero, depending on reinvestment rates.

You should be aware that investing small sums in zeros can be expensive. Markups are high and vary a great deal from dealer to dealer. If the maturity of the zero is short (under five years), the conventional coupon Treasury may actually be the better buy. Locking in a yield-to-maturity with a zero is an advantage only if the zero has a particularly attractive yield.

Before investing in zeros, you should carefully consider two unique aspects of these securities; namely, the tax treatment of zeros and their extreme volatility.

Even though the owner of a zero receives no interest payments prior to its maturity, the interest that is accrued (earned) is taxed annually as if it were actually paid out. (That interest is known as "imputed interest" or "phantom interest.") As a result of this feature, zeros are suitable mainly for two types of accounts: tax-sheltered accounts such as IRAs or Keoghs, and accounts taxed at low tax rates, such as accounts of children in a low tax bracket.

The volatility of zeros is unique. The basic explanation for the volatility of zeros is to be found in duration. As you will recall, bonds with long durations are more volatile than those with shorter durations. Because zeros have no coupons, their duration is the same as their maturity, far longer than that of ordinary coupon bonds with the same maturity. As a result, the volatility of zeros is much higher than that of ordinary coupon bonds with the same maturity.

To illustrate, let's look at Exhibit 6.2, which shows the percentage price changes that would occur to both zero coupon bonds and ordinary coupon bonds, both yielding 7%, if interest rates rise by 50 basis points, to 7.5%; by 100 basis points, to 8%; and by 200 basis points, to 9%.

As Exhibit 6.2 shows, zeros with two-year maturities are only slightly more volatile than ordinary coupon bonds. But as maturity lengthens, so does volatility. The volatility of the 30-year zero is more than two times that of the 30-year coupon security. If interest rates rise by 200 basis points, from 7% to 9%, the price of a zero with a 7% yield and a 30-year maturity would decline by approximately 43.8% ($4,380 for a $10,000 investment) compared with 20.6% for the coupon security ($2,060 per $10,000 investment).

If interest rates decline, the price of a zero coupon bond also appreciates at a higher rate than that of a coupon security with the same maturity and yield. Once again, price changes are most dramatic for zero coupon bonds with long maturities. Exhibit 6.2 also illustrates the percentage price changes that would occur to both zeros and ordinary coupon bonds, yielding 7%, if interest rates decline by 50 basis points, to 6.5%; by 100 basis points, to 6%; and by 200 basis points, to 7%.

Once again, price changes for the two-year bond are only modestly higher for the zero coupon bond compared to the regular coupon security. For bonds with intermediate or longer maturities, the sensitivity of a zero coupon bond to interest rate changes turns into a genuine bonanza at the longer end. For example, if interest rates decline by 100 basis points, the price of a zero coupon bond with a 30-year maturity rises by approximately 25% ($2,500 for a $10,000 investment). If interest rates decline by 200 basis points, the price of a zero coupon bond yielding 7%, with a 30-year maturity, goes up by an astonishing 79% ($7,900 for a $10,000 investment)!

Note that, as explained in the section on interest rate risk, the price changes that occur if interest rates fluctuate are larger if interest rates

EXHIBIT 6.2

Price Changes for a Given Change in Yields: Coupon Security vs. Zero Coupon Bond, 7% Yield

Change in Yields (Basis Points)	2 yr		5 yr		10 yr		30 yr	
	Coupon Bond	Zero Coupon Bond	Coupon Bond	Zero Coupon Bond	Coupon Bond	Zero Coupon Bond	Coupon Book	Zero Coupon Bond
+50	−0.9%	−1.0%	−2.1%	−2.4%	−3.5%	−4.7%	−5.9%	−13.5%
+100	−1.8%	−1.9%	−4.1%	−4.7%	−6.8%	−9.2%	−11.3%	−25.1%
+200	−3.6%	−3.8%	−7.9%	−9.2%	−13.0%	−17.5%	−20.6%	−43.8%
−50	+0.9%	+1.0%	+2.1%	+2.4%	+3.6%	+5.0%	+6.6%	+15.6%
−100	+1.9%	+2.0%	+4.3%	+5.0%	+7.4%	+10.2%	+13.8%	+33.7%
−200	+3.8%	+4.0%	+8.7%	+10.2%	+15.6%	+21.4%	+30.9%	+79%

decline than if interest rates go up. As is shown in Exhibit 6.2, for example, if interest rates go up by 200 basis points, the price of the 30-year, 7% zero declines by 43.8%. But if interest rates decline by the same amount (200 basis points), the price of the 30-year, 7% coupon bond appreciates by 79%. You can readily understand why anyone who anticipates that interest rates will decline buys zeros.

The price changes illustrated assume an instantaneous change in yields. In real life, as noted in the section on interest rate risk, changes of this magnitude would in all likelihood take months, or perhaps years. The numbers in Exhibit 6.2 would therefore have to be adjusted for time. For instance, if the interest rate change were to occur five years after the bonds were initially purchased, then five years would have to be subtracted from the age of the bond. Five years after the purchase date, the 10-year bond would have become a five-year bond, and so on.

Note also that the exact price swings illustrated in Exhibit 6.2 are accurate only for bonds with a 7% yield. Price changes would be somewhat higher or lower for bonds with different yields.

Note once again, however, that the interest rate changes illustrated are entirely plausible. Between September 1998 and December 1999, interest rates on the 30-year bond went from a low of 4.78% to a high of 6.75%. In the beginning of 2000, the interest rate on the long bond reversed steeply, declining to approximately 5.75% between January and the end of March.

In sum, while there is no risk to principal if you hold a Treasury zero to maturity, if you want to resell it before it matures, its value may have gone up a great deal or may have declined significantly.

Zeros for Investment Purposes

The peculiarities of zeros makes them ideal investments for several totally different purposes.

First zeros are ideal investments for tax-sheltered accounts such as IRAs or Keoghs, particularly if you would like to invest small sums periodically. Suppose, for instance, that you want to invest $2,000 annually in an IRA account. Because of the unique structure of zeros, $2,000 enables you to buy a much larger par amount of bonds, particularly if you are young and retirement is 20 or 30 years away. Furthermore, if the zeros are in a tax-deferred account, you can forget about paying taxes on phantom income. And finally, you can select maturities so that they coincide with any date you select. That can be the year you retire. Or you can build an annuity by buying bonds that will mature every year in succession starting with the year you retire and thereafter, for the next 15 or 20 years.

Second, zeros can be used to speculate on interest rate moves. As illustrated earlier, because of their extreme volatility, any change in interest rates has a dramatic impact on the price of zero coupon bonds, particularly those with long maturities. If you think interest rates are about to decline and you want to profit from such a move, you would buy zeros with long maturities. Then, if you are right, you will be able to resell your zeros with a significant capital gain. The legendary investor Warren Buffett was said to have made just such a purchase of zero coupon bonds with 30-year maturities in 1998, and for precisely this reason. Managers of many types of bond funds (or even of equity funds) routinely buy zeros to boost returns if they think interest rates are about to decline.

If you are wrong, on the other hand, and interest rates rise, then your downside risk is twofold. You may have to hold the zero to maturity (or longer than you expected). Also, and perhaps less important to you, there is the opportunity cost of not receiving the higher interest rate. There would be no risk of loss of principal, however, unless you actually decided to sell the zero. But, given the unreliability of interest rate forecasts, it is not advisable to buy zeros primarily in order to make interest rate bets unless you are prepared to hold them to maturity (or for a very long time) in the event that you are wrong.

Finally, zeros can be used to put aside money for a known future need such as a child's college tuition. Because reinvestment rates are locked in, the total return when the zero matures is known and guaranteed. The problem here would be the phantom interest generated by a Treasury zero, which generates annual taxes. You should be aware, however, that you can buy municipal zeros (they will be discussed in Chapter 7). Municipal zeros might be more appropriate for this type of use if you are in a high income bracket.

U.S. SAVINGS BONDS

The government still sells two types of savings bonds: Series EE and Series I. (The government no longer issues HH bonds.)

Savings bonds are described in detail in a continually updated Web site maintained by the Bureau of the Public Debt: savingsbonds.gov, as well as publicdebt.treas.gov. I will briefly describe some of the outstanding features of these bonds. If, after reading this section, you think savings bonds are for you, and if you have access to the Internet, that is your best source of the most current information. If you do not, then your local savings bank is your next best bet.

Both series I Bonds and Series EE bonds share a number of characteristics. Since they are direct obligations of the U.S. government, their credit quality is impeccable. Moreover, both of these series have attractive tax features. Interest income is exempt from state and local taxes. In addition, you may defer payment of taxes on *all* interest income until the bonds are redeemed, which makes these bonds very attractive for individuals who may not have other tax-deferred accounts. Finally, interest income of both I bonds and EE bonds, under certain circumstances, may be *entirely tax-free* if used to pay certain college expenses. This is called the education tax exclusion (described below). You can purchase either of these series in very small amounts (as little as $25.00) to amounts as large as $1 million. But each of these bonds has some unique characteristics. Their key features are described below.

Series EE Bonds

These are the first savings bonds that were issued. The government has changed the features of these bonds in order to make them more attractive. As a result, interest rates have varied widely since the inception of the program, depending on their issue date. Since 1997 these bonds earn 90% of the average rate of five-year Treasury notes sold at auction for the previous six months. Interest rates are reset every six months.

EE bonds are accrual bonds; that is, as with zero coupon bonds or bills, you do not receive interest income until you redeem the bonds at their maturity. EE bonds are sold at 50% of face value. For example, you would buy a $100.00 bond for $50.00. Interest accrues until the bond has reached its full face value. You cannot predict at the time you buy the bonds when they will reach face value, because that will depend on the interest rates prevailing while you hold the bonds.

EE bonds were originally sold with maturity dates ranging from eight to 17 years. But when the bonds reach maturity, most go into an automatic extension period, usually about 10 years. At the current time, most EE bonds can earn interest for up to 30 years. You need not hold EE bonds until they mature, however. EE bonds can be redeemed anytime after six months .But if you redeem EE Bonds prior to five years, there is a penalty, which is that you forfeit interest payments for the last three months.

EE bonds share the attractive tax features mentioned above. Taxes on these bonds are deferred until you actually cash in the bonds, as long as you hold the bonds for at least five years. EE bonds are also eligible for the education tax exclusion (see below).

EE bonds can now be purchased directly on line for face amounts of up to $1,000. They can also be purchased from your local bank. And employers can set up an automatic deduction plan called *EasySaver*. Minimum amounts that can be purchased are $25.00 ($50 face). The maximum amount is $5,000 ($10,000 face). There are no commissions of any type. The maximum that can be purchased during any one year is $15,000 purchase price ($30,000 face amount).

If you own EE bonds purchased prior to 1997 (or since that date, for that matter) and if you want to know what the bonds are currently worth or how much interest they are currently earning, you can, of course, check with your local bank. But there are also two sources of information on the Internet, both maintained by the government. One is called the *Savings Bond Wizard* (more about the Wizard below); and the other is called the *Savings Bonds Earnings Report*.

HH Bonds

The government stopped issuing these bonds in September 2004. Older bonds still outstanding may be redeemed through your local bank. Redeeming the bonds requires a signature guarantee. (There is a Web site to service HH bonds with links to TreasuryDirect.)

I Bonds

Series I bonds are the newest of the savings bonds. They were first introduced in September 1998. To remember the main feature of I bonds, think "I" and inflation. I bonds resemble TIPS. They are an accrual bond, meaning that you do not receive coupon interest while you hold the bonds. Interest is added to the bonds on a monthly basis and paid when the bond is cashed or redeemed. But, as with TIPS interest payments are adjusted for inflation based on the CPI-U. In effect, interest income grows at an inflation-indexed rate.

The earnings rate of I bonds is a combination of two separate rates: a fixed rate of return and a variable semiannual inflation rate. The fixed rate is set when the bonds are initially sold, and it remains the same throughout the life of the I-bond. But the inflation rate adjustment is reset every six months, in May and November, based on the CPI-U. In the unlikely event that deflation occurs, the value of the bond remains at its pre-deflation level. The formula for combining these two rates is somewhat complex. The two rates are not simply added. They are compounded. The exact formula is explained on the Treasury's Web site. In November 2009, I bonds were being sold with a combined interest rate of 3.36%, which is a combination of a fixed rate of 0.30% and a semiannual inflation rate of 1.53%. Fixed rates since the beginning of the panic of 2008 have been the lowest since the inception of the program: 0% in May 2008, 0.7% in November 2008, 0.10% in May 2009. But the combined rate has remained above 3%.

I bonds have several major advantages. Because interest rates of I bonds are indexed to inflation, the value of the bond rises with inflation, like that of TIPS. But in addition, the interest rate set at the time of issue guarantees a minimum return. Finally, and this is an important difference, because I savings bonds do not trade in the secondary market, the value of the bonds can never go down. The value of TIPS, on the other hand, fluctuates in the secondary market as interest rates change.

I bonds are sold for face amounts ranging from $50 to $5,000. They are purchased at face value: you pay $50 for a $50 bond.

I bonds can be bought directly through TreasuryDirect, at a local bank, or through an employer-sponsored plan such as *EasySaver*. (Paper securities are purchased through banks.) I bonds have a maturity of 30 years, but they can be redeemed any time after six months. Because these bonds are structured primarily as long-term investments, there is a small penalty for redeeming I bonds within five years of purchase: You would forfeit three months of interest if you cashed out your bonds within five years.

How have I savings bonds performed since their inception?

Buried in the TreasuryDirect Web site are two tables that show semiannual earnings on I savings bonds. (To find the most recent tables that show current values, go to "I Savings Bonds in Depth", click on "Tools," and then "Savings Bond Earnings Reports" at the TreasuryDirect Web site.) Exhibit 6.3 shows earnings for bonds that have been held for different periods. For purposes of comparison, I have included earnings for the most recent four-year period, with the lowest interest rates since the inception of the program, and for bonds purchased in 1998 through 2000 and held through 2010, issued when interest rates were higher than current rates. Earnings are shown on a $100 amount.

EXHIBIT 6.2

Earnings Report for I Bonds Held for Periods of up to 10 Years

Earning Period	Earnings to Date		when Held 5 Years			
Series I Bond Issue Dates	Start Date	End Date	Start Value	End Value	Current Earning	Since Issue
11/2009 – 4/2010	11/1/2009	5/1/2010	100.00	101.68	3.36%	3.36%
5/2009 – 10-2009	11/1/2009	5/1/2010	100.00	101.60	3.20%	1.59%
11/2008 – 4-2009	11/1/2009	5/1/2010	102.84	104.76	3.73%	3.12%
5/2008 – 10/2008	11/1/2009	5/1/2010	104.96	106.56	3.05%	3.20%
11/2007 – 4/2008	11/1/2009	5/1/2010	108.52	110.84	4.28%	4.16%
5/2007 – 10/2007	11/1/2009	5/1/2010	110.68	113.12	4.41%	4.15%
11/2006 – 4/2007	11/1/2009	5/1/2010	113.40	115.96	4.51%	4.28%
....						
....						
....						
11/2000 – 4/2001	11/1/2009	5/1/2010	170.32	175.88	6.53%	6.03%
5/2000 – 10/2000	11/1/2009	5/1/2010	179.68	185.72	6.72%	6.29%
11/1999 – 4/2000	11/1/2009	5/1/2010	182.68	188.64	6.53%	6.14%
5/1999 – 10/1999	11/1/2009	5/1/2010	185.60	191.56	6.42%	6.00%
11/1996 – 4/1999	11/1/2009	5/1/2010	190.36	196.48	6.43%	5.96%
9/1998 – 10/1998	3/1/2009	9/1/2010	196.52	202.92	6.51%	5.98%

Source: U.S. Savings Bonds report, www.treasurydirect.gov (tables were from November 2009).

Exhibit 6.3 is a bit confusing. Reading from left to right, the table shows:

- The issue dates for the I bonds, listed in six-month ranges
- The "start date" and the "end date" for the most recent six-month period for the first date in the range listed. (The "start value" is what the bond could have been redeemed for at the beginning of the most recent six-month reset period; and the "end value" is its value at the end of the six-month period.)

Note that while the current fixed rate is extremely low, older issues are continuing to earn higher rates because the fixed rate for those years was higher. Cumulative rates of return for 10 years show solid returns.

Note finally that a new program called Smart Exchange allows TreasuryDirect account owners to convert Series E, EE, and I Paper savings bonds to electronic securities in a special "Conversion Linked Account" within their online account.

Bonds to Set Up a Deferred-Tax Retirement Plan

Have I got a deal for you! I'm going to offer you a retirement plan with the following features:

+ You can invest any amount, from $50 to $5,000, and invest up to $10,000 per calendar year.

+ The amounts invested will accrue interest at a guaranteed minimum rate set at the time you buy; but an additional interest component will be added, which will be reset every six months, based on the inflation rate. In the event deflation occurs, the minimum interest rate will remain in effect. In the event interest rates rise, the value of this bond (*unlike that of any other bond, including Treasuries, that trade in the secondary market*) will not decline.

+ Interest and interest-on-interest will compound, tax deferred, until you choose to cash in some bonds, for income or for any purpose you choose. You can cash out any sum you wish, any time you wish, after six months. But you can also leave the money to compound for up to 30 years. Both purchases and withdrawals can be tailored to your needs.

+ Interest income is exempted from state and local taxes.

+ The credit quality of these bonds is of the highest quality. There is zero default risk.

+ You can buy these securities at no cost: no commissions of any kind. Furthermore, the organization that sells you these bonds will maintain your account free of charge to you.

+ You can buy these bonds in the privacy of your home, via the Internet. You can also set up an automatic withdrawal plan through your employer; or you can buy these bonds from your local bank.

Sound too good to be true? I have just repeated all the features I described above, because those are the features of I bonds. They bear repetition because this product is a sleeper: I have seen almost no mention of it in the financial press. Obviously, brokerage firms do not recommend I bonds even if they could sell them, because they can't make any money on them. Banks are unlikely to push I bonds; they compete with CDs, and banks don't make any money selling you I bonds. But if you compare the features of I bonds to those of other products designed to provide tax-deferred income, such as annuities, I bonds are likely to be the superior product.

One recent major change to the I bonds program, however, is that the maximum amount an individual can purchase has been lowered to $10,000 per calendar year per social security number ($5,000 in electronic form and $5,000 in paper securities). Note also that each of the partners in a couple can invest $10,000. Prior to this change, each individual was able to invest $60,000 per calendar year in I bonds ($30,000 in electronic form and $30,000 in paper form). Therefore, a couple was able to invest a total of $120,000 per calendar year. The current maximum changes the profile of the program significantly. It clearly is intended for middle class, rather than really affluent, investors. Nonetheless, I would suggest that if you are looking for a very safe, very predictable investment for some of the assets being put away for retirement, you should investigate I bonds before signing up for expensive and restrictive annuities, particularly if you are going to be investing in fixed-income instruments.

Savings Bonds for Education:
The Education Tax Exclusion

Both EE and I series bonds can be purchased to qualify for the education tax exclusion. That means, essentially, that either series of bonds can be used to save for a child's college education, tax free. If the proceeds from savings bonds are used to pay college expenses, no federal taxes are due. Note that only college fees and tuition qualify for the exclusion; board and room, books, and other miscellaneous college expenses do not qualify.

Under normal conditions, either series of savings bonds will in all likelihood be more advantageous than municipal bonds. Note, however, that the tax exemption holds only if the bonds are bought in the parent's name (not that of the child whose tuition will be paid). That may not seem logical, but that is the way it is. Also, to be eligible for the tax exemption, the parents' income must meet certain income restrictions. These caps are reset and pegged to the inflation rate. For the year 2008, the most recent year listed on the TreasuryDirect Web site, the full interest exclusion applies to joint incomes under $100,650, with partial exclusions for incomes up to $130,650 ($67,100 and $82,100 for single filers). Current guidelines are published in IRS Form 8815.

Once again, the details are somewhat complex. But the program is attractive enough to be of interest to most families in the middle income brackets.

FEDERAL AGENCIES

Most federal agencies that sell debt instruments are classified as *government-sponsored enterprises* (GSEs). These federal agencies are privately owned. They were created by Congress to reduce borrowing costs for sectors of the economy deemed essential, including farmers and homeowners. Because bonds issued by federal agencies are not direct obligations of the U.S. government, credit quality is deemed to be not as impeccable as that of Treasuries. As a result, bonds issued by federal agencies generally yield more than Treasuries with the same maturities by anywhere from 50 to 150 basis points, depending on maturity length, and current interest rates.

GSEs issue two types of instruments: discount notes (similar to T-Bills), with maturities under one year, and bonds, with maturities of two years or more. Zeros also exist for agency debt. Debt sold by the Federal National Mortgage Association (Fannie Mae or FNMA), Federal Land Banks, and Federal Home Loan Banks (FHLB) is exempt from state and local taxes. Other agency paper is not exempt.

The Agencies that are likely to be most familiar to you are the Government National Mortgage Association (GNMA or, more familiarly, Ginnie Mae); and the two Mortgage Associations: the Federal National Mortgage Association (FNMA, or Fanny Mae), and the Federal Home Loan Mortgage Corporation (Freddie Mac). Bonds issued by the GNMA have always had the explicit guarantee of the U.S. government. Up to the financial crisis of 2008, bonds issued by Freddie Mac and Fannie Mae had only an implicit guarantee. But since they are now almost entirely owned by the government (technically, they are under "conservatorship"), they now also have the explicit guarantee of the government, at least until their ultimate status is resolved. Bonds issued by these three agencies are described in more detail in Chapter 9, which deals with mortgage-backed securities.

Bonds issued by the three agencies involved with mortgages constitute an enormous market. Bonds issued by other government agencies constitute a much smaller market. The following are two of the better known Agencies:

Federal Home Loan Banks (FHLBs)

These are the 12 regional banks that back the nation's Savings and Loans (S&Ls). They are actually owned by the private S&Ls. Bonds issued by the FHLBs are known as *consolidated* bonds because they are joint obligations of the 12 Federal Home Loan Banks. That means that in the event one bank experiences financial difficulties, the other 11 banks are under a legal obligation to step in and cover any payments due by the weaker bank. The credit quality of these bonds is very high.

Tennessee Valley Authority (TVA)

The TVA was established by Congress in 1933 to promote the use of electric power in the Tennessee Valley region. It is the largest public power system in the country. The bonds issued by the TVA are not guaranteed by the government, but they are rated AAA, based on the status of the TVA as a wholly owned corporation of the U.S. government and the financial strength of the agency.

Both of these agencies issue a variety of bonds, both short and long term. The attraction of any of the Agency bonds compared with Treasuries is the higher interest rate. But at the time this is being written, spreads to Treasuries, particularly of short to intermediate agency bonds, are somewhat narrow—20 to 50 basis points. Minimums required for purchase vary from $5,000 to $10,000, depending on the agency.

One unusual feature of bonds issued by a number of Agencies is that they have what is called an "Estate" Feature. That feature allows the bonds to be redeemed at par plus accrued interest by the estate of the original bondholder after his death. (Technically, this is known as a conditional "put"). Since this feature is not available on all Agency bonds, if it interests you, seek out a knowledgeable broker; or look for it in the listings of online brokers.

Debt of any of these agencies can be purchased from banks or from brokerage firms. Beginning in March 2010, both FINRA.org/marketdata and

Investinginbonds.com are publishing trade data on Agency bonds, in formats similar to those published for corporate bonds (see Chapter 10). But note also that the price for agency bonds is quoted with the same conventions as Treasury bonds: par with fractions above par listed in 32nds of a point.

Note finally: one well-known agency, the Student Loan Marketing Association, colloquially known as Sallie Mae, was privatized in 2004. Subsequently, it experienced severe financial difficulty, and most of its bonds were downgraded, many to junk status.

Treasuries and Savings Bonds vs. Bank CDs

Insured CDs of banks are a popular alternative to short and intermediate Treasuries. No doubt the bank CDs owe their popularity to the fact that they are insured. Because both are extremely safe, let's go over some of the advantages and disadvantages of each.

Treasuries have the following features. They have no credit risk. They are more liquid than CDs. They can be sold any time with no interest penalty. There is no upper limit on the amount that is "insured." Finally, interest is exempt from state and local taxes. Their major disadvantage compared to CDs is that if you sell a two-to-five-year note before maturity, changes in interest rate levels may result in some loss of principal.

Note also that many large brokerage firms sell insured CDs. The advantage is that these firms stand ready to buy back your CDs if you need to resell before they mature. This feature makes them more liquid than ordinary bank CDs. But then, of course, the value of the principal in the CD fluctuates with interest rates.

SUMMARY

Treasury bills, notes, and bonds are the safest and most liquid debt securities that can be bought for any maturity. But even though the credit quality of all Treasuries is impeccable, longer dated Treasuries incur interest rate risk which rises as maturities are longer. Interest rate risk is negligible for Treasuries under two years, modest for Treasuries between two and seven years, and becomes significant after 10 years. Treasury Notes with maturities between three and seven years are particularly attractive investments for anyone looking for safety of principal and predictable returns. Treasuries of all maturities can be bought most efficiently and most cheaply through the TreasuryDirect Program.

This chapter also discussed Zeros, TIPS, and Savings Bonds. Zeros are sold at deep discounts, and mature at par: they are highly volatile. TIPS guarantee a real rate of return and protect against inflation. The Treasury is continuing to issue two categories of Savings Bonds: Series EE and Series I. Series EE bonds are sold at 90% of the average yield of five-year Treasuries sold at auction for the previous six months. Series I bonds are inflation-indexed securities. Both can be purchased for the education tax exclusion, provided certain income restrictions are met.

Questions to Ask When Buying Treasuries

How much interest rate risk am I assuming?

Where on the yield curve is the best current trade-off between yield and interest rate risk?

CHAPTER 7

Municipal Bonds

This chapter discusses

- ◆ Unique characteristics of municipal bonds
- ◆ When it pays to buy municipal bonds (taxable-equivalent yield)
- ◆ Credit quality: general obligation versus revenue bonds
- ◆ The rise and fall of municipal bond insurance
- ◆ Rating "recalibrations" by Moody's and Fitch
- ◆ Municipals with the strongest credit qualities
- ◆ Build America Bonds (BABs)
- ◆ Taxable Municipal Bonds
- ◆ Municipal bonds with special features
- ◆ Shopping for municipal bonds using the Internet
- ◆ Selecting municipal bonds

WHAT IS UNIQUE ABOUT MUNICIPAL BONDS?

Municipal bonds, "munis" for short, are issued by city, county, and state governments, as well as by enterprises with a public purpose, such as certain electric utilities, universities, and hospitals. For individual investors, the chief attraction of municipal bonds is that they are federally tax exempt. If you live in the state issuing the bonds, with a few exceptions, they are also exempt from state and local taxes, or, as the ads proclaim, triple tax free.

This is the only sector of the bond market where the primary buyers are individual investors. Overwhelmingly, munis deserve their popularity. Even though there are approximately 1.4 million issues outstanding, municipals are actually relatively uncomplicated securities once you understand the basics. Credit safety of municipals, moreover, is second only to that of Treasuries. Even though a number of municipal defaults have been highly publicized, the default rate of municipal bonds remains extremely low.

Between 2007 and 2009, however, the municipal bond market went through a veritable roller coaster ride. As with other sectors of the bond market, in 2008, munis tanked big time. The year 2008 was, in some respects, the worst year in the history of the municipal bond market. But 2009 was one of the best: most sectors of the municipal bond market rallied strongly.

From 2008 through the time this is being written (April 2010), several developments have taken place which are bringing major and probably permanent change to the municipal bond market. One is the failure of the major municipal bond insurance firms which, in effect, has resulted in the almost total disappearance of bond insurance from the municipal bond market. The second is the introduction of a new type of taxable municipal bond, Build America Bonds (BABs). BABs were intended initially to be a temporary program but they are proving so popular that proposals to either extend the program or make it permanent are under serious consideration by Congress. And the third is the adoption of a new ratings scale for municipal bonds, which will result in upgrades of most general obligation bonds and many others as well. Finally, the expansion of two Web sites: investinginbonds.com and EMMA.msrb.org (discussed at the end of Chapter 5) is bringing much greater transparency and much needed data and information to investors in the muni market.

This chapter will first cover the basic information that you need to understand when investing in municipals: namely, how to determine whether you will earn more from buying munis than from buying taxable bonds; and the differences in credit quality between general obligation and revenue bonds. It will then turn to the new developments in this sector. Finally, it will discuss and illustrate how to shop for municipal bonds using the Internet

Munis are not the right product for every investor. Let's see if they belong in your portfolio.

SHOULD I BUY MUNIS? (OR, TAXABLE-EQUIVALENT YIELD)

No one likes to pay taxes. But not everyone benefits from buying tax-exempt bonds. If you are in a low tax bracket, you may actually earn more by buying taxable bonds and paying the taxes. Yet a surprising number of individuals buy tax-exempt bonds when it makes no economic sense for them. It would appear that they are suffering from a disease called "taxaphobia."

If you are considering buying municipal bonds, your first step should be to determine whether you will earn more by buying munis or by buying taxable bonds. That decision is based on simple arithmetic. The method used most often is to calculate how much you would have to earn on taxable investments to earn as much as you net on municipal bonds. This is called the "taxable-equivalent yield." Exhibit 7.1 shows what some municipal bond yields are worth in various tax brackets.

The taxable-equivalent yield is easy to calculate The first step is to determine your exact tax bracket. The formula for computing the taxable-equivalent yield is

$$\text{taxable-equivalent yield} = \frac{\text{tax-exempt yield}}{(1 - \text{tax bracket})}$$

For example, suppose you are in the 39% tax bracket and you are considering purchasing a muni yielding 5% yield-to-maturity (YTM). To obtain the tax-equivalent yield, convert percentages to decimals. Your calculation looks like this

$$\text{taxable-equivalent yield} = \frac{.05}{1 - .39} = .082 \text{ or } 8.2\%$$

Translation: You would have to earn 8.20% in a taxable security in order to earn an equivalent yield.

If you are in the 15% tax bracket, on the other hand, the same calculation results in a taxable-equivalent yield on the same 5% muni of 5.88%. You may actually earn more by buying a taxable instrument.

Exhibit 7.1 provides a quick eye-view of taxable equivalent yields at the Federal level. But note that Investinginbonds.com and FINRA.org/marketdata both have "calculators" that enable you to determine tax equivalent yields.

Note also that in states with high state taxes, such as New York, California, Massachusetts, and Minnesota, demand for tax-exempt paper is often so high that you may earn more on out-of-state munis (federally tax exempt, but not exempt from taxes in the state where you live) than on munis from your own state. To determine which is your best option, compare yields on out-of-state munis to those of in-state munis on a tax-equivalent basis. Again, the "calculators" on Investinginbonds.com and

EXHIBIT 7.1

Tax-Exempt and Taxable-Equivalent Yields

TAX BRACKET	15%	28%	31%	36%	39.6%
TAX-EXEMPT YIELDS (%)	TAXABLE YIELD EQUIVALENTS (%)				
2.0%	2.35%	2.78%	2.90%	3.12%	3.31%
2.5	2.94	3.47	3.62	3.91	4.14
3.0	3.53	4.17	4.35	4.69	4.97
3.5	4.12	4.86	5.07	5.47	5.79
4.0	4.71	5.56	5.80	6.25	6.62
4.5	5.29	6.25	6.52	7.03	7.45
5.0	5.88	6.94	7.25	7.81	8.28
5.5	6.47	7.64	7.79	8.59	9.11
6.0	7.06	8.33	8.70	9.37	9.93
6.5	7.65	9.03	9.42	10.16	10.76
7.0	8.24	9.72	10.14	10.94	11.59

Source: investinginbonds.com Reprinted with permission.

FINRA.org/.marketdata enable you to determine tax-equivalent yields at the state level by typing in your federal tax bracket and the name of the state in which you live.

There are some additional fine points to remember when comparing taxable-equivalent yields. First, remember that Treasury and some federal agency debt are both exempt from state taxes. Particularly in high-tax states, either Treasuries or securities issued by certain agencies may net you more, net-after-taxes, than municipals. This is particularly true if you are buying very short maturities (two years or less) because the yield curve of munis tends to be more steeply upward sloping than that of taxable bonds. Also, if you are considering purchasing discount muni bonds, remember that the YTM for those bonds includes a capital gains component, which is federally taxable. Particularly if the discount is substantial, you may want to determine how much the capital gains taxes would decrease the total YTM.

As a rule, taxpayers in the highest tax brackets benefit from buying tax-exempt bonds; those in the lowest do not. Whether tax-exempts make economic sense for investors in the middle depends on the relationship between taxable and tax-exempt yields at the time of purchase (these change continually), as well as on current tax laws, and of course on your income. If tax laws change or if your income changes, then by all means, you should recalculate whether it continues to make sense for you to buy munis.

CREDIT QUALITY: GENERAL OBLIGATION VERSUS REVENUE BONDS

There is a good deal of confusion concerning the credit quality of municipal bonds. First of all, I would like to explain how munis are rated, and also clear up some common misconceptions.

Municipal bonds come in two varieties: "general obligation" and "revenue." General obligation bonds (also called GOs) are issued by states, cities, or counties to raise money for schools, sewers, road improvements, and the like. Monies to pay interest to bondholders are raised through taxes and some user fees. Revenue bonds are issued by a variety of enterprises that perform a public function, such as electric utilities, toll roads, airports, hospitals, and other specially created "authorities." Money to pay interest to bondholders is generated by the enterprise of the issuer. Electric utilities, for example, depend on the fees paid by users of electricity; hospitals depend on patient revenues; toll roads depend on tolls, and so on.

One misconception concerning municipal bonds is that GOs are much safer than revenues. There are strong and weak credits in each bond sector. The supposed safety of GOs is ascribed to the fact that they are backed by the taxing power of the issuer. Theoretically, that power is "unlimited" because bond indentures state that general obligation bonds are backed "by the unlimited taxing power of the issuer." In the real world, however, the power to tax is limited by political and economic considerations. The classic question any analyst has to ask is: In the event there is an economic crunch, who will the issuer pay, its teachers, police, or fire department, or the bondholders? If municipalities could tax at will, all GOs would be rated AAA, and as we know, this is not the case.

Similarly, the supposed lower safety of revenue bonds is based on the fact that issuers run businesses whose revenues cannot be predicted with certainty. Again, that bears little relationship to what goes on in the real world. Most electric utilities and toll roads can, and do, raise rates to pay for increasing costs. Consequently, many revenue bonds, particularly those issued for essential services such as electric power, sewer, or water, are high-quality credits. So are many toll roads or state authorities.

How much importance should you ascribe to differences in rating among sound quality credits (A or A+, or higher)? Not as much as you might expect. It's more important to understand what is behind the rating. Ratings of GOs are determined by the overall economic strength of the tax base compared to debt service requirements. AAA issuers have flourishing tax bases, a strong and diversified economy not dependent on a single industry, low levels of overall debt, and/or a strong tradition of prudent fiscal management. But factors other than the economy are also critical to GO ratings. One of them is size. Small cities or counties which come infrequently to market, even those with prudent fiscal management, are generally not rated higher than A. They may nonetheless be strong credits, particularly if you know the communities. Some wealthy communities have issued so little debt that they do not even have a rating!

Ratings of revenue bonds revolve around an analysis of revenues generated by sales, compared with money needed to cover interest payments (debt service). In practice, the rating is determined by a key ratio known as the "debt service coverage ratio," which is defined as the amount of money specifically *dedicated* to payment of debt service divided by the amount of debt service to be paid. This ratio is calculated for the past. How much money was actually available for debt service last year or for the past five years? It is also estimated for the future. How much money is going to be available next year, and the year after, and so on, for debt service? The past ratio is called "the historical debt service ratio."

An historical debt service ratio of at least two is generally required for an A rating. That ratio indicates that monies reserved for payment of debt service were equal to twice the amount needed for debt service. An historical ratio of five or six times debt service is considered fantastic. An historical ratio below one, indicating there wasn't enough money in the till to cover debt service, would almost guarantee a below investment-grade rating. Nonetheless, no matter how sound their management or how strong debt service coverage has been, revenue bonds are almost never rated AAA on their own merit. This does not make them unattractive investments—just the opposite. They yield more than GOs.

In the late 1980s, hospitals were viewed as particularly risky because of the stresses on the medical system. But even in this area there were some very strong credits; for example, teaching hospitals affiliated with outstanding universities, such as Massachusetts General, which is affiliated with Harvard University, or strong chains, such as the Sisters of Charity hospitals in the Midwest.

Also, in practice the boundary lines between revenue and general obligation bonds are sometimes fuzzy. For example, some counties and cities own hospitals and/or electric revenue plants, sometimes both. Therefore, in some instances, the revenue bonds they issue have both general obligation and revenue backing. These bonds are sometimes called "double-barreled" credits.

Among GOs, the weakest credits are found in two groups: GOs of large cities with deteriorating downtown cores and large social outlays, and older, small cities or districts with shrinking populations, a shrinking tax base, and deteriorating economies. Among revenue bonds, the riskiest bonds have been hospitals with strong dependence on government reimbursement (government programs do not cover hospital expenses in full); bonds issued by developers of nursing homes (many of these are highly speculative); and so-called private purpose bonds (also called industrial development bonds, or IDBs). These are issued by specially constituted authorities on behalf of private businesses.

The rating of a municipal bond is determined primarily by the specific revenues dedicated to debt service and by how much money is available to cover debt service compared with the cost of debt service. When you buy a municipal bond, it is important to get a very clear sense of the main factors underlying its rating. Who exactly is the issuer? Where does money to pay debt service come from? These factors should be specific. For example, in 1990, both the Port of Authority of New York and New Jersey and the Denver International Airport issued private purpose bonds on behalf of Continental Airlines, which subsequently declared bankruptcy. It is likely that many buyers of those bonds did not realize that Continental, whose financial troubles were well publicized, was responsible for debt service, and not the Port Authority of New York and New Jersey or that of the Denver Airport.

Therefore, you should get answers to very specific questions

- ◆ What are the revenues dedicated to debt service?
- ◆ How adequate are sources of revenue?
- ◆ For a utility bond, has the power plant been built and is it a going business? (If not, don't buy.)
- ◆ For a functioning utility, what is the historical debt service coverage ratio? (It should be at least higher than 2.)
- ◆ For a housing bond, where will the development be located, and how is real estate doing in that area? (If nothing has been built, the bonds may be very speculative.)
- ◆ If the bond is a GO, does the locality normally run a balanced budget, or does a deficit threaten continually?
- ◆ Finally, find out the rating history and not just the current rating. Has the rating been stable? Is the credit quality improving or is it deteriorating?

Much of this information is now available on the prospectus of most bonds, which are archived on EMMA. But any knowledgeable broker should be familiar with the outstanding credit features of specific bonds and should be able to answer these questions. If she can't, find another broker!

Finally, remember that the rating is only one of many factors to consider when buying munis. As always, maturity length and potential total return should be equally important considerations.

THE RISE AND FALL OF BOND INSURANCE

Between 2007 and 2008, the municipal market underwent several crises. The first was the failure of the major bond insurance firms.

Municipal bond insurance had its inception in the late 1980s. Bond insurance was an ingenious product. What made it really clever is the fact that default rates of municipal bonds are extremely low—the lowest of any debt instrument next to Treasuries. Within the industry, insurance has always been viewed primarily as a marketing tool. Even though insured bonds were rated AAA, they always traded like AA bonds.

Most individual investors rely on the ratings of the three major credit rating agencies, Moody's, S&P, and Fitch, to evaluate credit quality. Nonetheless, this does not eliminate investor concern about credit safety.

Enter the bond insurance firms. In return for a fee paid by the issuer, bond insurance firms guaranteed that in the event the issuer was unable to pay interest when due, or principal at the bond's maturity, the insurer would step in and pay. Initially, and for many years, the bond insurers were strongly capitalized and the major firms (MBIA, AMBAC, FGIC, and FSA) were all rated AAA. (A number of smaller insurers had somewhat lower ratings.) Consequently, the AAA rating was extended to the bonds under guarantee. As some wags put it, this was a way of making lemonade out of lemons. Bonds that would have received only investment-grade ratings, or possibly lower, were now rated AAA.

For the insurers, bond insurance was a dream product. As you would expect, the bond insurers screened bonds very carefully in order to insure only bonds that were unlikely to default. As a result, bond insurance firms suffered only minor losses and remained highly profitable. This seemed a win-win situation for issuers as well. The AAA rating of insured bonds promoted liquidity. And insured bonds were vastly popular with individual investors. Finally, bond insurance resulted in lower interest costs to issuers. And as insurance spread, its cost declined. Bond insurance became so popular that at the beginning of 2007 well over 50% of all municipal bonds came to market with insurance.

Why Bond Insurers Failed

At their inception and for many years, bond insurers were "monoline." What that means is that they insured only municipal bonds. But somewhere around 2000, the bond insurance firms began to extend insurance to taxable bonds. Unfortunately, many of these taxable bonds were tied to subprime mortgages. As the financial crisis of 2007 unfolded, it became clear that bond insurance firms would incur significant losses; and, furthermore, that these losses would severely damage their capital base and threaten their AAA rating.

Gradually, losses mounted in size. Initial efforts to recapitalize the bond insurance firms failed. Three of the major bond insurance firms: Ambac, MBIA, and FGIC were eventually downgraded to several notches below investment grade, in other words, to "junk" status. These three firms have essentially stopped writing bond insurance. As this is being written, only one firm, Assured Guaranty, retains a meaningful presence as a bond insurer. Assured Guaranty had acquired the insurer Financial Security Assurance (FSA) in 2009. The combined firms were renamed Assured Guaranty; or Assured for short. Assured is rated AAA by S & P and AA3 by Moody's.

Note also that even though Berkshire Hathaway had announced in 2008 that it would enter the market for municipal bond insurance, it has not insured any municipal bonds and it has no plans to do so.

Well over a year elapsed between the initial rumblings of trouble at bond insurance firms, and their ultimate downgrades. During that period, the bond insurance firms appealed for government help, on the grounds that if they failed, issuers would find it much more difficult to bring bonds to market. But even though this saga played a major role in depressing the municipal bond market for well over one year, there is no indication that the ultimate failures of the bond insurance firms permanently damaged the muni market. Bear in mind that the financial difficulties of these firms were related to defaults in their taxable bond portfolios, and not to their munis.

Nevertheless, the downgrades of bond insurance firms resulted in several major problems. The first had to do with ratings. Many bonds had been rated AAA only because of insurance. Now that the insurers had been downgraded (most to junk status or close), how would the rating agencies handle the ratings of insured bonds?

The solution was actually fairly straightforward. The great majority of insured bonds have a rating, referred to as the "underlying rating," which is the rating of issuers, based on their own claims paying ability, that is, before any insurance. Fitch's solution to this problem was to rate muni bonds based on their underlying rating, if that rating was higher than the current rating of the insurer; and to rate them at the insurer's rating only if the underlying rating was lower than that of the insurer. Other credit rating agencies essentially followed suit. Bear in mind that the bond insurers had insured only bonds they considered to be at least investment grade. After the downgrades of the bond insurance firms, the underlying rating of most municipal bonds wound up actually higher than that of the bond insurance firms. One important fact to bear in mind, however, is that the term "underlying rating" is now part of the rating information of municipal bonds.

A more significant problem was how the downgrades of the insurers would affect the price of insured bonds. Some price declines were bound to occur. For bonds that continued to be rated AA or A, price declines due primarily to the downgrades of the insurers should not have been major. Steeper declines in theory should have affected only the few bonds whose underlying ratings would now be below investment grade. Despite that, pricing of municipal bonds through 2007 and 2008 remained inconsistent and chaotic, partly as a result of the problems of the bond insurers, and partly due to the financial panic of 2008.

The final problem was whether the lack of bond insurance would permanently impair the ability of issuers to bring bonds to market; and whether it would raise the interest cost of new issues. But a record number of municipal bonds were issued in 2009, and yields actually came down as municipal bonds rallied.

As you would expect, the downgrades of the bond insurance firms greatly diminished demand for bond insurance. In 2009, only about 6% of muni bonds came to market with insurance, compared to well over 50% in 2007. Most of that, of course, is due to the downgrades of the bond insurance firms. Despite the low current demand for bond insurance, there is some speculation that some firms may attempt to create a new type of credit-enhancement business, primarily to serve the needs of smaller or marginal issuers whose credit quality may be too low to attract buyers based solely on their own (underlying) rating.

In any case, by the fall of 2008, the financial crisis became the bigger story. And the demise of bond insurers was relegated to the back pages.

"RECALIBRATIONS" OF MUNICIPAL BOND RATINGS

In April 2010, Moody's and Fitch both announced plans to change the entire rating scale in use for municipal bonds. This development was partly an outgrowth of the financial panic of 2008. But it is also justified by the default history of municipal bonds.

The rationale for the change is that the rating scales, as noted in Chapter 3, rating scales in use overstated the risk of municipal bonds. Ratings for munis use the same letter symbols as those used to rate corporate debt. They are the familiar letter symbols ranging from AAA for the highest credit quality, through investment grade, and all the way to junk. (These letter symbols were shown in Exhibit 3.3, in Chapter 3). The logical conclusion is that for any given rating, the risk of default is comparable for municipal and for corporate bonds; for example, that a municipal bond rated A has the same risk of default as a corporate rated A and so on.

In fact, historical default experience shows that the risk of default for municipals is significantly lower than that of taxable debt. The scales developed to rate municipal bonds had been based on comparisons of the financial strength of an issuer of municipal bonds to that of other issuers of munis. But observers have pointed out for years that if municipal bond ratings were based on actual default experience, then the ratings of municipal bonds would be significantly higher. A 2007 study by Moody's, for example, pointed out that general obligation bonds rated barely investment grade or just below had experienced default rates that were actually lower than those of AAA corporate bonds. A more recent study by Moody's, conducted in 2009, showed that between 1970 and 2009, rated municipal bonds experienced a total of 54 defaults (a default rate of less than 0.07%). Most of those defaults occurred in the housing and healthcare sectors.

For a number of years, different sources had called for a "unified" or "global" rating scale that would be based on actual default experience across different bond sectors. Bonds rated A, for example, would have the same risk of default whether they were corporates, or munis, or international bonds. Because municipal bonds have relatively lower rates of default, a "global" scale would result in significantly higher ratings for municipals. Congressional hearings held to investigate the ratings process gave further impetus to these proposals. In March 2010, both Fitch and Moody's announced that they would, in fact, change their rating scales for municipal bonds and adopt a "global" rating scale.

On April 5, 2010, Fitch announced that it was re-rating most municipal bonds. A few days later, on April 19, Moody's announced that it would roll out a new rating scale over a period of several weeks. To date, S&P has not followed suit. But it has declared that it has been using a global scale all along. If its ratings prove to be significantly out of sync with those of its competitors, it too may decide to change its scale.

The following changes were announced:

+ Bonds rated AAA would remain AAA.
+ Most general obligation bonds would be upgraded one, two, or even three notches.
+ Some revenue bonds would also be upgraded, one or two notches.

The bonds least likely to have any ratings changes are private purpose or "enterprise" revenue bonds, such as bonds for airports, sports stadiums, nursing homes, and the like. Ratings for these bonds have always been based on comparisons with similar corporate enterprises.

Ratings changes were extremely widespread. For example, with the exception of California and Puerto Rico, Moody's will rate bonds of all states at least AA; 14 states will be rated AAA. (Moody's is upgrading State of California bonds three notches, from Baa1 to A1.) Fitch announced it would "recalibrate" 38,000 bonds. About 3,750 CUSIPs not previously rated AAA would now be rated AAA. More than 7,500 CUSIPs would move up to AA.

Fitch is using the term "recalibrations" to emphasize a point, namely, that these "upgrades" do not denote a change in the financial strength of municipal bond issuers. Rather, these "upgrades" are based on the belief that the old scales overstated the riskiness of many municipal bonds. This is analogous to a college professor deciding that his scales for rating exams were too severe. And so, an exam that in the past would have been graded as a B will in the future be graded as an A. The answers on the exam have not changed. But the professor is giving it a higher grade.

Because the transition to new ratings is just beginning, it is too early to be sure about the impact of these "recalibrations" on the muni market. But certainly, the likelihood is that the changes will be positive. For one thing, the upgrades will allow some institutional buyers, who are prohibited from buying bonds below specified minimum credit ratings, to buy more munis. This should promote "liquidity." Some commentators are viewing the recalibrations as a vote of confidence in the muni market. Issuers are hoping that these "recalibrations" will result in lower borrowing costs. But it is not clear how individual investors will react to the changes. Bonds newly upgraded to AAA, for example, may trade with somewhat higher yields than bonds that had been AAA all along, just as in the past, bonds rated AAA because of insurance traded with higher yields than so-called AAA naturals.

There is, in fact, some irony in the fact that these changes in the rating scales are taking place at a time when budgets of many issuers of municipal bonds are under enormous strain, and almost daily one reads stories of cities and states being forced to cut budgets, with headlines warning that one issuer or another may not be "safe." About the only thing that is certain is that, for a while, at least, the changes in rating are bound to result in a fair amount of confusion.

Which Are the Safest, Highest Quality Bonds?

If you want to be sure that you are buying bonds with the highest credit safety, a few options are listed below.

If you are a belt and suspenders type, then your best bet is to look for pre-refunded bonds (sometimes called "pre-res" for short).

These pre-res, believe it or not, are as safe as Treasuries. The reason for that is that they are *backed by Treasuries held in escrow.* How can that be? Basically, pre-res are bonds issued when interest rates were higher. Issuers refund high coupon bonds if interest rates decline, much as a homeowner refinances a mortgage if interest rates decline. The way it works is this. Suppose a municipality issued bonds years ago, when interest rates were much higher than current rates, say, 6%. Suppose also that, due to the original call provisions, the municipality must wait several years before calling the bonds. How can that municipality lower its interest costs?

The answer is that the municipality may "refinance" by issuing new bonds at the current lower coupon rate (say, 4%). The newly issued bonds are known as "refunding" bonds. The municipality issues an amount of bonds sufficient to cover interest payments and to redeem principal of the older bonds (the 6% bonds) at the first call date. The proceeds from the sale of the refunding bonds (the 4% bonds) are used to purchase U.S. Treasury securities, which are then placed in an escrow account. The coupons of the Treasury bonds are used to pay the coupon payments on the older bonds (the 6% bonds), now called the "refunded" bonds. At the first call date, the remaining assets in the escrow account are used to redeem the refunded bonds.

The refunded bonds are totally free of default risk since monies to pay the bondholders are held in escrow and invested in Treasuries.

Whatever the initial rating of the bonds may have been, it now jumps to AAA. This is not automatic, however. Technically, the issuer has to apply for a new rating—because the rating agencies want their fee. In the event the refunded bonds are not rerated, they will generally trade like AAA bonds. The refunding bonds (that is, the newly issued 4% bonds), on the other hand, trade with the rating of the issuer.

Refunded bonds offer several other advantages. Maturities tend to be short; therefore, interest rate risk is low. Also, since most of these bonds trade at a premium, they offer higher cash flow and often, somewhat higher yields than other bonds with similar maturity and credit quality.

Another category of very safe bonds are those that are issued with the backing of an "umbrella." For example, a number of states issue bonds (primarily school bonds) on behalf of localities through very well-run and highly rated "bond banks." In effect, these bond banks are a type of quasi-insurance. Such bond banks operate in a number of states, including Maine, Virginia, New York, and New Jersey. Some of these bond banks take the form of a pledge that state aid payments would be reserved for payment of debt service in the event local school districts found themselves in financial difficulty. Other bond banks are actual funds dedicated to protection of debt service payments of bonds issued under their umbrella. The State of Texas, for example, issues bonds under the umbrella of its Permanent School Fund (PSF). This is a $22 billion fund, and it guarantees bonds issued by school districts. (Bonds issued under the PSF guarantee are rated AAA.) Some advisers also suggest buying bonds issued for essential services, such as water and sewer bonds, which have both general obligation backing, and revenue from operations dedicated to debt service (these are sometimes called "double-barreled" bonds).

Bear in mind finally, that some bonds still come to market with bond insurance. As noted above, this is a much smaller percentage of the bond market than prior to 2007. And the insurance will lose its value if the bond insurer is downgraded.

Note finally that any bond rated AA to AAA on its own merit is an extremely safe credit. Differences in ratings are often based on nuances. And as noted earlier, the actual default experience of municipal bonds has been extremely low. But if credit quality is one of your major concerns, then another layer of protection is added if you invest in bonds whose maturities are not longer than 10 years. The longer the maturity of a bond, the lower the visibility about possible economic changes to the credits of any issuer. Finally, it might be appropriate to remember April 2010 as the month the rating scales were changed. Investors may find it worthwhile to inquire whether a bond rating is pre- or post-April 2010.

Letters of Credit

Letters of credit (LOCs) are issued by banks and insurance companies as a form of credit enhancement. They are similar to bond insurance, but they do not confer the same degree of protection.

An LOC does not obligate the bank to actually take over interest payments. Rather, a letter of credit is a line of credit. It obligates the bank issuing the LOC to lend money to the issuer if the issuer does not have enough cash on hand to cover interest payments. But LOCs differ in the degree of "obligation" imposed on the bank. Some are irrevocable. Others obligate the bank to make the loan only under certain stipulated conditions.

LOC backing used to be fairly common. LOC backing is no longer a major factor in the municipal market. It is used primarily in connection with variable rate demand obligations, which are short-term debt primarily purchased by institutions.

Taxable Municipal Bonds

This is not a mistake. There have always been some municipal bonds that were taxable. Primarily, these were bonds issued for so-called private purposes; that is, purposes not deemed essential to the public good: for example, bonds issued to finance sports facilities, or certain types of housing bonds. But over the recent past, this was a diminishing category of bonds.

Build America Bonds (BABs)

Build America Bonds (BABs for short) are a new type of taxable municipal bond that was created as part of the "stimulus" legislation passed by the Obama administration at the beginning of 2009. Unlike prior taxable munis, the proceeds of these bonds were to be used for public purposes, primarily infrastructure projects, hence the name.

Bonds issued under the provisions of the Build America legislation benefit from a subsidy directly from the Treasury. The subsidy can take either of two forms. Issuers can choose to receive a direct subsidy of 35% of the coupon interest from the Treasury; or buyers of the bonds can benefit from a 35% tax credit.

For issuers, the attraction of BABs is that, even though the bonds are taxable, and therefore, interest expenses are higher than for tax exempt bonds, the 35% subsidy provided by the administration reduces the net interest cost of issuers to below that of tax exempt bonds.

Initially, these bonds were bought primarily by institutional investors. Buyers of the bonds were attracted by their high credit quality. In effect, BABs constitute a new asset class: a taxable bond with higher credit quality than many "regular" corporate bonds, but with interest rates that are competitive with those of corporate bonds. The same characteristics are attracting individual investors who are buying BABs to put away in tax-deferred plans such as IRAs or 401Ks. BABs are even attracting foreign buyers; a Toronto-based firm has launched a municipal bond fund dedicated to BABs, with a prospectus in French! Note also that the ratings of many BABs will be upgraded as a result of the change in the rating scales, and this can only make them even more popular.

The initial legislation for the program stipulated that BABs would be issued only during two years: 2009 and 2010. A variety of proposals have been made to extend the program, but gradually to reduce the subsidy, from the current 35% of interest costs to 30% in 2013. There are also a number of proposals to make the program permanent. In any case, BABs have been issued primarily with longer maturities (20–30 years). So they are likely to be around in the secondary market for many years.

BABs are callable. One possible trigger for the call would be a decision on the part of the government to stop paying the subsidy. Because BABs compete with corporate debt, which is taxable, call provisions are often the same as those in place for corporate bonds. One example is the frequent use of "make whole" call provisions. As the phrase "make whole" suggests, these provisions are designed to protect the original buyer against calls that would result in a loss of principal. Typical make whole provisions state that in the event there is a call, the bond would be at the higher of two prices: either par, or at a price based on a formula, typically, the price that would result in an interest rate set at the yield of the 10-year Treasury, plus 30 to 50 basis points. This type of call provision protects the buyer provided that the bonds are purchased at or close to par. In that event, the worst-case scenario is that the bonds are called at par. Therefore, there is no loss of principal. (Make-whole call provisions are discussed in more detail in Chapter 8, on corporate bonds.)

Because the BABs program has been so popular, there has been one unintended and unforeseen consequence, namely, many issuers are bringing out long-term bonds primarily as BABs. The result has been that the supply of long-term tax exempt bonds is shrinking.

Municipal Bonds with Special Features

Most municipal bonds come to market as serial bonds, with issues maturing at various maturities, from short to long. Below are some features that may be of interest.

Municipal Notes

Municipal issuers issue debt with maturities under three years, with names such as "revenue anticipation notes" (RANs), "tax anticipation notes" (TANs), or "bond anticipation notes" (BANs). As these names suggest, these securities are issued in anticipation of revenues from one of two sources: taxes or bonds. Notes are rated, but their ratings differ from those of long-term bonds. The higher quality ratings are "MIG 1" and "MIG 2" by Moody's and "SP 1?" or "SP" by Standard & Poor's.

Notes are purchased mainly by institutional investors, but they can be purchased in amounts as low as $10,000. And if the yield curve is normal (that is, upward sloping), these securities yield more than tax-exempt money market funds by perhaps 50 to 100 basis points.

Because the yield curve of municipal debt instruments is usually more sharply upward sloping than that of Treasuries, the yields of tax-exempt notes are comparatively low. They would be of interest mainly to individual investors in a high tax bracket, for parking money that will be needed within a period of less than one year. But limit your purchases of notes only to those with impeccable credit quality.

Municipal Zeros

Muni zeros are sold under a variety of names: "municipal multipliers," "principal appreciation bonds," "capital appreciation bonds," or zeros. Whatever their name, they share a number of features. They are issued at a deep discount from par. At maturity, they are redeemed at par. The difference between the issue price and par represents a specified compounded annual yield.

The volatility of municipal zeros is comparable to that of Treasury zeros. Volatility is particularly high for munis with long maturities. But there are some major differences between muni zeros and Treasury zeros. For starters, since muni zeros are federally tax exempt, no tax needs to be paid annually on "phantom" interest. Another major difference is that the credit quality of muni zeros varies with the issuer. For muni zeros, credit quality is critical because no interest is paid until the final maturity date.

If the zero defaults after several years, you would not have had the consolation of even a single interest payment. (This is one instance where bond insurance would make a lot of sense.)

In addition, muni zeros are subject to call. Muni zeros are called at stipulated *discounts* from par, and not, as some investors assume, at par.

At one time, muni zeros had the reputation of being expensive to resell. There is now a much more active secondary market for zeros. And markups are comparable to those of other munis. Remember, however, that the volatility of zeros makes them high-risk investments if you plan to resell. Because of this, they are appropriate purchases mainly if you plan to hold them to maturity.

Bonds with Put Provisions

A "put" is the exact opposite of a call. A put feature gives the purchaser the option of tendering (or "putting") a bond back to the issuer at stipulated intervals or dates at par. This is a form of protection for the bondholder since if interest rates rise, she can redeem her bond without incurring any loss of principal, and she can then reinvest the proceeds at a more attractive rate. Because of this feature, put bonds are less volatile than other long-term bonds, and they normally trade at or close to par. But since there is no free lunch, there are a couple of disadvantages. First, the coupon interest is usually lower than that of bonds with a similar maturity: total return may therefore be lower. And second, if interest rates decline, put bonds appreciate in value much less than other long-term bonds.

"Supersinkers"

"Supersinkers" are a variety of housing bonds with specifically designated maturities singled out for early retirement in the event mortgages are prepaid. This means that some of the bonds may be called early. The name "supersinker" derives from the fact that monies to retire the bonds accumulate in a "sinking fund." The retirement date is uncertain because prepayments are unpredictable.

The potential early call feature of supersinkers is considered attractive because, since there is not a specific call date, the yield of the bond—and its price—are determined by the maturity date, not by the uncertain call date. Supersinkers normally mature well before their maturity date. In effect, the purchaser earns a long-term yield on a short-term security.

Be very cautious, however, if a supersinker is selling at a high premium. An early call would result in a loss of principal.

MUNICIPAL BOND PRICING

Call Risk

Munis—mainly those with long-term maturities—are subject to call. You will remember that this means the issuer may choose to redeem a bond before its maturity date.

Call provisions on most munis are straightforward. Typical call provisions for 30-year bonds stipulate an initial call date 10 years after issue, at a price slightly above par (typically 101); and several additional consecutive call dates (in 15 years at 102, and so on). Housing revenue bonds, however, may have unusual call features. This can happen, for example, in the event that the money raised by the bonds is not needed for actual mortgages. The difference between those call provisions and ordinary call provisions is that no date is mentioned. The bonds may be called as early as a few months after issue, and this has happened.

Under normal circumstances, issuers are likely to call munis only if interest rates drop substantially. The higher and the more attractive the yield to the investor, the more expensive the interest for the issuer and the more likely it is that a bond will be called. As explained, be particularly careful to investigate call provisions for any bonds selling at a premium. Be doubly careful for housing bonds selling at a premium. Housing bonds are sometimes subject to extraordinary calls. A broker should quote both the YTM and the yield to the first call date (that will usually be lower than the YTM). In the event the bond is called, the yield-to-call becomes the actual return.

"Dollar" Bonds and "Basis" Bonds

Some munis are called "dollar bonds" because the price of these bonds is quoted in dollars. Other bonds are priced "to the basis." Instead of a dollar amount, the YTM is quoted. Therefore, the buyer has to work backward from the quoted yield to compute the price (the broker will pull out his trusty calculator).

"The Dated Date"

This is the date on which the bond begins accruing (earning) interest.

Markups

The author of a book on municipal bonds characterized pricing in the muni market as "let the buyer beware" or "what the market will bear."[1] For an individual investor, for bonds that are priced "fairly" commission costs may vary from under 1% ($100 per $10,000 of par) for actively traded issues with short maturities and high credit quality to about 4% ($400 per $10,000 par value bond) for inactively traded bonds with long maturities. If the markets are under stress, markups above 4% are not uncommon.

Small lots (under $25,000 par value) are considered a pain by brokers and are marked up accordingly. This makes them particularly expensive to sell. Brokers, in fact, have an expression for the pricing of these lots: they "punish the coupon." Translation: the commission costs for selling small lots are extremely high. Dealers who buy a small lot from you do so with the understanding that they are doing you a special favor. Paradoxically, the dealer will be anxious to get rid of small lots and will price them attractively for resale. What this means is that you can sometimes find attractive prices if you want to buy a small lot. But then, don't plan to resell!

When I wrote the first edition of this book (20 years ago), in order to research pricing inconsistencies, I pretended to be selling a number of small lots of munis that I had inherited. I called seven different firms to see what prices they would offer. Among the lots was a high-quality, widely traded New Jersey Turnpike bond; one very controversial credit, Philadelphia, whose financial difficulties were highly publicized at the time; and some infrequently traded issues.

I was offered prices all over the lot. The prices were closest on the New Jersey Turnpike bonds. This was not unexpected, since I live in New Jersey and New Jersey Turnpike bonds are actively traded. Nonetheless, even on this lot, offers varied by 150 basis points on a price of 98. Since I was "selling" a $40,000 par value lot, that translates into a price difference of $612 between the highest and the lowest offer. The largest difference occurred on an out-of-state housing bond (375 basis points, almost 4% or $1,500 on a $40,000 lot). A number of dealers refused to bid on some of the lesser-known names.

How much has that situation changed? In some respects, less than you might imagine. While writing an article about researching pricing of

---

1. James J. Cooner, *Investing in Municipal Bonds: Balancing Risks and Rewards* (New York: John Wiley & Sons, 1987), p. 44.

municipal bonds on the Internet, I decided to track the price of the same bond on different dealer Web sites, all of which were using the same electronic platform—in this case, Bond Desk. I assumed that different brokers using the same electronic platform would be offering the same bond at the same price. But that is not what happened. (I used CUSIP numbers, maturity, and call features to make sure I was tracking the same bond.) What emerged were patterns of pricing that differed markedly from broker to broker. So the same bond would be offered, say, at

> 101 by two firms
> 103 by another firm
> 103 to 105 by still another firm

As I found out when researching electronic platforms (discussed in detail in Chapter 2 of this book), dealers mark up their prices independently; and as a result, dealer markups can vary. Electronic platforms routinely mark up the price of any bond based on the instructions of the dealer selling the bond.

SHOPPING FOR MUNICIPAL BONDS USING THE INTERNET

Markups for municipal bonds continue to be hidden. So if you are shopping for municipal bonds, is there a way to determine if you are being quoted a fair price?

Just to be very clear, let's review the distinction between commissions and markups. Many brokers, particularly discount brokers, focus the attention of investors on their commissions. That is usually a small amount from $1.50 to $5 per bond. It is a fee for the service they render as brokers and that fee is broken out. The markup, on the other hand, is the difference between the price paid by a dealer when he buys a bond and the price at which the dealer sells you the bond. But that markup remains hidden. The price of a municipal bond is quoted net.

If I seem to be making much ado about markups, bear in mind that municipal bond trades of $25,000 to $50,000 are common. A 2% markup on a $25,000 lot is $500; it is $1,000 on a $50,000 lot. It is double those amounts for a 4% markup. In a market where municipal bond yields for intermediate to long maturities are in the 2% to 4% range, the markup is a definite concern. It can eat up six months to a year of interest income.

Thanks to the Internet, it has become much easier to become a better informed investor. The following are some suggestions to help you
make a more informed decision.

Step One: Get an Overview of the Market

If you do not follow interest rates regularly, the first step is to get an overview
of yields currently available in the municipal bond market. You can gain a
general idea by logging on to Investinginbonds.com. Click on "The
Municipal Market at a Glance." Under this heading, you will find a number
of items. You should focus on two of these. The first is a graph showing the
current shape of the yield curve in the municipal bond market. The second
is a table showing representative municipal bond yields. These two items are
published daily. Exhibit 7.2 shows both items on Friday, April 23, 2010.

Notice first that on this date, the yield curve was steeply upward
sloping, with yields starting well below 1% and rising to well over 4%.
Notice also where the break points are for yields that you would consider. If, for example, you are looking for a minimum yield of 3%, the
yield curve and the accompanying rates tell you that you need to look
somewhere in the neighborhood of 10 years. Bear in mind that these
yields are highly approximate. They are averages, culled nationwide.
Note also that the yields on this particular graph are for AAA bonds,
which have the lowest yields. Yields for lower quality credits would be

EXHIBIT 7.2

Municipal Market at a Glance

Representative Yields

MTY	INS	AAA	AA
3 M	0.30	0.25	0.25
6 M	0.33	0.26	0.26
1 Y	0.54	0.39	0.40
2 Y	0.99	0.74	0.82
3 Y	1.31	1.06	1.13
5 Y	2.10	1.75	1.85
10 Y	3.40	2.96	3.12
15 Y	3.88	3.42	3.58
20 Y	4.30	3.81	3.99
30 Y	4.53	4.11	4.26

04/23/10, 4:35 PM

S&P AAA Composite Yields

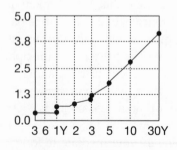

—•— Composite Yield
as of 06:00 Apr 24, 2010

higher. You can expect yields of individual bonds to vary from this table. But this is a starting point: it puts you somewhere in the ball park. (Similar tables are published on financial Web sites.)

Step Two: Do Some Comparison Shopping

You are now ready to do some comparison shopping. You have a number of different options.

The first option would be to look at one or more online broker Web sites, to see bonds being offered for sale. Chances are that you are not interested in looking at the thousands of bonds that trade daily. Rather, you are probably focusing on a number of criteria. Most online broker Web sites allow you to conduct a targeted search. The fewer criteria you select, the broader choice you will have. At minimum, your criteria for a search should include the state where you live, a range of acceptable maturities, and minimum credit quality ratings. To narrow the search further, add a couple of additional criteria, such as minimum yield or minimum coupon.

Your search will produce a list of bonds, typically in tabular form. The listing will look like Exhibit 7.3.

The source information clearly identifies BondDesk as the source of the data. Many online brokers typically add a disclaimer stating something like "All content on these pages has been supplied by .... (name of an electronic platform). XYZ brokerage services is not responsible for the accuracy of this data."

Most terms are self-explanatory, but reading from left to right, note in particular:

- ◆ Quantity: the total number of bonds for sale for that particular issue
- ◆ Min Qty (i.e., minimum quantity) the minimum number of bonds you can order at the listed price
- ◆ The CUSIP number of the bond; if you want additional information on this bond, this is the number you need
- ◆ The name of the issue and additional details, such as the tax status of the bond and call provisions, if any
- ◆ The coupon, set when the bond was issued
- ◆ The price, that is, the price posted by the dealer selling the bond
- ◆ The yield that will be the YTM that would result if the bond is bought at the listed dealer price. (The actual yield will be slightly lower after you add in the broker commission.)

EXHIBIT 7.3

Example of a Typical Municipal Bond Listing

Qty	Min Qty	ST	CUSIP	Issue	Coupon	Price	Maturity	Yield	Moody/ S&P	Credit Watch
410	10	NJ	650366BL4	Newark N J TAXABLE - Material Events - Subject to - Sinking Fund 04/19@100 - AGMC insured	5.853	04/01/2022	101.224	5.709	Aa3/ NR	/
1350	50	NJ	646080HG9	New Jersey St Higher Ed A Callable 06/18@ 100 - Subject to AMT - Material Events - Sinking Fund 06/14@ 100 - AGC insured	5.875	06/01/2021	109.99	4.394 (c)	Aa3/AAA	/
5	5	NJ	64580AAK7	New Jersey Health Care Fa Extraordinary Calls - Hospitals Use - Material Events	5.250	10/01/2018	109	3.982	Aa3/AA-	/
5	5	NJ	072887XF4	Bayonne N J Callable 07/15@100 - Material Events - AGMC insured	4.375	07/15/2021	102.975	3.741 (c)	Aa2/ NR	/
10	5	NJ	645918TG8	New Jersey Economic Dev A	5.000	05/01/2018	109.465	3.627	Aa3/AA-	/

Source: BondDesk Group, LLC. The bond content is presented by BondDesk Group, LLC. Reprinted with permission.

You may also encounter some terms which deserve additional comment.

"Material events." That is a warning that somewhere in the bond's history, one or more events have occurred which resulted in a change in the credit rating of the bond, and hence its price. If the phrase "material events" occurs along with the name of a bond insurance firm, it is safe to assume that the material event in question is the downgrade of the bond insurance firm. If that happens, also look for the phrase "underlying rating." That will be the bond's current rating. Note also that the same phrase "material events" could refer to some event affecting the financial strength of the issuer. Never buy any bond listed with this phrase without finding out what it refers to.

Tax status. BABs are now included in many listings for municipal bonds. You have to check carefully whether the listing you see is for a tax exempt muni; or for a BAB, which is taxable at the federal level. Note also that some bonds are subject to the alternative minimum tax (AMT).

Bond insurers continue to be listed. On many bond listings, this is a source of confusion since, as noted earlier, most bond insurance firms have been downgraded to below investment grade. Also, the phrase "material events" often applies to the downgrade of the bond insurance firm, rather than to the issuer of the bond.

On most broker Web sites, you can proceed to a more detailed screen. If you click on individual issues by name, a second screen will come up which will look like Exhibit 7.4.

Once again, BondDesk, an electronic platform, is identified as the source of the additional details. That information is followed by the same disclaimer as Exhibit 7.3.

Exhibit 7.4 gives more detailed information about the bond: dates when the bond may be called, dates when interest is paid, as well as a number of yields, including yield-to-maturity (YTM), the yield-to-call, current yield, etc.

You need to be very clear about several items.

Bond Rating

The first is the actual rating of these bonds. Ascertaining ratings is much more confusing than it used to be as a result of the downgrades of bond insurers, and also as a result of the recalibrations that took place in April 2010. Due to these two separate events, you will often see more than one rating, and this is the case with this particular bond. You need to figure out why there is more than one rating and what the different ratings mean.

EXHIBIT 7.4

Details of One Selected Bond from Exhibit 7.3

Actions
Back to Search Result
Description

Issue:	Bayonne N J Callable 07/15 @ 100 - Material Events			
Project/Addtnl Info:	NJ SCH BD RESERVE ACT PL1980			
CUSIP	072887XF4	Type:	Secondary Municipal	Moody/S&P/Fitch:	Aa2/NR/NR
Coupon:	4.375	Frequency:	Semiannually	Category:	General Obligation
Maturity:	07/15/2021	First Coupon:	07/15/2005	Delivery:	Book Entry
First Settlement:	12/22/2004	Next Coupon:	07/15/2010		
Dated:	12/15/2004	Last Coupon:			
Minimum Amount:	5,000.00	Denomination Amount:	5,000.00		
Collateral:				Orig Price/Orig Yield:	99.705 / 4.4
Blue Sky Restrictions:					
Reference material:					

Moodys Ratings Information

Underlying Rating: Baa 1
Long Term Rating: Aa 2 effective 04/23/2010
Short Term Rating:
CreditWatch:

S&P Ratings Information

Long Term Rating: NR
Short Term Rating:

Call / Sink / Put Features

Call Schedule:	07/15/2015 @ 100	
Next:	07/15/2015 at 100 on 30 days notice	Continuously Callable starting at

10/13/2009 - Fitch Rating Downgrade - FROM AA+ TO AA

Material Events / Use of Proceeds   Use: PRIM/SECNDRY ED

Security Notes

MOODY'S GLOBAL RATINGS RECALIBRATION ON 04/24/2010 FROM Baa3 TO Baa 1

Secondary Municipal Specific

				Tax		Subj State:
State:	NJ	Escrowed:	N	Fed Tax:	No	
Pre Refund:	N	Insurance:	AGMC	Subj AMT:	No	
Secondary Insurance:		Reinsurance:	No			
Enhancement:	ST SCH AID PROG	Bank Qualified:	No			
Revised Issue Price:	100	Market Discount Point:	97.25			

Offer

Price:	102.975	Settlement:	04/29/2010		
Yield to Maturity:	4.042	Duration:	4.669		
Yield to Call:	3.74				
Yield to Par:	-	Quantity:	5		
Current Yield:	4.249	Increment:	5		
Worst Yield:	Next Call	Min. Quantity:	5		

**Refer to Bond Calculator for bond yield details.
Source: BondDesk Group, LLC. The Bond content is presented by BondDesk Group, LLC. Reprinted with permission.

The first rating you see is identified as the "underlying rating," listed as Baa1 (under the heading "Moody's Rating Information"). As explained in the section on bond insurance, the underlying rating is the rating of the issuer, prior to any bond insurance.

But also notice, on the line below the underlying rating, there is a second, higher rating listed (Aa1). The two ratings are explained by two separate Notes, identified in the listing as "Security Notes." Under that heading, there is a phrase written in all caps: MOODY'S GLOBAL RATINGS RECALIBRATION ON 04/24/2010 FROM Baa3 to Baa1. That tells you that based on this recalibration, the rating was upgraded from Baa3 to Baa1, a two notch upgrade.

Under the same heading, note also that an insurance firm is listed: AGMC, Assured Guaranty Municipal Corporation, the one insurance firm still rated AA_3 by Moody's. The rating listed as the long-term rating is that of the insurance firm, AGMC. (As it happens, when I checked, I found out that coincidentally, Assured was upgraded one day prior to the recalibration upgrade of the issuer of this bond, Bayonne. The two upgrades are totally unrelated.)

To add to the confusion, other ratings are listed. For example, on 10/13/2009, there is a Fitch downgrade listed, from AA+ to AA. That downgrade applies to the insurer, and not to the issuer. More rating changes that took place in prior years are archived under "material events." All of those rating changes are primarily of historical interest. The most recent ratings are those that are in force.

So the bottom line is that the relevant ratings are the two most recent ones, the upgrade of the underlying rating of the issuer due to the recent recalibration and the most recent rating of the bond insurance firm. Note also that this particular bond does not have ratings either from S&P or Fitch. Remember that ratings cost money. A small issuer such as Bayonne often pays for only one rating.

Unfortunately, given the downgrades of the bond insurers in 2008, as well as the recalibrations of municipal bonds taking place in April and May 2010, determining the actual ratings of municipal bonds will require some detective work. After recalibrations are completed, by the middle of May 2010, bond listings on dealer Web sites should all carry a note such as the one in this listing indicating the upgraded rating, if any occurred, and the date of the recalibration.

The Many Meanings of Yield

The other item that needs to be very clear is what the various yields listed tell you.

If you are comparing several bonds that meet your criteria for maturity and credit quality, what should you focus on to pick the best buy?

It appears that some investors focus entirely on the price of the bond, assuming, for example, that a bond priced at 100 is a better buy than one priced at 102, regardless of the yield, simply because the bond is selling at a lower price. That is a mistake. Focus on price when looking up the trade history of a particular bond. But when comparing different bonds, to determine which bond is the better buy, focus on the yield-to-maturity (YTM). The general rule is that among bonds that are comparable with regard to maturity, credit quality, and call provisions, the bond with the highest YTM is the best buy.

Bear in mind that YTM quotes are estimates of what you will earn under certain conditions: whether you hold the bonds until they mature; whether you reinvest the coupons or spend them; and if you reinvest the coupons, the rate at which they are reinvested; and so on. (If this is not clear, please re-read the section on yields, in Chapter 4.) Occasionally, determining which bond is the best buy varies based on how you intend to use the bond. Suppose, for example, that you are buying the bond for income, and that you intend to spend the interest income and not reinvest it. Then you might look for a bond where the current yield is higher than the YTM or one that has a higher cash flow, such as a premium bond. For example, given the level of interest rates at the time this is being written, you are likely to run across some bonds quoting a YTM around 3% and a current yield of 4% or higher. Such a bond might suit your objective better than one quoting a higher YTM, but a lower current yield.

Note also that where call or sinking provisions are listed, the yield to call, or yield to sink, or yield to worst (sometimes the same as the yield to call) are also listed. But before worrying about the yield to call, bear in mind that if the coupon is low, the likelihood that the bond will be called is also low.

Note in passing that all Web sites are not equally detailed or helpful. Some Web sites make it easy for you to define your criteria and limit your search. Others supply only minimum information. Surprisingly, also, Web sites differ significantly in the number of choices that come up after you type in your criteria. As noted in Chapter 2, some firms apply proprietary screens that severely limit selection. If you are new to online searching of bonds, you may want to open accounts with several online brokers prior to settling on one or two.

Let's assume you find a number of bonds that match your criteria. You could, of course, simply decide that you like a particular bond and buy it. But you can now get actual trade data, which may suggest price targets lower than the listed dealer price. Different types of data are available at Investinginbonds.com and Emma.msrb.org. Both are free to all users. Let's start with Investinginbonds.com.

Price Data on Bonds: Investinginbonds.com

This Web site has become an indispensable resource. It was launched in 1991. Initially, it published prices of approximately 1,000 bonds that traded actively on the previous day. Gradually, the listings were expanded. Beginning in 2005, every municipal bond trade has been published, and these prices are available within 15 minutes of each trade.

Trading History of a Bond

Investinginbonds.com provides two types of pricing data. The first and the easiest to use is to simply look at the trading history of a bond. No matter how you zeroed in on that bond, whether your friendly broker offered it to you or whether you found it on an online site, before buying the bond, you should look up its trade history.

To look up the trade history of a bond, after clicking on "The Municipal Market-at-a-Glance," type the bond CUSIP number in the box labeled "Bond History." A brief listing will come up, that will look like Exhibit 7.5.

This particular trade history was listed on April 23, 2010 for a New Jersey Transportation Bond. Note that 1,852 trades are listed. That is actually a very high number of trades for a municipal bond. It denotes a very actively traded bond. Many municipal bonds, including some very high quality bonds, trade infrequently, perhaps less than a dozen trades in one year. That

EXHIBIT 7.5

CUSIP Search Results

ISSUER CUSIP	COUPON MATURITY	# OF TRADES
NEW JERSEY ST TRANSN TR FD AUTH SER A-FSA-CR 646136FB2	5.250 12/15/2021	1,852 trades

Source: Investinginbonds.com. Reprinted with permission.

is not a red flag. It simply means the bond was bought for income and has not been reoffered for sale.

When you click on the phrase "#. of trades" in Exhibit 7.5, a second screen comes up which shows all trades archived for this particular bond. The trade history will look like Exhibit 7.6.

The details that come up include the trade date, the exact time of the trade, the price at which the trade took place, and the yield that resulted from the trade. But trades are further identified as:

- Purchase from customer (an investor selling the bond to a dealer)
- Sale to customer (an investor buying the bond from a dealer)
- Inter-dealer (a trade between two dealers)

You can calculate the markup on a bond by subtracting the lowest price (usually a customer selling the bond to a dealer) from the highest price (usually a customer buying the bond from a dealer). Inter-dealer prices are considered the market price. In Exhibit 7.5, notice that the various trades

EXHIBIT 7.6

Trade Details for CUSIP: 646136FB2

RTNGS	ISSUER				ST	COUPON	
INS	CUSIP					MATURITY	NOTES
	NEW JERSEY ST TRANSN TR FD AUTH SER A-FSA-CR					• Non-taxable	
Insured	646136FB2				NJ 5.250	• Bond	
	Transportation/Combined					• Custodial receipt	

TRADE DATE	TRADE TIME	PRICE	YIELD	SIZE TYPE	TRADE
04/22/2010	11:25:30	110.050	4.151	20K	Purchase from Customer
04/22/2010	11:18:35	112.825	3.870	20K	Sale to Customer
04/21/2010	10:27:27	110.650	4.090	20K	Purchase from Customer
03/26/2010	09:16:07	110.809		35K	Inter-dealer
03/26/2010	09:16:07	112.684	3.890	35K	Sale to Customer
03/23/2010	14:06:00	111.216		35K	Inter-dealer
03/23/2010	14:06:00	111.216	4.039	35K	Purchase from Customer
03/23/2010	14:00:41	111.716		35K	Inter-dealer
03/23/2010	14:00:28	114.975	3.666	50K	Sale to Customer
03/23/2010	11:41:49	114.125	3.749	30K	Sale to Customer
03/23/2010	11:12:57	112.596	3.900	50K	Sale to Customer
03/23/2010	11:12:06	112.221		50K	Inter-dealer

Source: Investinginbonds.com. Reprinted with permission.

listed took place over approximately a one-month period. During that month, inter-dealer prices clustered around 110 ($1,100 per bond). Investors selling the bond to a dealer sold at prices close to the inter-dealer price. But investors buying the bond paid prices ranging from close to 112 ($1,120) per bond to about 114 ($1,140) per bond.

Note in particular that on 3/23/2010, three investors bought the same bond at three different prices. Indeed, two investors paid different prices for the same size lot: $50,000 par value bonds. But one investor paid 112.596 ($1,125.96) and the second 114.975 ($1,149.75). Translated into dollar amounts, one customer paid $56,298 ($1,125.96 × 50,000 bonds); and the second paid $57,487.50 ($1,149.75 × 50,000 bonds), or a difference in price of $1189, about 2% of the total price. Compared with the dealer price of about 110, this shows a dealer markup of 4%. Another way of looking at that price difference is that the lower purchase price resulted in a YTM quote of 3.9%, whereas the higher price resulted in a YTM of 3.66%.

Clearly, one customer overpaid for this bond. Since this bond has an intermediate maturity, an appropriate markup is typically in the range of 1% to 2%. Markups for longer maturities range from perhaps 2% to 4%.

Many online Web sites now have "hot" links directly to Investinginbonds.com that provide the trading history of a bond for 30 days. Of course, if a bond has not traded during that period of time, there will be no trading history.

If there are no recent trades listed for a bond, then the last price listed may be stale. That would indicate that you need to try to find comparables to estimate where the price ought to be.

Finding Comparables

How do you find comparables? This is the second type of price information you can find using Investinginbonds.com. Investinginbonds.com shows trade data for bonds trading close to real time. This is as close to a running tape for stocks as you will find in the bond market. What you want to find are the prices of bonds with characteristics that are comparable to those that you are considering for purchase.

To find comparables, go back to the start page of "The Municipal Market-at-a-Glance" and look for bonds trading "today." (There is also a complete summary of bonds trading the previous day.) Bonds come up based on a number of "sorts". The first "sort" is the name of the state whose bonds you are investigating. You then need to click on an additional "sort". "Sorts" include maturity, yield, coupon, and others. The first screen will look like Exhibit 7.7.

As the summary headings indicate, the data specify a number of details about the bonds that traded, including maturity date, call provisions, rating, the number of trades shown for that bond, either "today" or the prior day, and the high and low prices resulting from each trade. If you click on either "today" or "yesterday," a number of details appear, including whether the trades are customer buys, customer sells, or inter-dealer trades (details similar to those shown in Exhibit 7.6).

The problem here is not too little data, but too much. Because all trades are now listed within 15 minutes of each trade, the amount of detail can be overwhelming and confusing. Note also that finding bonds that are truly comparable requires a decent level of understanding of the trades you are consulting. To be truly comparable, bonds must have the same credit quality, virtually identical maturities, and very similar call provisions. But as noted elsewhere, other factors also come into play: the size of the lot, the direction of interest rates, and many other nuances, including whether the dealer just wants to get rid of a certain bond.

E X H I B I T   7.7

Data: Municipal Bond Prices

MUNICIPAL BONDS: NEW JERSEY REPORT								
Presently sorted by: Yield								
State: NJ								
Bond Traded: Today								
Sort by: Yield								
RTNGS								MORE INFO
INS	TRADE DATE	ISSUER CUSIP	ST	COUPON	CALL	CALL		SPECIAL
	TRADE TIME	SECTOR						PRICE
		SUBSEOTOR		MATURITY	DATES	PRICES	NOTES	INDICATOR
BBB S	04/28/2010	TOBACCO						
		SETTLEMENT			06/01/2017		• Non-	Today
		CORP N J		5.000	100.000	61.130	taxable	Full History
Baa3 M	16:03:31	RFDG-SR-SER 1A						
		ASSET-BACKED						Statements
		BONDS	NJ	06/01/2041		8.608	• Bond	Calculations
		888808DF6				• Book		
						entry		
						only		

Source: Investinginbonds.com. Reprinted with permission.

Looking for comparables requires patience. You need to narrow the number of trades that come up. I have had the best luck by sorting based on yield: a surprising number of bonds come up that have yields that are very close or even identical, down to several decimal points. But then, maturities and credit quality can be very different. You need to then focus on bonds that match other criteria that are important to you, such as maturity and credit ratings.

EMMA.msrb.org (EMMA): The Official Statement (OS) and Continuing Disclosure

If you are researching municipal bonds, you will want to get acquainted with EMMA: that is, EMMA.msrb.org. EMMA is the newest kid on the block; it was launched live on the Internet by the Municipal Securities Rulemaking Board (the MSRB) in July 2009. EMMA.msrb.org is intended to become the official repository of information and disclosure about the municipal bond market. It will be expanding its role as well as the information it will provide.

The trade activity details are identical to those provided by Investinginbonds.com. (That data actually originates with the MSRB). You can also search for information about any bond even if you do not know the CUSIP number. To locate a bond, type in the name of the issuer and the maturity of the bond. Then etc.

Once you log on to the Web site, you can search for information about any municipal bond by typing in its CUSIP number on the first screen of this Web site. When you type in the CUSIP, three tabs appear: Official Statement, Continuing Disclosure, and Trade Activity. Then proceed in the same manner as when you start with a CUSIP.

In addition, EMMA archives all Official Statements for municipal bonds issued since 2000. If you type in the CUSIP number of the bond as you will see the first page of the official statement, which will look like Exhibit 7.8. Note that Exhibit 7.7 shows the first page of the OS for the City of Bayonne general obligation bond shown in Exhibits 7.3 and 7.4.

You can download the entire official statement (OS). It contains as much information as is disclosed to the credit rating agencies. (In fact, the rating agencies base their rating primarily on the official statement.) Reading the OS is not the most fun you will have in your day, but it has all the information you will need to evaluate the financial strength of the issuer. Focus on revenues available for debt service and whether you think those revenues are adequate to cover debt service.

EXHIBIT 7.8

Official Statement of a General Obligation Bond Offered by the City of Bayonne

NEW ISSUE

RATING: Moody's "Aaa"
FSA Insured

In the opinion of McManimon & Scotland, L.L.C., Bond Counsel, assuming containing compliance by the City (as hereinafter defined) with certain covenants described herein, interest on the Bonds (as hereinafter defined) is not includable in gross income for federal income tax purposes under current law. In the opinion of McManimon & Scotland, L.L.C., interest on the Bonds is not an item of tax preference under Section 57 of the Internal Revenue Code of 1986, as amended, for purposes of computing the federal alternative minimum tax; however, interest on the Bonds held by corporate taxpayers is included in the relevant income computation for calculation of the 'ederl alternative minimum tax as a result of the inclusion of interest on the Bonds in "adjusted current earnings". No opinion is expressed regarding other federal tax consequences arising with respect to the Bonds. Further in the opinion of McManimon & Scotland, L.L.C., interest on the Bonds and any gain on the sale thereof is not includable as gross income under the New Jersey Gross Income Tax Act. See "TAX EXEMPTION" herein.

$55,309,000
CITY OF BAYONNE
In the County of Hudson, New Jersey

SCHOOL BONDS
School Bond Reserve Act (P.L. 1980, c. 72)
Book-Entry Issue
Not Bank Qualified
Callable

Dated: December 15, 2004   **Due: July 15, as shown below**

The $55,309,000 School Bonds (New Jersey School Bond Reserve Act P.L. 1980. c. 72) (the "Bonds") of the City of Bayonne in the County of Hudson, State of New Jersey (the "City") will be issued in the form of one certificate for the aggregate principal amount of the Bonds maturing in each year and will be payable at maturity in lawful money of the United State of America. Each certificate will be registered in the name of Code & Co., as nominee of The Depository Trust Company, New York, New York, which will act as securities depository ("DTC" or the "Securities Depository"). See "DESCRIPTION OF THE BONDS – Book-Entry Only System' herein.

Interest on the Bonds will be payable semiannually on the fifteenth day of January and July in each year until maturity, commencing July 15, 2005. The principal of and the interest on the Bonds will be paid to the Securities Depository by the City or its designated paying agent (the "Paying Agent"). Interest on the Bonds will be credited to the Participants of DTC as listed on the records of DTC as of each next proceding January 1 and July 1 (the "Record Dates" for the payment of interest on the Bonds).

The Bonds are subject to redemption prior to their stated maturities as set forth herein. See "DESCRIPTION OF THE BONDS – Redemption" herein.

The scheduled payment of principal of and interest on the Bonds when due will be guaranteed under an insurance policy to be issued concurrently with the delivery of the Bonds by FINANCIAL SECURITY ASSURANCE INC. See "BOND INSURANCE" herein.

▆ FSA

The Bonds are valid and legally binding obligations of the City and unless paid from other sources, are payable from ad valorem taxes levied upon all the taxable real property within the City for the payment of the Bonds and the interest thereon without limitation as to rate or amount.

MATURITY SCHEDULE
INTEREST RATES AND YIELDS OR PRICES

Year	Amount	Interest Rate	Yield	Year	Amount	Interest Rate	Yield
2006	$2,000,000	4.125 %	2.160 %	2016	$2,900,000	4.250 %	4.080 %
2007	2,000,000	4.125	2.340	2017	2,900,000	4.250	4.130
2008	2,000,000	4.125	2.500	2018	3,100,000	4.250	4.210
2009	2,100,000	4.125	2.880	2019	3,100,000	4.250	4.280
2010	2,100,000	4.125	3.150	2020	3,300,000	4.300	4.340
2011	2,100,000	4.125	3.520	2021	3,300,000	4.375	4.400
2012	2,300,000	4.125	3.680	2022	3,500,000	4.400	4.450
2013	2,300,000	4.250	3.820	2023	3,500,000	4.500	4.510
2014	2,500,000	4.250	3.940	2024	3,700,000	4.500	4.560
2015	2,700,000	4.250	4.040	2025	3,909,000	5.000	4.600

The Bonds are offered when, as and it issued and delivered to the Underwriter (as defined herein), subject to prior sale, to withdrawal or modification of the offer without notice and to approval of legality by the law firm of McManimon & Scotland. L.L.C. Newark, New Jersey and certain other conditions described herein. Delivery is anticipated to be at the offices of the City's Bond Counsel, McManimon & Scotland, L.L.C., Newark, New Jersey, or at such other place as agreed to with the Underwriter on or about December 22, 2004

UBS FINANCIAL SERVICES, INC.

Dated: December 2, 2004

Source: EMMA.msrb.org. Reprinted with permission of the Municipal Securities Rulemaking Board.

Note also that the only rating displayed on the official statement is the one issued when the bond was brought to market, in this case, 2004. The rating at the time was the rating of the insurer, FSA, which merged with Assured; this is the rating shown for Assured in 2010. The underlying rating would not have been shown. If you are looking at an OS for a bond trading in the secondary market, issued prior to 2008, in all likelihood, the rating will have changed. You need to check to find out the current rating.

The MSRB requires that all future statements of continuing disclosure will be posted on EMMA. At minimum, all issuers will be required to file at least one annual financial statement. Continuing disclosure is also supposed to also include any "material event" that will affect the value (hence the price) of the bond. The MSRB began archiving these annual disclosure statements in July 2009. But when you click on this tab, since the Web site has not been up and running for an entire year (at the time of writing), many CUSIPs do not show any continuous disclosure.

Finally, as mentioned at the end of Chapter 5, there is an "alert" feature on EMMA, which invites users to type in a CUSIP, as well as their email address, in order to receive alerts about any bond they own or are investigating. By all means, accept that invitation.

Talk to a Broker

As suggested earlier, before buying any bond, whether you are offered the bond by a broker you know or whether you found it online, it would be useful to investigate its trade history; and also to look for comparables. Once you have done that, you should have a pretty good idea of what you would want to pay for a bond. Clearly, for a bond showing recent trades if several prices are shown for customer buys, you would want to buy at the lowest customer buy price you see. Sometimes it is possible to do better. The price that is closest to the market price is the inter-dealer price. Yes, I know you are not a broker. But it is not unusual to find customer buys close to inter-dealer prices. Larger lots usually, but not always, will net you a better deal.

Does that mean that if you are logging on to a Web site that allows you to complete the trade online, you should skip talking to a broker?

As stated in Chapter 5, that is not the advice I would give. Broker listings are incomplete or may contain errors. They need to be double-checked. If you misunderstand any critical details, you have no recourse. You have assumed all the risks. Any broker should be willing to double-check all the features of a bond that ultimately affect return.

Second, some information may be confusing. As explained above, one of the more confusing items to zero in on is the current rating of the bond. Ratings are listed on broker Web sites, but they are not always accurate. I have seen many examples of bonds listed with AAA ratings that were no longer applicable. Most of the time, those were ratings in force when the bond was issued, and usually insured by an insurance firm that has been downgraded to below investment grade. You need to find out the underlying rating of the bond.

Double-checking municipal bond ratings will become easier sometime around 2011. At that time, the MSRB is planning to include complete rating information of municipal bonds on its EMMA Web site. But any broker can double-check the rating history on his Bloomberg professional terminal. A good broker can also help you sort out which bond among several is a better match for your objectives.

Third, a broker can help you bargain for a better price. Brokers have information displayed on their professional screens that is not available on investor Web sites. Some prices are firm and listed as such on the broker's professional screen. But in many cases, there is room for bargaining. Ask the broker to contact the dealer with an offer or to inquire what is the best price he can get. Market conditions vary. In a strong market, if supply is scarce, then there is less room to bargain. But much of the time, there is wiggle room. Selling a bond is costly. You need to ask a broker for several bids to get a good price. In a weak market, selling bonds can be extremely costly; and occasionally, for particularly illiquid bonds, impossible.

Note also that many brokers have access to pricing data that includes a "fair value" for any bond. In the recent past, there has been increasing emphasis on due diligence requirements and brokers are conscious that the NASD is cracking down on abusive practices. When I was researching broker pricing, one broker told me that that the house policy of his firm requires brokers to check "fair value" and prohibits them from selling a bond at a price that is outside of a 3% pricing band. While even that seems fairly wide, it is useful to check pricing against fair value, as well as the house policy.

Finally, firms expect you to call and they expect you to bargain. In fact, it is clear that many firms consider their Web sites just a means to get you to pick up the phone and talk to a broker; it is a way of getting you into the store. When you speak with a broker, that broker knows if the markup is excessive. To make the sale, the broker can use a number of tactics. He may offer to try to buy the bond at a more attractive price—he knows he can—to make you feel as if you are getting a bargain. Or, he may steer you to a bond in the firm's inventory as opposed to one listed by a dealer on an electronic platform—and again, with better pricing.

Buying at Issue

Researching the municipal bond market requires time. If you do not have the time, or the interest, there are definite advantages to buying at issue that is, when the bond is first brought to market. At that time, for a few days, the bond is priced at par (or at a uniform price) by all the dealers in the syndicate. The price remains at par until the bonds "break syndicate" and are allowed to trade at what the market will bear. During that time, moreover, prices—and therefore yields—are usually attractive because dealers are anxious to sell the bonds. The buyer also receives the longest possible call provisions.

Major brokerage firms that participate in bringing bonds to market usually have access to new issues. So do regional firms that specialize in bonds from your geographical area. Smaller brokerage firms, or discount brokers, may not have them. But if you are dealing with a firm that does not have access to new issues, ask where to find them.

SELECTING MUNICIPAL BONDS

Let's mention some additional factors you might want to consider before buying municipal bonds.

Other Tax Features of Municipal Bonds: The Alternative Minimum Tax (AMT); "de Minimis" Tax

While the exemption of interest income from federal income taxes is the main tax feature of municipal bonds, there are a number of additional wrinkles in the tax law affecting municipals that you should consider before buying municipal bonds.

One is the alternative minimum tax (also known as the AMT). The *Tax Reform Bill of 1986* provides for direct federal taxation of certain categories of municipal bonds. Only bonds specifically designated as "nonesssential" bonds, issued after August 7, 1986, are subject to this tax, and then only in the event that the individual investor's tax bracket makes him subject to the alternative minimum tax.

Because there is the possibility that the bonds may be taxable, however, these bonds yield somewhat more than other municipal bonds. Therefore, for those individuals not subject to the alternative minimum tax (and that's almost everyone not in the highest tax brackets), these bonds will result in a somewhat higher yield.

The AMT is of concern mainly to individuals with large incomes or very large municipal portfolios. If you are in that category, you need to calculate your tax bill in two different ways. The first is the standard method. The second requires a number of adjustments to taxable income and the addition of the amount of tax owed on the bonds subject to the AMT. The two tax bills are then compared. The higher tax is the one you pay. Whatever your tax bracket, you can avoid the AMT by making sure that you do not purchase bonds subject to the AMT.

Another tax wrinkle is the "de minimis" tax. Again, this tax is of concern mainly to individuals in the highest federal tax brackets. It is levied on discount bonds that are bought below a specified value and subsequently rise in price or are redeemed at par. That value is determined by multiplying the number of years outstanding until maturity by 0.25. For example, for a bond that matures in 10 years, that amount would be $97.50 (that is, a price of $975.00 for each $1,000 par value amount). If you purchase that bond at a price below $975.00, the difference between the purchase price and the selling price is treated as ordinary income for tax purposes, and not as a capital gain. This creates a tax liability when the bond is sold, and obviously the higher the tax bracket, the higher the liability. This tax liability lowers the real yield for the bond. The "de minimus" rule applies to any discount bond, whether it is an original issue discount bond or a bond selling at a discount in the secondary market. Therefore, if you are in a high tax bracket, you might want to check with your accountant before buying muni bonds selling at a deep discount.

Finally, note that even though munis are federally tax exempt, when you sell or redeem your municipal bonds, you may incur either a capital gain or a capital loss, and those create tax issues. Also, if your bonds have declined in value because interest rates have gone up, you may want to sell your bonds in exchange for other municipal bonds in order to generate a tax loss. This is known as a swap. Swaps are discussed in Chapter 14 of this book. If you are in a high tax bracket, or own a large portfolio of municipal bonds, or trade bonds actively, then tax issues become more complex and may require you to consult a tax accountant.

Investinginbonds.com has added an extensive discussion of tax information for all tax issues pertaining to municipal bonds.

Discounts versus Premium Bonds

Your broker telephones. She has just gotten some terrific bonds in inventory: one a discount and the other a premium. Both yield $4\frac{1}{2}\%$ to maturity. Which should you buy?

Well, you reason, I should buy the discount bond because if I buy the premium bond, at maturity, I will lose for each bond the amount of the premium over par.

Wrong, but a common misconception. If you are looking primarily for income—all other factors, such as credit quality and maturity, being equal—you should buy the premium bond. Premium bonds generally yield more than discounts. Here is why.

It is a common error to think that one "loses" the difference in price between par (the price of the bond when it is redeemed at maturity) and the amount of the premium. The YTM quoted for the premium bond is based on redeeming the bond at par. The premium is not lost. Even if the yield quoted for the premium and the discount bond are exactly the same, the discount bond yield includes anticipated capital gains. That capital gain is taxable, whereas the entire dividend yield of the premium bond is tax free. Hence, the net yield of the discount bond may actually be lower than the quoted ytm, whereas for the premium bond it will be the same.

The yield advantage is amplified by several additional factors. First, the premium bond has higher coupons. So you get a higher cash flow. If you are reinvesting coupons, you have larger amounts to reinvest every year and, therefore, more interest-on-interest. This makes even more sense at a time when interest rates at the longer end are low, by historical standards. If interest rates rise, you can reinvest interest income at higher rates. In addition, because many investors avoid premium bonds, they are usually offered with higher yields than comparable maturity discount bonds. Finally, premium bonds are less volatile than discount bonds, which protects principal in the event interest rates rise.

Therefore, if your style of investing is to buy and hold, muni premium bonds have distinct advantages: higher cash flow and lower volatility.

If you are buying premium bonds, however, you need to be particularly careful about call provisions, or sinking fund provisions. Many housing bonds, for example, are subject to special calls. An early call could result in a loss of principal.

Overall Strategy

You have decided to invest in munis. If you are seeking maximum income and safety, what should you buy?

Opinions differ on this. Some old hands in the industry would say: "Buy bonds rated AAA (for safety) with 30-year maturities and maximum call protection (for highest income)." My objection to long-term bonds has always been based primarily on the fact that long maturities expose the buyer to maximum interest rate risk. That objection is reinforced by rates currently in force (at the time of writing); high quality munis with 30-year maturities yield anywhere from 4.1% to 4.5%, significantly less than was the case even a decade ago. What are the chances that rates will remain at these levels for the next 30 years? Also bear in mind that if you need to sell these bonds, because of their long maturity, markups are likely to be very high.

On the other hand, because the yield curve remains extremely steep, high-quality munis with maturities of 8 to 12 years yield anywhere between 3% and 3.8%. The higher yields can be found on higher quality premium bonds, which also have the advantage of higher cash flows. Interest income on these bonds is anywhere between 80% to 85% compared with longer maturity bonds. But volatility of these bonds is significantly lower. Moreover, if you need to sell the bonds, markups are also lower than for longer term bonds.

To sum up: if credit safety is your main concern, the safest bonds are (in order of safety): pre-refunded bonds; bonds with credit enhancements such as a bond bank or "double-barreled" revenue backing; and bonds rated AA or higher. If you stick to maturities of 10 years or less, you also reduce volatility. For higher yield, buy premium bonds. Only buy 30-year bonds if yields are particularly attractive. If you buy 30-year bonds, only buy bonds with the highest credit quality.

If your total bond portfolio is small ($50,000 or less), it is difficult to put together a diversified portfolio of municipal bonds. You would be incurring high transaction costs. To maximize credit safety and minimize interest rate risk, for current income, consider pre-refunded bonds and keep maturities under seven years. For a small portfolio of municipal bonds, a high-quality short to intermediate bond fund might be a better option. (See Chapter 12 on bond funds.) Finally, make sure that tax-exempt bonds make economic sense for you. Particularly if your tax bracket is under 25%, check whether you might earn more by buying taxable bonds, particularly Treasuries, bought through Treasury Direct, savings bonds such as I bonds, or EE bonds, which defer taxes until they are redeemed.

If you have a large portfolio of municipal bonds, consult Chapter 15 of this book for strategies for managing large portfolios.

SUMMARY

Municipal bonds are the one sector of the bond market where individuals are the primary buyers, either through purchase of individual bonds or through purchase of funds. The primary appeal of these bonds is that they are tax exempt. Once you understand the basics, munis are relatively uncomplicated securities, and defaults are relatively rare. Moreover, the Internet provides information which should enable investors to select and buy municipals with more confidence that they understand what they are buying and that they are paying a fair price.

At the time of writing, however, the municipal market is at an interesting crossroads. On the plus side, the new rating scales (i.e., the recalibrations by Fitch and Moody's) can be viewed as a vote of confidence in the quality and safety of municipal bonds. The recalibrations will promote liquidity. Moreover, if as widely anticipated, tax rates are raised on more affluent families, that should also boost the appeal of munis.

But there are also minuses. One is the possibility of rising rates, which is a threat to the value of longer term bonds. Another minus is the budget problems of many issuers of municipal bonds. Virtually daily, articles appear with scary headlines such as "Are municipal bonds safe?" with the apparently obvious answer that due to budget woes, they are not. All it takes is for one default to happen, with widespread publicity, for the entire sector to be tarred, even if this is grossly unfair, and totally misleading.

My advice when it comes to munis has always been to buy high quality, short to intermediate bonds. I see no reason to change that advice. If you own a large portfolio, Chapter 15 lists additional strategies for managing bond portfolios.

Questions to Ask Before Buying
Municipal Bonds

When does the bond mature?

Who is the issuer?

What is the rating?

If the bond was issued with insurance, what is the "underlying" rating?

When was the rating issued? Is it pre- or post-May 2010 when the rating scales were "recalibrated"?

What is the source of revenue for debt service? Is it adequate to cover debt service? For a revenue bond, what is the debt service coverage ratio?

What is the yield-to-maturity?

Is the bond callable? Are there sinking fund provisions? When? At what price?

If the bond is callable, what is the yield-to-call? The yield to worst?

When did this bond trade last? At what price? was it a customer buy, a sell or an interdealer trade?

If there are no recent trades, can I find some comparables?

ADDITIONAL REFERENCES

Sources of information on the municipal bond market. For most investors, Investinginbonds.com and EMMA are the best resources. And they are free to anyone.

If you have a very large municipal bond portfolio, say above $500,000, you might consider a subscription to *The Bond Buyer*, which remains the bible of the municipal bond market. An online subscription to this daily publication costs about $2,850 per year. *The Bond Buyer* offers free two-week trial subscriptions. The online Web site allows free access to headlines, and some articles are available to nonsubscribers.

APPENDIX: THE NEW YORK CITY DEFAULT

Because stories about the financial problems of municipal bond issuers are particularly plentiful at the time of writing, it may be useful to review at least one highly publicized default that occurred in New York City in the 1970s. This default has almost receded into ancient history. And while no two defaults are exactly alike, the anatomy of this default is instructive.

In April 1975, New York City found itself in a cash crunch. As a result, the City deferred an interest payment on a short-term note. (Long-term bonds were never involved.) Technically, this delay constituted a default, and it was highly publicized. But the interest payment was ultimately made. No investor lost money unless he sold bonds that had declined in value because of the publicity surrounding the default. (Note: to this day, some New York City officials insist that there was never a real default.)

In September 1975, the State passed the Financial Emergency Act, putting the city under the authority of the Emergency Financial Control Board. The crisis was resolved through cooperation between three sectors: the unions, which agreed to use their pension funds for assistance; the state, which extended cash advances; and the banking community. Ultimately, the crisis was resolved through the creation of the Municipal Assistance Corporation (MAC), which was an entity created specifically for the purpose of issuing bonds on behalf of the city of New York. But note that MAC bonds were not obligations of the City of New York. The revenues to pay debt service were backed, not by the taxing power of the City but by the State of New York, and by a special lien on the city's sales tax (there were distinctions between the first and subsequent liens) as well as by a stock transfer tax.

In retrospect, New York City's default was not at all that surprising. The city's financial problems had been widely reported in the press. They included revenue shortfalls due to the city's economic decline; inability to contain spending within revenues; and poor fiscal management (for example, funding long-term expenditures through short-term borrowing). Under these circumstances, a downgrade should have been anticipated.

Because of the publicity surrounding the city's financial woes, and despite the fact that MAC bonds were not obligations of the City, the MAC bonds came to market with yields well above then-current market rates: 10% as compared to 8% for securities with comparable maturity and credit. From the beginning, MAC bonds represented a very solid investment. The bonds were secured by very strong revenue sources. Debt service coverage was predicted to be very strong and turned out to be even stronger than anticipated. In 1990, it reached 11 times on first lien bonds, and between four and five times on second lien bonds. MAC bonds were initially rated A, but because of the excellent historic debt service coverage ratio, by 1990 they were rated AA.

What can be learned from this episode? First, that defaults can and do occur and will continue to occur. Can they always be anticipated? In this case, yes. The city's financial troubles were well publicized and the default was preceded by several downgrades.

Finally, this episode demonstrates why it pays, literally, to be very precise about exactly which revenue streams back debt service. In this instance, MAC bonds were tarred by the woes of New York City, even though they were not obligations of the city and rated higher than direct obligations of the city. And that is the main reason why even though MAC bonds represented a very solid investment from the start, their yields were so high.

CHAPTER 8

Corporate Bonds

This chapter discusses

- ◆ The five groups of corporate bonds
- ◆ Risk factors of corporate bonds
- ◆ Corporate bonds with special features
- ◆ Junk bonds
- ◆ Buying corporate bonds
- ◆ Shopping for corporate bonds using the Internet

WHAT IS UNIQUE ABOUT CORPORATE BONDS?

Bonds issued by major corporations are known as corporate bonds, or corporates for short. They are commonly classified into five major groups.

Utilities. This group consists of both electric and telephone companies. These used to be highly regulated and, as a result, were considered among the safest of all corporate bonds. Since deregulation, that is no longer the case, particularly for bonds in the telecommunication sector.

Transportation. This group includes the bonds of airlines and railroads.

Industrials. This is the largest and most diverse of the five. It contains bonds of some of the premier corporations in the country, such as Exxon, General Electric (the oldest of the Dow components), and International Business Machines.

It also contains so-called junk bonds.

Finance. This group includes banks and insurance companies.

"Yankee" bonds. These are bonds issued by foreign issuers, but denominated in dollars. Yankee bonds will be discussed in Chapter 10, International Bonds.

Corporates are also classified on the basis of the security being pledged by the issuer as collateral for the bonds. The collateral may consist of mortgages (mortgage bonds); financial obligations (collateral trust bonds); or railway rolling stock (equipment trust certificates). Corporates that are not secured by any collateral are known as debentures or notes.

If you were to consider yield only, corporate paper would appear attractive. As a group, corporate bonds always yield more than Treasuries. And of course, that is the source of their appeal. However, for individual investors the higher yield is partly offset by the fact that income from corporate paper is fully taxable at every level: federal, state, and local.

More importantly, corporate bonds are far more risky than Treasuries, and far more complex. They are also subject to many more risk factors.

Credit quality of corporate bonds has been declining for the past couple of decades. There are very few AAA credits still left. Even Berkshire Hathaway has been downgraded to AA! Almost half of all corporate bonds are now classified as "junk" bonds, that is, below investment grade. And particularly for these bonds, credit quality is a genuine concern.

In addition, corporate bonds are subject to several different types of calls, known variously as calls, sinking fund provisions and refundings,

Also, in the 1980s, corporate bonds developed a unique set of risk factors, described in this section under the rubric: "event risk."

Finally, whereas yield is always higher for corporate paper than for Treasuries of the same maturities, over time, total return, particularly for lower-quality corporates, may be far lower.

This chapter will discuss the risk factors and the unique features of corporate bonds. A separate section will be devoted to junk bonds. The good news is that trade data as well as other information is now available for corporate bonds, on the Internet. So this chapter will discuss how to shop for and get pricing information on corporate bonds.

RISK FACTORS OF CORPORATE BONDS

Event Risk: How the Market Changed in the 1980s

The market for corporate bonds changed radically during the 1980s. This was due mainly to the emergence of the junk bond market and to the wave of takeovers, restructurings, and leveraged buyouts that swept corporate America in the 1980s, with devastating results to some bondholders. The phrase "event risk" entered the lexicon to designate the uncertainty created for holders of corporate debt by the takeover phenomenon. This wave of takeovers and restructurings resulted in massive downgrading. As a result of these events, the price of many corporate bonds dropped like a stone, sometimes also overnight.

As the 1980s progressed, and as takeovers involved ever larger companies, event risk loomed as an increasing menace. This uncertainty was compounded by the fact that takeovers were impossible to predict.

As a direct result of this turmoil, and in order to sell new debt, corporations found it necessary to add a variety of inducements—sometimes called "bells and whistles." Some, such as so-called poison pill provisions, were intended to prevent takeovers by making takeovers more expensive to the potential acquirer. Other innovations, such as floating-rate notes and put bonds, were intended to protect investors against interest rate risk (see below). Many of these bells and whistles have become permanent features of the corporate bond market.

During the 1980s, partly as a result of event risk, maturities in this sector became shorter. But occasionally, this trend reverses. During 1997 and 1998, for example, a number of corporations (Disney, for instance) issued 100-year bonds.

During the decade between 2000 and 2010, event risk due to takeovers has become less prevalent. But it has not disappeared. Major downgrades due to economic factors are also common occurrences.

Credit Risk

The credit quality of corporate issuers varies enormously, from AAA for some of the premier corporations in the country to as low as C for highly speculative junk.

Evaluating credit quality for corporates is a more complex process than for munis. The investor must analyze the financial strength of the company much as he would if he was buying stocks of the same company. Many factors need to be considered, including

- ◆ Overall economic trends
- ◆ Trends within the industry
- ◆ The relative ranking of the corporation within its industry
- ◆ The quality of its management

Note also one unique aspect of corporate bond ratings. When a corporation issues new stock, it immediately becomes undistinguishable from all previously issued stock of the corporation. But that is not the case for bonds. When a corporation issues bonds, each issue becomes a separate bond, with its own coupon, maturity date, call features, and seniority. Ratings are assigned to each individual issue, not to the issuer. Separate bond issues of a single issuer often have different ratings because bonds are ranked in order of priority for payment in the event of default. Senior debt is paid first. Less senior debt—either "subordinated" or "junior"—would be paid after the claims of senior issuers had been satisfied, and so on. As a result, senior debt generally has a higher rating than junior debt.

Rating changes among corporates can occur suddenly and can be major. This is partly the result of event risk. But it can also occur if a company runs into severe financial difficulties.

As one would expect, default rates of corporate bonds are lower in the aggregate during good economic times; and climb significantly during recessions. A study of annual default rates of corporate bonds between 1971 and 2009 shows that they have been as low as less than 1% a year (surprisingly, as recently as 2007); and as high as almost 13% in 2002. Note that bonds rated AAA or AA have had only rare defaults while those ratings were in force. But default rates rise after downgrades, and are progressively higher for lower rated bonds.[1]

Very short-term corporate debt (that is, commercial paper) has its own set of ratings. Standard & Poor's has the most categories, from A (highest quality) to D (lowest quality, and in default). "A" paper is further subdivided into A1 (strongest of the A group) to A3 (weakest). Moody's has three ratings: P–1 (strongest) to P–3 (weakest).

---

1. Data provided to the author by Professor Ed Altman, NYU Stern School of Business.

Call Risk

Like municipal bonds, corporate bonds are subject to call risk: that is, the risk that the issuer will redeem a bond prior to its stipulated maturity date. Calls take a number of different forms.

Like municipal bonds, corporate bonds may be called if interest rates decline, at a date stipulated in the indenture, and at a price also specified in the indenture, typically somewhat above par. Generally, bonds are protected against calls for a number of years, typically five or ten years, depending on the type of bond. Calls are usually unwelcome news for the investor because a rate thought to be locked in disappears, at a time when investment rates are lower.

A newer type of call provision has become popular because it provides protection against this type of unwelcome call. This call provision is called a "make-whole" call provision. As its name implies, its purpose is to make the original buyer "whole" in the event the bond is called. Under this type of call, a bond can be called at the higher of two prices: 100% of par, plus accrued interest; or a formula based on the Treasury yield at the time of the call plus a stipulated number of basis points. (The technical definition is that the call price is the sum of the present values of the remaining coupons and principal, discounted at a formula based on the yield of Treasuries of the same maturity plus an added spread, for example, 30 basis points.)

Formulas for make-whole calls differ for each bond. Note also that the call price changes as interest rates rise or fall; hence, the formula creates a floating call price. But it is a price which rises if interest rates decline. "Make-whole" provisions benefit the buyer because they make it expensive for an issuer to call a bond in the event interest rates decline. The bottom line is that if a bond is purchased at or close to par, and the bond is called, the worst case scenario is that it is called at par.

Some corporate bonds stipulate that they are subject to "conditional" calls; in other words, that the bond may be called in the event certain events occur. The most often cited is a change in tax laws, which affects the tax rates of the issuer.

Some bond indentures specify a type of call known as a "sinking fund." There is usually not an actual fund. But sinking fund provisions require that a certain percentage of bonds outstanding have to be to be retired every year regardless of interest rate levels. These calls may take place in several different ways. One is that the trustee chooses bonds to be retired by lot. Another possibility is that they are purchased by the issuer in the open market. Finally, sinking fund provisions may also allow the issuer to retire more bonds than initially stipulated. This is known as an "accelerated sinking fund" provision.

Corporate bonds may also be called under a number of contingencies designated as "refundings." In the event that the corporation can obtain sources of capital cheaper than the interest it pays on its bonds, it may use these proceeds to redeem (that is, to call) its bonds. These sources of cheaper capital include retained earnings, monies raised by selling assets, or proceeds from a stock offering. Refundings may occur only if they are stipulated in the bond indenture.

Sinking fund redemptions sometimes work to the advantage of the bondholders because some bonds are retired at par when interest rates have gone up and when the price of the bonds would normally decline. The lucky investor can then take his principal and reinvest it at higher interest rates. However, calls or refundings always protect the issuer and not the bondholders. Calls or refundings typically occur at a time when interest rates have dropped and when principal has to be reinvested at lower interest rates. Particularly onerous to bondholders are calls that occur when bonds are trading at a premium to the call price. Such calls can result in a loss of capital to anyone who purchased the bonds at the premium price.

CORPORATE BONDS WITH SPECIAL FEATURES

Put Bonds

A put feature gives the purchaser the opportunity to "tender" (that is, to resell) a bond back to its issuer at par, before the bond matures, at time periods specified in the indenture (typically every six months).

While a call protects the issuer, a put protects the investor. If interest rates go up, the bondholder can "put" the bond back to the issuer, that is, resell his bonds to the issuer at par, and reinvest the entire principal at a higher rate. Put features in a bond are designed to protect principal against interest rate risk. The ability to resell the bond to the issuer at par is intended to keep the bond trading at or close to par (assuming no credit deterioration). Effectively, the put feature turns the bond into short maturity paper at periodic intervals.

Another type of put is, not to interest rates, but rather, to takeovers. This put stipulates that the bond may be "put" back to the issuer if there is a "change of control." (This is also known as a "poison pill" provision.)

This type of provision always benefits the buyer of the bond. In the event of a takeover, the credit rating of the acquired firm changes to that of the acquirer. If the credit quality of the acquiring firm is lower than that of the acquired firm, then the credit rating of the acquired firm declines. But the put provision enables the investor to redeem the bond at par. On the other hand, if the credit quality of the acquiring firm is higher than that of the acquired firm, its credit quality goes up: The investor benefits because the credit rating of the bond goes up.

Note also a type of put known as a "conditional" put. This goes under several names such as a "survivor" option; or an estate provision. This "put" stipulates that if the owner of the bond dies, the estate may "put" the bond back to the issuer at par. (Some Agency bonds also have this feature.)

In practice, while put features have provided some protection against interest rate risk, they have not proved to be a panacea. If interest rates decline suddenly and steeply, the put provision may not prevent a price decline. There are also some undesirable features to put bonds. Typically, interest rates are lower than those of bonds with similar ratings and maturities—as you would expect, given their effectively shorter maturity. Moreover, put bonds trade like shorter paper, and this limits their upside potential in rising markets, when interest rates decline (compared to bonds with similar maturities but without the put features).

Floating-Rate Notes and Bonds

Like puts, floating interest rates on a bond are intended to provide protection against interest rate risk by maintaining bond prices close to par. Floating interest rates are far more prevalent in foreign markets than in the United States. They were introduced to the United States during the early 1970s.

The main feature of floaters is that the coupon rate is reset periodically, usually every six months, based on a stipulated benchmark. The benchmark used to reset the coupon is usually a short-term Treasury (the floater rate might be $3/4$ of a point higher). It may also be LIBOR (the London Interbank Offer Rate), which is a key rate for European investors. Sometimes floaters also have a "floor"; that is, a rate below which the coupon will not fall. Some floaters give the bondholder the option of exchanging the floater against a long-term bond, at specified intervals, though at rates which may not be as attractive as those of the long-term bonds.

The rationale for floaters is that as interest rates change, resetting the coupon rate at periodic intervals will tend to maintain the price of the bond at or close to par. In practice, this has tended not to work out quite as well as had been hoped, for a number of reasons. First, during times of extreme interest rate volatility, rates are not reset quickly enough to prevent price fluctuations. Secondly, the coupon rates of floaters are usually well below those of long-term bonds and often not very attractive when compared to shorter maturity bonds.

Floaters are issued chiefly by major banks, such as J. P. Morgan Chase and Citibank.

Convertible Bonds

As the name implies, convertible bonds are issued by corporations with the proviso (in the indenture) that they can be exchanged for the common stock of the corporation at a specified price. The buyer has the advantage of a fixed coupon and the potential to share in the possible appreciation of the stock.

If the price of the common stock does not appreciate, as long as there is no default, the downside risk is limited, since the buyer will continue to receive coupon payments and can redeem principal at maturity. In theory, convertibles are somewhat less risky than the common stock. But they have the potential of capital appreciation if the stock does well.

Because of this feature, the price of a convertible bond fluctuates mainly in tandem with the price of the stock, and not in response to interest rate changes. Analysis of convertible bonds is therefore more closely related to equity analysis than to bonds, but with its own unique twists. Convertibles are regarded as a very specialized form of investment. That kind of analysis, however, is outside the scope of this book.

Corporate Bonds with Equity Warrants

This feature gives a purchaser the right to purchase the stock of the issuer at a specified price at some future date. In effect, the purchaser of the bond is being granted options to buy the stock at what is hoped will be an attractive price at some future date. This type of structure is sometimes used by fast-growing companies with limited cash flow to attract buyers to its debt: it enables the issuer to pay a lower interest rate than might be warranted by its low credit quality. Amazon.com, for example, was able to issue bonds with equity warrants at very favorable interest rates in 1999, despite the fact that it was losing money and the bonds were rated as junk. The purchaser of the debt, on the other hand, is hoping that the price of the stock will rise quickly so that he may realize a profit.

JUNK BONDS

The moniker "junk bonds" is not new: It actually dates back to the 1920s, when it was used by traders to designate bonds of companies that suddenly fell into financial distress. These companies were also called "fallen angels."

At the current time, the term "junk bonds" encompasses a more diverse group of corporations than fallen angels. It designates bonds of any corporation rated below investment grade. Because the term "junk" is somewhat blunt, a large number of euphemisms are also used to designate these bonds: They are also called "high yield," "high income," "noninvestment grade," "speculative," or even "high opportunity" debt. I prefer the term "junk" because it is straightforward and unambiguous.

What sets junk bonds apart from other types of bonds is that, while they are fixed-income instruments, the primary risk factor is not interest rate risk but rather the risk that the company that issues the bonds may not survive. As a result, junk bonds tend to do poorly if the economy is in a slump, and perform better when the economy strengthens. Correlation of junk bond returns is higher with the stock market than with the bond market.

A Brief History of Junk Bonds

Junk bonds are not all equally risky. There are five ratings below investment grade, as shown in Exhibit 8.1. (This table should look familiar— it is the bottom half of the credit ratings table shown in Chapter 3, Exhibit 3.3.) These ratings designate bonds of companies that are in some degree of financial difficulty, ranging from somewhat speculative to outright default.

Junk bonds are unique because risk is almost entirely related to credit quality. Bonds in this credit category are typically issued with maturities in the 5-to–10-year range so that interest rate risk is relatively modest.

Up until the 1980s, this was a rather obscure and limited corner of the market; the province of a small number of specialists. The junk bond fund sector expanded dramatically in the mid–1980s. This was partly due

EXHIBIT 8.1

Junk Bond Ratings and What They Mean

Moody's	S&P	Fitch	What They Mean
Ba	BB	BB	Somewhat speculative; low grade.
B	B	B	Very speculative.
Caa	CCC	CCC	Even more speculative; substantial risk.
Ca	CC	CC	Wildly speculative; may be in default.
C	C	C	In default.

to the activities of Michael Milken, then of Drexel Burnham Lambert, who created a new type of junk bond, issued to finance mergers and acquisitions activity, including hostile takeovers and leveraged buyouts. These bonds received a huge amount of publicity. But the market's expansion was also due to the entrance of entirely new investors. A number of mutual funds were launched, which attracted significant demand from individual investors. Institutions, including banks (mainly thrifts) and insurance companies, also flocked to buy junk bonds.

The attraction of these bonds was, of course, their high yields. The difference in yield between Treasuries and lower-rated bonds is known as the "spread." The lower the credit quality of any bond compared to Treasuries, the higher the spread. In the 1980s, junk bonds sold at yields that were as much as 400 or 500 basis points higher than Treasuries with similar maturities. A body of thought developed among institutional investors and academics that a portfolio of junk bonds would ultimately provide higher returns than a portfolio made up primarily of higher-quality bonds. The reasoning was that, even in spite of potentially high default rates, the higher interest income would eventually result in higher total return than for more highly rated bonds.

But as astute investors might have predicted, rising demand for junk bonds eventually resulted in lower yields. The spread between junk bonds and Treasuries narrowed to about 200 basis points. But in 1989 and 1990, partly as a result of the exit of Drexel Burnham Lambert from the bond market, the price of junk bonds began to spiral down. Eventually, declines were horrendous.

When spreads between junk and Treasuries widened to about 700 basis points, some investors saw this as a compelling buying opportunity. Junk bonds (and junk bond funds) rallied briefly, only to decline in value again as the fear of an approaching recession spread. This time, the declines in price were even more horrendous.

In November 1990, spreads between junk and Treasuries reached 1,100 basis points—a truly amazing number at the time. During 1989 and 1990, the selling of junk bonds reached panic proportions. At the height of the panic, junk bonds were being sold for 30 to 40 cents on the dollar, with yields-to-maturity ranging from 20% to 40%.

The panic was overdone. In early 1991, a strong rally ensued.

Amazingly, this pattern of rally, crisis, and subsequent rally did not end at the beginning of the 1990s. During the decade of the 1990s through the present, junk bonds have gone on several similar roller coaster rides. Periods of outsize gains have alternated with periods of dramatic losses. Between 1998 and 2009, severe declines occurred twice: during the economic crisis of 1998, after Russia defaulted on its debt; and during the financial crisis that began in 2007 and lasted through 2008.

Prior to the beginning of the most recent crisis, in 2007, spreads to Treasuries had declined to about 260 basis points. Investors were once again behaving as if risk had ceased to exist. But in 2008, at the height of the financial panic, spreads to Treasuries widened to well above 25% (2,500 basis points), a new record. Declines in the price of many junk bonds were catastrophic, between 40% and 90%.

But once again, starting in 2009, junk rallied. For the entire calendar year of 2009, total returns of junk bonds were stellar once more, around 40% for an index of junk bonds. This was due to two separate factors. The first is that dividend yields of junk bonds were on average well above 25%, so interest income was very high. The second was that the extremely steep decline in yields resulted in a significant chunk of capital gains.

Should You Buy Individual Junk Bonds?

The junk bond sector has undergone many changes. Mergers and acquisitions activity ceased to be a major factor in the early 1990s. During the 1990s, prominent issuers of junk bonds included telecoms as well as start-up companies too weak financially to be rated investment grade, but nonetheless considered "growth" companies. These included now-failed firms such as WorldCom and Global Crossing but also firms that have prospered such as Amazon.com. The entire sector has continued to expand, partly due to a general decline in the credit quality of corporations. Throughout the 1990s, the percentage of corporate debt rated below investment grade varied between 22% and 30%, with the exception of

1998, when it reached 38%. But the percentage of debt rated below investment grade reached 49% in 2007.

At any one time, concentration of junk debt may be high in a particular industry. For example, in 2008, many banks, insurance firms, and
airlines were downgraded to junk status. As in the past some of these
companies will reemerge to profitability; others, like former industry
leaders such as Lehman Brothers, will go under. It is not clear, for example, whether General Motors will survive or will disappear like Pan Am
and Lehman Brothers.

So, where does this leave the individual investor? If you are looking
for high yields, should you consider buying individual junk bonds?

One key factor is the actual default rate of junk bonds. Each of the
successive crises in the junk bond market has been accompanied by
significant spikes in default rates, as shown in Exhibit 8.2.

This graph of defaults tracks the roller coaster ride in this market. In
1991, default rates peaked at around 11%; in 2002, they peaked at 12.8%.
Coincidentally, the default rate during the recession that began with the
financial panic in 2007–2008 also peaked close to 11%. (Exhibit 8.2 illustrates default rates and recessions from 1972 through December 2009.)

E X H I B I T   8.2

Historical Default Rates and Recession Periods in the
United States

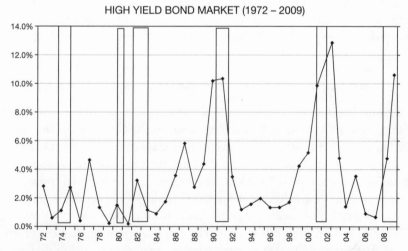

HIGH YIELD BOND MARKET (1972 – 2009)

Periods of Recession: 11/43 – 3/75, 1/80 – 7/80, 7/81 – 11/82, 7/90 – 3/91, 4/01 – 12/01, 12/07, 12/09

Source: E. Altman (NYU Salomon Center) and National Bureau of Economic Research. Material supplied to the author
by Professor Altman.

Defaults tend to peak just prior to the end of the recession and as of this writing, the recession does not seem to be over. The forecast of Professor Edward Altman of New York University, similar to that of the rating agencies, is that default rates will peak somewhere between 14% and 15%.[2] Note that defaults are higher in the most speculative categories of junk than in their higher credit quality peers. As is often the case in these situations, a rally in junk bonds began well prior to the end of the recession.

Given the history of this sector of the bond market, I consider buying *individual* junk bonds to be highly speculative for individual investors, and not worth the risk. Consider the following:

♦ Default rates are high and predicting which bonds are likely to default requires both expertise and a high degree of luck.
♦ Individual junk bonds are extremely illiquid—spreads are usually wide. Moreover, in the event the market seizes up, it is virtually impossible to sell a "junk" bond except at an extremely steep loss—a "markdown" that can at times reach 25% or 30%.
♦ Catastrophic price declines can occur virtually overnight.
♦ There is some salvage value to almost any defaulted bond. But this salvage value may be extremely low.

The primary buyers of junk bonds continue to be large institutional investors such as pension funds and insurance companies that need to diversify very large portfolios. Most individual investors do not have the same needs.

I would suggest individual investors buy individual junk bonds only if they have a very large bond portfolio ($500,000 in bonds) and if they can afford a loss, or can afford to take a long-term view and not sell during periods of negative returns. Junk bonds may also be considered attractive speculative vehicles for investors who have the stomach to buy them when spreads to Treasuries are wide—but be warned that such periods can last several years and that you can lose a lot of money while prices are declining.

---

2. Different methods are used to calculate default rates. Professor Altman of NYU calculates the default rate by comparing the value of defaulted bonds to the par value of junk bonds outstanding. Moody's rating service, on the other hand, calculates default rates by comparing the value of defaulted bonds to the principal value (that is, the market price) of junk bonds outstanding. Moody's also includes the debt of emerging markets in its calculations, whereas Altman does not. The two methods for calculating default rates result in different ratios. As a result, for any period you may see different ratios published for default rates of junk bonds.

Finally, for investors who would like to invest in this sector in much smaller amounts, because it would be utter folly to purchase junk bonds without diversifying, the most appropriate method is to invest through a bond fund. Regardless of how well or poorly managed any mutual fund investing in junk might be, at least a mutual fund will provide diversification. (Characteristics and returns of bond funds investing in junk are discussed in Chapter 12.)

To sum up: If you have a small bond portfolio (say under $50,000 total) and if you are investing in bonds primarily for income, despite their enticing high yields, junk bonds are a poor choice because they are high risk and volatile securities.

SHOPPING FOR CORPORATE BONDS USING THE INTERNET

The Internet has become an indispensable resource for researching corporate bonds, whether investment grade or high yield, prior to investing. The process is similar to that described for municipal bonds, in Chapter 7. The most comprehensive Web site for such a search, however, is FINRA.org/marketdata.

Corporate Bonds and FINRA.org/marketdata

FINRA.org/marketdata was developed and is maintained by the Financial Industry Regulatory Authority (FINRA), the regulator for all securities firms doing business in the United States. It was created through the merger of the former National Association of Securities Dealers (NASD) and member regulators functioning on the New York Stock Exchange. Reporting is done through TRACE, the acronym for Trade Reporting and Compliance Engine. Dealers are required to report all trades within 15 minutes of each trade: in other words, close to real time.

FINRA.org/marketdata went live on the Internet around 2007. This is a hugely comprehensive Web site, with data and information that encompass almost any regulated security that trades in the United States, including mutual funds, stocks, and options. It includes a tutorial that will help you navigate all of its resources. This section will focus on data and information that enable you to research corporate bonds. Many of these searches are similar to those described in the chapter on municipal bonds. But FINRA's Web site has some unique ways of presenting data. In addition, of course, many features of corporate bonds differ from those of municipal bonds. Therefore, in this section, I will focus primarily on aspects of researching corporate bonds that pertain mainly to corporate bonds and to this particular Web site.

Get an Overview

First of all, you would want to get an overview of the current state of the market for corporate bonds. You can do so by accessing the start page of the Web site. The exact web address is FINRA.org/marketdata.

Because the start page of this Web site encompasses both the stock and the bond markets, it is somewhat busy. Exhibit 8.3 shows the features of the start page that pertain to the corporate bond market.

The graph and data featured on this page are compiled at the end of every trading day. They summarize trading activity in both the Treasury and the corporate bond markets. Activity in the Treasury bond market is summarized by a yield curve; and yields at key points along the yield curve. The table titled "Corporate Bond Market Activity" shows how many corporate bonds traded, how many went up, how many declined, and so on. The idea is to give you a snapshot of the strength of the market, and of the direction of interest rates. If you click on the heading: "View: corporate bond" a second page comes up, which displays several lists of the most actively traded bonds: the most actively traded investment grade bonds; the most actively traded high-yield bonds; and the most actively traded convertible bonds, as well as their maturity, ratings, prices and yields. (This second screen is not shown.)

At the upper left hand corner of the start page (shown in Exhibit 8.3), you will notice a list of terms: company information, equities and options, bonds, mutual funds, and so on. To obtain another view of the bond market, click on "bonds." This will bring up a page with yield curves for several sectors of the bond market: Treasuries, corporates and municipals. The yield curve graphs show yields for different credit ratings: high grade and lower quality ratings. (These yield curves are not shown.)

Together, the various bond market exhibits provide a comprehensive snapshot of the yields and prices prevailing in the corporate bond market, for both investment grade and lower quality corporate bonds. This overview is a start. It will help you decide whether specific sectors of the corporate bond market appear attractive to you. The next step is to find bonds that are actually being offered for sale and determine whether you find them attractive. To do so, as for munis, you have a number of options. You can look at an online broker Web site to see specific bonds available for

EXHIBIT 8.3

FINRA Start Page

Last Updated: 5/6/2010

Search: [ ] [Equity ◄►] **Go**

Market Data
Company Information
Equities and Options
Bonds
Mutual Funds
Watchlist
Feedback

Market Data

Welcome to FINRA's Market Data Center. This comprehensive tool is designed to assist investors with market and investment research, both through the market data information provided as well as through the FINRA Investor Education material and tools.

U.S. Treasury BenchMarks

1 Month Bill	0.07%	-0.04
3 Month Bill	0.12%	0.04
6 Month Bill	0.17%	-0.03
2 Year Note	0.82%	-0.04
5 Year Note	2.22%	-0.07
10 Year Note	3.47%	-0.07
30 Year Note	4.32%	-0.07

More Yield Information

5%
4%
3%
2%
1%
0%

1M 3M 6M 2Y 5Y 10Y 30Y

FINRA TRACE Corporate Bond Market Activity   12:05 PM ET 5/6/2010

View: **Corporate Bond** | Agency Bond

	All Issues	Investment Grade	High Yield	Convertibles
Total Issues Traded	5,504	3,803	1,453	248
Advances	2,461	1,898	482	81
Declines	2,597	1,621	820	156
Unchanged	190	104	79	7
52 Wk High	406	311	86	9
52 Wk Low	51	35	13	3
Dollar Vol*	20,607	11,624	6,974	2,009

*Par value in millions

More FINRA TRACE Bond Market Inforamtion

Quick Bond Search

Bond   ⊙ Treasury
Type: ○ Corporate
       ○ Municipal

Symbol: [ ]

Yield: [Select... ◄►]
Coupon: [Select... ◄►]
Maturity: [Select... ◄►]

Search

- Advanced Bond Search
- Bond Center

Learn more

- Investor Alerts
- Investment Choices
- Protect Yourself
- Smart Investing

Market Data Tutorial
Learn more about the functionality and contest of this site

sale. And you can also search FINRA.org/marketdata to look for prices at which bonds actually traded. Finally, you can conduct a targeted search for comparables. This section will give examples of all three types of searches. You can do them in any order that makes sense to you.

Look for Bonds Offered on an Online Broker Web sites.

Let's start with a search on an online broker Web site. First, click on "corporate bonds" and then add general criteria such as maturity, and credit ratings. Exhibit 8.4 shows a sample of listings that you might have seen April 26, 2010.

As we saw with online municipal bond listings, the source information clearly identifies an electronic platform, BondDesk, as the source of the data. Once again, also, note the disclaimer, which identifies the platform as the source of the data, and which adds that

"XYZ brokerage services is not responsible for the accuracy of this data."

The headings of the listings are the same as those for municipal bonds and are mostly self-explanatory. But notice some differences:

- ◆ Qty (quantity): most listings show much larger numbers of bonds for sale than was the case for municipals.
- ◆ Min. Qty: Minimum quantity. Those are the minimum number of bonds you can order at the listed dealer price. Note that the minimum numbers vary a great deal. In many cases, the minimum order is much larger than was the case for municipals: 100 or even 250 bonds. Clearly, both the quantity offered for sale, and the size of the minimum orders, indicate that this continues to be primarily an institutional market. But nonetheless, as long as you order the minimum quantity specified, the price listed should be honored.
- ◆ The bonds list one or more of the call or put provisions explained earlier in the chapter, in the section on call provisions, such as "make-whole" call provisions, or "conditional" calls. You would need to inquire exactly how those provisions are worded and how they would impact any bond you may want to buy.

Clicking on the name of a bond brings up a second screen, with more detailed information about the bond. It will look like Exhibit 8.5, which shows additional details pertaining to one of the bonds listed in Exhibit 8.4: R. R. Donnelley & Sons.

EXHIBIT 8.4

Secondary Corporate Results

Qty	Min Qty	CUSIP	Issue	Coupon	Maturity	Price	Yield	Moody/ S&P	Credit Watch
500	2	78442FEJ3	Sim Corp Make Whole Call Only – Conditional Puts – Change of Control	8.000	03/25/2020	97.5	8.374	Ba1/BBB-	/
500	250	75913MAB5	Regions Bk Birmingham Ala	7.500	05/15/2018	101.693	7.218	Baa2/BBB-	/
100	100	026874BT3	American Int Group Inc Make Whole Call Only	8.250	08/15/2018	106.995	7.116	A3/ A-	/
132	1	98310WAE8	Wyndham Worldwide Make Whole Call Only – Conditional Puts – Change of control	7.375	03/01/2020	102.5	7.017	Ba1/ BBB-	/
2465	1	247131AF2	Delphi Financial Group Make Whole Call Only – Conditional Calls	7.875	01/31/2020	106.081	7.001	Baa3/ BBB	/
1000	10	257867AU5	Donnelley (R.R.) & Sons Make Whole Call Only – Conditional Puts – Change of control	11.250	02/01/2019	128.5	6.862	Baa 3/ BBB	/
25	1	57183MCD0	Marshall & Iisley Corp Sr. Callable 07/10@ 100 – Multi-Step Coupon – Conditional Puts – Death of holder	5.200	07/15/2018	92.5	6.841	Baa1/ BBB-	/
Edit Search		Build Ladder (New)	Build Ladder (add to Current)	Refresh	Next....	Last			

Source: BondDesk Group, LLC. The Bond content is presented by BondDesk Group, LLC. Reprinted with permission.

EXHIBIT 8.5

Bond Offering Detail

Action

Description

Issue:	Donnelley R R & Sons Co Nt 11.25%'19 Make Whole Call Only – Conditional Puts – Change of control			
CUSIP/ISIN/SEDOL:	257867AUS / US257867AU51/B3L67X9	**Type:**	Corporate	**Moody/S&P:** Baa3/BBB
Coupon:	11.25	**Frequency:**	Semiannually	**Category:** Industrial
Maturity:	02/01/2019	**First Coupon:**	08/01/2009	**Delivery:** Book Entry
First Settlement:	01/20/2009	**Next Coupon:**	08/01/2009	
Issue Date:	01/20/2009	**Last Coupon:**		
Minimum Amount:	2,000.00	**Denomination Amount:**	1,000.00	
Collateral:	Note			
Blue Sky Restrictions:				
Reference material:				

Moodys Ratings Information

Long Term Rating:	Baa3 effective 04/08/2009
Short Term Rating:	
CreditWatch:	

S&P Ratings Information

Long Term Rating:	BBB effective 03/13/2009 12:38:56 PM
Short Term Rating:	

Call / Sink / Put Features

Conditional Put Reason: Change of control

Security Notes

CALL @ MAKE WHOLE + 50BP

Corporate Specific

Issuer Full Name: R.R. Donnelley & Sons Company

Listed: Y   **Symbol:** DNY

Bid				Offer		
Price:	126.000		**Price:**	128.500	**Settlement:**	04/29/2010
Yield to Maturity:	7.193		**Yield to Maturity:**	6.862	**Duration:**	6.038
Quantity:	300		**Yield to Call:**	-	**Quantity:**	1000
Min Quantity:	10		**Yield to Par:**	-	**Increment:**	1
			Current Yield:	8.755	**Min. Quantity:**	10
			Worst Yield:	Maturity		

Source: BondDesk Group, LLC. The bond content is provided by BondDesk Group, LLC. Reprinted with permission.

Once again, note that the data is supplied by an electronic platform, and also note the presence of the disclaimer.

Several items deserve comment.

- ◆ Note that both the "bid" and the "offer" (also known as the "ask") are listed. Both are not always listed for all corporate bonds. But if both a bid and an offer price are listed for a corporate bond, that is an indication that bond is actively traded, and therefore, fairly liquid.

- ◆ A listed bid price also indicates that if you own this bond, and want to sell it, a dealer is willing to buy it at the listed price. Note, however, that even though both the bid and the offer prices are listed, that does not indicate that the same dealer is on both sides of the trade: they could be different dealers.

- ◆ The call provision listed is a "make whole call provision." make whole provision" specifies the bond may be called at either par; or at a price based on the make-whole call formula, whichever is higher. A "make whole" provision creates a floating call price. As a result, the price at which the call might be exercised cannot be stipulated. (More below about this call provision.)

- ◆ Note also that this bond is at the very bottom of the investment grade category. But since there has been no change in the rating scale of corporate bonds, there is no confusion about the rating.

- ◆ Notice finally that this listing includes three different ID numbers: the CUSIP number which is the ID number on U.S. exchanges; the "ISIN," which stands for International Identification Number; and "SEDOL", which stands for Stock Exchange Daily Official List. Those listings indicate the bond trades on exchanges other than US exchanges.

But the most striking aspect of this listing is the very high coupon (11.25%) and the price: not only premium, but a very high premium price: 128.50, in other words, $1285 per par value bond. The explanation of both the high coupon and the high premium price can be found in the date the bond was issued: January 2009. This was a time when the corporate bond market was deeply depressed. To obtain financing, the bond had to be issued with a very high coupon. But this listing is dated approximately one year and a half after issue, in May 2010, after a monster rally in the corporate bond market that started in 2009. Due to the enormous decline in interest rates of corporate bonds during the intervening year, the price of the bond has increased from par to 128.50; and the yield to maturity has declined to 6.8%.

How The "Make Whole" Call Provision Might Impact the Bond.

First, let's take a closer look at the "make whole" call provision. Because the bond is selling at a high premium, a make whole call at par would result in a significant loss of principal. But what are the chances that might happen?

Because I am not familiar with this type of provision, I asked my broker to walk me through some possible scenarios. For this particular bond, the make-whole call provision stipulates that the bond would be called either at a 50 basis points premium to the interest rate of the 10-year Treasury, or at par, whichever is higher at the time the bond is called. As I discuss this with my broker, the interest rate of the 10-year bond is around 3%. If the bond were to be called immediately, it would be called at a price which would result in an interest rate of 3.5%. That price would be about 160 ($1600) per bond. Clearly, it would not be in the interest of the company to exercise the call. That, you will remember, is the reason this type of call was created: to make it difficult for corporations to call a bond in the event interest rates decline; and to prevent the corporation from calling older bonds primarily to refinance at a lower cost.) In fact, it is reasonable to assume that the current high premium price of the bond is based partly on the assumption that the call will not be exercised any time soon.

But what would happen if interest rates were to rise? The premium to exercise the call shrinks as interest rates go up; and as time to maturity shrinks. If, for example, the call was exercised 3 years after the bond was purchased, and if over that period, rates were to rise by 300 basis points (a very plausible scenario), call would be exercised closer to 123 ($1230). If interest rates were to rise more than 300 basis points, then the call price would be lower still. So clearly, the call provision is not an immediate concern. But if interest rates rise, it would be a concern because the call price may decline to well below the current purchase price.

Suppose I Need to Sell the Bond Prior to Maturity?

Remember that bonds are redeemed at par, no matter where interest rates happen to be when you redeem the bond at maturity. For a premium bond, that means that every year, the price of the bond falls towards par.

Let us assume that interest rates stay exactly the same; and that you need to sell the bond in four years. The price of the bond would have declined to approximately 116.8 ($1168), a loss of about $120 per bond, prior to any markdown for the cost of selling the bond. But if interest rates were to rise, then the price would decline by a larger amount. The selling price would be even lower.

Elsewhere in the book, I point out that premium bonds can sometimes be extremely attractive purchases, because typically, they result in higher yields to maturity. But clearly, that has to be determined on a case by case basis. Clearly, what makes this bond appear attractive is the high coupon and the resulting high cash flow. But remember that this bond, like all bonds, will be redeemed at par. And (assuming you have reinvested coupons at the yield to maturity rate), your realized return will be the yield-to-maturity: 6.8%. One way of looking at the high premium of this bond (about 30% above par) is that you are paying for three years income up front. Moreover, selling the bond for any reason prior to maturity would probably result in a loss. And finally, the company issuing this bond is barely investment grade. So credit quality is a concern.

Look Up the Trading History of the Bond

Let's assume that you still want to buy the bond. You would then want to determine what you might want to pay for the bond. That dictates looking up the trade history of the bond as well as comparables.

To look up the trade history of a bond, you need to first find a "Bond Detail" page on FINRA.org/marketdata. This is a screen that contains basic details about bonds: the name of the issuer, the coupon, the bond's maturity date, as well as a graph with a trade history of the bond, and the last price at which it traded. (The date of that trade is not listed on that screen). Once you have located the "Bond Detail Page," to find the trade history of the bond, you would click on the phrase: "Search for bond trade activity"; the screen that would come up would look like Exhibit 8.6.

This page is similar to the trading history that was shown in Chapter 7, for municipal bonds. Exhibit 8.6 shows the exact time of each trade, the number of bonds traded, and also whose side of the trade is being recorded. "B" denotes a customer sale: a dealer buying the bond from a customer; "S" is a customer buy: a dealer selling the bond to a customer; "D," is an inter-dealer trade, always a sell. Trades shown in exhibit took place over a period of about two weeks. Inter-dealer prices were 128. Even though they were very large trades, customer buys (denoted by the letter S) were very close to 130. And one customer sell (denoted by the letter B) was 126.6, was close to 150 basis points lower than the inter-dealer price.

EXHIBIT 8.6

Bond Search Results

Quick Bond Search	Advanced Bond Search								
Select Bond Type	Treasury & Agency		Corporate	Municipal					
									Source:
Add to Watchlist									
Bond Symbol	Issuer Name	Coupon	Maturity	Calible	Moody's	S&P	Fitch	Price	Yield
HET.HP	HARRAHS OPERATING COMPANY INCORPORATED	10.00	12/15/2018	Yes	NR	CCC	NR	84.500	13.097
NWL.GT	NEWELL RUBBERMAID INCORPORATED	10.60	04/15/2019	Yes	Baa3	BBB-	BBB	137.398	5.200
DFS.GF	DISCOVER FINANCIAL SERVICE LLC	10.25	07/15/2019	Yes	Ba1	BBB-	BBB	124.035	6.644

Search Criteria			
Bond Type:	Corporate	Term to Maturity:	Between 7/28/2018 and 12/31/2019
Coupon Rate:	Between 10% and 12%	Coupon Type:	All
Days Since Last Trade:	1	Industry Group:	All

Source: FINRA.org/marketdata. ©2010 FINRA. All rights reserved. FINRA is a registered trademark of the Financial Regulatory Authority, Inc. Reprinted with permission from FINRA

Most of the other headings in the trade activity screen are self-explanatory. But note the term *modifier*. Under that term, you see different icons. If you "mouse over" the term, you will see an explanation of each icon.: "@" which is the most frequent icon, indicates a "regular" trade. Other icons designate terms of the sale that do not fit that description: trades conducted after hours, for example; or with an atypical settlement date.

Once again, note that some online Web sites now have "hot" links to the trading history of a bond for the prior 30 days.

Look for Comparables

This type of targeted search is one of the most popular searches on this Web site. You could, indeed, start your search for corporate bonds with this type of search. Typing in a broad set of criteria will generate a list of bonds that traded recently along with their yields and prices. Such a list can help you determine how and whether to continue your search. But note one feature of this search which is easy to miss: one of the "sorts" listed is "activity: bonds that traded within a certain period." In order to put together a list of bonds that traded recently, and whose price therefore is current, always type in that you want bonds that traded within one day or, at most four or five days. If you omit this step, you sometimes wind up with bonds where the most recent trade occurred months earlier. Those prices would be stale.

To generate a list of bonds comparable to the Donnelley bond we have been discussing, type in a list of criteria that are close, but not exactly the same. (If your criteria are too narrow, you may simply generate an error message. You can always start with broader criteria, and subsequently, narrow them.) After you click on "See Results," what will come up is a list of bonds, listed by issuer, and initially sorted by maturity. It will look like Exhibit 8.7 and it will have the same title as Exhibit 8.7.

Exhibit 8.7 shows only a small sample of the bonds that would have resulted from your search. (Note that the criteria used to generate the list of bonds are listed at the bottom of the exhibit.) To generate a list of premium bonds comparable to the Donnelley bond we have been tracking, I selected a maturity date range of about a year and a half, and a high coupon (10% to 12%) and generated a list of bonds that are also trading at premium prices. Note that the rating of the first bond in Exhibit 8.7, Harrah's puts it in a category well below investment grade, so I discard that one immediately as not comparable. Bonds that have ratings similar to the Donnelley bond have slightly higher ratings than the Donnelley bond. The most interesting comparable is the bond listed at the bottom, Discover. It has a somewhat higher credit rating, a somewhat lower coupon (10.25%), but also a somewhat lower price (124.035). But its listed yield is very close to that of the Donnelley bond, 6.64%. Note also that even though the date of the last trade is not listed on the screen, because I specified that I wanted to see bonds that traded within one day, ("days since last trade") the prices and yields are current for the date of the search.

You need not limit yourself to this type of search for comparables. For example, if, like me, you would be concerned about the very high premium price, you could do a different targeted search, specifying a maturity date within the same range, and a similar yield, but omit the coupon. By specifying a yield between 5% and 7%, I generated a list of bonds comparable in yield to the R. R. Donnelley bond, but trading much closer to par. Note, also, that when you do this type of targeted bond search, the bonds that come up are initially listed based on maturity. But you can manipulate the list by clicking on any of the headings in Exhibit 8.7, such as coupon, or yield. If you click on yield, the bonds are reordered based on yield. If you click on ratings, they will regroup based on ratings.

The Meaning of Yield on FINRA.org/marketdata

On FINRA.org/marketdata, unless otherwise specified, the yields that come up under any "yield" heading are always the yield-to-worst. This

EXHIBIT 8.7

Bond Trade Activity Search Results

Issue: DNY.HB Description: RR DONNELLEY & SONS CO Coupon Rate: 11.250 Maturity Date: 02/01/2019

Execution Date	Time	Status	Quantity	Price	Yield	Commission	Modifier	2nd Modifier	Special	As Of	Reporting
05/03/2010	15:31:11	T	2000	128.000	6.921	N	@				D
05/03/2010	15:31:08	T	2000	128.897	6.804	N	@				S
04/30/2010	17:16:00	T	5000	129.922	6.672	N	A				S
04/30/2010	13:37:14	T	10000	128.000	6.922	N	@				D
04/30/2010	13:37:11	T	10000	129.075	6.782	N	@				S
04/30/2010	13:37:11	T	10000	128.000	6.922	N	@				D
04/27/2010	14:26:00	T	7000	129.924	6.676	N	@				S
04/26/2010	14:17:00	T	10000	129.600	6.719	N	@				S
04/20/2010	13:58:58	T	1000000	126.641	7.112	N	@				B

makes comparing bonds on the basis of yield somewhat more difficult. For a premium bond, the yield-to-call is normally the worst yield. For a discount bond, the yield-to-worst is usually the yield-to-maturity.

But note that if you are starting from yields listed on online broker Web sites, unless otherwise specified, the yield listed under the column heading "yield" is the yield-to-maturity. (Other yields, including the yield-to-worst, are listed on more detailed screens). Remember also that if the bond has a make-whole call provision, the call price will remain unspecified; but that might indeed turn out to be the yield-to-worst.

Evaluating a bond on the basis of its yield-to-worst is considered more prudent than looking at the best case scenario. But the worst case scenario is not necessarily the most probable one. Moreover, comparing several bonds on the basis of their yield-to-worst means that you are comparing yields at different dates. Therefore, comparing bonds on the basis of their individual yield-to-worst could be somewhat misleading. I would still seek out the yield-to-maturity to determine which appears to be the best buy.

Searching for Bonds with Incomplete Information

The FINRA Web site enables you to look up detailed information on bonds whether you have the CUSIP number, or less precise information such as the name of a company or an issuer. You would look for a "Bond Detail Page." To look for a corporate bond, go to the start page of the FINRA.marketdata Web site (shown in Exhibit 8.3), click on "bonds," then on "corporate". If you have the CUSIP number, you can use the "quick bond search." Type the CUSIP number, click on "see results" and a bond detail page will come up. If you do not have a CUSIP number, you can type in the name of a company, and a list of several different bonds issued by the company will be displayed.

Note another characteristic of the FINRA Web site. On some screens, you will see a letter symbol next to the name of a bond. FINRA assigns its own symbols to bonds. For example, the Donnelley bond we have been tracking was assigned the symbol DNY.HB. These symbols may be used instead of a CUSIP number, but only on the FINRA Web site.

Additional Search Information

The type of targeted search illustrated in Exhibit 8.7 is not limited to corporate bonds. You can conduct similar searches for municipal bonds; and for Treasuries and agencies. For example, for municipal bonds, start with bonds, but instead of "Corporate", click on "Municipals", and then type in the appropriate criteria: state, maturity, credit quality, etc. And don't forget to select bonds that traded within one or a few days! But remember that that whatever type of bond you are researching, the yield displayed in the FINRA Web site is always the yield-to-worst, not just for corporate bonds, but also for municipals, and for Agencies.

Note also that a lot of the data (including price data) on both corporate and Agency bonds can also be accessed on Investinginbonds.com. Much of that data actually is a feed which originates with FINRA, through its TRACE engine.

Finally, I have not discussed EDGAR, a Web site maintained by the Securities and Exchange Commission (SEC). EDGAR archives disclosure documents, including the prospectus and annual reports, of all corporations, both foreign and domestic, whose securities trade in the US. EDGAR has been considered somewhat difficult to navigate, but it is being redesigned to become more user friendly.

Company Information Center

FINRA has a unique search feature for researching the various securities issued by corporations. Again, go to the start page (shown in Exhibit 8.3), and under "market data," the first option that comes up is "company information." If you type in the name of a corporation, the page that comes up lists the most recent price of the stock (along with a graph), as well as information on all the securities that are outstanding for this corporation, including a graph of the stock price, options outstanding, bonds, company profile, recent news headlines about the company, and recent SEC filings. This enables you to link information on any security of the company to other securities of that company. For example, is an example of such a page: it shows information for Intel. (Because of space limitations, the news headlines, under the MarketWatch heading, were abbreviated.)

Buying Corporate Bonds: Talk to a Broker

As noted elsewhere, many online brokers now allow you to research and buy bonds online without discussing the trade with a broker. There is no need to repeat the caveats discussed in Chapters 5 and 7. Given the fact that corporate bonds are in many ways more complex than municipals, and as a group, more risky, all the caveats that apply to purchasing municipal bonds apply in spades to corporates. I would suggest talking with a broker, hopefully, a knowledgeable broker, before buying corporate bonds.

When to Buy Corporates

To some extent, the price of corporate bonds follows interest rates up and down. But total return of corporate bonds, particularly of junk bonds, is often more highly correlated with the stock market than with the bond market. Comparing the total return of corporate bonds to that of Treasuries, yields inconsistent results. If the economy is strong, investment grade corporates sometimes have higher total returns than Treasuries, because yields are higher. But during recessions, corporate bonds often decline in price. The lower the credit rating of a corporate bond, the more it declines. Moreover, during periods of uncertainty, or recessions, "flight to quality buying" sends Treasury bonds soaring. This, for example, was the case in 2008, when Treasury prices soared; and all other sectors of the bond market tanked. To be sure, this was an extreme example, but it is not unique.

When is a good time to buy corporate bonds? For investment grade bonds, you would want to buy corporates when the yields are higher than those of Treasuries by a significant amount: say at least 150 basis points for maturities in the 5 year to 10 year range.

If you are a trader, you would want to buy corporate bonds when they are unpopular and spreads to Treasuries are wide. The widest spreads will always be found in the high yield (junk) bonds sector. But remember that those are volatile and speculative securities.

Once again, the best example of when to buy is to be found in the 2007–2008 financial crisis. Toward the end of 2008, when fear dominated the markets, spreads to Treasuries of both investment grade corporates and junk reached record levels. Total return of both investment grade corporate bonds and junk bonds in 2009 was extremely high. (Examples of these returns will be seen in Chapter 12, on bond funds.)

As this is being written (in May 2010), spreads of corporate bonds compared to Treasuries have narrowed significantly compared to where they were in 2008. In the 5 to 10 year maturity range, investment grade corporate bonds yield around 200 to 300 basis points (2% to 3%) more than Treasuries. Those are reasonably attractive spreads. But bear in mind that one reason for the wide spread is that Treasury yields are at record lows. If interest rates on Treasuries rise, then the spread to Treasuries of corporates will narrow. As always, you have to decide whether the spread is wide enough to compensate you for the additional risk you are taking on.

Tables comparing aggregate returns for corporate bonds with those of Treasuries often show that that those returns are higher for corporate bonds than those of Treasuries of comparable maturities. But bear in mind

EXHIBIT 8.8

Company Information Detail: Intel

Company Information Detail

Intel Corporation (Q:INTC)
Last: 21.51   Change: -6.66 | -2.99%
Quote Information

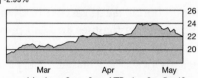

	Mar Apr May	
	1dy 1mo 3mo 6mo YTD 1yr 3yr 5yr 10yr	
Open:		22.15
High:		22.38
Low:		19.91
Yield:		2.93
P/E Ratio:		19.73
Market Cap:		119.68 B
Volume:		160,695,866
Shares Out:		5.56 B

Search: [INTC]   [Equity]   Go

Company Profile   Add to My Watchlist
Intel Corporation   Web site
2200 Mission College   Phone: (408) 765-8080
Boulevard,
Santa Clara CA 95054-1549   Fax: (408) 765-9904

Industry: Semiconductor-Broad Line
Employees: 79,800

Intel Corporation is a semiconductor chip marker, which develops advanced integrated digital technology products, mainly integrated circuits, for industries such as computing and communications. The company also develops platforms that are designed and configured to work together to provide an optimized user computing solution compared to components that are used separately. It offers products at various levels of integration, to allow its customers flexibility in creating computing and...

More Company Profile Information

Dividend: 0.16
EPS: 1.09
M=Millions   B=Billions
More Equity Information

Options

Symbol	Last	Change	Strike	Symbol	Last	Change
INTC100522C00022000	1.30	+0.28	22.00	INTC100522P00022000	0.19	-0.09
INTC100522C00023000	0.45	+0.05	23.00	INTC100522P00023000	0.41	-0.27
			23.26			
INTC100522C00024000	0.17	+0.03	24.00	INTC100522P00024000	1.03	-0.33
INTC100522C00025000	0.06	+0.01	25.00	INTC100522P00025000	1.83	-0.18

Bonds issued by Intel Corporation

Symbol	Coupon	Coupon Type	Call	Maturity	Rating Moodys/S&P/Fitch
INTC GD	2.95	Fixed	No	Dec 2035	NR/A-/NR

More Bond Information
MarketWatch News for Intel Corporation
Tech stocks begin week with broad gains-
MarketWatch.com
SEC Fillings

Filling Date	Document Date	Type	Category	Amended
04/14/2010	04/14/2010	8-K	Special Events	
04/13/2010	04/13/2010	8-K	Special Events	

that the aggregate total return of the corporate bond sector is boosted by the fact that it includes lower-rated corporate bonds, which yield more than higher quality debt. Indeed, some professionals feel that for individual investors, high-grade corporates do not have a spread to Treasuries that is wide enough to compensate individual investors for some of the uncertainties of corporate bonds, such as credit downgrades should the corporation run into economic difficulties and call provisions.

As a group, corporate bonds are somewhat less predictable than munis, for all the reasons described above. The yield advantage over Treasuries is further diminished by the fact that Treasuries are exempt from state tax. As a rule, this is worth about 50 to 60 basis points. For individuals in the higher tax brackets, corporate bonds are most appropriate for purchase in tax-sheltered or tax-deferred accounts (IRAs, Keoghs). For those of you who want to buy corporate bonds, here is a list of appropriate precautions:

- Only buy investment grade bonds. This is a shrinking group. You need to check ratings.
- Monitor the ratings.
- Buy only if the spread to Treasuries of comparable maturity is wide enough to compensate you for the additional risk. For bonds with maturities of 5 to 10 years that should be at least 200 basis points for high quality bonds; and higher than that for lower quality bonds.
- Stick to maturities of 10 years or less. Some of the best buys at the time this is being written are probably in shorter maturities: say two to three years: at these levels, Treasury yields are particularly low. And there is better visibility on credit quality of corporates for short maturities.
- Investigate call and sinking fund provisions before you buy.

SUMMARY

Some of the highest yields in the taxable bond sector are to be found in the corporate bond market. But they are trickier to buy than other taxable bonds because they are subject to many uncertainties. Bonds of corporations that are commonly described as "junk" have the highest yields but should not be purchased unless you have a high degree of expertise in analyzing these bonds.

As this chapter should have shown, investing in corporate bonds requires time, and some expertise. Moreover, it would not be prudent to invest in corporate bonds without diversification. Unless your portfolio is large enough to permit adequate diversification (say at least $100,000), if you want to invest in corporate bonds, a conservatively managed bond fund or ETF may be your best bet.

QUESTIONS TO ASK BEFORE BUYING CORPORATE BONDS

What is the company profile?

What is the credit rating?

What are the call provisions? The sinking fund provisions?

What is the spread to Treasuries of a similar maturity?

When did the bond last trade? At what price? At what yield?

Has the credit rating changed?

CHAPTER 9

Mortgage-Backed Securities

This chapter discusses

- The unique nature of GNMA cash flows
- How prepayments affect GNMA cash flows
- The vocabulary of GNMA returns
- CMOs and other sons of GNMA
- Agency backing of mortgage-backed securities. Ginnie, Fanny, and Freddie.
- Collateralized debt obligations (CDOs) and collateralized debt swaps (CDSs)
- The financial crisis of 2007–2008
- The current state of the mortgage backed and asset backed securities market

The financial crisis of 2007 and 2008 began in the mortgage-backed sector of the bond market. Between 2008 and 2009, much of the activity in this sector ground to a halt. And this is one sector of the market that remains under the shadow of that crisis. Yet the securities in this sector, which are tied to the housing industry, have become part and parcel of the taxable bond market; and at some point, every sector of the market is likely to re-appear, even though some changes are likely.

Let's start with a capsule history of the securities that make up this sector of the bond market, up through the crisis of 2008–2009.

The first mortgage-backed securities (MBSs) were issued in the 1970s under the name of GNMAs (popularly called Ginnie Maes). They consisted of mortgages that were repackaged to be sold as bonds. In 1983, a new structure was developed that was intended to lessen some of the uncertainties associated with GNMA cash flows: These were known as collateralized mortgage-backed obligations (CMOs). In the late 1990s, cash flows such as credit card debt, car loans, boat loans, and the like were repackaged into bonds similar in structure to both GNMAs and CMOs, called asset-backed securities (ABS). Between 2000 and 2007, there was an explosion in the number of CMOs.

In 2003, two new fiendishly complex asset-backed instruments made their appearance: CDOs (collateralized debt obligations) and CDSs (collateralized debt swaps). Both of these were intended for institutional use. By 2007, the bonds and derivatives based on these securities had become the largest segment of the taxable bond market, dwarfing the market for Treasuries and corporates by far, and also dwarfing the market for conventional GNMAs and CMOs.

Toward the end of 2007, cracks developed in the very foundations of this market, namely, the mortgages repackaged into bonds. The cracks were due to a new type of mortgage, so-called subprime mortgages. These cracks spread to virtually every sector of the asset-backed and mortgage-backed securities market that did not benefit from government guarantees. During 2008–2009, sectors of this market froze. For example, no new collateralized mortgage obligations (CMOs) were issued. Instead, during these two years, much of the activity in this sector consisted of the Federal Reserve purchasing well over 1 trillion dollars of mortgage-backed securities. Those purchases ended in March 2010.

GNMAs and CMOs remain the prototypes for all mortgage-backed and asset-backed securities. Understanding GNMA cash flows is basic to understanding any of the other instruments. This chapter will begin with a discussion of the fundamental characteristics of GNMAs and GNMA cash flows, and then discuss how these were repackaged into CMOs.

This chapter will also briefly discuss asset-backed securities, CDOs, and CDSs. Despite their complexity, and the controversy surrounding their use, new CDO and CDS securities are being issued and traded. However, new regulations are under consideration that might affect both the structure of these securities and the way they are traded.

Finally, we will briefly discuss the state of the mortgage-backed market at the time this is being written.

WHY GNMAs ARE UNIQUE

GNMAs were the earliest mortgage-backed securities, first issued in 1970.

GNMAs were, and continue to remain, mainly an institutional product. The minimum required to purchase a new GNMA is $25,000, although older GNMAs can be purchased for less. Banks, insurance companies, and pension funds, as well as mutual funds, are the primary buyers of GNMAs.

The appeal of GNMAs to individual investors is based on a number of factors: impeccable credit quality (GNMAs have the unconditional backing of the U.S. government); high cash flow (unlike other bonds, interest is usually paid monthly); and higher current yield than Treasury securities. But there is never a free lunch. If GNMAs yield more than Treasuries, then they must have features that make them less desirable than Treasuries. And this, of course, is the case.

In reality, GNMAs are complex securities. Anyone who tells you GNMAs are simple does not understand the product. While they have no credit risk whatsoever, they are not riskless. Like other bonds, they expose the buyer to interest rate (and price) risk. More importantly, when you buy an individual GNMA, you will not know the exact amount or the timing of its cash flows, or indeed, how long the GNMA will be outstanding. Finally, each GNMA is unique. Two GNMAs with similar coupons and quoted maturities may ultimately perform very differently.

Analysis of a GNMA is totally different from that of any other fixed-income instrument. Analysis focuses on two elements: the probable longevity of the security—that is, how long coupon payments are likely to continue—and its total return. Both are uncertain. Professional investors rely on extensive statistical analysis in their decision process. Individuals usually do not have access to these models.

Analyzing GNMA cash flows requires mastering a whole new set of conceptual tools and vocabulary. But you should not purchase individual GNMAs (or any other mortgage-backed security) unless you are prepared to spend some time mastering the peculiarities of these securities. Within the scope of this chapter, I can only cover some basics.

Note also that GNMAs are taxable both at the federal and at the state level. Since Treasuries are exempt from state taxes, this erases some of the yield advantage that GNMAs have compared to Treasuries, particularly in states with high tax rates.

GNMA Cash Flows

The easiest way to start is to describe how a GNMA security is created. GNMA stands for "Government National Mortgage Association," which is an agency of the U.S. government within the Department of Housing and Urban Development (HUD). That agency does not issue bonds. Rather, its role is that of an insurer and facilitator.

The process of creating GNMA securities (or as they are also known, GNMA pools) begins when a builder or a developer puts up a development. At the point where the builder has obtained financing and sold a number of houses to individual homebuyers (who have obtained individual mortgages), the builder—or more precisely, the mortgage originator—applies to the GNMA for a pool number and GNMA backing. Only mortgages insured by the Veterans Administration (VA) or the Federal Housing Administration (FHA) are accepted. Because these mortgage payments are insured by government agencies, GNMA is able to unconditionally guarantee timely payment of interest and repayment of principal. The mortgages are then bundled together by a servicer into one pool totaling a minimum of $1 million. Pieces of this pool are then sold to investors. You might consider this pool as similar to a mutual fund, except that in this case the fund is made up entirely of mortgage payments. Exhibit 9.1 illustrates how this process works.

When you buy a GNMA (colloquially known as "Ginnie Mae" or "Ginnie" for short), you are buying a percentage amount of the pool. This pool consists of mortgage payments, which have been repackaged (the Wall Street word is "securitized") in order to create a debt instrument with a fixed coupon. Through the magic of investment banking, individual mortgages have been transformed into debt instruments. But the cash flows of GNMAs differ from those of other bonds. The cash flows of GNMAs are exactly those of the underlying individual mortgages "passed through" from the original homeowners to the purchaser of the Ginnie Mae security. (That is the reason that mortgage-backed securities such as GNMAs are sometimes also called "pass-throughs.")

Let's take a closer look at a typical GNMA pool. Each pool is made up of mortgages bundled together because they share a number of characteristics. All mortgages are fixed rate; they are issued for 20 to 30 years and at the same interest rate, based on prevailing interest levels. The servicer acts as a middleman. He receives the mortgage payments made by homeowners and sends them to the purchasers of GNMA securities, charging $1/2$ of 1% for his services. As a result, the coupon rate of GNMA securities is $1/2$ of 1% lower than the homeowner's interest cost. For example, 8% mortgages would be bundled together into GNMAs with a $7^1/2$% coupon. (There are also adjustable rate pass-throughs, but that's another topic.)

When you buy a GNMA, the payments you receive are percentage amounts of those sent by homeowners to their bank. Each homeowner

EXHIBIT 9.1

Origination of a GNMA Pool

GNMA Pool Organization

Mortgage lender gives commitment to the home buyer.

Mortgage lender obtains guarantee from GNMA.

Buyer settles on house; mortgage is obtained.

Lender pools similar mortgages and delivers to securities dealer but retains responsibility for servicing.

Securities dealer sells mortgage pools, in whole or in part, to investors and advises GNMA of new owners.

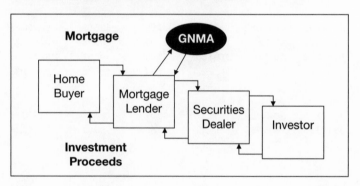

After the pool is originated, the lender collects monthly payments of principal and interest from the home buyer by the 30th of each month and forwards them to GNMA.

GNMA disburses payments to investors by the 15th of the following month whether or not payment has been received from the home buyer.

Source: T Rowe Price Associates. Reprinted with permission.

sends a fixed monthly amount to his bank that includes both interest and principal. On a 30-year mortgage, during the first few years a small fraction of the monthly payment pays down principal. That percentage gradually increases through the life of the mortgage based on a preset schedule, called the "amortization schedule." As the amount paying down principal increases, the amount of interest correspondingly declines. Exhibit 9.2 shows the cash flows for a mortgage with a servicing fee. (The assumptions are that the mortgage loan totals $100,000. The term

E X H I B I T   9.2

Cash Flow for a Mortgage with Servicing Fee

Month	Beginning Mortgage Balance	Monthly Mortgage Payment	Net Interest for Month	Servicing Fee	Principal Repayment	Ending Mortgage Balance
1	$100,000.00	$840.85	$750.00	$41.67	$49.19	$99,950.81
2	99,950.81	840.85	749.63	41.65	49.58	99,901.24
3	99,901.24	840.85	749.26	41.63	49.97	99,851.27
4	99,851.27	840.85	748.88	41.60	50.37	99,800.90
...	...	...	...	...	...	...
...	...	...	...	...	...	...
...	...	...	...	...	...	...
98	92,862.54	840.85	696.47	38.96	105.69	92,756.85
99	92,756.85	840.85	695.68	38.65	106.53	92,650.32
100	92,650.32	840.85	694.88	38.60	107.37	92,542.95
...	...	...	...	...	...	...
...	...	...	...	...	...	...
...	...	...	...	...	...	...
209	74,177.40	840.85	556.33	30.91	253.62	73,923.78
210	73,923.78	840.85	554.43	30.80	255.62	73,668.16
...	...	...	...	...	...	...
...	...	...	...	...	...	...
...	...	...	...	...	...	...
357	3,297.89	840.85	24.73	1.37	814.75	2,483.14
358	2,483.14	840.85	18.62	1.03	821.20	1,661.95
359	1,661.95	840.85	12.46	0.69	827.70	834.25

Source: Frank Fabozzi, ed., *The Handbook of Fixed Income Securities*, 5th ed. (New York: McGraw-Hill, 1997), p. 508. Reprinted with permission.

of the loan is 30 years—equal to 360 months. The servicing fee is 0.5%; the mortgage rate is 9.5%.)

This is the first aspect of GNMA monthly cash flows, which differentiates them from those of other fixed-income instruments. Every month you receive some principal and some interest. When the last payment has been made by the last homeowner in a GNMA pool, the entire principal has been paid back. (There is not a large sum remaining to be redeemed as there is when other bonds mature.)

Bear in mind that the principal payments are not income. The principal payments received each month are your own money being returned to you. If that is not immediately obvious, consider the following analogy. Suppose you lend someone $100 to be repaid in ten equal monthly installments with interest. Each month you would receive $10 worth of principal, in addition to the interest payment. At the end of the 10 months, your entire principal would have been repaid; no more would be forthcoming. But clearly, the $10 repayment of principal paid out each month is simply repayment of $1/10^{th}$ of the loan amount being returned to you.

HOW PREPAYMENTS AFFECT GNMA CASH FLOWS

But the story does not stop here. Remember that your GNMA is made up of small pieces of many mortgages. Few homeowners hold mortgages for 30 years. Whenever a home is sold, its mortgage is prepaid in full. Homes may be sold for many different reasons. Some of these reasons have to do with lifestyle decisions. Homeowners may buy a larger house. They may retire or divorce. Or they may have to move because of a job change or a birth or a death in the family.

But homeowners may also prepay a mortgage for economic reasons. If interest rates decline, many homeowners refinance their mortgage in order to reduce monthly payments. For owners of GNMA bonds, this is the key factor to keep in mind. It ties prepayments directly to declines in interest rates.

Whenever a mortgage is prepaid, the prepayments are *passed through* directly to the holders of GNMAs. Prepayments radically complicate GNMA cash flows. Much of the time, payments on a GNMA cease well before the original term of the mortgage loans. Whenever a mortgage is prepaid, a number of things happen. First, you get back some principal. But bear in mind that you receive interest only on the principal amounts that remain outstanding. Therefore, as principal comes back to you, your interest income decreases. Moreover, if many of the mortgages in your GNMA pool are paid down, interest payments on those mortgages cease altogether. As a rule, prepayments speed up the return of principal and shorten the amount of time a GNMA remains outstanding. As a result, even when GNMAs are made up of 30-year mortgages, they are viewed by the market as intermediate, rather than as long-term, securities.

In addition, due to the unpredictable timing of prepayments, no pool behaves exactly like the average. As a result, when you buy a GNMA, you cannot predict either the timing or the speed of prepayments. You also cannot know the final date when all payments cease. This, in turn, means that any yield quotes are, at best, highly inexact estimates.

Let's sum up the differences between GNMA cash flows and those of other bonds. When you buy a bond, you receive interest payments in the form of coupons, usually twice a year. At the bond's maturity, you receive a much larger sum, the principal, which is redeemed in full in what is in effect a large balloon payment. You know at the time of purchase exactly how much you will receive for each coupon payment; the dates of these coupon payments; and the date of repayment of the principal balloon.

Payment schedules for GNMAs, however, differ radically from the above. You receive a check each month that consists of some principal and some interest, based on the amortization schedule. Principal is paid off not in one balloon at the bond's maturity, but carved up into little monthly increments. Whenever mortgages are prepaid, the amount of principal you receive increases; but concurrently, the amount of interest declines. GNMA payments continue until the last mortgage in the pool is paid down. At that point all payments cease. No one, not the servicer, not the builder, and not the GNMA, can predict with certainty either how long it will take before all mortgages are prepaid or the timing and size of prepayments. So while a GNMA has a stated final maturity date, when you buy a GNMA, you cannot know how much you will receive each month or how long it will take before that particular GNMA is paid down.

In the bond market, however, you are compensated for uncertainty: All these uncertainties are one reason that GNMAs yield more than Treasuries. Another reason is that the interest rate on the underlying mortgages is higher than concurrent interest rates paid by Treasury securities.

How Do Interest Rate Changes Affect GNMAs?

GNMAs, like any debt instrument with a fixed coupon, react to changes in interest rate levels. But again, they do so in their own unique way. Once again, prepayments are the complicating element. Elsewhere in the book, I emphasized that when interest rates decline, the value of your bonds goes up, and that when interest rates rise, the value of your bonds declines. That volatility is directly tied to maturity length. But for GNMAs that relationship is modified. Here is why.

Suppose, for example, that interest rates decline substantially. In that event, homeowners are likely to rush to refinance their mortgages. If you own a GNMA, this is bad news. First, prepayments are likely to speed up dramatically. A large percentage of your GNMA pool is likely to be paid down far earlier than you assumed. And secondly, you get lots of principal back, just when rates are lower. Now you have to reinvest at lower rates. The result is: Not only won't your GNMA appreciate in price as much as other bonds with similar maturities, but in some cases your GNMA may actually decline in value. Also, the total return you earn on the GNMA is likely to be substantially lower than you initially antici-pated for two reasons: You will be reinvesting large amounts of money (the principal being returned to you) at much lower rates than the coupon interest of your original GNMA, and because of this, the price of your original GNMA is likely to have declined. As a result, in rising mar-kets the upside potential of GNMAs is more limited than that of other bonds with similar maturities.

Now suppose interest rates rise. This also is bad news. First, pre-payments slow so that the life of your GNMA pool is likely to increase. In this instance, you will have to hold on to your GNMA longer than you anticipated. What is more, at this juncture, the coupon of your GNMA is lower than rates currently available in the market. Therefore, you guessed it: The price of your GNMA is likely to decline more steeply than that of other intermediate bonds.

Both of the preceding scenarios are simplified. Premium, discount, and par GNMAs react differently to interest rate changes. Also, volatility in the face of interest rate fluctuations is cushioned for GNMAs by the fact that the market treats them as intermediate, rather than long-term, instru-ments. But interest rate changes may create a kind of "heads I lose, tails I lose" situation. In rising markets, GNMAs underperform other bonds. In declining markets, they may decline somewhat less, but not much less than other bonds. So while GNMAs yield more than Treasuries on a cur-rent yield basis, when total return is considered, there are time periods when individual GNMAs may not perform as well as Treasuries. Moreover, the total return of an individual GNMA, as we shall see, is far more uncertain than that of Treasuries.

THE VOCABULARY OF GNMA RETURNS

Let's assume you are being "shown" a GNMA pool, that is, an individual GNMA security. Your broker will no doubt be looking at a *Yield Table,* derived from a Bloomberg (professional) terminal. This is very different from the free *Bloomberg* Web site available on the Internet. The Bloomberg (professional) database has become ubiquitous in the trade. It contains an extraordinary range of data concerning all types of securities. For GNMA securities, each Bloomberg GNMA Yield Table is based on cash flow sce-narios contributed by several leading brokers. In effect, it represents the consensus estimate of the cash flow patterns and returns for that particu-lar GNMA security. If you are shown a quote on paper, it will look like Exhibit 9.3. The quote will look busy and confusing. But it contains a lot of information that is not self-explanatory.

EXHIBIT 9.3

Yield Table for a GNMA Pool from a Bloomberg Terminal

GN704426

Mtge **YT**

5.5% 3/15/39 ADV: <PAGE>

LOANS : 134

Vectors
99 <Go>

66
<GO> 36296XSPO   MBS : GNSF I
6.000(342)15 WAC (WAM) WALA MAY10

65
<GO> GNSF 5.5 N

MAY 1mo	590P	17.70
'10 3mo	833	23.3
6mo	1112	27.9
12mo	1132	21.9
Life	1175	20.5

3/1/09:	23,068,501	next pay	6/15/10	(monthly)
5/1/10:	17,380,240	rcd date	5/31/10	(14 Delay)
factor	0.753418690000	accrual	5/1/10-	5/31/10

CA	TX	GA	OTHR
30.6	13.1	6.3	49.9

YIELD TABLE

B. Median:
Vary **1**
PRICE **32**

5/20/10

	0bp 508 PSA	+300bp 137 PSA	+200bp 167 PSA	+100bp 262 PSA	-100bp 918 PSA	-200bp 1143 PSA	-300bp 1192 PSA
106-21	2.9990	4.4987	4.3898	4.0267	1.0523	-.1733	-.4601
AvgLife	2.95	8.78	7.72	5.47	1.57	1.21	1.15
Mod Dur	2.68	6.41	5.82	4.46	1.52	1.20	1.14
DateWindow	6/10- 11/15/38	6/10- 11/15/38	6/10- 11/15/38	6/10- 11/15/38	6/10- 10/15/31	6/10- 9/15/25	6/10- 8/15/24

214

Exhibit 9.3 shows a GNMA with a 5.5% coupon, based on 6% underlying mortgage interest rates. The number at the very top (GN704426) is the pool number of the GNMA. That number is assigned by the GNMA when the developer obtains GNMA backing. The other long number (36296XSP0) is the CUSIP number which identifies the specific GNMA. The date (3/15/39) is the final maturity date for the GNMA, that is, the date when the very last mortgage in the pool will be totally paid down.

What follows is an explanation of the terms which you need to understand in order to evaluate the GNMA.

Face Amount, Factor, and Remaining Balance

These terms do not appear on the quote, but the corresponding numbers do. They are in the top box, on the left. The *face amount* is the initial amount of mortgage principal ($23,068,501) still outstanding for this particular security. Expressed as a decimal, the *factor* (0.753418690000) is the percentage of the mortgages in the pool that has not been paid down. (Factors are published by the GNMA for all outstanding GNMA mortgage pools.) Factors change over time. The *balance* ($17,380,240) is the principal amount of the original mortgages that has not been paid down, in dollars. The balance is calculated by multiplying the face amount by the factor. It is, in a sense, the current par value of this particular pool.

Next Pay, Record (rcd) Date, and Accrual

These are bookkeeping terms. *Next pay* (6/15/10, monthly) is the next date you would receive a check. As specified, the check will be paid once a month. *Accrual* indicates the amount of time interest has already accrued. Like accrued interest on municipal bonds, it will be added to the current offering price, when you buy the GNMA. The *record date* (5/31/10) is the date of record for the origination of the pool. The "14 delay" notation simply indicates that the servicer of the GNMA pool sends the check 14 days after receiving mortgage payments.

Current Offering Price

The current offering price (106.21) is stated in multiples of 100, as it is for any other bond. As is the case for Treasury bonds, the number after the decimal (.21) should be read as 21/32nds. The price therefore, would be $1060 plus 21/32 times $10.00, that is $1065.60. Even though this is a fairly recent GNMA, because it was issued with a coupon that is somewhat higher than one that would be issued at the time this is being written, it is trading at a premium. (GNMAs, like other bonds, can trade at a discount, at par, or at a premium.)

Prepayment Assumptions

For GNMAs, yield quotes are meaningless unless they are tied to specific prepayment assumptions. You will notice that several yields are quoted, starting with 2.9990 (2.99%) through -0.46 (negative 0.46%). Each yield is listed under a specific prepayment assumption, which is listed as "PSA" plus a number. This requires an explanation. Let's first explain how to interpret *prepayment assumptions* and PSA.

Prepayment assumptions have gone through a number of different formulations. The basic method used has been to compare the prepayment history of each pool to a benchmark. During the early 1990s, the benchmark most often used by brokers selling GNMAs to individual investors was based on the data compiled by the Federal Housing Administration. Periodically, the FHA published updates of past prepayment patterns, based on the latest nationwide figures. The GNMA maintained statistics for each pool, expressed as a percentage of current published "FHA experience"; that is, the latest FHA data. If prepayments were an exact match of FHA experience, the pool was said to prepay at 100% FHA experience; if at twice the speed, it was said to pay at 200%.

Using FHA experience as a yardstick, however, proved cumbersome because, whenever data were revised, so was FHA experience. In other words, the yardstick (FHA experience) kept on changing. To cope with this shortcoming, two other models came into use. The first to be developed was known as "constant prepayment rate" (CPR). As its name implies, CPR is a constant.

Prepayment patterns, which change continually, are expressed as multiples of CPR. The CPR for any period is the percentage of mortgages outstanding at the beginning of the period which terminate during that period. For example, if a pool of mortgages prepays at a constant rate of 1% per month, then 1% of the outstanding balance (in addition to scheduled principal repayments) will be prepaid each month.

Currently, the industry standard is the Public Securities Association (PSA) model. That model combines features from both of the preceding models. It is based on data published by the FHA. And like CPR, it assumes a rate of prepayment of principal. But that rate is not *one* constant. Rather, it is expressed as a series of prepayment rates for the entire life of the GNMA pool. The PSA benchmark (denoted as 100% PSA) assumes a series of CPRs that begin as 0.2% in the first month and increase by 0.2% each month thereafter. These prepayments level 30 months after mortgage origination to 6%. If a particular GNMA pool is said to prepay at 200% PSA experience, that would mean that for the first 30 months, principal would prepay at 0.4%, leveling off to 12% after 30 months.

An older GNMA pool will have a prepayment history. Older and new pools will both list a number of future prepayment scenarios.

Yield

The *yield*, technically, is called the *cash flow yield*. The yield is comparable to what is known for other bonds as yield-to-maturity. YTM, as you will recall, takes into account all the cash flows earned by a bond: interest; interest-on-interest (assumed to be based on reinvestment at the initial YTM rate); and redemption of the security at par.

You can readily see why quoting such a yield poses problems for a GNMA security. There is simply no way to predict when the mortgages that make up the GNMA will be paid off, or when prepayments will begin. This is where the prepayment assumptions become relevant. In order to quote a yield for a GNMA, estimates have to be made about prepayment possibilities. So instead of quoting just one yield, a typical Bloomberg quote, like the one above, lists a range of prepayment assumptions, based on specific PSA speeds. Those PSA speeds themselves are tied to a range of scenarios about changes in interest rate levels. This is very concentrated information. Starting from left to right, read:

0 bp. That means, if interest rates stay flat, we assume 508 PSA. The yield would then be 2.99%.

Next +300 bp. Read: if interest rates go up 300 basis points, PSA speeds slow down to 137. The yield would be 4.4987.%.

Let's move to the last number (–300 bp). Read: if interest rates decline by 300 bp, then prepayments speed up rapidly. We then assume a PSA speed of 1192. The yield would then actually be negative, that is, minus .46%.

None of these yields should be interpreted as a prediction of the actual return. Rather, the different scenarios indicate a possible range of returns, depending on what happens to interest rates, and how those changes affect prepayment speeds. In this particular example, because the the GNMA is selling at a premium, there is a significant range of possible yields. The range of possible yields would be equally wide for a GNMA trading at a discount. If a GNMA trades close to par, on the other hand, the range of possible yields is much narrower, with little difference between the lowest and the highest yield.

The reason the range is wider for a premium (or a discount GNMA) is that yield quotes are based on the assumption that prepayments occur at par, and that the GNMA is redeemed at par. Since the GNMA in Exhibit 9.3 is selling at a premium, faster prepayments would actually result in a loss of principal, and therefore, a negative yield.

Average Life and Duration

Duration (in this quote) is a measure of the volatility in the price of the bond in response to changes in the level of interest rates. But note that for this security, it is tied to another term, *average life*. Average life is a technical term that pinpoints the approximate point in a GNMA's life when half of the principal will have been paid back. If you are considering buying individual GNMAs, this number is important. The market prices GNMAs based on these midpoint measurements and totally ignores the final stated maturity date of the mortgages. In effect, this number is the market's estimate of how long the GNMA will remain outstanding.

If you are comparing a GNMA to other securities (Treasuries, for example), you would compare the cash flow yield of the GNMA to the YTM of a Treasury whose final maturity was about the same as the average life of the GNMA. For example, compare the cash flow yield of a GNMA with an estimated average life of two years to the YTM of a two-year Treasury; and one with an estimated average life of 12 years to a 12-year Treasury.

Note that the term "average life" is somewhat confusing. Even though the market treats this number as if it denotes the anticipated longevity of the security, in reality, average life describes the average number of years that each principal dollar will be outstanding. Average life is weighted for time and is related to speed of prepayments. The higher the prepayment speed, the shorter the average life.

In Exhibit 9.3, take a look at the numbers listed as possibilities for average life: they range from 2.95 years to 1.15 years. This is actually a fairly narrow range. This series of numbers pinpoints very precisely the risk you incur when you buy this security. It is impossible to predict how long it will remain outstanding. If interest rates go up, prepayments slow down. The GNMA then becomes a much longer security. If interest rates decline, on the other hand, prepayments speed up. The GNMA becomes much shorter.

Window

This is the date when you would start receiving payments and prepayments of principal. For GNMAs, the window is always open. That means you start receiving principal payments immediately. On this security, if you assume interest rates stay flat for the entire life of the GNMA—a most unlikely possibility—(the 0 bp assumption), you would receive principal for almost 30 years: from 6/20/10 to 11/15/28. If, on the other hand, you assume interest rates decline (–300 bp assumption), and if, as a result, pre-payments occur much more rapidly, most of the principal would have been repaid by 8/15/24. (As we will see later, for CMOs, there is a lock-out period so that the window is defined more narrowly.)

The only yield measurement that is computed for GNMAs exactly like that of other bonds is current yield, which, as you will remember is coupon divided by price. In Exhibit 9.3 the yield, 5.5%, is divided by the price, which is close to 100. Therefore, current yield is approximately also 5.2%.

Before proceeding further, a few important caveats are in order.

1. *Your total return will differ from any of the quoted yields.*

    GNMAs are sometimes purchased because the quoted yields appear high when compared to other high-quality credits such as Treasuries. So let's review the assumptions underlying the yield.

    This will make clear why it is highly unlikely that yield will actually be earned.

    The assumptions underlying the yield are:
    ◆ That all interest received will be reinvested rather than spent. Spending monthly payments will lower return.
    ◆ That interest and principal payments will be reinvested at the same rate as the quoted yields. This is highly unlikely for individual investors, particularly if the quoted yield is high. If, for example, the yield is 6%, and monthly checks are swept into a money market account, which yields less, then that too will lower the actual return.
    ◆ Quoted yields are tied to specific prepayment assumptions. In the event prepayments speed up or slow down substantially, the total return will differ considerably from any of the stated yields. Prepaid principal may be returned at a lower—or higher—price than your cost, resulting in capital gains or losses. Also, both principal and interest will then be reinvested at rates differing from the cash flow yield quoted at the time of purchase.
    ◆ Bear in mind that prepayment speeds will affect the price at which you can sell the GNMA if you need to sell before the GNMA is retired. Suppose, for example, that interest rates decline. Prepayments will speed up and that will shorten the

life of your GNMA. But this shorter life will not result in the same price changes for all GNMAs. If, for example, you bought a premium GNMA, and prepayments speed up, the principal is returned at par, and therefore, at less than your cost. Also, you now have to reinvest returned principal at a lower interest rate. In that event, if you need to sell, you sell at a loss. On the other hand, if you bought your GNMA at a discount, and prepayments speed up, principal is returned to you faster than initially anticipated, and at a price higher than your cost. This means you can sell at a profit.

2. *Don't confuse cash flow yield and monthly cash flow.*

   Yield measures only interest income. Cash flow is the total monthly check you receive, which includes three different items: regularly scheduled principal payments, prepayments of principal; and interest. Some dealers (or mutual funds) lump together both interest and principal and call it monthly income. That results in inflated yields. Remember that the principal is your own money that is being returned to you. It is not income.

3. *Bear in mind that prepayment patterns are not predictable.*

   Prepayment patterns have proved remarkably difficult to predict. During the early 1990s, the assumption, based on FHA experience, was that after 12 years only 17% of 30-year mortgages would still be outstanding. This assumption is no longer used.

Intuitively, the pattern of prepayments you might expect would be: low prepayments in the early years of a mortgage, acceleration thereafter; and finally, a leveling off in the later years. But significant changes in interest rates (and therefore in mortgage rates) have played havoc with prepayment assumptions. Large declines in interest rates such as those that occurred in 1993 and in 1998 caused massive prepayments and resulted in chaotic conditions in the GNMA market. Even this factor, however, is not consistent across GNMA pools. Some homeowners may behave in ways that do not seem to make economic sense. They may, for example, not refinance even if interest rates decline, because they may not be able to afford the cost of getting a new mortgage. They may also pay off existing mortgages with very low mortgage rates, just for the satisfaction of knowing they own their home free and clear. They may move for any number of reasons. All of this makes prepayment patterns of any one pool impossible to predict accurately.

One final note. Much of the preceding discussion may appear academic and irrelevant. But the reason for its inclusion is simple. GNMAs are purchased mainly for their higher yield compared to other securities with high credit quality. Therefore, it is important to understand how prepayments will affect your total return. The quote illustrated in Exhibit 9.3 is intended to clarify the uncertainties you face when you buy a GNMA. I have gone into a lot of details because if you are considering buying a GNMA you should insist on seeing a detailed yield table, such as the one shown in Exhibit 9.3. Some brokers quote only one yield. But that is misleading.

Before turning to other mortgage-backed securities, let us note that all the terms used to describe GNMAs apply equally to all securities that are described in the remaining sections of this chapter. If you are considering purchase of any mortgage-backed security, you should insist at least on a verbal description of the key terms in the yield table, and better still, on being shown a quote on paper.

Differences among Par, Discount, and Premium GNMAs

Because GNMAs have been issued since the mid–1970s, GNMAs are available with coupons ranging from 4% to 10%. Whatever the coupon, yields are clustered somewhere around 4% at the time this is being written. As a general rule, you can estimate the yield on GNMAs will be somewhere around 1/2 of 1% lower than the cost of 30-year mortgages. New GNMAs are constantly coming to market. Consequently, you can purchase GNMAs trading at a discount, at a premium, or at par. Each has advantages and disadvantages.

The *par GNMA* is the easiest to understand. GNMAs normally trade at par only when they are issued. They would therefore have no prepayment history and would be priced based on average expectations. Typically, for GNMAs with underlying mortgages of 30 years, average life might be anticipated to be about 12 years. Nonetheless, the Bloomberg will list a variety of prepayment assumptions and cash flow yields. Since none of the mortgages in par pools have yet been prepaid, par GNMAs are likely to be outstanding longer than either discount or premium GNMAs. Note that at the current time, you can also find GNMA pools based on underlying mortgages of 15 years or of seven years. Average life for these would be considerably shorter than for the GNMAs based on 30-year mortgages.

Discount GNMAs have coupons that are lower than current interest rates on mortgages. If interest rates remain stable, prepayments are less likely to speed up, since coupon rates are lower than current rates. Mortgages would be prepaid mainly for considerations other than interest rates. Therefore, cash flow is a little more predictable than for par GNMAs.

On the other hand, discount GNMAs are more interest rate sensitive than either par or premium GNMAs. This translates into steeper price increases or declines as interest rates fluctuate. Again, the reason for this is to be found in prepayment patterns. If interest rates decline, prepayments occur faster than anticipated. This boosts total return because prepaid principal which was purchased at a discount (since this is a discount GNMA) is returned at par. But if interest rates rise, prepayments slow. Average life becomes longer, and the longer maturities cause price declines to accelerate. Discount GNMAs then plummet in price.

Premium GNMAs were issued at a time when interest rates were higher than current rates. They, too, are older pools. In the event that interest rates rise, the high coupon acts as a brake and cushions against declines in price. Therefore, premium GNMAs are a hedge against rising rates.

But the high coupon can be a disadvantage if interest rates decline, particularly if the fall is steep. In that event, prepayments can speed up significantly. You will then have to reinvest both principal and interest at significantly lower rates. In all likelihood, you will hold the GNMA for less time than you initially expected. Ultimate total return will then be far lower than initially anticipated.

Also, steep declines in interest rates constitute a particular risk to anyone who purchases a GNMA at a premium. That is because the principal amounts of the mortgages, purchased at a premium (remember: this is a premium GNMA) are prepaid at par. Speedier prepayments always translate into capital losses for premium GNMAs. If the prepayments occur shortly after purchase, this can result in a very significant loss of principal.

Varieties of GNMAs

While GNMAs on single-family homes were the initial prototype, the market expanded to include a variety of GNMA pools. The cash flows of any of these pools are analyzed in the same manner, but the underlying mortgages differ. These are the main types still in the market.

GNMA I pools. Those are the "plain vanilla" GNMAs, such as the prototype just analyzed. They are composed of 12 (or more) fixed-rate 20-to-30-year mortgages and they total at least $1 million face value, all issued at the same interest rate.

Midgets. Those are composed of underlying mortgages with a 15-year maturity. Average lives would be much shorter than for GNMA I pools. Because of this maturity difference, GNMA midgets trade at a premium to regular GNMAs with the same coupons.

GNMA II pools. These have been issued only since 1983. They differ from GNMA I pools in a number of ways:

◆ They are larger than GNMA I pools.

◆ They are based on multiple rather than single issuer pools.

◆ They have a wider range of interest rates than the original.

The larger size of the pool serves to even out prepayments somewhat. But because of the varieties of coupons and maturities, they are more difficult to analyze than GNMA I pools. They generally yield a bit more for that reason.

GNMA GPMs. GPM stands for "graduated mortgage payments." These are based, not on fixed rate, but on graduated mortgage payments. The cash flows are even more complex than for ordinary GNMAs. Also, the market for these is smaller and less liquid than for ordinary GNMAs.

GNMA mobile homes. These are based on mortgages for mobile homes. They have a shorter history than other GNMAs and have not been as exhaustively analyzed.

Stripped Mortgage-Backed Securities

Like any other bond, mortgage-backed securities can be stripped.

Several types of strips exist, including interest-only (IO) strips and principal-only (PO) strips. There are also two classes of "floaters": floaters and inverse floaters. These are strips with floating rates. The coupon of a floater moves with interest rates. The coupon of an inverse floater moves in a direction counter to interest rates. These strips are all extremely sensitive to interest rate changes, and they are all highly volatile.

To understand some of the reasons behind the extreme volatility, ask yourself what would happen to any of these strips if interest rates move up or down. Let's use the interest-only strip as an example. An IO has no par value. Bear in mind that interest rate payments continue only on mortgages that remain outstanding. Therefore, the IO will receive interest payments only as long as underlying mortgages remain outstanding. Clearly, if interest rates decline, prepayments will speed up. As a result, interest payments to the interest-only strip will diminish and possibly disappear altogether. In this instance, a decline in interest rates, which ordinarily causes bond prices to rise, can lead to disastrous price declines for interest-only strips. On the other hand, if interest rates rise, the IO strip may also decline.

Strips based on mortgage-backed securities are as volatile as the more volatile zero coupon bonds, but much less predictable. I mention these securities only to alert you to their existence and to their volatility. Any detailed analysis of these securities is beyond the scope of this book. They are used primarily by managers of institutional portfolios, as a tool for hedging. Using them as standalone securities is highly speculative.

CMOS AND OTHER SONS OF GNMA

Between the late 1990s and 2007, the mortgage-backed sector underwent enormous changes. By the end of the 1990s, GNMAs were no longer the largest segment of the mortgage-backed market. Several developments were responsible. Initial variations were of three kinds

◆ Asset-backed securities based on cash flows other than
   mortgages
◆ Restructured cash flows
◆ Who backs the mortgages

Asset-Backed Securities Based on
Cash Flows Other Than Mortgages

Almost any type of loan can be repackaged and resold as an asset-backed bond. Beginning in the late 1980s, many types of loans in addition to mortgages were so repackaged. The largest segment of that market was based on credit card loans. Smaller sectors were based on automobile loans, mobile homes, and the like.

Credit card loans currently make up the largest segment of the asset-backed market. Bonds created out of these loans may be very short: under one year. But the structure of asset-backed loans backed by credit cards is different from that of mortgage-backed securities. A large number of factors affect the credit quality of these loans. Among them are the underwriting standards of the credit card company; the number of credit card holders who fail to pay off their credit card loans; and the structure of the security, which differs considerably from that of other asset-backed or mortgage-backed securities.

Pass-through securities backed by these types of debt instruments expanded significantly between 2000 and 2006 although they remained primarily institutional products. But they too were repackaged into collateralized debt obligations (see below) and, as such, also were part and parcel of the ongoing credit crisis of 2007 and 2008.

Restructured Cash Flows: Collateralized Mortgage Obligations (CMOs)

Let us now look at the repackaging of GNMAs into collateralized mortgage obligations (CMOs).

Repackaging GNMAs into CMOs actually goes back to 1983. Another term that is now used interchangeably with CMOs is "REMIC," which stands for "real estate mortgage investment conduit."

Initially, this innovation was intended to eliminate some of the uncertainties arising from the unpredictability of prepayments. For many years, it was considered CMOs did, in fact, achieve that goal. CMOs were so successful that they became a larger sector of the market than GNMAs.

CMOs consist of cash flows from mortgage-backed securities that have been diced and sliced and redivided (in Wall Street terms: "restructured"). The cash flows of the underlying securities are redirected and reconstituted into a series of bonds with more predictable average lives and prepayments than the original.

CMOs are based on much larger pools than GNMAs, ranging in size from $50 million to $1 billion. Each deal has features unique and specific to that particular CMO. The key difference between older mortgage-backed securities and CMOs is that CMO payment streams are redistributed to a number of different "tranches" ("tranche" is a French word meaning slice or portion). A CMO may have as few as three or as many as 50 different tranches.

The simplest CMOs are what would be called today *sequential pay* or "plain vanilla" CMOs. To illustrate how that works, let us assume that we are putting together a CMO, comprised of several GNMA pools. The CMO will have three tranches. All three tranches receive interest payments.

Unscheduled prepayments, however, are sent *sequentially* to each tranche. The first tranche (or slice) receives all unscheduled prepayments made, say, during the first three years. Thereafter, that tranche is retired. In effect, it would be sold initially as a bond with an approximate three-year maturity. Unscheduled prepayments made during the next three years then go to the second tranche. That tranche is then retired, say, in eight years. The third tranche would then receive all remaining prepayments. The whole idea is to make the time the CMO remains outstanding more predictable. Investors seeking shorter-term maturities would buy the earlier tranches. Investors seeking longer-term securities would invest in the later tranches. The buyers of the later tranches would initially receive only interest payments. They would not receive prepayments until earlier tranches had been retired.

In all CMOs, interest payments vary with the perceived riskiness of the tranches. The shortest and least risky tranches receive lower interest payments. Longer or riskier tranches receive higher interest payments. The more uncertainty, the higher the planned interest payments. But remember that due to prepayment uncertainties, the timing of all payments remains uncertain.

Companions, Planned Amortization Tranches, and Targeted Amortization Class

The sequential CMO structure seemed to solve many of the uncertainties associated with GNMA pools. But once more, interest rates failed to cooperate. In 1993, interest rates declined precipitously. As a result, massive prepayments occurred: average lives of CMOs shortened dramatically. In 1994, however, interest rates did an about-turn. The Federal Reserve Bank raised interest rates seven times. Suddenly, prepayments slowed down to a crawl.

This is the exact reverse of prepayment risk, and in fact it has been given a name: *extension risk*. That risk is based on what happened to the anticipated prepayment patterns of CMOs in 1994. Since prepayments dried up, the average lives of CMOs became totally unpredictable. Tranches that were issued with anticipated average lives of two or three years suddenly were treated by the market as if their maturity had been extended to much longer terms. The price of these tranches plummeted.

To further limit this risk, another innovation occurred in the structure of CMOs. Two new types of tranches were created: *planned amortization class* (PAC) and *companions*. The idea behind these two types of tranches is that the role of the companion is to protect the cash flows of the PAC tranches by absorbing either earlier prepayments or later prepayments. This is accomplished by redirecting prepayment cash flows that occur either too early or too late for the desired maturity of the PAC tranche to the companion tranche. Because it absorbs unscheduled or unwanted prepayments, the companion tranche is clearly the more volatile, and riskier, of the two types of tranches. For that reason, it usually sells with a higher yield. Companion tranches with the least predictable prepayment patterns have the highest yields.

The structure of CMOs divided into PACs and companions varies with each deal, as does the number of tranches. The schedule of principal prepayments is based on prepayment rates known as "PAC bands." These bands are targeted at a percentage of PSA speed: for example, 95% of PSA speed for early prepayments and 240% of PSA speed for later prepayments. This would enable the issuer to target cash flows to the PAC in a tighter maturity range. The average life of the PAC, theoretically, is then much more predictable; much less elastic than it would be without the PAC bands.

A similar but somewhat less tightly defined structure involves tranches called *targeted amortization class* (TAC) and companions. You may also encounter the term "busted PAC," which indicates that the companion bands of a PAC have already absorbed all the prepayments that could have been targeted to it. As a result, the PAC is now "busted." That means that it is now trading without support, very much like older GNMA pools: it has become a less predictable, less liquid security, and for that reason it is likely to be quoting a higher cash flow yield.

Note also that as the market has continued to evolve, ever more complex structures have been devised. Some CMOs now come to market with several layers of PACs and several layers of companions.

The "Z" or Accrual Tranche

There is one more type of tranche that you might encounter: the "Z" or "accrual" tranche. The CMO structures described earlier (sequential pay, PAC, TAC, and companion) all redirect prepayments of principal. The Z or accrual tranche redirects payments of both principal and interest.

Think of the Z as resembling zero coupon bonds. A Z tranche receives no payments of any kind—either interest or principal—until specified tranches are retired. (This is called interest and principal lockout.) When the CMO comes to market, the Z tranche has a very small face value. During the years of principal and interest lockout, the Z tranche generates coupon interest at the same coupon rate as other tranches in the CMO, but this coupon interest is not paid out. Interest payments are said to "accrete," which is another way of saying they are added on to the original price of the Z bond, on a monthly basis. Once the classes preceding the Z bond are paid down, the Z bond begins to receive both principal and interest payments, based on the "accreted" value.

When Z tranches first came to the market, they were typically the last tranche of any CMO deal and invariably, therefore, had extremely long average lives. That is no longer the case: Z bonds can now be placed at different stages of the CMO structure. Z tranches have much the same appeal as zero coupon strips: during the accretion phase, there is no reinvestment risk. But because the average life of Z bonds (particularly those which are the last tranche of a CMO deal) is difficult to predict, these can be extremely volatile. For that reason, the yield is high: the higher the uncertainty, the higher the yield.

Let's sum up some of the key points concerning CMOs.

CMOs are a structure compatible with any guarantor. There have been CMOs backed by GNMA, FNMA, FHLB, and private corporations. Some older CMOs that have become illiquid have been recycled into newer CMOs.

With the exception of Z (accrual) tranches, most CMOs pay interest monthly. Most CMOs have a principal lockout period, during which only interest payments are received. The period during which payments of principal are received is known as the "payment window." Both the payment window and the lockout period may change once the CMO is outstanding, depending on what happens to interest rates and how those changes in interest rates affect prepayments.

While companion tranches and Z tranches are designed to lessen the uncertainties associated with cash flows of CMOs, they limit but do not eliminate prepayment risk. Sudden sharp changes in interest rate levels can play havoc with planned maturity structures and cash flows.

Advantages and Disadvantages of the CMO Structure

The CMO structure was intended to lessen some of the cash flow uncertainties inherent in older pass-throughs. This is particularly true for PACs and for earlier tranches in sequential pay (plain vanilla) deals. These tranches protect the buyer from both interest rate risk and prepayment risk. As a result, they yield less than later tranches or companion tranches.

If you wanted to lock in a higher yield for a longer period of time, you would buy the later tranches of a sequential pay deal. By so doing, you would enjoy, in effect, a kind of call protection, since the later tranches cannot receive any principal repayments until earlier tranches are retired. For higher yield, you could also buy either companion tranches or Z (accrual) tranches.

Finally, let's put the risks of CMOs into even plainer English. The intention behind the CMO structure was that, given their high credit quality, you could assume that you would get your money back. You just could not be sure precisely when you would get it back, particularly for later tranches in sequential pay CMOs, companion tranches, or Z tranches. The theory was that, in spite of the complex nature of CMO deals, CMOs as a group would better meet the needs of individual investors than GNMAs: Their structure would result in a higher degree of predictability than older pass-throughs. In addition, they could be purchased for as little as $1,000 minimum investment.

AGENCY BACKING OF MORTGAGE-BACKED SECURITIES: GINNIE, FANNIE, AND FREDDIE

Up until the late 1990s, all CMOs were backed by government agencies. In addition to the GNMA, the two others were the Federal National Mortgage Association (FNMA), colloquially known as Fannie Mae and the Federal Home Loan Mortgage Corporation (FHLMC), colloquially known as Freddie Mac. Up until 2006, securities backed by any of these agencies were perceived to be equally creditworthy. But from the beginning, they operated somewhat differently and had different government backing.

The oldest of these is actually Fannie Mae, which was created by Congress in 1938 to provide liquidity for the mortgage market. In 1968, the original FNMA was separated into two different organizations: GNMA and FNMA. The third agency, Freddie Mac was initially owned by the 12 Federal Home Loan Banks. But in 1989, it too became a private corporation, much like FNMA.

All three agencies were created by Congress in order to increase the amount of capital available for housing loans. But they operate differently. GNMA remains a government agency. As noted above, it buys mortgages insured by FHA and the VA. Those mortgages are repackaged and guaranteed by the GNMA.

Both Fannie Mae and Freddie Mac were rechartered by Congress as private institutions to establish a secondary market for conventional mortgages, that is, for loans that were not insured by either the VA or the FHA.

Neither Fannie Mae nor Freddie Mac actually issues mortgages. Fannie Mae buys mortgages from mortgage lenders such as banks and mortgage companies. Those are repackaged into mortgage-backed securities including CMOs. Fannie Mae finances these purchases by issuing its own debt instruments: bills, bonds, and notes. Fannie Mae is one of the largest issuers of debt. Up until 2006, Fannie Mae's securities sold at a spread to Treasuries of perhaps 50 to 100 basis points. Freddie Mac operates in a manner similar to Fannie Mae.

But the differences do not end there. GNMA has always been, and remains, a government agency. Its securities enjoy direct government guarantees. Both Fannie Mae and Freddie Mac are what are known as government-sponsored enterprises (GSEs). They are both publicly traded corporations whose stock trades on the New York Stock Exchange. However, they both have the ability to borrow directly from the U.S. Treasury. Up until the financial crisis of 2007, that ability conferred an *implicit* AAA rating on the debt of both of these agencies. Essentially, up to the middle of 2007, the market treated the securities issued by the three agencies as equally creditworthy. In fact, the largest segment of that market were the bonds issued by Fannie Mae.

But bear in mind that the mortgages purchased by Fannie Mae and Freddie Mac were not insured. Between 2003 and 2006, many of these mortgages turned out to be "subprime" (see below). Both Fannie Mae and Freddie Mac suffered devastating losses.

How CMOs Changed:
Private-Label Mortgages

Between 2003 and 2006, several new types of securities were created that further transformed the market for mortgage-backed securities. The first development was the creation of CMOs that did not have agency backing. These were known as "private-label" pass-throughs.

Between 2000 and 2007, there was a huge expansion of this sector of the market. Private-label CMOs were issued by banks, by investment banks, and by thrifts. Initially, these private-label CMOs were based on so-called jumbo mortgages. These were very large mortgages typically taken out by affluent homebuyers. Prepayment patterns for these mortgages were somewhat different than those of less affluent buyers. But credit quality was not affected. Neither was liquidity. These private-label CMOs were rated by the rating agencies, and for a number of years, the ratings were mainly AAA and AA.

Starting in 2003, new types of mortgages became the basis for a large and ever-increasing number of private-label CMOs. These were mortgages issued with much looser underwriting standards than those that had prevailed in the past. To quote an authority on the bond market, "These loans are primarily classified as 'limited documentation,' where the borrower is missing a standard credit history, documented source of income, or some other standard input used in credit scoring models".[1]

In other words, most of these new mortgages were variations of "subprime" mortgages, going under euphemistic names. Many mortgages also had "bells and whistles" such as teaser rates designed to reset at a later date (at which time payments might go a lot higher) or 100% financing (meaning mortgages were issued without any down payment). These bells and whistles made it easier to take out mortgages, but much more difficult to actually repay them. In the industry, these mortgages also went under the nickname NINA mortgages (standing for "no income, no assets"). Another term for these mortgages was "liar loans."

Why would banks issue mortgages using such loose underwriting standards? Not to worry: It was assumed housing prices would continue to rise. In the event borrowers were unable to pay, the banks could repossess the house and be made whole. But also remember: Few banks kept the mortgages on their books. Most mortgages were promptly sold and repackaged into some kind of mortgage-backed security.

These private-label pools had no agency backing of any kind. Nonetheless, even mortgage-backed securities based on liar loans or NINA mortgages continued to be rated mostly AA and AAA. Rating agencies justified the ratings by pointing to "credit enhancements," primarily "overcollateralization." What that means is that assets generating cash flows dedicated to paying debt were higher than the sums required for servicing the debt; for example, 125% of the amount needed to service debt.

In retrospect, it is clear that the high ratings were based on faulty assumptions. Most CMOs were made up of very large pools that were geographically diverse. The rating agencies assumed that it was highly unlikely that losses would take place at the same time in all parts of the country. But that is what, in fact, happened. It also became clear, in retrospect, that the mathematical models used to evaluate the risk profiles of subprime mortgage pools were elegant and sophisticated—but the data used in building the models was flawed or insufficient. Many models were based on as little as five years of data.

---

1. Fabozzi, *The Handbook of Fixed Income Securities*, McGraw-Hill, 2005, p. 567.

It is estimated that by 2006, approximately 50% of mortgage-backed securities were based on subprime mortgages. In 2006, housing prices began to decline everywhere in the United States. As housing prices began to decline, many of the homeowners who had bought NINA or other subprime mortgages suddenly realized that they owed more on their mortgages than the house was worth. Many of the homebuyers just walked away. Suddenly, servicers ceased receiving cash flows. This started a chain reaction of losses. CMOS, which had been rated AAA by the major rating agencies were downgraded to junk virtually overnight. The price of these securities plummeted.

What made these losses particularly troublesome is that it was impossible to estimate the extent of current and future losses. As a result, it became nearly impossible to rate any security based on potentially problematic losses, and equally impossible to price it. Since many of these securities were part of bank capital, or collateral to back financing, the capital base of many institutions started to crumble.

COLLATERALIZED DEBT OBLIGATIONS (CDOs) AND COLLATERALIZED DEBT SWAPS (CDSs)

From 2003 onward, two more types of pass through securities were developed: collateralized debt obligations (CDOs) and collateralized debt swaps (CDSs). These were much more complex than GNMAs or CMOs.

CDOs

In one sense, collateralized debt obligations are simply a more evolved, more elaborate form of CMOs. Their structure is similar to that of CMOs. CDOs consist of extremely large pools of debt obligations subdivided into tranches consisting of senior tranches and less senior tranches. The main differences between CMOs and CDOs is that CDOs were made up of much larger pools; and each pool was much more complex. As is the case with CMOs, each CDO is unique. And the number of tranches varies with each deal.

What makes these instruments so fiendishly complicated is that each of the tranches of cash-generating assets was itself incredibly complex. To quote Fabozzi, again, a CDO "is an asset backed security (ABS) backed by a diversified pool of *one or more* of the following types of debt obligations: investment-grade and high-yield corporate bonds, emerging market bonds, residential mortgage-backed securities (RMBS), commercial mortgage-backed securities (CMBS), asset-backed securities, real estate investment trusts (REIT) debt, bank loans, special-situation loans and distressed debt, or *other CDOs* [italics mine]"[2] In other words, each tranche is itself a highly complex pool of assets with a unique and complicated risk profile, including, in the case of a so-called "CDOs-squared," the riskier tranches of other CDOs.

In simpler language, CDOs were subdivided into tranches, each with its own rating, risk profile, and pricing. But given the incredible complexity of the deals, in actuality, the "analytics" behind these profiles amounted to little more than guesswork: mathematical models built (like the analytics underlying simpler CMOs) on faulty assumptions and insufficient data.

Credit Default Swaps: CDSs

On to the final type of mortgage-related security: credit default swaps (CDSs). These are also called "synthetic CDOs." In simple language, CDSs were bets that some CDOs were going to go bust. They were a type of insurance, but a rather weird type of "insurance." What is unique about CDOs is that, much of the time, the CDOs were owned by a third party (in other words, not owned by the buyer of the insurance). Why would anyone buy insurance on a security they did not own? Well, there is a very neat explanation for that. If the CDO went bust, the owner of the CDO took a big hit. But the purchaser of the CDS (i.e., the owner of the insurance) would get to collect on the "insurance."

Of course, in the daily press or professional literature, that was not the way these securities were described. Instead, they were described in mysterious and somewhat impenetrable jargon. But if you understand the nature of the product, the jargon becomes clear. Again, to quote Fabozzi: "A *synthetic* CDO is so named because the CDO does not actually own the pool of assets on which it has the risk. Stated differently, a synthetic CDO absorbs the economic risks but not the legal ownership of its reference credit exposures.... The building block for synthetic CDOs is a credit default swap, which allows counterparties to transfer the credit risk but not the legal ownership of underlying assets. A protection buyer purchases protection against default risk on a reference pool of assets. Those assets can consist of any combination of loans, bonds, derivatives, or receivables".[3]

---

2. Frank Fabozzi, et al., The Handbook of Fixed Income Securities, 7th Edition, McGraw Hill, 2005, p. 669.

3. Fabozzi, *Fixed Income Securities*, 2005, p. 669.

In some respects, these transactions were analogous to transactions surrounding any insurance. "The CDS is a contract between a protection buyer and a protection seller. Under this agreement, the protection buyer pays a premium to the protection seller in return for payment if a credit event (typically bankruptcy, failure to pay, or restructuring) occurs with respect to the reference entity."[4] Note the allusion to "the reference entity." Fabozzi's wording reiterates that the "insurance" is taken out on assets owned not by the buyer of the insurance, but by a third party.

Note also another major difference between swaps and conventional "insurance" contracts. Insurance companies are required to hold reserves against the insurance they sell, in case they need to pay out claims. Sellers of swaps were not required to have any reserves against the swaps (some claim the reason they were called swaps rather than insurance was precisely in order to skirt the requirement to hold reserves against potential claims).

The motivation of the protection seller is easy to understand: That party makes money by selling the insurance. Moreover, if the insurance seller considers it unlikely that "a credit event" will ever occur, then that seller of credit default swaps may assume he is engaging in a virtually riskless transaction. That was the assumption of most sellers of swaps.

The motivation of the buyer of protection is less clear. The most charitable interpretation is that buying swaps may be viewed as analogous to "shorting" a stock which is also not "owned"; in other words, as a kind of hedge against a decline in some sector of the mortgage-backed or CDO market. But a more cynical view is that swaps basically amounted to bets that some CDOs (or other mortgage-backed asset) would go bust. This was legalized gambling. Moreover, if a firm had good information, or thought it did, that the portfolio holdings of some firm such as Lehman Brothers had lots of troubled assets, then a smart move, to "short" Lehman Brothers, would have been to buy CDSs against it.

Whatever their motivation, swaps became the fastest growing segment of the asset-backed market. It was, moreover, an international market. (In fact, swaps seem to have originated in Europe.) The market for swaps at one time dwarfed any other market in existence. By some estimates, it was several times higher than the GDP of the entire planet. (These estimates, it should be noted, are based on "notional" amounts of the swaps. The concept of "notional" amounts can be defined by analogy: Suppose you buy fire insurance for your house worth $500,000 at a cost of $1,000 per year. The "notional" amount of the insurance is the value of the house. The

---

4. Fabozzi, *Fixed Income Securities*, 2005, p. 699.

actual cash outlay for the insurance is $1,000.) Basically, estimates of the "notional" amounts of swaps result in extraordinarily large numbers that are all over the map. While the exact numbers are uncertain, what is certain is that the numbers were so large as to be virtually beyond comprehension.

THE FINANCIAL CRISIS: 2007–2008

The financial crisis, in retrospect, includes very clear event milestones. The crisis that began with defaults in subprime mortgages took a sudden and giant step forward when the U.S. Treasury under Secretary Henry Paulson forced the sale of Bear Stearns to J. P. Morgan. This was followed by the bankruptcy of Lehman Brothers.

The market seized up almost immediately. Why? A multitude of reasons. First, many CDO and CDS securities were so complex that rating them, or pricing them, was basically guesswork. Rumors began to spread that assets on the books of certain institutions including a number of well-known investment banks and commercial banks were difficult to value or full of uncertain losses. Firms were unable to obtain credit; hedge funds pulled their money out of investment banks; and so on. Firms stopped trading with other firms because they feared they would not be repaid. Banks stopped lending because they feared the loans would not be repaid. As soon as suspicions became rampant that a firm was trying to sell assets in order to raise cash, this was taken as a sign that that firm was in dire financial straits. Such a firm trying to sell assets, or borrow, found that buyers evaporated or bids came in at fire sale levels—and declined from there.

There is no need to go into details about the "bailout" that brought an end to the panic. Suffice it to say that in order to keep the financial system of the country afloat, the federal government injected massive amounts of money into the largest banks and a number of major financial institutions such as AIG. As part of the bailouts extended by the government to financial institutions, both Fannie Mae and Freddie Mac were basically taken over by the government. As this is being written technically, both are under "conservatorship"; they are about 80% "owned" by the government (i.e., the U.S. taxpayers). As a result, all bonds issued by both agencies still have an explicit government guarantee. At some point in the future, however, both agencies may be re-privatized. But there is as yet to real information about the future structure of either Fannie or Freddie. The future status of the implicit government guarantee will depend on how Fannie and Freddie are reorganized.

At the time of writing, proposals are being considered for legislative reforms designed to prevent another crisis, but final legislation has not been passed. Some of the proposals under consideration would affect CDOs, CDSs, and Fannie and Freddie. But at this point, proposals are still vague.

CURRENT STATE OF THE MORTGAGE-BACKED AND ASSET-BACKED SECURITIES MARKET

At the time this is being written, while the atmosphere of crisis has abated, the mortgage-backed and asset-backed securities market remains deeply scarred by the financial crisis. Millions of mortgages remain in default; and more foreclosures are on the horizon. And numerous question marks overhang the future of this sector of the bond market.

The first question is how the eventual unwinding of this crisis will affect interest rates. In 2008–2009, much of the activity in this sector of the market has centered on the Federal Reserve. Beginning in 2008, as part of the "bailout" program, the Federal Reserve undertook a program of buying mortgage-backed securities from banks and from other major financial institutions. The Federal Reserve purchased well over 1 trillion dollars of these securities. These purchases include the so-called "toxic assets"; you will remember that these were the various securities that were defaulting because they were based on subprime mortgages. The Federal Reserve made these purchases for several reasons: to keep mortgage rates low and also to inject "liquidity" (i.e., money) into the financial system. The Federal Reserve, as planned, stopped buying mortgage-backed securities in March 2010. One major question mark hanging over the bond market is what the Federal Reserve plans to do with all of these securities.

At the time this is being written, the Federal Reserve has not let it be known what its exit strategy is likely to be. The Federal Reserve has actually been selling some of these securities all along to hedge funds and to some large mutual fund groups. It could continue these sales. It may sell its entire remaining portfolio at some future date. But it could also hold on to many of these securities until they mature, i.e., until the mortgages are retired. The Federal Reserve is weighing its options carefully because massive selling of these securities could trigger a rise in interest rates. So this uncertainty will continue to overhang the mortgage-backed market in all likelihood for a number of years.

A second question mark concerns the regulation of the CDO and CDS securities, which are blamed for much of the crisis. Prior to the financial crisis, and up to the time this is being written, both CDOs and CDSs were being traded completely over the counter with no regulations of any kind. CDOs and CDSs have always been institutional products, designed for large financial institutions. They were never intended for individual investors. That market is quietly continuing to operate—largely out of public view. We might note in passing that the cost of CDSs appears to have become an accepted proxy for measuring risk. Discussions concerning the finances of an institution often allude to the fact that the costs of insuring swaps on that institution are rising as proof that it is experiencing increasing financial difficulties. One proposal being contemplated is the creation of an exchange that would place certain requirements on the trading activity of CDOs and CDSs and other derivatives. This is being resisted by many large financial institutions because trading these securities has been, and presumably continues to be, hugely profitable. If an exchange is created by new financial regulations, that may bring more transparency to the market. But at the moment, this is very much up in the air.

You may well wonder why, since CDOs and CDSs are institutional products, they are described in this chapter. There are two reasons for this. One is that these securities played a major role in the financial crisis of 2008 and 2009. At the time of writing, they are continuing to be issued and traded without any regulations. A second reason is that the history of this market is that at some point securities designed for institutions are re-packaged for individual investor consumption. These are volatile and extraordinarily complex products. And that is not likely to change.

A third question mark concerns the future of the CMO market. During 2008 and 2009, this sector of the market had largely ground to a halt. Basically no new CMOs were issued during this period, although older ones continued to be traded, largely among institutional investors and hedge funds. Nonetheless, at the time of writing, a couple of new CMO deals appear to be in the pipeline. They are being structured very carefully with high-quality underlying mortgages. If these deals are successful, this market may begin to revive and operate as it did in the past, with CMOs being re-packaged for individual investor consumption. This is likely to happen, moreover, if interest rates rise, and as investors seeking higher yields begin to dip their toes in this market.

Finally, for individual investors, this market remains dramatically different from its incarnation prior to the financial crisis. Private label CMOs, or CMOs backed by Fannie and Freddie, that had been the backbone of this market between 2000 and 2007 are simply not available to individual investors. I consulted a number of brokers to try to find out why. One reason I was given is that it is not clear what type of mortgages had been repackaged in these securities; do they include subprime mortgages, for example? Another is that brokers are unable to tell investors what tranches are in the CMO; is it a more risky or a less risky tranche? (Remember that CMOs may hold 50 to 100 tranches.)

At the time of writing, the brokers I consulted were selling only the plainest and most straightforward GNMA I pools—no GNMA II pools, no CMOs, no asset-backed securities. When and how this market will come back is unclear.

Note also that as this is being written online brokers do not list mortgage-backed securities on their Web sites. If you would like to investigate buying a mortgage-backed security, you need to ask a broker to find such a security.

Note, however, that investors can buy Fannie Mae and Freddie Mac agencies. Those are not mortgage-backed securities. Rather, those are debt issued by both of these agencies. As long as Fannie and Freddie are under government conservatorship, these agency securities carry the explicit guarantee of the government and are rated AAA. Note also that the price of these securities is now being published along with that of other agencies both on FINRA and on Investinginbonds.com.

Finally, note that getting price or trading information on mortgage-backed securities will continue to be difficult. As noted in Chapter 5, FINRA will undertake a pilot project gathering data on mortgage-backed securities in 2011, but not for public dissemination.

Tax Considerations

In case this market comes back, you need to be aware of the particular tax treatment of these securities. Taxes on any type of mortgage-backed security are a bit of a nightmare. Interest on any mortgage-backed security is subject to federal and state taxes. Return of principal is not. Therefore, make sure you know how much of your cash flow is interest and how much is principal. If you own any pass-throughs, it is essential to maintain good records. Otherwise you will overpay your taxes.

In addition, if you sell your mortgage-backed security before final payments cease, you may incur either a capital gain or a capital loss (depending on the difference between the price you paid and the price at which you are selling). When prepayments occur, they too may subject you to a capital gain or a capital loss.

Because the tax considerations of pass-throughs are complex, if you have a large portfolio of these securities, it is advisable to consult with a tax adviser or accountant.

SUMMARY

In conclusion, mortgage-backed securities offer the buyer certain advantages, such as credit safety, monthly payments, and a high cash flow. GNMAs were the first and remain the prototype for mortgage-backed securities. But they had significant disadvantages. Prepayment patterns proved remarkably difficult to predict. As a result, total return was uncertain; and reinvestment risk very high. At the time of writing, government backing behind GNMAs has held up that sector of the market. But bear in mind that the government guarantee does not eliminate either prepayment risk or interest rate risk.

CMOs were intended to reduce some of the cash flow uncertainties associated with GNMAs. The subprime mortgage crisis, however, introduced a totally unanticipated risk: default risk. CMO credit ratings went from AAA to junk virtually overnight. And between 2008 and 2009, the CMO market ground to a halt. How long it will take for it to recover is still unclear.

Some brokers are selling GNMAs, but only the plainest, easiest to understand GNMA 1 pools, which are those basically made up of 30-year mortgages, all issued with the same mortgage rate. The following are some the points you would want to remember before buying a GNMA:

- It makes no sense to buy GNMAs unless the yields are higher than Treasuries by a meaningful amount. That level varies with interest rates. But it should be higher than 100 basis points.
- Ask to see cash flow yield based on a variety of prepayment assumptions. Make sure those assumptions are spelled out in terms of prepayment speeds.
- Remember to compare GNMAs to Treasuries on the basis of the estimated average life and not the stated final maturity.

If you want to purchase such a security, be sure to buy it from a broker, who will show you a yield table and discuss possible prepayment assumptions. Be sure that you understand how faster or slower prepayments would affect the particular security you are considering. Would the security go up in price or down in price if interest rates rise (or if they fall)? Would faster or slower prepayments mean you would hold the security longer or less time?

At the time of writing, one reason CMOs are hard to find is that no new ones have been issued between 2008 and 2009. When new ones begin to come to market, the critical issues will be the underwriting standards of the mortgages, the size of the deal, and the seniority of any tranche you are considering. If these points are not clear, then do not buy.

Fannie Mae and Freddie Mac bonds are sold by both of those agencies. But bear in mind that both Fannie and Freddie sell two types of bonds, agencies and mortgage-backed securities. Brokers are selling agency securities, which are bonds issued by both agencies in order to buy mortgages. At the time of writing, they are AAA, based on the fact that both Fannie and Freddie are 80% owned by the government. Trading information about these securities is listed on FINRA along with that of other agency securities. If you want to buy agency bonds, I would suggest you stay with short maturities, given the uncertain future of these agencies. But mortgage-backed securities issued by either of these agencies, whether in the form of GNMAs or CMOs), are still not being sold by most brokers to retail investors.

FINRA will undertake a pilot project gathering information about mortgage-backed securities in 2011, initially not for public dissemination. Hopefully, at some point, this will bring more clarity and transparency to these securities.

If you have a small portfolio of bonds (say under $50,000), then if you want to invest in this sector of the bond market, your best bet remains to do so through a conservatively managed bond fund.

QUESTIONS TO ASK BEFORE PURCHASING A PASS-THROUGH

What kind of yield is being quoted (current yield, cash flow yield)?

What are the prepayment assumptions?

If prepayments speed up (or slow down), how will that affect this security? Will it mean that the security will be outstanding for a longer (or for a shorter) period of time?

How will that affect the value of this security?

For a CMO: how is this deal structured? What type of tranche am I being offered: is it a companion? A PAC? A TAC? A Z (accrual) tranche?

What is the first payment date?

To whom could I sell this security if I need to resell? Do you make a market in this CMO?

ADDITIONAL REFERENCES

If you want to find out more about these securities, the definitive book is Frank Fabozzi, ed., *The Handbook of Mortgage Backed Securities*, 4th ed. (New York: McGraw-Hill, 2005). This book is brought up to date periodically. But the most recent edition was updated prior to the financial crisis of 2008–2009.

CHAPTER 10

International Bonds

This chapter discusses

♦ The international bond market: an overview
♦ Currency risk
♦ Categories of international bonds
♦ Emerging markets debt: Brady bonds
♦ Buying individual international bonds
♦ Is there a case for investing in foreign bonds?
♦ Obtaining information on international bonds

Over the past 25 years, as economies worldwide have become increasingly interdependent, there has been an explosion in trading of bonds issued in multiple currencies and trading in countries other than that of the issuer. The bond market has become truly international, embracing debt of corporations and governments from every corner of the globe. Moreover, as economies worldwide seek to expand and develop, the less developed component of the international bond market is likely to continue to grow in importance.

For individual investors in the United States, is there a case to be made for investing in bonds issued in countries other than the United States or denominated in currencies other than the dollar?

That case can be summarized as follows:

♦ Returns from international bonds often do not correlate with those of U.S. bonds. This is the diversification argument. Even though international bonds may be risky, they can lower the total risk of a portfolio.

- ◆ This case is strengthened by the fact that the value of bonds denominated in foreign currencies goes up when the dollar declines in value. As a result, investing in international bonds provides a hedge against a falling dollar.
- ◆ Total returns of bonds in this sector may be higher than those that can be earned on U.S. bonds.

Each of these arguments has validity or, at least, has been valid at some point over the past 25 years. Whether it applies to you, and to your portfolio, is another matter.

Because this is such a broad topic, this discussion can cover only the basics: Who are the issuers? How does currency risk affect return? What are the characteristics of emerging market debt as opposed to debt of more developed countries? What is the best way to invest in this sector of the bond market?

THE INTERNATIONAL BOND MARKET: AN OVERVIEW

First, let us define this sector of the bond market.

International bonds are issued by an incredibly broad variety of issuers. They include governments both of developed and less developed countries; supranational institutions such as the International Monetary Fund (IMF) and the World Bank; regional supranational agencies such as the Asian Development Bank; and corporations (both national and multinational) from every corner of the globe. Bond issues vary in size from tiny (less than $100 million) to many billions; and financing structures and techniques are as complex as any in the United States.

But, from the point of view of a U.S. investor, the first surprise is that international bonds are not all denominated in foreign currencies. Because the U.S. bond market is the largest, most liquid bond market in the world, many foreign institutions, including governments and corporations, issue bonds denominated in U.S. dollars.

On the other hand, U.S. multinational corporations also issue bonds denominated in foreign currencies such as the euro or the yen.

This intermingling of issuers and currencies has resulted in a somewhat confusing terminology; so first, let's define some of the key sectors of the international bond market from the point of view of a U.S. investor. The following are some of the terms you will encounter:

Vocabulary of International Bonds

Domestic bonds. The term "domestic" is one of the more confusing terms in this market. In the international bond market, "domestic" does not mean "issued in the United States." Rather, the term "domestic" refers to bonds that are issued within a foreign country in that country's currency. Examples would be bonds issued in baht in Thailand, or in pesos in Mexico. These bonds are issued, underwritten, and traded under the regulations of the country of issue.

   Foreign bonds. Again, this term must be translated to an international context. The term "foreign" is used to designate bonds that are issued by a borrower located outside a country (any country) but which are intended primarily for local investors. Examples include Samurai bonds, which are issued in Japan for Japanese investors by issuers located outside Japan; and Bulldog bonds, sterling-denominated bonds issued for consumption in the UK by non-British issuers.

   The U.S. version of this market are "Yankee" bonds, which are dollar-denominated bonds, issued and traded within the United States, registered with the SEC, denominated in U.S. dollars, but which are issued by institutions outside the United States. Yankee bonds are issued primarily by governments with very high credit ratings (such as Italy, the province of Ontario, the province of Quebec, or Hydro-Quebec).

   Foreign-pay bonds. For U.S. investors, any bond issued in a currency other than the U.S. dollar is a foreign-pay bond. Foreign-pay bonds are probably the first type of bond any individual investor thinks of when he thinks of the international bond market. At the present time, the primary trading market for foreign-pay bonds remains outside the United States, in the country of origin of the bonds.

   Eurobonds. Again, this term does not mean what you might initially assume. It does not necessarily have anything to do with the European Union. Eurobonds are issued simultaneously in a number of foreign markets in a variety of currencies, including U.S. dollars, euros, Japanese yen, etc. "Euro" has come to mean "offshore." London has become the center of the Euromarket. In practice, the euromarket is dominated by foreign, that is, non-U.S. investors. Issuers in that market include sovereign governments, large corporations, and supranational agencies such as the IMF.

   Eurobonds are not registered with the SEC even when they are denominated in U.S. dollars. For that reason, U.S. investors are unable to participate in the primary market (that is, they cannot buy at issue), although they can buy these bonds in the secondary market (that is, after they start trading).

Eurodollar bonds are eurobonds, denominated in U.S. dollars. In other respects they are issued and trade like other eurobonds, that is, primarily offshore. Major issuers in eurodollar bonds include sovereign governments, large corporations, and supranational agencies.

Global bonds are hybrids. They may be issued and traded in the United States or offshore, in the euromarket. Most global bonds are denominated in U.S. dollars.

From the point of view of any U.S.-based investor, two critical factors stand out.

Currency Denomination

The first factor is whether a bond issued in a country other than the United States is denominated in U.S. dollars or in a foreign currency.

A wide variety of foreign borrowers issue debt denominated in U.S. dollars. These include sovereigns, supranational agencies, and large foreign corporations. Perhaps surprisingly, they also include debt issued by so-called "emerging" markets.

The critical factor for U.S. investors is that, regardless of the issuer, bonds denominated in U.S. dollars tend to track U.S. interest rates. (One important exception are Brady bonds, and subsequent issuers of emerging market bonds, which are discussed below.) Investing in foreign bonds denominated in U.S. dollars may present U.S. investors with an opportunity to earn higher yields than would be available on U.S. bonds with comparable credit quality and maturity.

As noted earlier, international bonds issued in a foreign currency are called *foreign-pay bonds*. It remains difficult for U.S. investors to buy individual foreign-pay bonds. But you can invest in foreign-pay bonds through bond funds and exchange-traded funds.

Credit Ratings and Credit Quality of International Bonds

A second critical factor is the credit quality of international bonds. At one extreme are bonds with very strong credit characteristics. Those would include, for example, sovereign bonds issued by foreign governments of unimpeachable credit quality such as Japan, France, the UK, or the Netherlands; supranational agencies such as the IMF or the World Bank; or certain foreign multinational corporations with international reputations and strong balance sheets.

At the other extreme are the bonds of so-called emerging markets. Emerging markets are defined in a variety of ways, but traditionally, the most accepted definitions have been based on a country's gross domestic product or per capita income. Emerging market countries, in a nutshell, are poor or very poor. Since they began trading, bonds issued by emerging market governments or by corporations located in emerging markets have been viewed by U.S. investors as a subsector of the market for riskier "junk" bonds: potentially high return, but extremely volatile and high risk. Some proponents of this sector, however, regard this view as needing to change: They argue that countries such as China, India, Brazil, and Russia, in the past viewed as highly speculative, should be regarded as having economies with strong growth potential and developing capital systems (more on emerging market debt below).

The major rating agencies—Moody's, Standard & Poor's, and Fitch—all rate foreign bonds. The largest segment of that market consists of bonds issued by foreign governments (sovereigns). The credit rating evaluates both the ability of the government to pay as well as its willingness to pay.

It is not a given that a government that is able to pay its debts will always be willing to do it: some defaults are rooted in a political situation where a government will simply decide to renege on its foreign debts. Suppose, for example, a foreign government is asked to cut spending in order to pay foreign investors. That may be impossible, for political reasons. Some countries may simply be unable to collect taxes. Another important factor is that, to pay off debt denominated in a foreign currency, a country needs to have a supply of reserves in the foreign currency. This is usually obtained through trade, mainly exports.

How frequently do foreign governments default on their bonds? The answer may surprise you. Between 1970 and 1996, for example, a survey conducted by Standard & Poor's of the debt of 113 governments numbered 69 defaults on foreign currency debt. (Note that Standard & Poor's counts any debt restructuring as a default.)

For sovereign governments, Standard & Poor's assigns separate ratings to debt denominated in the local currency and to debt denominated in a foreign currency. That is due to the fact that defaults are much more common on debt denominated in foreign currency than on debt denominated in the local currency. In the survey just cited, while 69 countries defaulted on debt denominated in foreign currency, only eight defaulted on debt denominated in local currency.

As is the case with the U.S. market, however, ratings change. For example, in 1996, Malaysia was rated AA+ and Thailand AAA. That was one year before the Asian crisis and ensuing defaults. More recent defaults have taken place on emerging market debt since the Asian crisis: Russia defaulted on its debt in 1998; Ecuador in 1999; Ivory Coast in 2000; and Argentina in 2001. The default on Argentina's debt was the largest—totaling $95 billion of debt, denominated in U.S. dollars, including multiple bond issues.

At the time this is being written, one of the biggest news stories in the international bond market is the crisis facing Greek debt, which has raised the specter of a default. European countries are getting together to fashion a "bailout" package, but its outcome is very much in doubt. There is also fear that the debt of Portugal and Spain is also in jeopardy. Finally, the rating agencies have issued warnings that the debt of some of the major developed countries such as Britain and Japan is not immune; and that indeed, the debt of these countries may be downgraded from AAA to AA some time in the not-too-distant future.

CURRENCY RISK

Foreign-pay bonds are subject to the same type of risks as all bonds, namely, interest rate and credit risk. But they are also subject to a risk unique to this sector, namely, currency risk.

Another term for currency risk is "exchange-rate risk." If you have traveled outside the United States, you have experienced a form of currency risk. You know that at different times a dollar will buy a larger amount, or a smaller amount, of the foreign currency, and that will affect the cost of hotel rooms, restaurant meals, and so forth.

Despite the fact that the symptoms of impending currency changes are well known, changes in the relative values of currencies are notoriously difficult to predict. Sudden, dramatic changes in currency values sometimes occur without any apparent warning. The impact of a currency crisis, such as the meltdown that occurred in Asia in late 1998, can result in very steep losses. Virtually overnight, some bonds lost as much as 50% or more of their value. Those declines were followed by virtual collapses of the equity markets of the countries involved. Yet just a few months earlier, those economies were being hailed as participants in the "Asian miracle."

Currency risk, however, is not limited to emerging markets. Shifts in the value of the currencies of well-developed countries also occur, although generally in a more orderly fashion, over a longer period of time. Still, those changes can also be major. For example, over the last two decades, one dollar has purchased as many as 200 yen and as few as approximately 80.

Over short periods (a year or less), fluctuations in the value of currency are often the most significant component of total return, dwarfing both interest income and changes in price resulting from interest rate movements. Bear in mind that you have to convert the price of an international bond into the foreign currency when you initially purchase the bond; and again, you have to convert the price of the bond into U.S. dollars when you sell. This creates risk at both ends of the transaction. It is not unusual for a bond to have a positive return in the local currency, and a negative total return in dollar terms, and vice-versa. This can be illustrated by Exhibit 10.1, which shows how foreign currency impacts total returns of the International Bond Index developed by Citibank.

EXHIBIT 10.1

Average Annual Returns of International Bond Index by Components

	CONTRIBUTION TO RETURN			
Year	Income	Domestic Capital Gain	Foreign Currency	Total Dollar-Converted Average Annual Return
1985	8.1%	2.7%	21.6%	35.0%
1986	7.4%	3.6%	18.1%	31.4%
1987	7.2%	0.4%	25.5%	35.1%
1988	7.6%	−0.5%	−4.4%	2.3%
1989	7.7%	−4.9%	−5.7%	−3.4%
1990	8.3%	−3.5%	10.2%	15.3%
1991	8.1%	5.8%	1.7%	16.2%
1992	7.9%	4.8%	−7.3%	4.8%
1993	7.6%	9.3%	−2.1%	15.1%
1994	7.4%	−10.0%	9.6%	6.0%
1995	7.1%	8.5%	2.9%	19.6%
1996	6.7%	3.0%	−5.3%	4.1%
1997	6.2%	2.3%	−11.9%	−4.3%
1998	5.7%	3.3%	7.9%	17.8%
1999	5.1%	−5.0%	−4.9%	−5.1%
2000	4.8%	0.9%	−7.8%	−2.6%
2001	4.4%	0.4%	−8.0%	−3.5%
2002	4.1%	2.8%	14.0%	22.0%
2003	3.7%	−1.5%	16.0%	18.5%

Source: Frank Fabozzi, et al., *The Handbook of Fixed Income Securities*, 7th Edition, McGraw Hill, 2005, p. 407. Reprinted with permission.

Exhibit 10.1 shows that between 1996 and 2003, the income component and the domestic components of total return were minor compared to the component of foreign currency changes. For example, in 1985, and 1987, total return of the index in excess of 30% was due primarily to foreign currency component exceeding 20%. For the three years between 1999 and 2001, negative returns of the index were due once again to a negative foreign currency component.

Note also that the impact of foreign currency changes is somewhat diminished by that of the fact that Exhibit 10.1 shows total returns of an index rather than individual countries. When Mexico devalued its currency, or after the meltdown that occurred in Asia in late 1998, virtually overnight, some bonds lost as much as 50% or more of their value. At about the same time, the value of Russian bonds plummeted to near zero after the Russian government defaulted.

If you decide to invest in international bonds, do you want to see the dollar rise against foreign currencies, or do you want to see it decline against those currencies? The answer is: You want to see the dollar decline against the foreign currency you are buying. (Note that Exhibit 10.1 shows that, for dollar-based investors, foreign currency returns are negative if the dollar strengthens against the foreign currency; they are positive if the dollar declines against the foreign currency.)

Note also that many bond funds that invest in foreign-pay bonds use hedging techniques to reduce currency risk. If you are investing in such a fund, you need to know whether that fund hedges, and to what extent: Hedging reduces the volatility caused by currency changes. But if you are investing in a fund of foreign-pay bonds in order to hedge against the dollar, then you would want to invest in a fund that does not hedge.

EMERGING MARKETS DEBT: BRADY BONDS

Emerging Markets Debt

While they have been viewed as the most volatile sector of the bond market since their inception, the returns of emerging market debt have often been the highest of any category of bonds. A brief history of this sector will explain the factors behind the returns.

Brady Bonds

For many years, emerging market debt was synonymous with Brady bonds: Emerging market debt owes its success to the development and evolution of the market for Brady bonds.

Brady bonds had their origin in the defaults of a number of Latin American countries. In 1982, Mexico declared a moratorium on debt payments. A number of other Latin American countries followed suit. This left several of the largest U.S. banks holding about $100 billion of loans in default.

"Brady" bonds are named after the former U.S. Treasury Secretary Nicholas Brady, who played a leading role in solving what had become a major international debt crisis. The Brady plan developed a number of structures that enabled the banks to swap the defaulted loans for bonds issued by the Latin American governments involved in the defaults. The basic formula called for a steep write-off of the loan amount and also stretched out repayment of the debt over a period of as much as 30 years. In return for this debt relief, the governments issuing the bonds agreed to implement a program of reforms to their economies. The entire program was developed jointly by the U.S. Treasury, the World Bank, and the IMF. In order to attract American investors, the bonds were to be issued in U.S. dollars. Not surprisingly, they paid very high yields, between 15% and 25%.

The initial Brady plan offered banks a variety of options for restructuring their loans, resulting in several different types of bonds. In addition, Brady bonds incorporated a number of attractive features, the most important of which was that the principal of many Brady bonds was collateralized with U.S. Treasury zeros, purchased at the time the Brady bonds were issued, in an amount sufficient to cover the principal value of the bonds. In the event of a default, the collateral would be paid not at the time of the default but on the original maturity date of the bonds.

Despite initial skepticism, and an enormous amount of volatility, the Brady bond program turned into one of the most remarkable success stories in international finance. During the late 1980s and the decade of the 1990s, a large and liquid market developed for trading these bonds. Initially, Brady bonds were purchased primarily by large institutional investors such as pension funds or hedge funds. Subsequently, the market expanded to include a wide variety of mutual funds: initially, mutual funds specializing in emerging market bonds, but also, and less obviously, "high-yield" (junk) bond funds, and international stock funds, both "value" and "growth."

The enormous success of the Brady bonds can be judged by the following:

◆ As interest rates declined in the United States, and as demand grew for Brady bonds, yields collapsed. As a result, in early 2007, spreads to U.S. Treasuries narrowed to as little as 2% to 4% on much emerging market debt.

- The Latin American countries initially involved in the Brady program were able to retire their Brady bonds well before the initial maturity dates.
- Initially, the entire Brady bond sector, along with all other markets considered "emerging," was rated as junk. The sovereign debt of many of these countries has been upgraded. Mexico, for example, is now rated investment grade. Russian sovereign bonds went from default to investment grade within the space of five years.
- Initially also, the entire Brady bond sector—and indeed, the entire emerging market debt sector—experienced very sharp price moves, either up or down, as one unit. For example, the Asian debt crisis of 1998 sent bond prices plummeting in all emerging markets worldwide. This is no longer true. Increasingly, countries are viewed on a stand-alone basis.
- This has become a continually expanding market—new countries are constantly entering the market for emerging debt, and new investors are entering the market as well, including individual investors, mainly through bond funds.

The Impact of the Brady Bond Model on Debt of Emerging Markets

While it was initially developed to solve the Latin American debt crisis, the Brady plan has been extended to emerging market governments in every region of the globe. The formula remained similar to the original Brady plan: In return for capital and debt forgiveness or debt relief, governments of underdeveloped countries agreed to economic reforms demanded by the IMF and by the World Bank. In addition, many of the structures adopted for Brady bonds were also extended to debt issued by new entrants in the emerging debt market.

While in the 1990s, the Latin American countries were the core of emerging markets, that market has become much more diverse geographically. It now includes many Asian countries, such as China, India, and South Korea. It also includes some of the "emerging" economies of Eastern Europe (such as Poland and Czechoslovakia) and some of the Baltic countries. Between 2000 and 2007, many of these countries, as well as some Latin American countries, benefited significantly from rising commodity prices. Many of these countries were able to retire their dollar-denominated debt. The trend in these countries is now to issue debt denominated in the local currency.

When they were initially issued, the high yields of Brady bonds were the largest component of total return. During the last five years, however, by far the largest component of total return was capital appreciation, due both to upgrades in credit quality, and to a collapse in yields. For example, bonds issued by the Russian government went from default to investment grade in just five years. Bonds of many countries that export oil or other commodities were upgraded as the price of oil soared (including countries such as Venezuela, Brazil, Nigeria, and Kazakhstan). The debt of countries such as Poland, Hungary, Thailand, and Malaysia was upgraded based on expectations of a worldwide improving economy led by the United States. Similarly, declines in interest rates occurred in all international markets. These factors resulted in the outsize returns enjoyed by emerging market bonds of many countries' markets, but were particularly large in the debt of emerging markets whose credit quality was upgraded.

Because of their very high returns, there is now a subtle shift occurring in the way the debt of "emerging" markets is being viewed. Emerging market countries and their debt are being viewed as areas of the world economy that will experience the fastest growth. Many financial advisers are routinely advising individual investors to include some percentage of "emerging market" debt in their bond portfolio.

Does that mean that emerging market bonds should no longer be viewed as potentially high risk? I do not think so. Most U.S.-based individual investors know very little about emerging market countries. Often, the markets are extremely thin, and one or two issuers may dominate particular markets. Capital markets are poorly developed and political risk is often high. Finally, many of these bonds are highly illiquid, and if the market seizes up, the illiquidity itself is the cause of major losses.

The most recent default, that of Argentina, provides a useful case study. As stated above, Argentina defaulted on $95 billion of debt in 2001. Prior to 2001, Argentina had pegged its debt to the U.S. dollar, and had been hailed as a model of fiscal discipline. After its default (and partly based on the Brady bond model), Argentina "restructured" its debt, but with a very steep write-off: paying somewhere around 35 cents on the dollar. Creditors holding about $20 billion refused to go along with the restructuring and are suing the government (this happened in late 2009). The lawsuit is preventing Argentina from accessing global bond markets, and therefore, from raising needed capital. That may result in further damage to the economy of Argentina.

Similarly, at the time this is being written, the debt of Greece has suddenly begun dominating the news. A "bailout" package is being structured by the IMF (the International Monetary Fund) and a number of European countries. But suddenly, the market is being gripped by fear that the problems will spread to other countries in Europe, such as Spain and Portugal. And flight to quality buying is once again centering on U.S. Treasuries.

BUYING INDIVIDUAL INTERNATIONAL BONDS

International bonds denominated in U.S. dollars can be purchased from most brokerage firms that sell taxable bonds. They are listed along with U.S.–issued corporate bonds. You may need to do some rooting around the Web site to find the bonds. On the Web site I use most often, you click successively on Bonds, Secondary Market, Advanced Search, Corporate, and then finally, under "categories", on Foreign Issuers. What then shows up is an extremely broad variety of offerings, in all maturities, with credit ratings from the very highest quality (AAA) to bonds well below investment grade or in actual default (D rating). Note that many bonds that in the past were considered risky "emerging market debt," for example bonds issued by Mexico or Brazil, are now investment grade. Others remain below investment grade.

Exhibit 10.2 shows just a few of the bonds that you might have seen on your favorite online Web site on May 6, 2010.

You will note that the format of the bond listing is identical to that of U.S.–issued corporate bonds. The provisions in the indenture are also the same type of provisions that you see on U.S. corporate bonds. For example, call provisions include "conditional calls" and "make-whole calls" (defined in the chapter on corporate bonds).

Note that the source information for this listing is the same as those illustrated both for municipal bonds and for corporate bonds: an electronic platform, in this instance, BondDesk. Once again, also, note the disclaimer, which identifies the platform as the source of the data, and which adds that "XYZ brokerage services is not responsible for the accuracy of this data."

One of the striking aspects of these bonds is their yields (in this case, the YTM). The bonds shown in Exhibit 10.2 are barely investment grade and they are long term, meaning that interest risk is high. Yet the yields are below 6% at a time when 30-year U.S. Treasuries are yielding around 4.25%—a spread to Treasuries below 200 basis points. That might make sense for a bond like Hydro-Quebec, rated Aa2/A+. But bonds issued by Brazil or Mexico are also sporting the same spreads to Treasuries. The likely explanation is that these bonds were being offered for sale after a massive rally in all types of taxable debt that had been ongoing for about a year. Yet the narrowness of the spreads, and the very long term nature of the bonds, may look to some (including myself) like a giant red flag.

EXHIBIT 10.2

Secondary Corporate Results

Qty	Min Qty	CUSIP	Issue	Coupon	Maturity	Price	Yield	Moody/S&P	Credit Watch
6	6	448814FH1	Hydro-Quebec	8.250	01/15/2027	125	5.877	Aa2/A+	/
500	100	105756BR0	Brazil Federative Rep Make Whole Call Only	5.625	01/07/2041	96.45	5.876	Baa3/BBB-	/
500	100	29081YAB2	Embraer Overseas Ltd Make Whole Call Only - Conditional Calls	6.375	01/24/2017	102.75	5.871	Baa3/BBB-	/
241	1	105756BB5	Brazil Federative Rep	8.250	01/20/2034	130.25	5.869	Baa3/BBB-	/
250	1	872456AA6	Telecom Itaila Cap S.A. Make Whole Call Only - Conditional Calls	7.175	06/18/2019	109.179	5.858	Baa2/BBB	/
300	1	02364WAPO	America Movil Sab De Cv Make Whole Call Only - Conditional Calls	6.125	11/15/2037	103.683	5.854	A2/A-	/
159	1	780097AL5	Royal SK Scotland Group P Conditional Calls	5.000	10/01/2014	96.745	5.85	Baa2/BBB-	/
100	10	03938LAM6	Arceiormittal Sa Make Whole Call Only - Conditional Calls	9.850	06/01/2019	127.825	5.848	Baa3/BBB	/
30	1	29081YACO	Embraer Overseas Ltd Make Whole Call Only - Conditional Calls	6.375	01/15/2020	104.001	5.828	Baa3/BBB-	/
243	1	893830AT6	Transocean Inc Make Whole Call Only	6.800	03/15/2038	113.358	5.824	Baa2/BBB+	/
150	1	91086QAG3	United Maxican Sts Mtn Be	8.300	08/15/2031	130	5.821	Baa1/BBB	/
88	1	136385AE1	Canadlan Nat Res Ltd Make Whole Call Only	6.450	06/30/2033	107.963	5.819	Baa2/BBB	/
253	1	893830AF6	Transocean Inc Make Whole Call Only - Conditional Calls	7.500	04/15/2031	120.251	5.814	Baa2/BBB+	/
20	10	786609AC1	Saga Peta Asa	7.250	09/23/2027	115.58	5.812	Wr/AA-	/
225	1	947075AB3	Weatherford Intl Ltd Make Whole Call Only	6.500	08/01/2036	109.591	5.784	Baa1/BBB	/
250	2	03938LAM6	Arceiormittal Sa Make Whole Call Only - Conditional Calls	9.850	06/01/2019	128.386	5.778	Baa3/BBB	/
500	2	65535HAB5	Nomura Holdings Inc Conditional Calls	6.700	03/04/2020	106.844	5.775	Baa2/BBB+	/
439	2	71645WAN1	Petrobras Intl Fin Co Make Whole Call Only - Conditional Calls	7.875	03/15/2019	114.5	5.758	Baa1/BBB-	/

EXHIBIT 10.3

Bond Offering Detail

Description

Issue:	Brazil Federative Rep Glbl Bd 5.625%41 Make Whole Call Only			
CUSIP/ISIN/SEDOL:	105756BR0/US105756BR01/B4TL852	**Type:**	Corporate	**Moody/S&P/Fitch:**	Baa3/BBB-
Coupon:	5.625	**Frequency:**	Semiannually	**Category:**	Government
Maturity:	01/07/2041	**First Coupon:**	01/07/2010	**Delivery:**	Interchangeable
First Settlement:		**Next Coupon:**	07/07/2010		
Issue Date:	10/07/2009	**Last Coupon:**	07/07/2040		
Minimum Amount:	1,000.00	**Denomination Amount:**	1,000.00		
Collateral:	Debenture			
Blue Sky Restrictions:				
Reference material:				

Moodys Ratings Information

Long Term Rating:	Baa3 effective 10/06/2009
Short Term Rating:	
CreditWatch:	

S&P Ratings Information

Long Term Rating:	BBB- effective 02/09/2010 08:41:24 AM
Short Term Rating:	

Call / Sink / Put Features Corporate Specific

Issuer Full Name: Federative Republic Of Brazil
Listed:

Symbol:

Bid			Offer	
Price:	94.750	**Price:**	95.350	**Settlement:**	05/11/2010
Yield to Maturity:	6.001	**Yield to Maturity:**	5.956	**Duration:**	14.298
Quantity:	186	**Yield to Call:**	-		
Min. Quantity:	1	**Yield to Par:**	-	**Quantity:**	64
		Current Yield:	5.899	**Increment:**	1
		Worst Yield:	Maturity	**Min. Quantity:**	1

For additional details about these bonds, click on the name of the bonds. The screen that will come up with look like Exhibit 10.3. Once again, the details for the bond should look thoroughly familiar. The ratings are those of the U.S. rating agencies.

Note that both the "bid" and the "offer" are listed. But the spread between the bid and the offer is unusually narrow: 60 basis points, that is, well under 1%, even though this is a bond that is long term (maturing in 2041) and barely investment grade. The very narrow spread between the bid and the offer, as well as the narrow spread to Treasuries mentioned above, clearly point to a bond that is in high demand. Why that is the case escapes me. But as this is being written, there seems to be a very high demand for debt that a few years ago would have been considered too risky.

You are now able to research foreign bonds denominated in U.S. dollars on FINRA.org/marketdata, as you would any U.S.–issued corporate bond, to get more detailed information on the bond, as well as its trade history.

Why might you want to buy international bonds denominated in U.S. dollars?

Two possibilities: one would be to speculate by buying bonds with very high yields in markets that have potential for appreciation. (Brady bonds were all initially dollar denominated and rated as the lowest form of junk; ultimately they proved to be outstanding speculations. But of course, many highly speculative bonds are losers.)

But note that clearly, the bonds listed in Exhibit 10.2 do not have very high yields, which brings up the question of whether you are being compensated for the risk.

At the other end of the spectrum, since the yields of higher quality credits are roughly in line with those of U.S. corporate bonds, such bonds would be of interest mainly to individuals who want to diversify a large portfolio of taxable bonds.

Buying Individual Foreign-Pay Bonds

For U.S.–based investors, buying foreign-pay bonds is far more difficult than buying U.S. dollar–denominated bonds. I called a number of large international banks, as well as brokerage firms that have international operations to find out if this could be done.

The response I got from Merrill Lynch was typical: If you are considered a "high net worth" client of the firm, your broker can obtain foreign-pay bonds for you. But you have to show a specific need and be very clear about what you want and why. It is the policy of Merrill Lynch to discourage (or, as the broker put it, "not to encourage") individuals to buy foreign-pay bonds. Rather, the official policy of Merrill Lynch is to suggest that if you would like to invest in foreign-pay bonds, you should do so through bond funds. Exceptions would include foreign nationals living in the United States who might want to invest in currency of their own country or U.S. citizens doing business abroad. In such cases, Merrill would put you in touch with a branch office in the country of interest. Similarly, if you are a wealthy citizen of a Latin American country, a bank such as JPMorgan Chase can service your needs. But, in most instances, at the current time, individual investors will find buying foreign-pay bonds difficult.

Foreign Currency CDs

If you want to invest in a foreign-pay bond primarily to hedge against a falling dollar, or in order to add a foreign currency dimension to your portfolio, an online bank named EverBank (www.everbank.com) offers an interesting option: certificates of deposit (CDs) denominated in foreign currencies. These are called World Currency CDs. This product actually has a fairly long history. World Currency CDs were first offered in the 1980s by a small bank named the Mark Twain Bank, which was purchased by EverBank in the year 2000. EverBank is strictly an online bank.

Like many CDs, World Currency CDs are offered for periods of three months, six months, or one year. The CDs are insured by the FDIC against a bank failure (at the present time, $250,000 is insured until December 31, 2013). What is unique about these CDs, however, is that they are denominated in foreign currencies. EverBank offers a broad variety of options. The first is to invest in a single currency. Currently being offered are CDs denominated in major currencies, such as the euro and the Japanese yen; the currencies of smaller countries, such as the Czech koruna and the Danish krone; and more speculative currencies, including the Mexican peso and the South African rand.

Another option is to buy a basket of currencies tied to a particular theme. At the present time, EverBank offers several choices. One, called the "commodity" CD is tied to currencies of countries that produce commodities: Australia, New Zealand, Canada, and South Africa. Another, tied to gasoline, is called the "petrol" CD. Soon to be introduced is a "prudent" CD, which will invest in a basket of strong currencies.

The currencies offered, and their combinations, change frequently. The required minimum investment is $10,000 for a CD denominated in a single currency; and $20,000 for one denominated in several currencies.

Interest is paid on these CDs in the foreign currency. A few CDs offer significantly higher interest rates than are currently available on more conventional CDs. As I am writing this, the highest are denominated in South African rands (4.88% for a three-month CD) and the Mexican peso (4.04% for a three-month CD). Obviously, these are speculative currencies. The rates appear high only because current U.S. interest rates on CDs are below 1%.

Rates on CDs denominated in stronger currencies are in line with U.S. interest rates, and may be extremely low (for example, CDs denominated in Japanese yen, from three months to one year, 0%—that is not a misprint; a Canadian dollar CD, also from three months to one year—a scarcely more generous 0.10%).

Why, you might reasonably ask, would anyone want to invest in any of these CDs?

Well, the answer for both high and low interest rate CDs is that total return is governed primarily not by the interest earned on the CD, but rather by the movement of the currency against the U.S. dollar. If the dollar rises against the foreign currency, the CD suffers a capital loss. Of course, if the dollar declines against the currency, the CD earns a capital gain. Because changes in the value of a foreign currency are often steep and unpredictable, volatility of returns can be high. Note that the FDIC insurance protects against a bank failure: it does not protect against losses to the market value of the CD due to changes in the values of the foreign currency.

Foreign Currency ETFs

ETFs provide still another vehicle for investors who want to hedge against a falling dollar. The structure and characteristics of ETFs are discussed in Chapter 14. But this is an appropriate place to note that you can buy a very broad variety of currency ETFs.

- Single currency ETFs are available for currencies as diverse as Australia, Brazil, Britain, Canada, China, the Euro, India, Japan, Mexico, New Zealand, Russia, South Africa, and Switzerland, and more are on the way.
- Multi-currency ETFs provide exposure to regions such as emerging markets, and Asia.
- More speculative currency ETFs include leveraged ETFs which provide double exposure to the Euro and to the Japanese yen; and inverse currency ETFs, which allow you to double short the

Euro and the yen. Both of these are extremely risky. (This is explained in Chapter 14.)

IS THERE A CASE FOR INVESTING IN INTERNATIONAL BONDS?

Given the unpredictable nature of exchange rates, and therefore, the unpredictability of returns in this sector, is it possible to make a case for investing in international bonds?

Proponents of investing in this sector voice a number of arguments. The first is diversification. This is based on the fact that total returns of international bonds do not correlate exactly with the total return of U.S. bonds. According to modern finance theory, holding assets whose returns are not closely correlated lowers the volatility of the total portfolio even if each of the assets is volatile. While this argument has some merit, applying it to a bond portfolio is appropriate mainly for very large, extremely diversified portfolios of bonds, such as those of insurance companies, pension funds, and the like. For individual investors with a few bonds or even a few bond funds, the diversification argument is irrelevant and particularly so if the objective for investing in bonds is safe, predictable income.

Another argument is that a portfolio that includes international bonds may earn higher total returns. There is no question that during some time periods, portfolios of international bonds would have earned higher total returns in dollars for U.S. investors than portfolios holding only U.S. bonds. These time periods can always be selected with hindsight. But, as Yogi Berra is reputed to have said, making predictions is very difficult, especially for the future. In the case of international bonds, selecting the appropriate bonds for higher total returns means you have to be right about timing (when to buy the international bonds). You also have to be right about which currency or which international market to choose. The strongest case for potentially higher returns can be made for investing in emerging market bonds. But as we saw, this is a very high-risk, extremely volatile market.

The final argument for investing in international bonds, which seems to be the most relevant to individual investors, is that, in effect, this represents a way for individual investors to hedge against a falling dollar, should the dollar go into a serious decline. Again, predicting the value of the dollar against other currencies is not for amateurs. While "experts" have been predicting that the dollar must decline against many foreign currencies, timing this decline has proved elusive. Many foreign investors continue to regard the dollar as a reserve currency.

The most recent argument that the dollar must decline is based on the enormous deficit incurred as a result of the stimulus package and the bailouts of the financial system incurred after the financial panic of 2008. If you think this argument has merit, and if you feel the need to hedge against this possibility, then that is probably the strongest argument in favor of deploying some percentage of your bond portfolio to international bonds.

On the other hand, if you are investing in bonds mainly in order to have a safe and predictable income stream, then the arguments for investing in foreign bonds are not very convincing. If your portfolio is large, or if you feel you have enough information to be able to speculate in an informed manner, then including foreign bonds for a percentage of your portfolio may make sense. In either case, at the moment, the easiest method for investing in international bonds is through bond funds and ETFs, but only for a small portion of your portfolio. If you are primarily interested in speculating on higher returns, then the potentially highest return sector is in emerging market bonds.

OBTAINING INFORMATION ON INTERNATIONAL BONDS

Information about international bonds in the U.S. printed media is somewhat sporadic. It usually appears when a crisis is brewing. But once again, the good news is that there are significant sources of information on the Internet.

The most impressive Web site is Investinginbondseurope.org. This Web site is the result of a partnership between the Association for Financial Markets in Europe (AFME); the SIFMA Foundation for Investor Education; European members of AFME; and European market makers. It is targeted to European investors and therefore it can be accessed in five languages (English, French, Italian, Spanish, and German). It is also readily available to U.S. residents via the Internet.

This Web site is a sister site of Investinginbonds.com and its format was purposely designed to look very much like Investinginbonds.com. The start page bears the familiar format of "The market-at-a-glance" with similar graphs and cleverly positioned question marks to guide the novice investor. Much of the information is genuinely new because European bond markets are not clones of the U.S. bond market.

On this Web site, you can discover the main types of bonds issued by governments and corporations in European countries. The Web site has links to numerous Web sites, including the largest issuers in various countries. A "resource center" in the header of the start page has hot links to Web sites as diverse as the European Central Bank and European Securities Regulators.

You can even search for trading data on an enormous variety of actively traded bonds issued in the more developed European countries, as well as in the less developed countries of Europe (now called "emerging Europe"). That data can be found on BondMarketPrices.com, under the heading"*xTrakter*." Trade data is generally end of the day trading data and not provided in real time. It includes high and low prices and some information about spreads.

The Web site includes many tools such as calculators for currency conversions and rules that govern suitability of bond investments for individual investors. Note that foreign issuers have tax treaties with the United States. and that many foreign bonds have mandatory withholdings for tax purposes that can be as high as 30%.

Another site that has extensive information on foreign markets, including data on stocks and interest rates in those markets, is Bloomberg.com. The Bloomberg professional terminals have extensive news coverage on markets worldwide. Many of the articles and some of the data that appear on the Bloomberg professional network also appear on Bloomberg.com. Bloomberg (Bloomberg.com) publishes daily price and yield information for representative issues of international bonds, including Canadian, French, German, Italian, Japanese, and UK government bonds, in maturities ranging from 30 months to 30 years, depending on the maturity structure of the bonds of a particular country.

SUMMARY

The international bond market has grown tremendously in the last decade. It is likely to continue to grow in importance because of the enormous capital needs of the underdeveloped world, and of developed economies which seek to catch up with the United States. International bonds are subject to the same risks as U.S. bonds, namely, interest rate risk and credit risk. But another far more major risk is currency risk. Total return of international bonds is highly unpredictable.

If you want to invest in foreign-pay bonds, the best alternatives are bond funds. They now come in three different flavors: mutual funds; closed-end funds; and the newest kid on the block, exchange-traded funds. Those will be discussed in later chapters.

PART THREE

Investing through Funds

Bond funds were latecomers to the mutual fund universe. Few bond funds had their inception prior to the 1980s. Subsequently, bond funds underwent explosive growth. During the decade of the 1980s, more money flowed to bond funds and to money market funds than to stock funds. This reversed in the 1990s, partly due to the spectacular bull market in stocks, which marked that decade. But starting in 2009, the trend reversed once more, with money going to bond funds at an unprecedented rate: In fact, for most of 2009, about 10 times as much money went into bond funds as into stock funds.

What lies behind these enormous cash flows to bond funds? That is not totally clear. Returns of most categories of bond funds were high for most of 2009. But returns of stock funds were far higher during the same year. A more likely factor may be the perception that bonds are a lot safer than stocks. After the losses suffered in stocks in 2008, investors may just have been looking for safety.

If that is what lies behind this rush into bond funds, investors may be in for another rude awakening. Bond funds, just like stock funds, differ enormously in the degree of safety they provide. Potential total return is equally variable.

Advertising of many bond funds focuses on two themes: high yield and safety of principal. Ads indicate only in fine print that assets invested in bond funds can go down as well as up. Many investors do not realize that they can lose money even in funds investing in securities guaranteed by the U.S. government. Sadly, many investors come to this realization only after the value of their fund has gone down. Returns for some categories of bond funds are almost as variable and as difficult to predict as those of equities.

The purpose of this part of the book is to enable you to evaluate bond funds in a more informed manner. These chapters will tell you which funds can indeed provide safe predictable income; which funds are volatile (go up and down in price) and why; and which funds might provide higher total return, but at what risk.

The next four chapters are an attempt to provide detailed information about bond funds. Chapter 11 provides an overview: how investing in funds differs from investing in individual bonds; costs; researching funds and the like. Chapters 12 and 13 define categories of open-end bond funds—ordinary mutual funds—and discuss historical returns and risk factors of funds in different sectors of the bond market. Chapter 14 discusses three alternative types of bond funds: closed-end bond funds, unit investment trusts, and the newest bond funds, namely, exchange-traded funds (ETFs).

CHAPTER 11

Bond Mutual Funds:
An Overview

This chapter discusses

- ◆ Differences between bond funds and individual bonds
- ◆ How much will I earn? Measures of bond fund returns
- ◆ The costs of investing in bond funds
- ◆ Why the NAV of your bond fund will go up and down
- ◆ Some guidelines for selecting, buying, and monitoring bond funds
- ◆ Taxes and bond funds

DIFFERENCES BETWEEN BOND FUNDS AND INDIVIDUAL BONDS

Bond Funds Defined

Bond mutual funds are technically known as open-end funds. Each fund is comprised of a portfolio of bonds that is managed by an investment adviser—technically known as the management company. These management companies are better known to individual investors as mutual fund "families" or groups. Some of the better known fund groups are Vanguard, Fidelity, T. Rowe Price, etc.

The mutual fund's price per share, also called its net asset value (NAV), varies daily. An open-end fund has three main characteristics:

- ◆ An investor can buy or sell shares in that fund on any business day at the closing price per share: its net asset value (NAV) on that day.

- ◆ The portfolio changes continually both because investors buy and sell shares and also because the manager buys and sells bonds.
- ◆ The price per share can be expected to go up and down sometimes daily, and with it the value of your assets in the fund will go up and down.

There are many differences between bond funds. The most obvious difference is that they invest in different sectors of the bond market; for example, there are corporate bond funds, international bond funds, municipal bond funds, and so on.

Funds differ both in degree of riskiness and potential total return. Riskier funds sometimes generate higher total return. But as a general rule, expect that the higher the riskiness of the fund, the higher the unpredictability of return. This chapter and the next will discuss the various factors that affect both riskiness and total return.

Why Individual Bonds and Bond Funds Are Totally Different Investments

While you can invest in any sector of the bond market either through a bond fund or by buying individual bonds, the two are radically different investments.

The main difference is that an individual bond has a definite maturity date and a fund does not. If you hold a bond to maturity, on that date it will be redeemed at par, regardless of the level of interest rates prevailing on the bond's maturity date. Assuming a default has not occurred, you get back 100% of the principal invested in the bond. You have also earned a predictable income for the period that you have held the bond, consisting of the coupon interest and, if coupons were reinvested, of interest-on-interest.

This is not the case with a bond fund. Bond funds are comprised of a great many issues. While a number of individual issues may remain in the portfolio until they mature, there is no single date at which all the bonds in the portfolio of the fund will mature. Most bond funds are actively managed, which means that the portfolio changes continually. But, and this is an important but, most bond funds maintain a "constant" maturity. For example, a long-term bond fund will always remain long term, somewhere between 15 and 25 years. The maturity of a short-term bond fund, on the other hand, will always be short, that is, somewhere between one and three years. Consequently, unlike an individual bond, the NAV of a fund does not automatically return to par on a specified date. Rather, the NAV of the fund will move up and down in response to a variety of factors, including changes in interest rates, credit quality, and for international bonds, currency values.

What this means is that you cannot know, at the time you purchase a bond fund, what its NAV will be when you want to sell it. The price at which you will sell your fund will be determined by conditions prevailing in the bond market at the time of the sale. This price may be higher than your initial cost, or lower, depending on what has happened to the value of the underlying portfolio. The fact that you can sell fund shares any day you wish does not mean that you can sell at the price you paid. (This is discussed in greater detail in the section on interest rate risk, below.)

HOW MUCH WILL I EARN?

How much you earn in a bond fund is measured by three different numbers: NAV, yield, and total return. The NAV tells you, every day, what your investment in the fund is worth. Yield is a measure of the distributions (that is, the interest income) that the fund generates. Total return sums up what you have earned from all of the cash flows of the fund. Bond fund advertising focuses on yield. But total return is actually the more meaningful number. So let's first clarify what these three numbers really tell you.

Net Asset Value

The price per share of a bond fund, its net asset value, varies daily, like that of any mutual fund. The NAV is the closing net asset value for the day. To determine the NAV, the value of all the assets in the fund (less any minor liabilities) is tabulated at the end of each trading day. The total net assets (TNA) are then divided by the total number of shares outstanding, and the resulting number is the net asset value per share for that day. Any change in NAV translates directly into a corresponding change in the value of your assets in the fund. If you own 1,000 shares of a fund whose NAV is $10 (for a total value of $10,000), and the NAV declines to $9.95 the next day, then your assets in the fund will have declined to $9,950, $50 less than the previous day. If the NAV goes up by 5 cents, then your assets in that fund increase to $10,050.

While this point may seem elementary, I stress it at the outset because there is a widespread misconception that somehow if you are investing in a fund of high-quality bonds such as Treasuries or other government-guaranteed securities, then your invested principal cannot decline in value. That is not the case. A bond fund is not a certificate of deposit. With the exception of money market funds whose NAV remains a constant $1 per share, the NAV of all bond funds should be expected to go up and down, and with it the value of your assets in the fund will go up and down.

Newspapers no longer print the NAV of most bond funds every day. Most still print NAVs of the largest bond funds. But the closing price of any fund can be found, daily, on the fund's Web site. Financial Web sites also publish the NAV of mutual funds, as does FINRA/market data. (If you do not have access to the Internet, all funds have a toll-free number that you can call.) You can monitor the value of your funds as often as you care to.

Bond Fund Yields

When you invest in a bond fund, you receive interest income which is generally posted at the end of every month. You may choose to receive it in cash or to reinvest it to buy additional shares. The interest income constitutes the income portion of your fund, and that is the number measured by yield.

As we saw in the discussion of individual bonds, the key number quoted to buyers of individual bonds is the yield-to-maturity (YTM). As we saw in Chapter 4, the YTM of an individual bond is an estimate of how much you will earn from all cash flows of the bond assuming the bond is held to maturity and also assuming interest income is reinvested at the YTM rate. In other words, the YTM quote for an individual bond assumes a known date when you get return of capital in full. But as mentioned above, there is no single date when all the bonds in the portfolio mature and are redeemed; and, therefore, there is also no date when all the bonds in the portfolio are redeemed at par. Since a bond fund does not have a maturity date, it cannot quote a YTM. Instead, it quotes a yield, known as the SEC standardized yield.

The standardized SEC yield is a snapshot of the actual returns of the fund for the past 30 days. By far the greatest portion of the SEC yield consists of the interest income accrued by the fund for the past 30 days. In addition, however, the 30-day SEC yield includes minute increases in the price of bonds in the portfolio as they rise toward par (this would be the case for discount bonds) or (for premium bonds) minute declines as the price of these bonds falls toward par. The SEC yield also reflects the fund's expenses during the 30-day period, which are subtracted from the gross income received. Because the SEC standardized yield only measures interest income thrown off by the bond fund for the last 30 days, the two yields—YTM for an individual bond and the 30-day SEC yield—are not comparable.

The main reason for the existence of the 30-day SEC yield is that it is a standardized formula. It ensures that yields are calculated by all funds using the exact same formula. Prior to the imposition of the SEC standardized rule in 1988, it was not uncommon for funds to manipulate and inflate yield quotes. Now, if you are comparing two GNMA funds or two municipal bond funds, and if you ask for the SEC yield for the same 30-day period, you know the quotes are exactly comparable for the past 30 days.

There is a second type of yield quoted for bond funds, which is known as the distribution yield. The distribution yield is based solely on the dollar amount of dividends distributed for the previous month. The distribution yield is comparable to the current yield you would be quoted for an individual bond, that is, dividend income divided by price. Unlike the SEC yield, however, it does not include any change in the value of individual bonds as they rise or fall toward par. If you are comparing several funds, make sure you know whether they are quoting the distribution yield or the SEC yield.

Bond funds are marketed to investors on the basis of yield. That is what all the ads trumpet. But yield is only one of the factors that determine total return. Other factors are equally important. As we shall see below, if you focus primarily on yield, you are ignoring risk factors that are as important, or more important, in determining total return.

Total Return

The yield quoted by bond funds—whether the distribution yield or the 30-day SEC yield—is a measure of the fund's current dividend distributions. Its biggest limitation, however, is that it does not include any decline (or increase) in the value of principal caused by declines (or increases) in the fund's NAV. Over long holding periods, the only measurement that accurately measures a fund's actual return to you is total return.

Total return of the bond funds consists of

* Dividends
* Capital gains distributions, if any
* Interest-on-interest earned by reinvesting interest income
* Plus or minus any changes in NAV

Changes in NAV have a major impact on total return. Suppose, for instance, that you are tallying total return for the past year. Assume that your fund's dividend yield was 5%. Further suppose that the NAV of your fund has declined by 10% at the end of the year. This will translate directly into a 10% decline in the value of all your assets in the fund including your initial investment and any reinvested income. Total return for the year will be

* Dividend distributions: +5%
* Decline in the value of principal: −10%
* Total return: − 5%

If you had invested $10,000 at the beginning of the year in this fund, at the end of the year your investment (including dividend distributions) would now be worth approximately $9,500.

On the other hand, suppose that the fund's NAV goes up by 10%. Then the total return calculation would look like this

* Dividend distributions: +5%
* Principal gain: +10%
* Total return: +15%

Under this scenario, if you had invested $10,000 at the beginning of the year, your investment would now be worth $11,500. Whether your fund has gone up in value, or gone down in value, in either case, if you sell the fund, the change in value is said to be "realized". If you do not sell your fund, it is said to be "unrealized"

Note that for both of the above examples, whether the NAV has gone up by 10% or down by 10%, the bond fund would continue to advertise approximately the same yield—about 5%. (The yield quote would actually rise somewhat if the NAV declined.) But there would obviously be a major difference in the total return under the two different scenarios and, consequently, in the value of your investment in the fund at the end of the year.

If you are researching a bond fund, whatever your source of information may be, the returns listed are total returns, rather than yield. It is critical that you understand this distinction because investors sometimes equate total return with yield. To compound the error, that number is sometimes taken as a forecast of future returns. There is a cliché in investing that past returns do not guarantee future returns. That is particularly true for bond funds, as we shall see below.

Total Return, Two Ways

Data on bond funds usually include total returns for periods longer than one year, ranging anywhere from 3 to 10 years.

That said, there are several ways total return is reported. The convention, in all cases, is to assume that interest income, as well as capital gains distributions, is reinvested.

Cumulative total return simply adds all returns, including interest income, interest earned by reinvesting interest income, plus or minus any changes in NAV. A cumulative return for 10 years adds up returns from year 1 through year 10, and displays the total amount.

More often, however, returns are displayed through a graph, which shows "annual" total returns. The display seen most often lists "average annual returns" for certain specified periods. Less often, you will see actual annual returns listed for every year. Exhibit 11.1 shows why this distinction is important.

Exhibit 11.1 shows returns of the same fund, presented in two different ways, in Graph A and in Graph B, for the same time period, from 12/31/1999 to 12/31/2009.

Graph A shows average annual returns of about 4.8% over a 10-year period. That number is calculated by adding up all annual returns from 1999 to 2009; adjusting for compounding and then dividing that number by 10. (Note that average annual returns are given for several other time periods as well: three years and five years. Actual total return is listed for the most recent one-year period. That is the number illustrated in the column with the "10 years" number.)

Graph B displays the *actual* total returns for each year. This graph shows that annual returns included gains of about 17% and 14% for 2003 and 2009, respectively; losses of close to 5% and close to 10% for 2001 and 2008; and gains of about 5% for other years. In other words, actual total return on a year-to-year basis was highly variable.

FIGURE 11.1

Annual Returns, Two Ways

Graph A

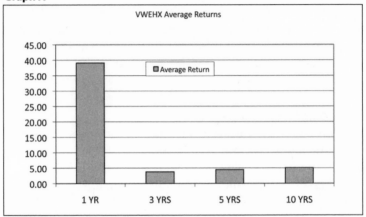

Graph B

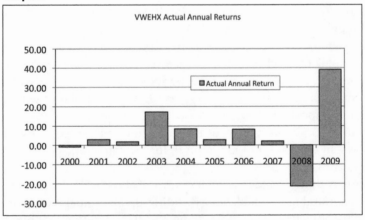

Source: Lipper, a Thomson Reuters Company. Graphs supplied to the author and reprinted with permission.

These two graphs show why the distinction between "average" annual total return and "actual" annual total return is important. "Actual" annual data show the actual total returns of a fund for every calendar year. These data also show how variable these returns have been in the past—and presumably, how variable they are likely to be in the future. "Average" returns, on the other hand, smooth out returns. In addition, "average" annualized returns are accurate only for assets that have been in the fund for the entire period (or the various periods) that is "averaged." In other words, three year average returns would apply to your investment only if you owned the fund for the specific three years noted in the graph. If you owned the fund for two years, then your actual returns for that period may be quite different than what is shown for three years, particularly if the fund is a volatile fund.

For reasons unknown, data concerning past total returns of bond funds are displayed more often with the "average" format, perhaps because that "smooths" out returns. But actual returns are much more accurate and in my opinion, more useful. Actual returns are listed in the prospectus of most funds, and those are usually also available online. Morningstar and FINRA.org/marketdata also list actual annual returns. Note that actual total returns are most often displayed not in a graph, but rather in a table format.

Why Tables of Returns Overstate Returns

One additional note concerning total return: Tables of total returns, either averaged or actual, overstate returns in a number of ways. Commissions or loads are not subtracted from the total returns of load funds. Neither are taxes. There is some movement in the direction of adjusting total returns for both of those factors. But, in all fairness, those returns would vary significantly from investor to investor, depending on the exact date the fund was purchased and on tax brackets. Just be aware of how your own tax situation or the timing of your purchases would affect the total returns listed.

Finally, if you are comparing total return numbers for different funds, make sure you are comparing total returns computed in the same way and over the exact same period of time. Sometimes, particularly for volatile funds, and volatile years, even a difference of a few weeks can make a significant difference in the total return of a fund.

THE COSTS OF INVESTING IN BOND FUNDS

There are two types of fund expenses. The first, called "shareholder fees," are what used to be called "commissions" or "loads." They may be deducted from your investment when you buy a fund or when you sell your fund. The second, known as the "fund operating expenses," are deducted daily from fund assets before the NAV is calculated.

The issue of fund expenses has been discussed exhaustively by John Bogle, the founder of the Vanguard Mutual Fund Group and one of the truly distinguished men in the mutual fund industry. His best known book, *Common Sense on Mutual Funds,* was recently updated and reissued by John Wiley & Sons. In his book Bogle places fund expenses front and center. The case is overwhelming that investors should make fund expenses one of the primary criteria in selecting bond funds. Here is why.

What Is a Load?

A load is a sales commission. The mutual fund industry has been very creative in creating many different types of loads.

The simplest loads are still the commissions paid at the time of purchase. They consist of a percentage of the money invested and are deducted from the amount you invest at the time of purchase. Standard commissions vary between 4% and 5.75%. Some so-called "low-load" funds charge less, between $1^{1}/_{2}$% and $3^{1}/_{2}$%.

But now the matter becomes more complicated. Some funds charge graduated amounts. For instance, the commission might be 4% if you invest less than $100,000. It may decline to $3^{1}/_{4}$% for up to $250,000 and to $2^{1}/_{2}$% if you invest more than $250,000. Some load funds, incidentally, deduct commissions not just from the initial sum you invest, but also from every amount invested subsequently including reinvested distributions.

Another form of commission is charged when you sell shares. These loads go under a variety of names, including "exit fee," "back load," "deferred sales charge," "redemption fee," "contingent deferred sales charge," and the like. These fees are usually higher for shorter holding periods. They decline if you hold a fund for longer periods of time. For example, you might pay a stiff 6% exit fee if you hold the fund for only one year. The back load might drop to 5% after two years, to 4% after three years, and so on until it disappears if you hold for five to seven years.

In addition, many funds have added a variety of charges that fall somewhere between a commission and annual expenses. They are more insidious because you, the shareholder, may not be aware of either their existence or of their true cost. Some funds now charge shareholders an annual fee for the cost of advertising and selling new shares. These fees, known as 12b–1 fees, are imposed in addition to the usual annual fund expenses and are deducted directly from assets invested in the fund. For no-load funds, 12b–1 fees are capped at 25 basis points ($1/_{4}$ of 1%), although few no-load funds actually charge any 12b–1 fees. For load funds, 12b–1 fees are capped at 75 basis points ($3/_{4}$ of 1%).

To complicate matters further, some fund groups are listed with an alphabet soup of fees and commissions. These fund groups offer different classes of shares: Class A, Class B, and Class C. These groups allow you to choose the poison you prefer. Class A shares generally charge a front-end commission (or load). Class B shares may charge a 12b–1 fee and a deferred sales charge. Class C shares may not charge either a front or a back load, but then will charge a higher 12b–1 fee. *These distinctions vary from fund group to fund group.* But they are continuing to multiply.

How Loads Eat into Total Return

Suppose you are investing in a fund yielding 5%. Let's assume you pay a load (or commission) equal to 5%. There are two ways in which this reduces total return. The first is that, particularly in a low interest environment, a load as low as 3.75%—which is considered a low "load"—eats up all or most of the entire interest income for year one. (Obviously, the higher the load, the greater the "loss.") The second is that 5% is deducted from the monies that you invest. Only 95% of principal is actually invested. Therefore, less of your money earns interest for as long as you own the fund.

The ultimate effect of commissions on total return depends partly on how long the fund is held. If you hold a fund for one year or less, a 4% to 5% load may eat up the entire year's worth of interest income. So would a back load of 4% to 6%. But if you plan to hold a fund for five years or more, an initial commission may be cheaper in the long run than an equivalent percentage as an exit fee. The latter will represent a percentage of a larger amount each year you own the fund if the fund does well.

Surprisingly, if you plan to hold a fund for over five years, the most expensive form of commission may be the 12b–1 fee. Consider, as an example, that you have invested in a fund that levies an annual 12b–1 fee $3/4$ of 1%. If you hold the fund for 10 years and multiply the annual fee by 10 times, this results in a commission cost equivalent to 7.5%. Actually, that number understates the true cost of such a plan because, if your assets in the fund increase annually, each year you are charged a percentage of ever-larger amounts.

Annual Fund Operating Expenses:
The Expense Ratio

Broadly defined, fund expenses are all the recurring expenses that are charged against assets in a mutual fund. They would include transaction costs for buying and selling bonds, salaries for management, overhead expenses, mailing costs for reports to shareholders—in short, all the costs associated with running the bond fund. These expenses are deducted directly from the monies invested in the bond fund. If you divide total annual expenses by the total amount of assets in the fund, the resulting number is what is known as the "expense ratio." For example, if a fund has $1 billion in assets and the total cost of managing the fund is $10 million, the expense ratio will be 1% ($10 million divided by $1 billion, or 100 basis points). If the total cost is $5 million, the expense ratio will be $1/2$ of 1% (50 basis points). The expense ratio is commonly stated in basis points. Obviously, if all other factors are equal, the lower the expense ratio, the higher the total return of the fund.

Fund expenses vary all over the lot. The low cost leader is Vanguard, with annual expenses of around 20 basis points (1/5 of 1%) for its bond funds. A number of fund groups maintain subgroups which cap annual expenses at approximately 50 basis points ($1/2$ of 1%): for example, T. Rowe Price for its Summit Funds and Fidelity for its Spartan Funds. The high end of the range is approximately 2% in annual expenses (not including 12b–1 fees). When you see total returns listed for a bond fund, operating expenses have already been deducted.

Why Fund Expenses Matter!

Are there any advantages to buying load funds?

The only benefit would be the advice that you may get if you are dealing with an experienced broker.

It is one of life's clichés that you usually get what you pay for. Therefore, you might assume that bond funds that charge commissions or have higher annual expense fees somehow do a better job for their shareholders than the lowest-cost bond funds. You might expect, for example, that load fund groups (mutual fund groups that charge commissions) would compensate their shareholders with lower annual expenses. But precisely the opposite is true. As a group, the no-load funds are low-expense leaders. Many load funds charge higher annual expenses. Investors in load funds (of whatever stripe) wind up doubly penalized: a percentage of their assets is lost to commissions, and on an annual basis higher management expenses come directly out of total return.

In the current low interest environment, with long Treasuries at approximately 4%, the difference between annual management expenses of 20 basis points and 1.5% is eye-popping. To illustrate: Assume you invest $10,000 in a fund yielding 4%, or $400 a year. A fund with an expense ratio of 20 basis points would deduct annual expenses of $20 from interest income of $400, posting annual interest income of $380. A fund with an expense ratio of 1.5% would deduct $150 returning $250. That is a $130 difference, *or approximately 32% of total return for year one.*

Obviously, once again, I am using an example where differences in expenses are very large, to make a point. But it should be clear that particularly over long holding periods, differences in expense ratios compound to lower returns by significant amounts.

A further, potentially even more significant drawback of load funds, or of funds with high expense ratios, is that in order to be able to post yields competitive with those of low cost funds, the managers of higher cost funds must pursue somewhat riskier strategies. In the world of bonds, one can always reach for higher returns by taking on more risk. To use a sports analogy, high-expense funds begin the race with a large handicap. Much of the time, this translates into inconsistent returns. Outstanding returns for one year are often followed by much less stellar returns in subsequent years.

To be sure, costs are only one of a number of factors that make up total return. But the evidence is clear that over long periods of time, lower-cost funds investing in higher-grade securities consistently rank above higher-cost competitors in total return.

The obvious conclusion is that, as a first cut, investors should consider as potential candidates for their investments only those bond funds that have low expense ratios (under 50 basis points), no commissions of any kind, and no 12b–1 fees. Remember also: it makes little sense to invest in a high-cost fund if a less risky lower-cost fund is available that posts similar returns.

WHY THE NAV OF YOUR FUND WILL GO UP AND DOWN

Before you invest in any bond fund, you need to consider potential risks to capital. This section will discuss the most significant risks you incur when investing in bond funds.

This section will discuss some of the major risks associated with investing in bond funds. Since bond funds are debt instruments, they are subject to the same risks as individual bonds. But bond funds are also subject to a number of unique risks. Let's examine them now.

Interest Rate Risk

For most bond funds, the chief risk is interest rate risk A bond fund responds to changes in interest rates like an individual bond. If interest rates rise, the NAV of a bond fund declines. If interest rates decline, NAV goes up.

How much NAV goes up or down is tied directly to maturity length. Bond funds invest in a specific segment of the yield curve: short (three years or less); intermediate (3 to 10 years); or long term (15 to 25 years). As the average maturity of a bond fund increases, so does volatility. Volatility of NAV is negligible for funds with very short maturities, but very high for long-term bond funds. Maturity in bond funds is weighted by the size of each issue in the portfolio. For that reason, the term "average weighted maturity" is used to describe the maturity length of a bond fund portfolio.

This aspect of bond fund investing is the one that has been most puzzling to novice investors. The widespread misconception exists that money invested in high-quality credits (AAA municipal bonds, GNMAs, or Treasuries, for example) is totally risk free. At the risk of being tiresome, I repeat: that guarantee extends only to credit quality. For bond funds investing in high quality credits such as GNMAs or Treasuries, credit risk is virtually nonexistent. But interest rate risk is alive and well. In fact, if you buy individual bonds which you intend to hold to maturity, you can ignore interest rate risk because you know what the bond will be worth when it matures. But you cannot afford to do that when investing in bonds through funds.

Moreover, with bond funds, interest rate risk does not diminish with time, as it does for individual bonds. To illustrate this basic difference, let us assume that you are considering buying either a bond fund with an average maturity of 10 years; or an individual bond with the same maturity. Every year, the maturity of the individual bond declines by one year: In five years, it will be a five-year bond; in seven years, it will be a three-year bond. Moreover, as it approaches maturity, every year, the price of the individual bond rises (for a discount bond), or declines (for a premium bond) toward par no matter what is happening to interest rates. The bond fund, on the other hand, maintains a "constant" maturity (with some minor variations). Therefore, interest rate risk remains equally constant, as long as you own the fund.

Duration: How to Estimate Volatility

Because interest rate risk is such a major source of volatility for bond funds (that is, NAV going up and down), interest rate risk is one of the key factors you need to consider before investing.

Surprisingly, it is not difficult to estimate potential volatility. What you need to know before you buy a bond fund is its duration. Duration used to be considered an arcane concept. But at the current time, duration is usually listed in any analysis of a bond fund. Morningstar lists it; and so do the summaries bond funds post on their own Web sites.

Duration, as we saw in the section on individual bonds, is a reasonably accurate measurement of the sensitivity of a bond to interest rate changes. The same holds true for bond funds. A fund's duration can be used as a rough guide to determine how much the NAV of a fund is likely to move up or down in response to a change in interest rates of 100 basis points (1%). That change is approximately equal to the duration of the fund.

As an example, let's suppose you own a fund investing in long-term Treasuries. Let's assume the fund has a duration of eight years and is yielding 6%. If the yield were to rise to 7% (a move of 100 basis points), then you can expect that the NAV of the fund would decline by 8%, that is, by the duration of the fund.

Moves of this magnitude are not unusual. Larger moves have occurred. Between September 1998 and January 1999, the yield on the Treasury's long bond went from a low of approximately 4.8% to a high of approximately 6.7%, a move of almost 200 basis points within the space of a few months. As a result, the NAV of bond funds investing in long-term Treasuries declined sharply, by as much as 15% to 20%. (The exact number varied from fund to fund based on the exact makeup of each fund, its exact duration, and its expense ratio.)

Average-weighted maturity of bond funds and duration are closely related. But two funds with identical average-weighted maturities may have different durations, based on whether the fund invests in premium or in discount bonds, zeros, derivatives, and so on. Broadly speaking, premium bonds shorten duration and cause volatility to decline. Discount bonds or zeros lengthen duration and cause volatility to rise. Treasury Inflation Protected Securities (TIPS), which have very low coupons, also are highly volatile.

Typically, for most bond funds, duration is lower than average-weighted maturity. Below are some general parameters of the relationship between duration and average-weighted maturity.

Bond funds with short maturities (one to three years) have a duration of one to two years. Volatility in response to changes in interest rates is low.

As duration increases, so does volatility. The duration of
   intermediate bond funds with average maturities of 8 to
   12 years ranges between four and five years.

The duration of long-term bond funds, whose average maturity
   ranges from 15 to 25 years, varies from six to eight years.

The most volatile funds are those which invest in zeros. For these
   funds, duration and average maturity are identical. Therefore,
   the NAV of a bond fund with a duration of 25 years may move
   up or down by as much as 25% in response to every 100 basis
   points (1%) change in yield.

As we saw in Chapter 4, these guidelines are approximate. Also, as
with individual bonds, changes in NAV are larger if interest rates decline
than they are if interest rates rise. (In other words, the NAV of a bond
funds goes up more if interest rates decline than it goes down if interest
rates rise.) Nonetheless, for bond funds whose major risk factor is interest
rate risk, duration numbers provide better information concerning
the potential volatility of the fund's NAV (and therefore its potential
riskiness) than any other kind of information. Duration is particularly
useful because it is a forward-looking number, as opposed to total return,
which tells you what happened in the past: Duration enables you to
predict how exposed you are to changes in the level of interest rates.

How Some Funds Destroy Principal

In prior editions of this book, I labeled this concept "NAV erosion." I am
using the terms "destruction of principal" because I decided the previous
term was not strong enough to describe some of the strategies used by
some bond funds, which result in significant and, occasionally, catastrophic losses of principal.

What I mean by destruction of principal are declines in NAV that
represent a permanent loss of principal. There is a big difference between
this type of loss and a change in NAV due primarily to changes in the
level of interest rates. If you buy a long-term bond fund when interest
rates are at 5%, you know that if interest rates rise to 6%, the NAV of your
fund will decline. But if interest rates return to 5%, you have the right to
expect that at that time, the NAV of your fund will again be what it was
when you bought the fund. In the meantime, you would have earned the
interest income and interest-on-interest on reinvested dividends.

Many bond funds, however, do not meet this test. If you compare their NAV at intervals of several years when interest rates were roughly at similar levels, you may be in for a major shock. The NAV of many funds is well below what it was in earlier years when interest rates were at similar levels.

As an example, one strategy prominent years ago was the practice of stuffing the portfolio of a fund with premium bonds. This was done deliberately even though the fund managers were fully aware that when these bonds were called, or sold, at par or below, each redemption would result in a loss of principal and, therefore, a loss of NAV. In effect, these managers sacrificed principal in order to advertise a higher yield. Sadly, many taxable bond funds sold to the public at that time as particularly safe investments, for example, government bond funds and GNMA funds, were among the most flagrant abusers.

More recently, many of the largest disasters involve the use of "sophisticated" or "state of the art" strategies based on "quantitative models" or derivatives. Derivatives first came to the public's attention in 1994 when many bond funds suffered steep declines which were attributed to their use.

First of all, let us define derivatives. A "derivative" is any financial instrument which derives its value from another instrument. It cannot be priced independently. The term, however, is a catch-all that covers a very broad spectrum of financial instruments, some fairly well known (such as options and futures) and others so obscure and arcane that only professionals using them understand them. New derivatives are constantly being created, and unfortunately, even if I understood them all, there are far too many derivatives for me to discuss them in detail.

Derivatives are an important tool for managing bond fund portfolios. But derivatives may be used in two radically different ways. They may be used to hedge against losses. Or they can be used in an attempt to boost yield, and therefore total return. Hedging raises costs, but it normally reduces risk. Using derivatives to boost yield, however, is a double-edged sword. It is in the nature of derivatives to magnify both losses and gains. When derivatives work as intended, the gains can be significant. Derivatives, however, often behave in totally unanticipated ways. In that case, losses can be major.

As an example, some of the significant gains of municipal bond funds in 1992 and 1993 were due to the use of derivatives known as "inverse floaters." (Inverse floaters are floating-rate bonds designed to rise in price as interest rates fall.) As interest rates declined in 1992 and

1993, inverse floaters performed as hoped, resulting in gains for some municipal bond funds.

One problem with derivatives, however, is that even the most experienced managers cannot anticipate the conditions that might cause their strategy to backfire. When interest rates turned up in 1994, the price of inverse floaters plummeted. The municipal bond funds that had souped up returns in 1992 and 1993 with inverse floaters became the biggest losers of 1994. (Chapter 12 describes additional examples of funds marketed as low risk, which tanked because of strategies largely based on derivatives.)

Avoiding these disasters can be difficult. One reason is that, as long as the strategies work, fund management receives kudos and money pours into the funds. The problem is that in many cases, investors are simply not warned that the same strategy can backfire.

In addition, the prospectus of a fund may not really give you any clues. One red flag to watch for are returns that seem high compared to similar funds for the same period. Try to find out how the fund earned the higher returns. Be suspicious of any fund that promises to use "sophisticated" or "state of the art" quantitative strategies or economic models. Those phrases, or others like them, imply the use of derivatives to boost yield. Be an aware consumer. Above all, be skeptical of promises that sound too good to be true. If you don't like or fully understand the strategy of the fund, find another fund.

"Sell-Off" Risk

What would happen if too many investors want to sell their shares on the same day and if there are no buyers? Could a risk exist for bond funds which would be the equivalent of a run on the banks?

Bond funds, like other mutual funds, permit investors to redeem their shares any time they wish. This has worked well because most of the time the money to meet redemptions is available. New money comes into funds on a daily basis. And managers keep some cash on hand for the purpose of making redemptions. Most of the time the daily redemption of shares does not materially affect the fund.

But what happens if there are more sellers than buyers? Then the manager has no choice except to sell some of the securities held by the fund. In weak markets, even normally liquid securities become illiquid, that is, hard to sell. Managers are forced to sell their best, their most liquid, holdings first. If the decline continues, eventually, managers are forced to sell holdings no one wants, at fire sale prices.

The preceding paragraph written as a theoretical possibility for prior editions of this book, constitutes an almost perfect description of what happened in the bond market in 2008.

The bond market had experienced a number of episodes of massive selling prior to 2008, which had resulted in steep losses. But prior to 2008, the steepest sell-offs were usually limited to a particular sector of the bond market which was experiencing problems specific to that sector. Two of the most severe sell-offs involved the riskiest sectors of the bond market. In 1989 and 1990, due to the collapse of Drexel Burnham Lambert, which had almost single-handedly created the junk bond market, junk bonds went into a tailspin. During that time, the NAV of some junk bond funds declined by as much as 50% (that is, $5,000 per $10,000 investment) within a six-month period. In 1998, the bottom fell out of bonds of emerging markets, and NAVs of bond funds in that sector declined by 50% or more.

Less severe sell-offs hit all sectors of the bond market during 1994 and 1999: During both of these years, interest rates rose in the Treasury market, and as a result, all sectors of the bond market experienced losses.

The year 2008, however, is in a class of its own. Massive flight to quality buying of Treasuries caused an enormous rally in Treasuries. But every other sector of the market experienced a sell-off of epic proportions. Sellers could not find any buyers. This severe imbalance between buyers and sellers resulted in trades at fire-sale prices: Buyers shunned any type of risk. As a result, many sectors of the bond market experienced losses whose magnitude was out of all proportion to the actual riskiness of the securities involved.

One remarkable fact, however, is that despite the panic, and even though many bond funds suffered significant losses, most bond funds maintained "operations." Despite the panic, investors in bond funds were able to sell shares, but unfortunately, in many cases, with very steep losses.

Of course, once again, the other side of the picture is that many sell-offs present speculative opportunities once the waves of selling have run their course. But there is no way to know when a decline has run its course except in retrospect, and there is no guarantee that all declines will eventually reverse.

Credit Risk

With the exception of funds investing primarily in bonds that are below investment grade (such as bond funds investing in junk bonds or debt of emerging markets), credit risk is usually a less significant factor for holders of bond funds than it is for holders of individual bonds. Bond funds are, by their nature, diversified. The larger the fund, usually, the more diversified it is. Most large funds hold dozens (sometimes hundreds) of different issues. Particularly if those securities are investment grade or higher, diversification becomes an important safety factor. Few issues comprise more than a small percentage of total assets (usually less than 2%). In addition, many funds are monitored for credit quality by in-house credit analysts. Deteriorating credits may be sold before the problem becomes significant.

This is one clear advantage bond funds have compared to individual bonds: you can boost yield without incurring significant credit risk by investing in bond funds whose portfolio is primarily in investment grade bonds. But you do not have to limit yourself to buying only bonds with the highest credit quality (as you might wish to do with individual bonds). But note that in comparing one bond fund to another, it would not make sense to purchase a fund with a high expense ratio and riskier bonds if a lower expense fund with a less risky portfolio provides an equal or higher yield.

What Happens to Your Money If a Management Company Goes Belly Up? Is There Any Fund Insurance?

The issue of investor protection was addressed in the Investment Company Act of 1940, which continues to regulate mutual funds. Basically, the regulations governing mutual funds make it extremely unlikely that any fund can actually go bankrupt.

In order to explain why, it is helpful to look at the structure of mutual funds. The typical structure consists of a management company (the mutual fund group) that manages a group of funds. The individual mutual funds and the management company are separate entities. The management company functions as an investment adviser. It manages the assets of individual funds. But it does not actually hold the assets of these funds. Also, each fund is actually set up as an individual corporation or business trust. The assets of the individual funds are kept entirely segregated from those of the management company. The securities in those funds are held in trust by a custodian such as a bank—again, not by the management company. A transfer agent usually maintains and administers the individual accounts.

This type of structure is mandated by the Investment Company Act which requires that securities held in mutual funds must be held in the custody of a bank or other approved custodians. If the management company (the mutual fund group) were to find itself in financial difficulty, the assets of the individual funds would continue to be held by the custodian and would remain segregated from those of the management company. All of this is very strictly regulated by the SEC. It is, therefore, unlikely that the financial misfortunes of a management company would adversely affect assets held in mutual funds.

In addition, the Investment Company Act stipulates that mutual funds cannot "pledge, mortgage, or hypothecate" fund assets. So it appears unlikely that a fund could find itself in a position where liabilities exceed assets, the typical condition leading to bankruptcy.

But you should be aware that that mutual funds are not covered by the Securities Investor Protection Corporation (SIPC). SIPC covers individual securities and cash held by brokerage firms. (Many mutual fund groups also function as brokers, and individual securities held by the broker arm are covered by SIPC.) Most mutual fund groups, however, carry insurance in the form of a "blanket fidelity bond" to protect assets under management against possible fraud or malfeasance on the part of employees.

Of course, bear in mind that there is no protection of any kind against market risk. If a fund loses money because the manager invested in a sector of the market that tanked big time, unless you can prove you were deliberately misled about the policies of the fund, there is no recourse of any kind.

SELECTING, BUYING, AND MONITORING BOND FUNDS

Should I Buy a Fund or Individual Bonds?

This question is frequently asked but the answer need not be an either/or proposition. There is a place for funds and for individual bonds in any portfolio: Each can play a different role.

Some Advantages of Funds

Funds offer a number of advantages compared to individual securities. They enable an investor to buy a diversified portfolio cheaply and efficiently. They are convenient. They simplify collecting and reinvesting dividends as well as record-keeping. They offer liquidity. If you want to resell, you always have a ready buyer.

Perhaps more importantly, if you would like to invest in securities that are complex and require a lot of expertise, then it makes sense to invest in those through funds. As a rule, the greater the expertise required to navigate within certain sectors of the bond market, the better off you would be choosing a fund, as opposed to individual securities. For example, if you want to invest in junk bonds, or in any international bonds (whether high quality or emerging market debt), then do so through a mutual fund. Due to the unique nature of mortgage-backed or asset-backed securities and some of the complex features of corporate bonds, it makes sense to invest in those through funds as well.

Even if you feel comfortable buying individual bonds such as Treasuries or munis, you may want to include funds in your portfolio in order to diversify core holdings.

Note also that, on a total return basis, for investors who buy and hold over long periods of time (more than five years) and who reinvest dividends, certain features of funds boost their return when compared to individual securities. Any large fund can buy securities more cheaply than any individual. Also, a mutual fund distributes dividends monthly. This is an advantage both if you rely on dividend checks for income and if you reinvest. More frequent compounding also boosts return. So does reinvesting at higher than money market rates. The higher reinvestment rate and monthly compounding of higher-yielding bond funds boost total return over long holding periods. Over very long holding periods (10 years or longer), bear in mind that interest income and interest-on-interest comprise the greatest part of total return.

Advantages of Individual Bonds

The main difficulty with bond funds is that you cannot be sure that you will recover principal in full when you need to sell a fund. If preservation of capital along with a reasonable level of income are your paramount concerns in purchasing bonds (in other words, if you are unwilling to lose any part of principal, and want to be certain to at least earn the coupon), then you should buy individual bonds. The intermediate range (five to 10 years) provides anywhere between 80% and 90% of the return of long term bonds, with far less volatility. The maturity range, of course, varies with the shape of the yield curve.

If you want the highest degree of safety, whether you are investing $10,000 or one million dollars, put that money in a laddered portfolio of short to intermediate Treasuries (and include a percentage of TIPS, for inflation protection). This is as safe as anything can be in this world. The main advantage to buying individual securities—rather than a fund investing in those securities—is that, as noted above, you are guaranteed return of your entire principal at maturity. Note also that your return will not be reduced by fund expenses.

As a rule, if you are investing less than $50,000 (total) in bonds, and if you are buying securities other than Treasuries or high quality short maturity munis, then you might feel more comfortable buying mutual funds rather than individual securities. But then, particularly if this is money you cannot afford to lose, confine your investments to short or intermediate bond funds investing in very high-quality bonds—Treasuries or the highest credit-quality municipals. If your portfolio is larger, and you are able to buy individual securities at a good price (without excessive commissions), then individual securities may be a better option, particularly if you prefer to buy and hold rather than to trade.

These, however, are guidelines. All choices involve trade-offs. Funds and individual securities are different enough so that your choice can be governed by what feels most comfortable for you.

Finally, one important reminder. Don't expect conservatively managed bond funds to outperform significantly their sector of the bond market. They generally don't. This, however, is not meant as a criticism of funds. Nor does it lessen their usefulness to individual investors. It means only that individuals should realize that performance of bond funds will in all likelihood track that of the sector of the bond market in which they invest.

Volatility and Total Return: Short Term and Long Term

I have stressed potential volatility as a risk factor for a number of reasons. The main one is that you can avoid unnecessary losses if you understand the potential volatility of an investment.

When investing in bond funds, one simple rule is that you should never buy a long-term fund (or any fund whose NAV is going to be volatile) for short holding periods. If you are going to need the money within a short time interval, say one to five years, major changes in NAV will clearly affect total return far more than interest income.

On the other hand, over long holding periods (10 years or longer), as long as you are investing in conservatively managed funds, income produced by reinvesting interest income, if compounded, becomes the main component of total return. The reason for this can be explained through the concept of duration. Theoretically, there is a point corresponding to the duration of your bond fund at which changes in NAV become less relevant to total return. For example, if you own a fund with a duration of eight years, that point is reached when the cash flows correspond to that duration. If during that eight-year period, interest rates go up, you will be buying shares at a lower price, but you will be receiving higher interest income. If interest rates decline during that eight-year period, then the NAV of your fund will go up. In fact, if interest rates rise, this eventually ought to result in higher total return (even if NAV declines) because you are reinvesting at higher rates.

On the other hand, even over long time intervals, total return is never guaranteed. A catastrophic decline such as the one that occurred in 2008, particularly if it occurs toward the end of the holding period, can devastate what had been solid returns for many years.

Finally, and most important, consider your comfort level with volatility. A lot of advice in fund literature advises investors to match investments to their tolerance for risk. But investors often overestimate risk tolerance. A real loss often makes you realize your risk tolerance is not quite as high as you thought it was. Don't buy any volatile fund if you are not comfortable with a certain amount of volatility and uncertainty. The risk is that a steep decline can cause you to panic and sell out at the worst possible time.

SOURCES OF INFORMATION CONCERNING BOND FUNDS

The problem nowadays is not finding information. Rather, it is information overload. The financial press, magazines, newspapers and newsletters, finance channels on television, and the Internet all issue barrages of information about mutual funds. Most of the information concerns equity funds, with occasional attention paid to bond funds, usually after a particular sector has had a good run. Unfortunately, much of this information is hype and not very useful. Some excellent sources of information do exist, however, and these will be discussed below.

Why Not Just Buy the Fund That Had the Highest Return Last Year?

A great deal of the information published concerning mutual funds consists of rankings of top-performing funds. Most financial publications periodically issue lists of top-performing funds, some as often as every month or every three months. So a legitimate question would be: Why not just buy the bond funds that had the highest total returns last year?

The main reason would be that, for bond funds past performance simply does not predict future performance. Generally, bond funds track the sector of the market in which they are invested. If a particular group of funds does well one year and conditions change, so will returns for these funds. If, for example, interest rates go up in a particular year, then bond funds with short maturities will be standouts that year. If interest rates decline, long-term funds, or funds investing in zeros, will be the winners. Next year's conditions will dictate winners and losers next year.

Another caveat is that the top-performing funds in any group are likely to be the riskiest funds in that group. In order to have a higher total return than funds investing in comparable securities, a fund manager has to take on more risk. According to one of the leading experts on bond funds, Michael Lipper,[1] if a fund manager wants to be at the top of his respective peer group, he has to be willing to take the chance that next year he will be at the bottom. Very few funds turn up as top-performing funds year after year. Moreover, you are unlikely to be able to predict from a list of past winners which are likely to be next year's winners.

Finally, the objectives and investment policies of the top-performing funds may not be appropriate for your investment needs. If the top-performing funds are volatile, and you need stable, predictable income, then those funds are not for you.

Instead of looking for only top-rated funds, look for conservatively managed funds that have operated for at least five years (more is better) and preferably through both strong and weak markets. You want to look for funds that have held up relatively well during bear episodes and that have done okay during bull markets. Basically, you are looking for consistent performance and relatively conservative management. Those would typically be funds that rarely if ever are the top fund in their peer group; but that show up year after year in the top 20% of their peer group in rankings by either Lipper or Morningstar. Conservative management is a somewhat subjective term. But it should include such policies as prudent rather than aggressive risk taking: investments in higher quality credits; and a low expense ratio. In the long run, those are the funds most likely to preserve both capital and income.

---

1. Quoted in *The Handbook of Fixed Income Securities*, ed. Frank J. Fabozzi and Irving M. Pollack (Homewood, Ill.: Dow Jones-Irwin, 1987), p. 492.

Morningstar

One of the most ubiquitous sources of information on mutual funds, including bond funds, is Morningstar. Chances are that you have seen references to it in advertisements for funds or on the Web. One of its virtues is that its target audience is the individual investor.

Morningstar started out as a newsletter about mutual funds. It now has information on virtually every type of investment that is traded. Currently, it is available in two forms: as a printed newsletter, which comes out on a monthly basis; and on the Internet. Both are now available in many public libraries. The printed version publishes a detailed, one-page analysis of major mutual funds, including bond funds. Major funds are reviewed once a year. These one-page summaries contain a lot of information: fund objectives, expense ratios, average-weighted maturity, duration, an analysis of the manager's past track record, and actual annual total returns for 10 years or since inception for more recent funds. A style box, which looks like a tic-tac-toe box, summarizes the sensitivity of the fund to changes in interest rates and its credit quality.

The Internet version comes in two flavors: a free Web site and a more in-depth "premium" version available for a monthly fee. The "premium" subscriber version is more complete and it is updated monthly.

What's in the "Stars"?

The feature of Morningstar's analysis that has received the most attention is its star ratings: Morningstar awards from one to five stars to selected funds. Over the years, Morningstar has changed its formula for awarding stars. At the present time the main determinant for awarding stars is performance: the top rating (five stars) is awarded to funds that are in the top 10% of a narrowly defined peer group. A number of additional factors enter into the star rating, as well as a risk adjustment developed by Morningstar and proprietary to it.

These star rankings have become ubiquitous. Any fund that is rated four or five stars trumpets this fact in advertisements. Surveys indicate that many individuals buy only funds that have earned four or five stars from Morningstar.

Whatever their merits may be in other situations, you should be aware of the limitations of star rankings concerning bond funds. Like other bond funds, four- and five-star funds track the sector of the market in which they invest. The list of five-star bond funds, for example, includes many long-term municipal bond funds and these go up in up markets, and down in down markets, as do other bond funds in the same sectors. More important, the criteria used by Morningstar to award stars will not necessarily point you to funds that are the best fit for your personal objectives.

Note also that Morningstar's database is limited. Many bond funds are not included. Moreover, Morningstar has its own formula for calculating yield: It bases that number on distributions (interest and capital gains) over a 12-month period and NAV at the beginning of that 12-month period. That calculation differs significantly from the formula for calculating the standardized 30-day SEC yield. Therefore, yields posted by Morningstar may differ from those posted by the fund or by other sources such as Lipper.

Morningstar, however, does supply some very useful information. But instead of looking at the stars, focus on the expense ratio, the duration of the fund, its credit quality (those two are summarized by the style box), and the table of actual annual returns for the past 10 years.

Many financial Web sites have links to Morningstar, mainly to generate lists. It is much more useful to go directly to the Morningstar Web site.

The Dow Jones newspapers (*Barron's, The Wall Street Journal*) use the Lipper database to compile their fund rankings and returns. Many other publications, including *The New York Times* and many financial Web sites, use the Morningstar database. This can be somewhat confusing because Morningstar and Lipper classify funds based on different criteria. Also, the Lipper database includes many funds not rated by Morningstar. As a result, you will sometimes see different funds turn up as the top-ranked or top-performing fund in a given objective. Also, at one time Morningstar did not separate funds by maturity. It now does that on its Web site. But newspapers using Morningstar data do not necessarily make use of that distinction.

Finally, note that many financial publications, both in print and on the Internet, publish weekly tables of fund returns and fund rankings compiled by Lipper and grouped according to their objectives. For bond funds, the objectives are those defined in Chapters 12 and 13.

Lipper Reuters "Fund and ETF Screener"

The Lipper group has developed an online fund screener that is totally different from that of Morningstar. It uses the entire Lipper database which lists all funds, including open-end, closed-end, and ETFs for both stocks and bonds. A short web address that will work is funds.us.reuters.com, typed into Google. (The complete web address is http://funds.us.reuters.com/US/screener/screener.asp.)

To search for funds, you would first select the Fund classification and profile of the type of fund you are researching: bond, equity, open end, ETF, and the like. You will then type in criteria that include:

- Total expense ratio
- Total return (over certain periods, such as 3 years, 5 years, etc.)
- Consistent returns
- Preservation of capital
- Tax Efficiency

The screener is totally quantitative. But the criteria selected may suggest funds you might not have considered. For example, if you are trying to find a taxable bond fund that will have low volatility and preserve capital, the fund screener may suggest funds with low duration, low expense ratios, that have had a consistent record of returns over a selected holding period.

Getting Information Directly from Mutual Fund Groups

Mutual fund groups provide a lot of useful information. It is available for free, directly from the mutual funds themselves. Investigating a fund need not be a lengthy process, and it may save you a lot of grief.

Years ago, material was supplied by mutual fund groups mainly through a document, written in stilted language, called a "prospectus." The language and format of the old prospectus were dictated by legal requirements. While the prospectus supplied lots of good information, it was often difficult to read and confusing.

The good news is that the prospectus has undergone a significant transformation. In 1996, the SEC approved changes to make the prospectus easier to read and more useful to prospective shareholders. In lieu of the old prospectus, many fund groups now publish a very short document (two to four pages long), formally known as a "profile," which contains a lot of the key information you would want to know before buying a specific fund.

In addition, the Web sites of most fund groups generally provide the same type of information in a very succinct format. Exhibit 11.2 shows as an example the Vanguard High Yield Tax Exempt Bond fund. It provides a summary of the objectives, risk profile, and past performance of the fund. Much of the information is self-explanatory. Note that performance

EXHIBIT 11.2

Example of Bond Fund Information Available Online

 Vanguard

Vanguard High-Yield Tax-Exempt Fund Investor Shares (VWAHX)

Product summary

- Seeks to provide a high and sustainable level of current income that is exempt from federal personal income taxes.
- Invests up to 20% in non investment-grade securities.
- Generally offers the highest yield of Vanguard's municipal bond funds but is subject to the highest risk of principal fluctuation.
- Maintains a dollar-weighted average maturity of 15 to 25 years.

Price and performance

Price as of 06/09/2010	$10.46
Change	$0.00 0.00%
SEC yield as of 06/09/2010	3.94%

Fund facts

Asset class	Long-Term Bond	
Category	High Yield Muni	
Expense ratio as of 10/31/2009	0.20%	This is **82% lower** than the average expense ratio of funds with similar holdings.*
Minimum investment	$3,000 ⓘ	
Fund number	0044	
Fund advisor	Vanguard Fixed Income Group	

Risk potential

Less risk   More risk
Less reward   More reward

Average annual performance ↻ Quarter-end I Month-end
As of 03/31/2010

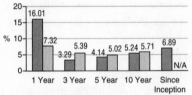

■ High-Yield Tax-Exempt Inv
□ Barclays 10 Year Municipal Index** (Benchmark)

Hypothetical growth of $10,000
As of 05/31/2010

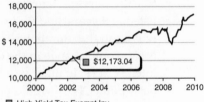

$12,173.04

■ High-Yield Tax-Exempt Inv

> The performance data shown represent past performance, which is not a guarantee of future results. Investment returns and principal value will fluctuate, so that investors' shares, when sold, may be worth more or less than their original cost. Current performance may be lower or higher than the performance data cited. See performance data current to the most recent month-end. Click to view standardized returns, fees, and expenses.

Portfolio composition
Distribution by credit quality† (% of fund)
as of 04/30/2010

	High-Yield Tax-Exempt Inv
AAA	17.3%
AA	27.4%
A	34.4%
BBB	13.7%
BB	0.3%
B or Lower	1.8%
NR	5.1%
Total	100.0%

Characteristics
as of 04/30/2010

Fund total net assets	$6.7 billion
Number of bonds	745
Average maturity	9.8 years ⓘ
Average duration	7.0 years ⓘ

* Source: Lipper Inc. as of 12/31/2009.

**Includes investment-grade (rated Baa or above by Moody's) tax-exempt bonds that are issued by state and local governments and have maturities of 8 to 12 years.

† Derived from data provided by Moody's Investors Service and Standard and Poor's.

© 1995–2010 The Vanguard Group, Inc. All rights reserved. Vanguard Marketing Corp., Distrib. Terms & conditions of use I Security Center I Obtain prospectus I Careers I Vanguard.mobi I [–] Feedback I Enhanced Support

Source: Vanguard Funds. Reprinted with permission.

information is shown as "averaged" rather than actual. "Actual" year-by-year data is shown at the beginning of the prospectus, which is also available online.

In evaluating this or any other bond fund, you would want to focus on a number of key items:

- Make sure that you understand the objectives and key policies of the fund. They are spelled out under the heading of "product summary."

- Some of the key information about the fund shown in Exhibit 11.2 is listed under "Portfolio Composition": This is a breakdown of the credit ratings of the portfolio. If you add them up, you will see that 92.6% of the portfolio is rated investment grade or higher. (BBB is the lowest investment grade.) This is important because, as noted elsewhere, many funds with the phrase "high yield" in the fund name, invest primarily in bonds that are below investment grade.

- Equally important, under "Characteristics," average maturity is listed (9.9 years) and so is the average duration (7.0 years). You will recall that duration is a rough guide to how much the fund's NAV would change in the event of a 100-basis-point change in interest rates. In other words, if interest rates went up by 100 basis points, NAV would decline approximately 7%; in the event interest rates decline by 100 basis points, the fund's NAV would go up by about 7%.

- Together, these two pieces of data summarize the risk profile of the fund very clearly: Credit risk is low because the makeup of the portfolio is high quality; but interest rate risk is moderately high.

- Either the prospectus or the profile on the Web site should also list any expenses imposed for buying shares in the fund, or redeeming them. Because these expenses are borne by investors in the fund, commissions are also called "shareholder expenses." A true no-load fund lists no shareholder expenses of any kind.

- The profile does list the expense ratio of the fund in basis points. Those are the management expenses for running the fund: They are not commissions. This fund group (Vanguard) gets very high marks for low fund expenses.

In addition to the profile of the fund, you would want to check

- The procedures for buying and for redeeming shares
- The procedures for receiving or reinvesting dividends
- Available services (check-writing privileges; buying or redeeming shares by phone or over the Internet; switching privileges, again by phone or over the Internet)
- Whether the fund can be used for tax-deferred plans such as IRAs or Keoghs

Mutual funds are required to publish a number of additional documents, which can be requested separately. One, called the Statement of Additional Information (SAI), is technical and can be somewhat difficult to read. It includes information, such as a list of all the individual securities in the fund as well as audited financial statements. Once you buy a fund, the management company will routinely send you annual and semiannual reports, which discuss the performance of the fund and relate it to current conditions in whatever sector of the market the fund is invested.

Many mutual fund families also produce an enormous amount of information concerning a wide range of topics, such as guides to IRA accounts and planning kits for asset allocation or saving for retirement, with detailed questionnaires. Some of these planning kits (which are available for free from the mutual fund groups) are good enough to be used by financial planners, who, incidentally, may obtain them for free from the mutual fund groups and then charge you for their use.

All of the information supplied by funds is now available both in printed form and on the Internet. All mutual fund groups now have a Web site, and many of these are extremely well done. Finally, mutual fund groups all have toll-free numbers, and you can discuss any questions you may have with real persons, some of whom may be genuinely helpful.

Buying No-Load Funds

By that, I mean 100% no-load funds, with no 12b-1 fees. You can still buy funds the old-fashioned way: directly from the fund groups. Here is a list (in alphabetical order) of some of the larger fund groups that have a variety of no-load bond funds, along with their toll-free telephone numbers.

American Century Investors   Fidelity (800 544 8888)
   (800 345 2021)
Black Rock (800 441 7762)   Invesco (800 959 4246)
Columbia (800 426 3750)   Schwab (866 232 9890)
Dreyfus (800 373 9387   T. Rowe Price (800 225 7720)
DWS (800 728 3337)   Vanguard (800 662 7447)
Federated (800 341 7400)

The expense ratios of the Vanguard funds are consistently the lowest in the industry. Several fund groups (for example, T. Rowe Price and Fidelity) have introduced subgroups of funds with low expense ratios. While the funds listed do not charge 12b–1 expenses, and do not, as a rule, have either exit or redemption fees, they occasionally impose nuisance fees on specific funds (junk bond funds, for example) to discourage trading. Before buying a fund, it is prudent to double check. Because they do not earn commissions, most brokers do not sell no-load funds.

The procedure for buying no-load funds directly from the management companies is simple. All mutual fund groups have a toll-free number staffed by personnel whose job it is to answer questions from current and potential shareholders. If you are interested in one or more funds, telephone and ask for information. You will be sent a prospectus and usually additional information concerning the funds. If, after reading this information, you still have questions, then telephone the fund's marketing people and ask those questions.

The entire procedure has become even easier since the advent of the Internet. By now, most mutual fund groups have a Web site. You can read and download any needed information and forms directly from the Web. In order to actually invest in a fund, however, you still are required to fill out some forms and usually to mail or fax them in. The funds need your original signature and need to ask if you have read the prospectus. (That can be the profile described earlier.)

In addition, a number of fund "supermarkets" now make it possible for you to buy no-load funds in one spot. A number of discount brokers also sell no-load funds: Schwab was the first, and remains the best known. But bear in mind that discount brokers charge a small fee for this service. In addition, several large no-load fund groups (including Vanguard, T. Rowe Price, and Fidelity) have established discount brokerages, and they too sell no-load funds other than those of their own group, again, usually, for a modest fee. This enables you to put all your accounts under one umbrella. But there are some drawbacks to these fund "supermarkets."

First, although the fees for buying or selling no-load funds may appear tiny, they add up. In addition, frequent sales generate taxes, which should be added to your transaction costs. Also these supermarkets may not send you all the statements a management company normally sends, and those are needed for your tax records.

TAXES AND BOND FUNDS

Suppose you invested $10,000 in the "many happy returns" bond fund three years ago. You sell the shares today for $20,000. What are the tax consequences?

Simple, you say: the difference between my purchase price and my sale price is $10,000. That represents a capital gain, and it will be taxed at the current long-term capital gains rate. Simple, but wrong. And yet, it appears, a very common error.

To calculate your tax liability, you have to determine what is called in financialese the "cost basis" of your shares. This includes not only the money you initially invested, but also dividend income that is reinvested, as well as capital gains distributions. All mutual funds send periodic reports to shareholders which list all taxable capital gains distributions. These are also reported by the mutual fund groups to the IRS. You, the shareholder, must report these annually on your tax forms, whether the fund has gone up in value or down in value. Taxes are paid annually on all taxable distributions.

Let us assume that during the three years that you owned the fund you received dividends totaling $1,000 annually, as well as capital gains distributions of $500 two years in a row. Dividends and capital gains together add up to $4,000. To determine the "cost basis" of your shares, when you sell all the shares in your fund, the total amount of the distributions (that is, dividends plus capital gains) has to be added to the $10,000 that you initially invested. The cost basis rises to $14,000 (instead of $10,000). This lowers your tax liability since you have already paid taxes on the $4,000 of interest income and capital gains. To determine your tax liability at the time of sale, subtract the cost basis ($14,000) from the sale price ($20,000). You owe taxes on capital gains of $6,000—not $10,000.

The procedure I have described briefly is known as the "average cost basis." It is the method used most commonly to determine your tax liability for the sale of shares in a mutual fund. Calculating the cost basis, particularly for funds held for a long time, can be complicated and onerous. Some mutual fund groups now calculate this cost basis and report it to you routinely (but not to the IRS) when they send you summaries of annual transactions. Others do not. But if you are faced with the sale of shares in a fund held for a long time, it pays to inquire whether the fund group can supply the data.

You are not obligated to use the "average cost basis" to determine your tax liability. It is possible to use other methods to determine taxes due (for example, designating certain shares for sale). And if your portfolio is large, you should consult a tax adviser to determine which method is most beneficial.

If you are selling only part of your shares—not all the shares in the fund—this procedure has to be modified somewhat in order to determine the cost basis of the shares you are selling. The important point to remember is that all distributions, including dividends paid out by municipal bond funds that are not taxable, should be added to your cost basis. This raises the cost basis and lowers taxes due.

When you switch money out of one mutual fund into another, even within the same family of funds, this is considered a sale for tax purposes and will create a tax liability, which may be either a capital gain or a capital loss. Note also that if tax exempt mutual funds distribute capital gains, even though interest income from these funds is exempt from federal income taxes, capital gains are taxable at whatever capital gains tax rate is applicable to you.

Finally, there are tax consequences to owning funds, even if you just hold them and sell nothing. Each fund generally sends out exact tax information on dividend and capital gains distributions at the end of each year. Dividends are federally taxed as ordinary income (unless the fund is a municipal bond fund). Capital gains distributions are federally taxable, at the rate on capital gains.

It is a good idea to inquire about the schedule for capital gains distributions before you buy a fund. If you buy a fund just prior to a capital gains distribution, you are taxed immediately, even if you have owned the fund for one day or if the fund immediately declines in value.

Paper losses or paper gains create no tax liabilities, but you may want to sell a fund in which you have a paper loss, either to redeploy assets or to offset a capital gain. Similarly, you may want to protect a capital gain by selling shares.

It is essential to maintain good records if you own mutual funds. A simple method is to keep all your records for one fund in one folder and keep those together as long as you own the fund. Even if you do not do all the computations yourself, an accountant will need this information to compute your tax liability accurately.

SUMMARY

QUESTIONS TO ASK BEFORE BUYING A BOND FUND

What securities does the fund hold? What are its objectives and investment policies?

What is the average maturity of the fund?

What is the credit rating of most of the securities in the fund?

What has been the total return for the last year? For the last three years? For the last five years?

How much has the NAV varied from year to year? Am I comfortable with that amount of volatility?

What has been the fund's dividend yield? What has been its 30-day SEC yield?

Is there a commission? An exit fee? A 12b–1 plan?

What are annual expenses?

How long has that fund existed? Has it existed long enough to have a meaningful track record?

How does its track record compare to those of similar funds?

What services are available to shareholders?

CHAPTER 12

Money Market Funds and Tax-Exempt Bond Funds

This chapter discusses the risk factors and past performance of the following types of bond funds:

♦ Money market funds: taxable and tax-exempt
♦ Bond funds whose price goes up and down: "plain vanilla" funds and more speculative funds
♦ Tax-exempt bond funds: short-term, intermediate, long-term, high-yield

Selecting a fixed-income fund can appear thoroughly bewildering. As of December 2009, excluding money market funds, the Lipper survey of fixed-income funds (the most complete survey of those funds) listed well over 8,000 open-end bond funds (this total includes exchange-traded funds [ETFs] and money market funds); how is an investor to choose?

This chapter is a start. It classifies bond funds based on risk factors and potential volatility. This chapter will discuss characteristics and average annual returns of money market funds and tax exempt bond funds for a variety of time periods, ranging from one year to 10 years, though Dec. 31, 2009. Taxable bond funds will be discussed in Chapter 13.

Let's first look at a group of bond funds that are among the oldest in the industry, but that you may not even consider to be bond funds: money market funds.

MONEY MARKET FUNDS

Prior to 2008, I thought that this section would need very few revisions; after all, since their inception, money market funds have become ubiquitous and until the fall of 2007, they were considered virtually riskless.

What changed? In September 2008, Lehman Brothers declared bank-ruptcy. On September 16 of that week, the Reserve Primary Fund, the oldest money market fund in existence, was found to be holding debt of Lehman Brothers, which had become worthless overnight. On that day, the Reserve Primary Fund officially "broke the buck," meaning that its net asset value (NAV) declined to about 97 cents a share. Compared to some of the losses experienced by stocks and bonds around this time, this was not a major loss. But among money market funds, whose entire reason for being was that the price per share never declined below $1 per share, this was an earthquake. A run on the fund began, primarily fueled by institutional investors, and the fund suspended all redemptions that day. (To add a brief epilogue: The Reserve Primary Fund then closed and began liquidating assets in order to repay investors. This fund was in dispute with the SEC for about one year; but after several distributions, by the end of June 2010, investors in the fund had recovered about 99% of the money invested in the fund.

Back in September 2008, the failure of the Reserve Primary Fund sparked a panic: a run on money funds suddenly loomed as a real possi-bility. Such a run, moreover, would have caused significant disruptions to the short-term commercial paper market, which companies use to fund their day-to-day operations.

In order to prevent the panic from spreading, then – Secretary of the Treasury Henry Paulson issued a federal guarantee for money market funds, up to a limit of $250,000. This immediate response was successful in preventing a run on money funds. That guarantee was due to expire in September 2009, and it did expire, as planned.

But whereas the atmosphere of panic subsided, the failure of the Primary Reserve Fund sparked a number of proposals for changing regu-lations that govern money funds. We will discuss below a number that have already been adopted, as well as some that remain under consideration. First, this section will briefly discuss how money market funds work.

How Money Market Funds Work

Money market funds occupy a unique place among fixed-income funds. They are the only funds whose NAV does not go up and down: it remains a constant $1 per share. The principle behind money funds is very simple. Money funds invest in a variety of debt instruments with very short matu-rities, usually three months or less. As these securities mature, they are replaced with other equally short instruments. The value of the principal does not change, but the interest income varies as interest rates change.

Since their inception, money market funds have ranked among the safest of all investments.

Money market funds were among the first fixed-income funds, and they remain extremely popular. They have become ubiquitous. As this is being written, in May 2010, approximately 70% of all the money in taxable bond funds is still invested in money market funds despite the extraordinarily low yields still prevailing at this time: from about five basis points annualized yield to about 30 basis points for the highest yielding institutional funds. Note that about 60% of that amount is institutional money: Institutions of all types use money funds to park cash for short periods of time.

As a group, money funds have been an extraordinarily successful product. They have been profitable both for shareholders and for the companies offering them. Despite the enormous sums slogging around this market, it has proved remarkably free of scandals, scams, and losses. It is probably almost a forgotten fact that before money market funds existed, individual investors seeking risk-free investments were limited to passbook savings accounts at miserly regulated rates. The major innovation of money market funds was that they made available to the individual investor the high money market yields previously available only to institutional investors. In an environment of rates close to zero (and in some cases, at zero), this statement sounds absurd. But the big innovation of money market funds *was* that these funds made available to individual investors the highest yields available on the shortest debt paper: securities with maturities averaging three months or less.

By law, the maturity of money funds cannot exceed 90 days. (New regulations going into effect late in 2010 will require that to be shortened to 60 days.) Note that some money market funds occasionally keep their maturity at 50 days or less, particularly if they anticipate that interest rates may go up soon. Because of their short maturity, money funds respond very quickly to changes in interest rates. If interest rates rise, so does yield. If interest rates decline, so does yield. This quick response is an advantage if rates are going up; a disadvantage if they are going down.

Money funds are offered in two different guises: taxable and tax-exempt. Both groups can be further subdivided.

Taxable Money Market Funds

Taxable money market funds include the following categories:

General funds. This is the largest group of money market funds. They invest in a variety of short debt instruments, including short-term

Treasury bills, insured CDs, commercial paper issued by corporations, federal agency debt, "repos" (which are overnight loans), foreign obligations, and a constantly growing list of short-term debt instruments.

Treasury-only money market funds. This subgroup buys only Treasuries. The yield of Treasury-only money funds is lower than that of money funds investing in commercial paper issued by corporations. The exact amount varies with interest rate levels. On the other hand, interest income is exempt from state taxes. This exemption may bring the net-after-tax yield close to that of the more diversified money funds, particularly in states with very high state taxes. The added advantage, for risk-averse investors, is the impeccable credit quality of the securities in the fund.

Government money market funds. A third variation are money market funds labeled "government" money market funds, which include not only Treasuries, but also very short-term agency debt.

Taxable money market funds are offered by brokerage firms and by mutual fund groups. Most mutual fund groups offer at least one taxable money market fund. The larger mutual fund groups offer both taxable and tax-exempt money funds, and often a choice among several taxable and tax-exempt money funds. Minimums required to invest are typically low: $1,000 is typical. Money market equivalents offered by banks are known as money market accounts. Bank money market accounts are insured to the limit provided by FDIC insurance (currently back to $100,000 per account). Money market funds offered by brokerage firms and by mutual funds are regulated as bond funds by the SEC. They are not covered by insurance.

Money market accounts offered by banks tend to have lower yields than those offered by brokerage firms, primarily because they are insured. But if the insurance helps you to sleep better at night, by all means take your money out of the bank's passbook account and put it in its insured money market fund. You will still boost your yield (compared with a passbook account) and have a totally safe investment. Initial deposits required are low. Note, however, that Treasury-only money market funds offered by brokerage firms invest in direct obligations of the Treasury and are therefore just as safe as bank money funds, but they usually offer higher yields. Note also that in addition, there is no limit on the amount that is "insured."

Yields and Returns of Taxable Money Market Funds

The yield quoted for money market funds is a standardized SEC yield, based on interest income for the preceding seven days and annualized. That number may be simple or compounded. In the past, yields typically clustered around the yield of the 3-month Treasury bill (which, as you will remember, had been the average maturity of the funds). Yields were somewhat higher for general funds, somewhat lower for Treasury and bank money funds. As mentioned above, new regulations will require that the average maturity of money market funds be lowered to 60 days. When those regulations go into effect, yields will then cluster around the yield of the 2-month Treasury bill.

During the 1980s, yields of money funds were extremely high: they actually briefly reached 20% in 1981. Between the 1990s and 2008, yields varied between a high of 6% and a low of 2%. Beginning in September 2008, when the Federal Reserve lowered the discount rate, at the start of the financial crisis, yields have declined to an all time low, less than 10 basis points for some funds, and actually zero for many funds.

Bear in mind that with short-term interest rates between zero and 15 basis points, the annual expenses for managing the funds exceed interest income, even for funds that invest in commercial paper, whose interest income is somewhat higher than that of Treasury-only funds. Many fund sponsors are absorbing management fees in order to prevent yields from going negative. Nonetheless, since the beginning of 2009, approximately 63 money market funds have exited the business or merged with other funds. Many more funds will be forced to exit the business if ultra-short interest rates do not rise. But it is not clear as this is being written when the Federal Reserve is likely to begin raising short-term rates.

In more "normal" times, money market fund yields tend to cluster in a tight range, within about 50 basis points of each other. Nonetheless, some money funds underperform the averages by more significant amounts. The key, as you would expect, is the expense ratio. The low-cost leader is Vanguard, with an expense ratio for money funds ranging from less than 15 basis points to 30 basis points, depending on the fund. Among other fund groups, expenses average about 50 basis points although they reach 100 basis points for a few.

Tax Exempt Money Market Funds

Tax-exempt money market funds also come in two different flavors:

General tax-exempt money market funds. This group invests in short-term debt instruments exempt from federal taxes without regard to geographic origin.

Single-state tax-exempt money market funds. These funds invest in debt instruments of one state only. They are tax-exempt to residents of that state, as well as federally tax-exempt.

Tax-exempt money market funds are offered by mutual fund groups. They remain extremely popular: approximately 40% to 45% of all assets in tax-exempt bond funds are in money market funds. Despite the extremely low yields that have prevailed in these funds since 2008 (well under 10 basis points), very few assets have exited the funds. Regulations that govern tax-exempt money market funds are similar to those that govern taxable money market funds.

To date, these funds have an impeccable record of safety. No tax exempt money market fund has ever "broken the buck." Nonetheless, you should be aware that there is no insurance of any kind that covers these funds.

To determine whether a taxable or a tax-exempt fund makes more sense for you, you need to do some simple arithmetic. You have to calculate the net-after-tax yield; the calculation is the same as for municipal bonds (see Chapter 7). Although no one likes to pay taxes, except for individuals in the highest tax brackets, the net-after-tax yield of taxable funds is often higher than that of tax-exempt money market funds. That is because yields of very short tax exempt paper are extremely low. The same arithmetic needs to be done to determine if single-state tax-exempt money funds are best for you. Whether they make sense for you depends on both your federal tax bracket and your state's tax rate.

How Safe Are Money Funds?

Prior to 2008, that question seemed almost silly: Money funds were regarded as virtually riskless. That perception was based partly on the tight regulations that govern money funds. Money funds are required to be broadly diversified, and restrictions are placed on the type of securities that funds may buy. The tight regulations and short maturities resulted in an enviable record of safety.

Nonetheless, even prior to 2008, on a number of occasions—in 1990, 1994, and 1999—a number of taxable money market funds were found to hold short-term debt of corporations that defaulted. The confidence of the investing public in money funds is built on the widely shared belief that NAV will not "break the buck" (that is, that the share price will not drop below $1). To prevent any erosion of confidence, the parent companies of the money funds in question chose to absorb the loss by actually buying the defaulted paper.

Still, the question arises: Why did these potential losses occur at all? In the preceding examples, the managers of the funds in question bought somewhat riskier paper in order to boost the yield of the funds by only marginal amounts. Some, no doubt, were attempting to compensate for high expense ratios.

As a result of the financial crisis of 2008, a number of new regulations were proposed, which are intended to bolster the safety of money market funds. The following have already been adopted:

◆ The average weighted maturity will be reduced to 60 days instead of 90 days

◆ The minimum credit quality of commercial paper is being raised

◆ At least 10% of assets in the fund will have to be in assets that mature in one day

◆ At least 30% of assets in the fund will have to be in assets that mature in one week

◆ The funds will have to report the value of their assets per share more often.

One proposal is still under consideration; namely, allowing the price of money market funds to "float." This is by far the most controversial proposal. Proponents feel that if investors anticipate that the NAV might occasionally decline to below $1 per share, then such an event would not cause a panic. Opponents of the proposal feel that allowing the price to float would in effect, destroy money market funds as they currently exist, turning them into ultra-short bond funds. The major concern is that money funds seeking to boost yields would take on too much risk.

What Percentage of Your Portfolio Should You Keep in Money Market Funds?

Because of their safety, and convenience, money market funds have become a permanent alternative to bank passbook and checking accounts, as well as a place to keep liquid cash or contingency reserves. Over long stretches of time, however, returns of money funds have been significantly lower than those of stocks or of longer-term bonds and bond funds. Moreover, while safety of principal is high, money funds carry a very high income risk, as well as significant reinvestment risk. Two questions then arise: Should you maintain a permanent percentage of your portfolio in money funds? And if so, how much?

The attractiveness of market fund yields compared to other investments varies with interest rates and with the shape of the yield curve. If the yield curve is flat or inverted, yields may compare favorably with those of longer-term instruments, but usually only very briefly. There are also occasional periods when money market funds have had better total returns than other bond market investments. That happens if interest rates are rising on longer term debt, as was the case in 1994 and 1999. For example, for the 1999 calendar year, money market funds all had positive total returns whereas most longer-term bond funds posted negative total returns (total return of long-term bond funds of all varieties was down as much as 10% to 12%).

This is not intended as a suggestion that investors try to "time" the market by going entirely into cash (i.e., into money funds) whenever they feel worried about the bond market or the stock market. There is no evidence that anyone has ever consistently succeeded in timing the market. What this suggests, however, is that most investors need to hold a certain percentage of their assets in extremely safe assets such as money market funds or very short-maturity fixed-income securities in order to be able to ride out episodes when the stock market or the bond market, or both, are going through troubling times. Some financial advisers feel that for retirees, this should equal whatever amount is needed to meet expenses for at least one year.

Over longer time periods, however, real returns from money funds are not likely to keep up with inflation. Money market funds are not appropriate as long term investments except for a small portion of your portfolio (not to exceed 20%).

To sum up, for parking money over short periods of time, if safety is your main concern, then invest in Treasury-only money market funds or bank money market accounts that are insured. General money market funds (or if you are in a high tax bracket, tax-exempt money market funds) provide slightly lower safety margins but somewhat higher total returns.

Finally, let's look at how money market funds have performed over the years. Exhibit 12.1 shows the average annual total returns of general and Treasury-only taxable money market funds; as well as average annual returns of tax exempt money market funds. Average annual returns are shown for 2008, 2009 and for 5-year and 10-year holding periods, through December 31, 2009.

EXHIBIT 12.1

Average Annual Total Returns of Taxable and Tax-Exempt Money Market Funds for 2008, 2009, and for 5-year and 10-year Holding Periods through December 31, 2009: All Distributions, Dividends, and Capital Gains Are Assumed to Be Reinvested

	2008 (12/31/2007– 12/31/2008)	2009 (12/31/2008– 12/31/2009)	5 Years (12/31/2004– 12/31/2009)	10 Years (12/31/1999– 12/31/2009)
General Money Market Funds	2.04%	0.17%	2.66%	2.47%
U.S. Treasury Money Market Funds	1.12%	0.03%	2.26%	2.25%
Tax-Exempt Money Market Funds	1.69%	0.16%	1.80%	1.76%

Source: Lipper, a Thomson Reuters Company. Material supplied to the author and reprinted with permission.

These returns are shown partly to remind readers that under normal circumstances, the yield and total return of money market funds exceeds zero. These returns are of interest for two additional reasons:

- First, as Exhibit 12.1 shows, average annual returns of general money market funds exceed those of Treasury-only funds by slight margins for longer-term holding periods. (But note that if a Treasury-only money fund has a particularly low expense ratio, its total return may be higher than that of a general money market fund.)
- Note also that on a taxable equivalent basis, for someone in a 25% tax bracket, the 5-year and 10-year average annual total return of tax exempt money funds would have been higher than that of taxable funds. (1.89% equates to 2.52% for someone in a 25% tax bracket.)
- Finally, the total returns of all types of money market funds will serve as reference points when we look at the total returns of longer-term, riskier bond funds. As we will see, while most longer-term funds have had higher total returns than money funds, some of the more volatile and riskier funds have occasionally failed to perform as well.

Alternatives to Money Market Funds

If you want to keep a significant amount of money in very safe instruments for somewhat longer time periods, there are some alternatives to money funds, which can boost yield without significant risk. One would be to invest in a combination of Treasury bills and short-term notes (two years or less), through Treasury Direct (see Chapter 6). Another would be to invest in three-month, six-month, or one-year certificates of deposit (CDs). Their yield is usually higher than that of bank money market funds. (Brokerage firms shop the country for insured CDs with the highest yields.) Still another alternative would be to invest in so-called jumbo CDs. Those require minimum investments of approximately $100,000. Most brokerage firms also shop the country for the highest jumbo CD yields, and they can sell them to you. (Yields of jumbo CDs are listed in the newspaper along with those of money market funds.) But note that while CDs are insured, and while yields may be higher than those of money funds, there may be penalties if you want to sell early.

There are no insured equivalents for tax-exempt accounts. One alternative would be to purchase very high-quality, tax-exempt bonds maturing in one year or less; or tax-exempt notes maturing in one year or less: tax anticipation notes (known as TANs) and revenue anticipation notes (RANs); or ultra-short bond funds, with average-weighted maturities under two years.

Keeping Informed about Money Funds

Coverage of money market yields is spotty and ever changing in the printed media. On the Web, the most complete information on money market funds, including yields, different types of funds, and where to find the highest yields, is to be found on http://www.imoneynet.com. Barron's publishes some of the data from imoney.net on the weekend.

BOND FUNDS WHOSE PRICE GOES UP AND DOWN: "PLAIN VANILLA" AND MORE SPECULATIVE FUNDS

For any sector of the fixed-income market, you can buy either a fund or an individual security. There are funds that invest in municipal bonds, funds that invest in Treasuries, funds that invest in corporate bonds, funds that invest in GNMAs, funds that invest in international and emerging market bonds, and so on.

As stated earlier, with the exception of money market funds, the price of all bond funds can be expected to go up and down, some by a little, many by a lot. This chapter and the next will discuss in detail why this happens, which bond funds are less volatile and why, and which bond funds are most volatile and why. The purpose of this analysis is to give you some idea of the potential total returns and volatility of the various categories of bond funds.

What's in a Bond Fund Name?

A number of factors complicate this analysis. To begin with, there is no general agreement about the riskiness of certain categories of bond funds such as junk bond funds. The Securities and Exchange Commission, the major rating agencies, and the Investment Company Institute have all tried to come up with a system of ratings that would give individual investors some indication of the types of risks they incur when they buy bond funds. To date, no agreement has been reached by all parties.

A second complicating factor is that there is also not one single, generally agreed-upon classification for bond funds. The two main purveyors of data on bond funds, Morningstar and Lipper, come up with different categories. Another word for categories is "objectives." I have adopted the Lipper database and classification because it is more complete.

Moreover, one of the more mysterious aspects of investing in bond funds is that determining exactly how to classify any bond fund is not always obvious. That is because the names of many bond funds obfuscate, rather than make clear, exactly in what corner of the bond world the bond fund invests.

For starters, the name of a fund may be so general that it offers no clue concerning the type of securities in a bond fund, their maturity, their credit quality, and therefore, the main risk factors of the fund. The name, after all, is a marketing device, designed to attract investors. Any number of confusing possibilities exists. So-called "government" or "government-only" funds are a prime example. These funds may be invested primarily in Treasuries or primarily in GNMAs. They may also include agency securities, or zeros. Or they may include a combination of all of the above. In all cases, the name implies the highest credit quality and very little risk. But of course, we know that interest rate risk affects government securities to the same extent as any other securities of the same maturity length. I shall point out additional instances of confusing fund names where appropriate.

Also, many bond funds invest in more than one sector of the bond market. Occasionally, the name of the fund indicates as much. That would be the case, for example, for funds labeled "multi-sector" or "total return" bond funds. But even when the name of a fund mentions a specific corner of the bond market, that does not mean that the fund owns only that type of bond. Whatever their name, many bond funds include a range of maturities and a variety of credits, from high to low. Many bond funds also include a sprinkling of lower credit quality but higher yielding securities in order to boost their advertised yield or, they hope, their total return. Such securities may include high-yield debt, derivatives, or even stocks. This may boost total return in good times but exacerbates declines in weak markets. Moreover, these lower-quality securities may not be listed in the general information about the fund.

Lipper's definitions of categories (Lipper's term is "objectives") are fairly narrow. The Lipper organization decides, based on their own criteria, which category a fund belongs to. (This is important to fund managers because Lipper's rankings, within a group, in part determine their salaries!) Even so, these definitions, with their quantified criteria, point up how difficult it can be to characterize a fund based only on its name. The Lipper categories generally specify that, to be put into a specific category, 65% of all the bonds in a fund should clearly belong to that category. For example, for a fund to be classified as a corporate bond fund, 65% of the securities in that fund should be corporate bonds. But that means that, for many Securities funds, 35% of all the bonds in the fund belong to a different category. For some funds, the total is higher.

In practice, mutual fund families label their funds much more loosely than does Lipper. A prime example are the labels "high-yield" and "high income," which are used with different meanings in different mutual fund groups. Some fund families label their longest-term funds "high yield" or "high income" to indicate that they will have high yields because they invest in long-term bonds. However, credit quality for these high-yield funds may be very high. Other fund families designate funds as "high yield" or "high income" because they invest in lower-quality, and hence higher-yielding, bonds. (Note also that even within Lipper's classification there is room for some overlapping.)

In order to come up with some indication of risk factors for different bond funds, I have subdivided Lipper's classification into two basic groups: "plain vanilla bond funds," and "more speculative" funds.

"Plain vanilla bond funds" are the most straightforward to describe and understand. For these funds, interest rate risk—and therefore maturity length—is the primary determinant of both a fund's volatility and its total return. All longer term municipal bond funds can be classified as "plain vanilla" funds. Many taxable bond funds can also be classified as "plain vanilla" funds. Those would include bond funds that invest in treasury or agency debt; or in a variety of investment grade bonds.

I am calling the second group "more speculative" funds because their risk factors are more complex. Total returns for these funds vary the most from year to year and from fund to fund within a single category. Bond funds placed in this group include junk bond funds, international bond funds, emerging market debt bond funds, and multi-sector bond funds. All taxable bond funds, whether "plain vanilla" or speculative, will be discussed in Chapter 13.

Lipper divides bond funds into two main groups: taxable and tax-exempt. In this chapter, we will discuss tax exempt bond funds: those, by definition, invest in bonds that are federally tax exempt.

"Plain Vanilla" Funds: Estimating Volatility

For this group of funds, both total return (dividends plus any change in the share price) and volatility of share price (that is, how much share price goes up or down) are related directly to the average maturity length of the fund's portfolio. This is due to two factors. Assuming a normal "upward-sloping" yield curve, dividend yield is higher for longer maturities, lower for shorter maturities. Therefore, funds with longer average maturities normally yield more than funds with shorter maturities.

But higher yield always comes at a cost. The cost here is that the share price of funds with longer average maturities goes up and down more steeply in response to interest rate changes than that of funds with shorter maturities. As noted in the preceding chapter, a bond fund responds to changes in interest rates very much like an individual bond.

You can estimate the potential volatility of these bond funds by using the concept of duration. Duration was discussed in Chapter 4 and also in Chapter 11. Duration is a measure of a bond's sensitivity to changes in interest rates. The concept of duration works equally well for bond funds. The general rule is that for every 100 basis point change (1%) in the level of interest rates, the NAV of a bond fund will rise or fall by that fund's duration. For example, assume a fund has a duration of 8 years. If interest rates rise from 6% to 7%—that is, 100 basis points—the NAV of that fund would decline in value by approximately 8%. A decline in interest rates of the same magnitude would cause the NAV of the fund to rise by approximately the same amount.

The amount is approximate, and as our discussion in Chapter 4 indicates, exact amounts differ based on the level of interest rates. Changes in NAV are higher when interest rates are lower: For example, if interest rates rise from 4% to 5%, that is a higher percentage change in the level of interest rates than if they rise from 8% to 9%. Changes in NAV are also larger if interest rates fall than if they rise. But the general rule is an approximate but useful guide to the potential volatility of a bond fund.

Over short-term holding periods (one to two years), particularly if interest rates are volatile, changes in NAV, rather than interest income, often dominate total return. As a result, for short-term holding periods, the total return of long-term funds is unpredictable. If interest rates decline, the NAV of the fund will rise. Therefore, total return will be higher than interest income. If interest rates stay the same, NAV will not change and total return will be the same as interest income. If interest rates rise, the NAV of the fund will decline. Therefore, total return may be lower than interest income.

Over long holding periods, however, say 10 years or more, long-term funds should have higher total returns than shorter-term funds. That is due primarily to the fact that over a long stretch of time, the income portion of the funds (dividend income plus interest-on-interest earned by reinvesting interest income) should dominate total return. But that needs to be qualified. Because of the high interest rate risk of long-term funds, during a period such as the 1970s, when interest rates climbed inexorably for most of the decade, long-term funds would be poor investments. Given the low level of interest rates as this is being written, there is the likelihood that at some point, long-term interest rates will start going up. How much, or when, no one knows. Also, as we shall see below, an abysmal year such as 2008 significantly reduces or even wipes out what had been very solid returns for the entire preceding decade.

MUNICIPAL BOND FUNDS

As stated above, all municipal bond funds can be classified as "plain vanilla." Municipal bond funds were among the earliest bond funds.

Some had their inception in the 1970s. Their popularity declined some-what during the second half of the 1990s, when the spectacular bull market in stocks made bonds appear far less attractive. Nonetheless, approximately one-quarter of all the assets in bond funds remain in the municipal sector. The major attraction of these funds is that interest income is federally tax-exempt (but subject to state taxes if you do not reside in the state issuing the bonds). The municipal corner of the bond market is much less diverse, much more homogeneous than the taxable sector. It is also the only sector of the bond market that is dominated by individual investors.

Before discussing these municipal bond funds in greater detail, let's look at Exhibits 12.2 and 12.3. Exhibit 12.2 displays total returns of municipal bond funds for 2008, and for 5-year holding periods through December 31, 2008. Exhibit 12.3 displays total returns of municipal bond funds for 2009 and for 5-year and 10-year holding periods through December 31, 2009. (Total return is the average annualized compounded total return, based on reinvestment of all dividends and capital gains distributions, if any, plus changes in share price.)

I included both time periods for several reasons. So let me state clearly what I am trying to show.

- First, I want to illustrate total returns for two years (2008 and 2009), each of which was an outlier: 2008 (the year of the panic), which saw devastating losses in all sectors of the bond market other than Treasuries; and 2009, which was an almost complete reversal of 2008, with outsize gains in many sectors of the bond market.
- I also wanted to illustrate how returns in volatile years, can impact total returns, both up and down, going as far back as 10 years: this is important, for example, if you are looking at average annualized returns for longer holding periods.
- Finally, I included "principal only returns" for both 2008 and 2009 to illustrate how NAV is affected by changes in the level of interest rates. "Principal only" returns indicate percentage changes in NAV only—dividend income is not included.

Let's briefly take a closer look at the various categories of municipal bond funds, beginning with Lipper's definitions.

E X H I B I T   12.2

Average Annual Total Returns of Municipal Bond
Funds through December 31, 2008: All Distributions,
Dividends, and Capital Gains Are Assumed to Be
Reinvested

	2008 (12/31/2007–12/31/2008)	2008 (Principal Only)	5 Years (12/31/2003–12/31/2008)	10 Years (12/31/1998–12/31/2008)
Short (1–2 Years)	0.12%	−3.35%	1.66%	2.85%
Intermediate (2–5 Years)	−1.79%	−5.37%	1.85%	3.35%
General	−9.09%	−12.80%	0.53%	2.44%
Single State (Average)	−7.09%	−10.63%	−1.11%	2.83%
High Yield	−25.11%	−29.07%	−2.48%	0.57%

Source: Lipper, a Thomson Reuters Company. Material supplied to the author and reprinted with permission.

E X H I B I T   12.3

Average Annual Total Returns of Municipal Bond
Funds through December 31, 2009: All Distributions,
Dividends, and Capital Gains Are Assumed to Be
Reinvested

	2009 (12/31/2008–12/31/2009)	2009 (Principal Only)	5 Years (12/31/2004–12/31/2009)	10 Years (12/31/1999–12/31/2009)
Short-Term (1–2 Years)	5.26%	2.94%	2.53%	3.20%
Intermediate (2–5 Years)	10.75%	7.08%	3.39%	4.60%
General	16.85%	12.01%	2.91%	4.59%
Single State (Average)	15.52%	N. A.	3.02%	4.57%
High-Yield	30.80%	23.16%	1.48%	4.42%

Source: Lipper, a Thomson Reuters Company. Material supplied to the author and reprinted with permission.

- The largest subgroup is the category of *general municipal bond funds*. General municipal bond funds are the most broadly diversified municipal bond funds: by type of bond (general obligation, revenue); geographically (they include bonds from many states issuing tax-exempt bonds); and by credit quality (although Lipper stipulates that at least 65% of bonds in the general municipal bond category must be investment grade).

- *High-yield municipal bond funds* invest at least 50% of their portfolio in lower-rated municipal bonds. This stipulation differentiates high-yield municipal bond funds from the general funds. In other words, the credit quality of *Lipper's high-yield* fund category is largely below investment grade.

- *Short, short-intermediate, and intermediate* municipal bond funds all have weighted average maturities shorter than the long-term funds. The average-weighted maturity of short municipal bond funds is three years or less, that of *short-intermediate* funds is three to five years, and that of *intermediate* funds is five to 10 years. In other respects, these funds are broadly diversified: geographically, by type of bond, by credit quality, etc.

- *Single-state municipal bond funds* invest primarily in bonds of one state. They are exempt from federal taxes and also from state and local taxes to residents of the state in which they are issued. Lipper lists single-state funds for 27 states. Most of these are long-term funds but there are now intermediate and short-term funds in this group for some of the larger states such as California and New York.

What These Tables Show

To make sense out of the data in both Exhibit 12.2 and Exhibit 12.3, bear in mind that most so-called "general" or "national" tax exempt bond funds are long term. The chief risk in these funds is interest rate risk. The only municipal bond funds that are not long term are those specifically identified by their shorter maturity length: "short" and "intermediate" funds. Interest rate risk is much lower for these funds. But there is no doubt that 2008 will be remembered as the year that holding bonds with any whiff of risk, whether interest rate risk, or credit risk, translated into losses. In fact, in 2008, losses in tax exempt "high yield" funds were as high or almost as high as those posted by corporate high yield ("junk") funds, even though default rates of lower quality tax exempt bonds are much lower than those of corporate bonds.

When you analyze returns shown in Exhibits 12.2 and 12.3, a number of facts stand out:

- As shown in Exhibit 12.2, the funds experiencing the largest losses were the riskiest funds the funds with the longest average weighted maturities, whether general or single state; and the high-yield funds.

- By far the worst performers were the "high-yield" funds. (Bear in mind that Lipper's "high-yield" category comprises bond funds that hold at least 50% bonds rated below investment grade [such as tobacco bonds or private enterprise bonds such as nursing homes]). In 2008 losses for this group were unprecedented for municipal bond funds: averaging 25% (− 25%). Better performing "high yield" funds posted returns of −12% to −13%; whereas those investing in the riskiest bonds experienced truly shocking results: losses −30% to −50%.

- Note also that the losses of both general (long-term) and high-yield funds so devastated total return that they wiped out what had been solid returns for up to 10 years. As shown in Exhibit 12.2, average 10-year total returns for high-yield funds (as a group) actually declined to being barely positive (average compounded annual returns of 0.57%) for the entire 10-year period through December 31, 2008.

- In 2008, many of the general and single-state tax-exempt funds experienced losses that were nearly as high as those of the high-yield funds. (Those losses disappear into the averages.) It bears repeating that those losses were primarily due to the fact that many "general" funds are long-term funds.

- There was a complete reversal in 2009. As shown in Exhibit 12.3, high-yield and long-term funds (both general and single state) posted significant gains in 2009 (an average gain of almost 31% for the high yield funds; and almost 17% for the general funds). But even with these outsize gains, through December 31, 2009, average total return of both of these groups remained below that of lower risk intermediate funds for both the 5- and 10-year holding periods.

- The sweet spot for both 2008 and 2009 was the intermediate funds whose average-weighted maturity ranges from 5 to 10 years. As shown in Exhibit 12.2 average annual total return for this group was close to flat for 2008 (some of the better performing intermediate funds actually posted small gains in 2008), a very good performance for 2008. And as shown in Exhibit 12.3, average total return for 2009 was a gain of close to 11%. This combination resulted in these funds posting the highest average total returns of any groups for both the 5-year and the 10 year holding periods, through both December 2008 and December 2009.

- The category of short funds (the group with a maturity of 1 to 2 years) provided a genuine safe harbor. The better performing funds in this group actually had positive total returns in 2008; and rallied into 2009. For the 10-year periods between 1998 and 2008, average annual total return for this group of funds was actually higher than that of the high yield group (an average gain of 2.85% for the short funds, compared with an average gain of only 0.57% for the high yield group. For the 10-year period between 1999 and 2009, because of the significant gains of the high yield funds in 2009, average annual total return of high yield funds regained its advantage over the short funds: as shown in Exhibit 12.3, an average annual total return of 3.2% for the short funds, compared to 4.42% for the high yield group).

- Both the losses of 2008 and the gains of 2009 were primarily due to changes in NAV. The principal-only column of Exhibit 12.2 shows average losses in NAV of close to 30% for the high-yield sector; and close to 13% for general and single-state funds. In 2009, the principal-only column shows average gains of about 23% for the high yield group; and 12% for the general group. As also shown in Exhibits 12.2 and 12.3, changes in NAV were much lower for groups with shorter maturities.

One final but important note. Although I am showing "principal only" returns only in Exhibits 12.2 and 12.3, the same pattern will be repeated for all bond funds throughout both chapters. For "plain vanilla" bond funds with shorter maturities, changes in NAV are either negligible (for the shortest funds) or modest (for intermediate funds). Changes in NAV are the largest component of total return and of volatility for longer-term funds, particularly at a time such as the present when interest income is at historically low levels.

More on Selecting Municipal Funds

Let us now take a closer look at the individual categories of municipal bond funds.

General, Long-Term Tax-Exempt Bond Funds

The general, long-term tax-exempt bond funds are the veterans of the industry. A few had their inception in the 1970s. This remains by far the largest group of municipal bond funds. These funds are highly diversified geographically. But it is a dirty secret of the bond fund industry that what sells funds is yield. The general bond funds invest in bonds with the longest average weighted maturity—typically in the 16-to–25-year range. Duration is somewhere between 6 and 10 years. That long duration has been the main contributor to the volatility of these funds in good times and in bad times. In good years, when interest rates are declining, the long duration of these funds magnifies the rise in NAV. When interest rates rise, on the other hand, the long duration of these funds magnifies losses.

The most aggressive funds, which feature the highest yields, invest in the longest-term bonds. They may also add a sprinkling of lower-quality credits in order to boost yields further. As a result, short-term swings in NAV are highly unpredictable and can be violent. Losses in 2008 of some of the more aggressively managed long-term muni funds approached those of high-yield tax exempt funds. More conservatively managed long-term funds invest primarily in high quality credits; and duration tends to be somewhat shorter, under seven years. Volatility of these funds is lower: the more conservatively managed funds do a better job of protecting principal and achieve higher total return with lower risks for long-term investors.

Tax-Exempt High-Yield Bond Funds

As noted above, the term "high yield" is somewhat confusing. For taxable bonds, the term "high yield" designates funds that invest in bonds rated below investment grade. Despite the similarity in name, there is simply no credit quality analog in the municipal sector to the "high yield" or junk bonds issued by corporations. Tax-exempt high-yield funds hold issues in the riskier sectors of the tax-exempt market (for instance, tobacco bonds, nursing homes, private activity bonds such as airport bonds, unrated bonds, and the like). Credit quality for these funds clusters around investment grade, or just below. But that is a far cry from corporate junk bonds. The default rate of municipal bonds even in the lower credit quality range has been very low.

Moreover, all "high yield" bond funds do not invest in the same credit-quality range: many funds with the words "high yield" in their name invest primarily in bonds with high quality credits, but longer maturities. Only the most aggressive funds invest primarily in the lowest quality credits. To evaluate the credit quality of a high-yield fund, the key is to look at the portfolio makeup: If the credit quality of the fund includes upwards of 50% investment grade bonds, or higher, whatever the name of the fund, credit risk is modest to low.

Lipper's criteria limit this group to funds whose portfolio is at least 50% below investment grade. These are clearly the most aggressive funds in the municipal sector, investing in the lowest credit quality bonds. Some may also add derivatives to their portfolio.

As a result, the range of returns in this sector is the widest of any group of municipal bond funds. In 2008, for example, the best performing muni high-yield bond funds experienced losses ranging from 15% to 18%; whereas the worst fared much more poorly with losses of 30% to almost 50%.

One more note of caution regarding the perils of investing in bond funds with the highest quoted SEC yields: At the end of 2008, one municipal high-yield fund, the Oppenheimer Rochester Municipal bond fund, was quoting a yield of 13.8%. Total return for this fund in 2008 was a loss of almost 50% despite the high yield. (If you add back interest income for 2008, that translates into a decline in NAV of slightly more than 60%.) A lucky speculator who bought the fund at the beginning of 2009 could have cashed in a very handsome profit because total return for 2009 exceeded 50%. But in spite of the outsize gains of 2009, average annualized total return for the for the 10-year holding period through December 31, 2009 was 2.29%, a few basis points higher than the average annualized return of tax-exempt money market funds; and lower than the average annualized return of ultra-short tax-exempt funds.

Short and Ultra-Short Bond Funds

A number of well-managed fund groups offer municipal bond funds that limit average-weighted maturity to anywhere between one and three years. The duration of these ultra-short bond funds varies between one and two years. This remains a fairly small group of funds although a few are among the oldest in the industry.

The rationale behind these funds is that this maturity sector will capture a higher yield than is available in money market funds, but that the very short duration will produce negligible volatility. Bear in mind,

also, that due to the very short maturities of these funds, the entire portfolio of bonds matures and turns over within less than three years. As a
result, risk to principal is extremely low. But one drawback is that reinvestment risk is significantly higher than for longer-term funds.

These funds have generally achieved their objectives. Volatility has
been dramatically lower than for longer-term funds: as was shown in
Exhibit 12.2, ultra-short funds had positive total returns in 2008. Total
returns were also positive both in 1994 and in 1999, two years when a rise
in interest rates caused significant declines in long-term funds. And, again
as shown in Exhibit 12.3, because of the stable NAV, average annual total
returns for the five- and 10-year marks are much closer to those of longer-
term funds than you might expect.

Compared to money market funds, on the other hand, performance
is sometimes less than optimal. Most of the time, total returns and yields
of very short tax exempt funds are higher than those of tax exempt money
market funds. Occasionally, however, if short-term interest rates are rising, the NAV of short-term funds declines; and as a result, both the yield
and the total return of tax exempt money funds may exceed that of very
short-term funds, at least for a while.

These ultra-short municipal bond funds make sense for you if you
are trying to lift yield and total return above that of money market funds,
while incurring minimal risk to principal. They are particularly attractive
when interest rates are unstable and the future trend of interest rates is
particularly cloudy.

On the other hand, as I write this, interest rate levels are below 1% for
these very short funds. When short-term rates rise, as they are likely to do
sometime within a year or two, the rise in rates is likely to cause the NAV
of the ultra-short funds to decline. Because interest income is so low, any
decline in NAV might translate into a net loss for the year. Because duration is low for these funds (one or two years at the most), risk of loss of
principal is not very high. But in this environment, money market funds
might actually prove to be better buys, at least for a time: Interest income
for money market funds will rise as interest rates rise on short-term rates.

Insured Municipal Bond Funds

I have not included the returns of insured municipal bond funds in either
Exhibit 12.2 or Exhibit 12.3. The reason for that is that, as we saw in
Chapter 7, the major bond insurance firms have been downgraded to well
below investment grade; and most insured bonds now trade based on their
underlying rating, which in many cases is higher than that of the insurer. It

seems clear that bond insurance is no longer viewed as conferring any degree of protection. A number of mutual fund groups have merged their insured bond funds with their general bond funds. But some insured bond funds continue to exist.

Unless bond insurance re-emerges as a force in the municipal bond market, buying a municipal bond fund because of insurance makes no sense. If high credit quality is one of your major criteria for choosing a municipal bond fund, then choose among the many funds that invest in bonds with very high credit ratings such as AAA or AA. That will give you higher credit quality than you would get by investing in "insured" bond funds. For added safety, stick to funds which are intermediate, whose duration is no longer than five years.

2008 AND 2009 BOND FUND RETURNS: SOME PERSPECTIVE

In a very real sense, both of these years were outliers: well outside the range that would be considered "normal."

There have been a number of bad years in the municipal bond market: 1994 and 1999 come to mind. But 2008 is in a league of its own—without any doubt the worst year ever in the municipal bond market. Bear in mind, however, that losses experienced in 2008 did not result (as had been the case in 1994 and 1999) from a lengthy and sustained rise in interest rates. Rather, they were due to a combination of factors unique to 2008: the demise of the bond insurance firms; an unprecedented widening of credit quality spreads resulting in lower quality credits being marked down out of all proportion to real risk; and perhaps most important, to a severe imbalance between buyers and sellers—a market where sellers could find no buyers except at fire sale prices.

To sum up, in 2008, losses in some muni funds (particularly in the high-yield and long-term bond funds) were unprecedented. But they were due to highly unusual circumstances, which "punished" risk out of all proportion to the real risks involved.

The extraordinary declines in municipal bond prices on the one hand; and on the other hand, the equally extraordinary declines in Treasury *yields*, created a situation where munis had become amazingly cheap, based on the ratio of yields of munis to Treasuries of the same maturity. As noted elsewhere, municipal bonds are considered cheap when their yields are somewhere between 85% and 95% of Treasuries at the longer end of the yield curve, meaning ten years or higher. In December 2008, ratios were anywhere between 150% and 300% of Treasuries at every point along the yield curve. Municipal bond yields had rarely been close to 100% of Treasuries, and such situations lasted only a few days. The ratios reached on December 2008 were unprecedented, but they were the end point of a decline that was months in the making.

The situation was ripe for a major rally. And in 2009, municipal bond funds rallied for most of the year.

At the end of 2009, the ratios between munis and Treasuries were back to what would traditionally have been considered "normal." If you see articles (as I still occasionally do) telling you that municipal bonds and bond funds are amazingly "cheap" compared to Treasuries, you need to realize that that was the case at the end of 2008. That situation reversed completely in 2009. Municipal bonds and bond funds may still be appropriate investments for you. But they are no longer amazingly cheap. In fact, as I am writing this, because of the gains of 2009, munis are actually somewhat expensive compared to Treasuries.

SUMMARY

Municipal bond funds had their greatest popularity in the late 1980s and early 1990s. This coincides with their highest returns. During this period, on a net-after-tax basis, municipal bond funds provided individual investors with higher total returns than virtually any other bond funds. Those generally high returns were due to two factors: the very high interest rates that prevailed during most of the 1980s and early 1990s; and the general trend of declining interest rates during those years. In addition, as a group, these funds did a good job of preventing erosion of principal. The better-managed municipal bond funds should continue to do just that.

You should not expect, however, that a municipal bond fund will somehow perform a lot better than its sector of the market. In general, municipal bond funds track their sector of the bond market. If interest rates rise significantly, the NAV of even the best managed municipal bond funds will decline, and sometimes significantly. Losses are unlikely to be as high as those that occurred in 2008; but in a rising interest rate environment, declining NAV diminishes total return. While managers of long-term bond funds shorten or lengthen maturities to some extent in order to insulate the fund against market declines, these changes are at the margin. Major changes in maturity would dramatically alter the yield of the fund. And the yield is one of the major factors that attracts investors.

Both Exhibit 12.2 and Exhibit 12.3 list average total returns for the group. Clearly, all municipal bond funds are not created equal. The best-managed funds have higher total returns than the averages; the worst are a lot lower. Among funds in the same group (for example, high yield, or intermediate), differences in total return are due to some extent to the factors analyzed in the preceding chapter: expense ratios, and credit quality. But they are also due to the policies of the fund with regard to how aggressively they manage the fund, either by attempting to boost yield by buying riskier credits, or derivatives. The largest differences in total return occur in the most aggressively managed funds.

In prior editions of this book, I noted that despite sometimes violent declines when interest rates rose steeply, over most long term holding periods (10 years or more), total returns of long-term and high-yield muni funds on average exceeded those of shorter-term funds. Whether that continues to be the case will depend entirely on what happens to longer-term interest rates.

But there are a number of factors other than interest rates that will affect municipal bonds and bond funds. One factor that would depress the municipal bond market is a prolonged recession or a slower economic recovery than is currently anticipated. States and local governments are experiencing financial difficulties which are much in the news at the time this is being written. A prolonged recession would lead to lots of downgrades. That does not necessarily imply that many more municipal bonds will default. Default rates of municipal bonds were extremely low even during the Great Depression. But nonetheless, downgrades and news stories about downgrades depress the market.

On the other hand, one factor that would increase demand for municipal bonds is a tax increase at the federal level. That would make municipal bonds more attractive to a larger group of investors; and higher demand always translates into price support for the market.

As stressed throughout, because of their higher volatility, both long-term municipal bond funds and high-yield tax exempt funds should be viewed as potentially volatile and therefore more risky than intermediate- or short-term funds. Investors seeking the highest possible income should be cautious about holding most of their bond portfolio in long-term bonds or bond funds. In the current environment, it would seem prudent to hold some of your fixed-income portfolio in shorter-term bonds and bond funds; or in short-term cash or cash equivalents such as one- or two-year CDs or Treasuries.

CHAPTER 13

Taxable Bond Funds

This chapter discusses:

- ◆ "Plain vanilla" taxable bond funds: short, intermediate, long
- ◆ TIPS Funds
- ◆ GNMA funds
- ◆ More speculative bond funds: "junk," multi-sector, international, and emerging market bond funds
- ◆ Miscellaneous bond funds: index funds and loan participation funds

Taxable bond funds are much more diverse in their makeup than municipal bond funds and this makes them much more difficult to categorize and define. To get some idea of the potential number of combinations, consider first all the different taxable bonds available to U.S. investors: corporates, governments (the United States and foreign governments), federal agencies, and mortgage-backed and asset-backed securities. Consider further that every sector of the taxable bond market comes in short, intermediate, or long maturities. Consider that credit quality for taxable bonds ranges from impeccable to junk and to companies in default. Finally, consider that many taxable bond funds invest in more than one sector of the bond market, and to boot, many use a variety of derivatives either to hedge or to leverage total return. This gives you some idea why taxable funds are much more difficult to categorize than tax-exempt funds. Also, as we shall see, given the diverse management policies of these funds, patterns of total returns are not as clear cut in this group as they are in the tax-exempt groups.

I am dividing this section into two main groupings. The first are the "plain vanilla" funds, defined in the previous chapter—those whose risk factors derive primarily from the average-weighted maturity and the average credit quality of the fund. This grouping includes funds investing in a variety of corporate bonds and government debt; as well as mort- gage- and asset-backed securities

I am calling the second grouping "more speculative funds." Those are the most volatile bond funds, with the most variable returns. They include "junk" bond funds, international bond funds, and emerging mar- ket bond funds.

Before discussing these categories, let's again address the issue of fund names. Some fund names give you very precise information about the portfolio of the fund. A label such as "Long-term Treasury" or "Short- term corporate" identifies the primary holdings of the fund; their credit quality; and a probable maturity range. But many taxable bond funds are not so clearly named. Indeed, many names seem intended to mislead rather than to inform. A "government" bond fund, for example, may invest in U.S. Treasury bonds, federal agency bonds, GNMA bonds, or zero coupon bonds, in any combination. Many "government" bond funds (including funds with names like "government-only") in fact, invest mainly in GNMA bonds. Some fund names, such as "corporate," "income," and "high income," are even more vague. These funds may hold corporate bonds, Treasuries, government agency paper, GNMAs, and so on, again in any combination. The name of these funds does not give you a clue about the actual securities in the fund. More importantly, the name tells you nothing about the average weighted maturity of the fund or the credit quality of its portfolio. In fact, some "income" funds invest in stocks as well as bonds. Before investing in any bond fund, it is imperative to investigate what securities the fund holds, their credit quality, and the maturity or duration of the fund. If you fail to do this, you will have no idea of the risks you are incurring.

DOMESTIC "PLAIN VANILLA" TAXABLE BOND FUNDS

"Plain vanilla" taxable bond funds invest in a broad variety of U.S. debt rated at least investment grade. But once again, the names of specific funds sometimes make it difficult to determine, just by looking at the fund name, what the portfolio holdings may be or their maturity sector. Unless otherwise specified with a name such as "Treasury Only," many of the bond funds in this grouping invest in a broadly diversified portfolio, which includes corporate bonds, agency debt, mortgage-backed securi- ties, and perhaps some Treasuries within the specified maturity sector.

(Note: Once again, I am using the Lipper categories because those are used most widely by fund groups and by the financial media. In compiling these tables, I have omitted a few of the smallest categories.)

The chief risk factor for these funds is our old friend: interest rate risk, determined by average-weighted maturity and duration. The Lipper organization groups these funds according to their own criteria, and based on the following maturities:

- ◆ Ultra-short funds (90 days to one year)
- ◆ Short-intermediate: one to three years
- ◆ Intermediate: five to ten years
- ◆ Long: ten years or more

Exhibit 13.1 illustrates the average total return of "plain vanilla" taxable bond funds both for 2008 and for 2009; and for 5-year and 10-year holding periods through December 31, 2009. (Total return is the average

E X H I B I T   13.1

Average Annual Total Returns of "Plain Vanilla" Taxable Bond Funds for 2008, 2009, and for 5-Year and 10-Year Holding Periods through December 31, 2009 (All Distributions, Dividends, and Capital Gains Are Assumed to Be Reinvested)

	2008 (12/31/2007– 12/31/2008)	2009 (12/31/2008– 12/31/2009)	5 Years (12/31/2004– 12/31/2009)	10 Years (12/31/1999– 12/31/2009)
Ultra-Short				
(1 Year or Less)	−5.96%	5.28%	2.05%	2.88%
Short-Term (1-3 Years)				
U.S. Treasury	6.57%	0.65%	3.69%	4.22%
U.S. Govt.	−3.04%	4.37%	3.47%	4.00%
Short-Term Investment				
Grade (1-3 Years)	−5.77%	9.61%	3.02%	3.88%
Intermediate Investment				
Grade (5-10 Years)	−4.43%	12.89%	3.90%	5.51%
Long-Term (>10 Years)				
U.S. Treasury	19.92%	−6.47%	4.76%	6.24%
Corporate A Rated	−5.88%	15.18%	3.47%	5.45%
Corporate BBB Rated	−8.84%	21.13%	4.04%	6.11%

Source: Lipper, a Thomson Reuters Company. Material supplied to the author and reprinted with permission.

annualized compounded total return, based on reinvestment of all dividends and capital gains distributions, if any, plus changes in share price.) Because annualized total returns have been averaged, volatility and variability of returns show up primarily in the stark contrasts between the losses of 2008 in all sectors of taxable bond funds other than Treasuries as well as in the steep gains of 2009.

This discussion will begin with the shortest categories, and end with the longest.

Ultra-Short Funds

These funds invest in investment grade bonds with very short maturities: 90 days to one year. Ultra-short funds are marketed as being almost as safe as money market funds, but with higher yields. The short maturity of these funds significantly reduces interest rate risk. When coupled with high credit quality, these funds ought to produce modest, but safe returns, just like their tax exempt counterparts. And indeed, some funds in this group have done just that.

But unlike their municipal counterparts, some ultra-short or short corporate bond funds have been disappointing or extremely poor performers. Indeed, a number have produced downright disasters. As you might guess, the culprit has been the attempt to juice up total return through a variety of "sophisticated" strategies.

Disasters in this group have not been limited to the recent past. Lipper has eliminated two categories of bond funds that belonged to this category, which were discussed in the prior edition of this book, precisely because even though they were initially marketed as very low risk funds, returns were abysmal. The first was the so-called "short world, multi-market funds." These were popular in the early 1990s. At the time these funds were launched, they had a dual strategy: They would invest in short-maturity foreign-pay bonds whose yields were higher than those of U.S. bonds with the same maturities. Currency risk was to be eliminated through hedges against the foreign currencies. Initial returns were high because interest rates at the time on short maturity bonds were higher abroad than in the U.S.; and also because at the time, the dollar was declining. But the strategy turned sour for two reasons: First, interest rates declined on the foreign bonds; and second, the dollar started rising against foreign currencies. As losses mounted, assets exited the funds.

A second category, also popular in the 1990s, and marketed as a low-risk alternative to money funds, was that of bond funds investing in ARMs (adjustable rate mortgages). These funds also had extremely disappointing returns. Only a few funds in this group still exist, with little in the way of assets.

The most recent disaster in this group are the "yield plus" funds. As shown in Exhibit 13.1, the average annual total return for the group in 2008 was a negative 5.96% (in other words, a loss of close to 6%). For 2008, which was a disastrous year for most bond funds other than those investing in Treasuries, a loss of 6% may not appear particularly disastrous. But what makes it disastrous is that the average negative returns of the entire group are the result of losses posted by approximately 40% of the funds in this group. One of these was a very popular fund managed by Schwab, under the name "yield plus". Indeed, between 1999 and 2008, this fund was the most popular Schwab bond fund, with assets under management of over $13 billion dollars. For the calendar year 2008, that fund posted losses of over 35%. It posted an additional 15% loss in 2009. The reasons for the decline are somewhat in dispute, but it would appear that, in spite of the fact that it was marketed as a short term fund, a substantial percentage of the assets of the fund were invested in longer term mortgage backed securities, some of which were based on sub-prime mortgages. Furthermore, it would appear that the sales literature for the fund did not accurately disclose the holdings of the fund. Similar funds suffered losses that were almost as large (a number of these were called "adjustable rate" funds). Investors in the Schwab fund are suing Schwab, claiming they were misled.

These disasters do not extend to all ultra-short funds. Bond funds in the top 20% of this group all had positive total returns, ranging from 1.5% to 4.20%. And bond funds in the second and third quintile experienced much more modest losses, ranging from 1 1/2 to almost 7%. But the disasters in the bottom 40% were enough to bring down the averages for the entire group. The difference between the disasters and the more successful funds is that the latter invest in higher quality credits, or in bonds that have a government guarantee such as Treasuries or agency debt.

If you decide to invest in a bond fund with a very short maturity, make sure that you check both the maturity and the credit quality of the fund. The periodic disasters in this group are clear evidence that in the world of bonds, you can always get somewhat higher yields by taking on some added risk. But if you are looking for very safe returns, don't jeopardize principal by investing in a fund with added enhancements such as "structured" securities or derivatives you don't understand. There is no way of knowing when these may blow up.

Of course, if you want to invest in Treasuries, the simplest alternative is to buy individual Treasuries through Treasury-Direct, as described in Chapter 6. Because Treasuries have no credit risk, there is no need for diversification. And if you buy short maturity Treasuries that you hold to maturity, you recover principal in full.

Short U.S. Government and Treasury Funds (1 to 3 Years)

This is the second group shown in Exhibit 13.1. This group invests in bonds with slightly longer maturities than the ultra-short funds—1 to 3 years. Exhibit 13.1 shows two types of funds in this maturity range: Treasury only funds, which invest almost entirely in Treasuries; and a U.S. government category, which includes agency debt as well.

This is a small group of funds, but it deserves to be larger. The range of returns in this group is remarkably narrow. As shown in Exhibit 13.1, most funds in this group show positive returns for every period illustrated, including 2008, 2009, and 5- and 10-year holding periods. Interest rate risk for this group is low and credit quality is high.

In 2008, the short maturity Treasury-only group had average total returns above 6%, well in excess of their interest income, as plummeting yields on short-term Treasuries caused the NAVs of the funds to soar. But in 2009, total returns of short term Treasury-only funds were barely positive in 2009, due to a rise in Treasury yields. But the high returns of 2008 elevated the average annual returns for 5 years and for 10 years.

If interest rates are stable, you would expect yield and total return to be somewhat higher for the U.S. government category than for the Treasury only group, and that is the typical pattern. For example, as shown in Exhibit 13.1, average annual total return of the government grouping was positive in 2009 (almost 4 1/2%) and as a result, total return for this category was close to that of the Treasury-only group, for both the 5-year and 10-year holding periods.

Short and Intermediate Investment Grade Funds

Funds in both of these categories invest in a broadly diversified group of bonds that are rated investment grade or higher. The primary distinction between the short and the intermediate grouping is that the short grouping invests in bonds with maturities of 3 years or less; whereas the intermediate category invests in bonds with maturities of 5 to 10 years.

The short investment grade grouping includes many funds with the phrase "low duration" or "short term" as part of their name. Once again, these funds are intended to produce returns that are higher than money market funds, without too much risk; and with low volatility of returns.

Interest rate risk for this group is modest, and credit risk should also be modest. As shown in Exhibit 13.1, total returns were unusually high in 2009 (an average gain of 9.61%), due to the enormous rally in investment grade debt that took place in 2009. Total returns are also positive for both the 5-year and 10-year periods, but lower than those of the Intermediate investment grade category (see below).

Note, however, that average annual total return for this group was negative in 2008, an average loss of 5.77%. There is a broader range of returns in this group than the averages suggest. Approximately half of the funds actually had positive returns in 2008. But the funds in the lower half of the group included at least one downright disaster: one fund showing a loss of 69% (due to investments in subprime mortgages), and several others with losses exceeding 25%. Most funds in the lower half of the category experienced much smaller losses, ranging from a loss of 5% to a loss of 10%. But the combined losses of the funds in the lower half of this category lowered the averages for the entire group.

Intermediate Investment Grade Funds (5 to 10 Years)

The intermediate investment grade grouping deserves special comment. At the time this is being written, this group is the largest in the taxable bond fund grouping: It holds approximately 40% of all the assets in tax-able bond funds. That is partly due to the fact that this group includes two extremely large taxable bond funds: the Pimco Total Return Fund, which is the largest bond fund (and the largest of all mutual funds, with over $220 billion in assets); and the Vanguard Total Return Bond Index Fund, which has close to $80 billion in assets. But this group also includes a very large number of smaller bond funds (a total of 580 funds in 2009).

This is an attractive group of funds. Average weighted maturity for the group is between 5 and 10 years, but even for funds with a 10-year weighted average maturity, duration is below 5 years, so that interest rate risk is modest. Total return of funds in this group is benchmarked to the Barclays Capital U.S. Aggregate Index; and many of the funds in this group either track the index very closely, or with a few variations. This is true, for example, of the Vanguard Total Return Fund, which tracks the index closely (it holds well over 7,000 bonds). The Pimco Total Return Fund tracks the largest U.S. categories of the index but includes some bonds not in the index in order to boost total return. As this is being written, for example, it includes a sprinkling of international and emerging market debt. Both of these funds have solid long-term records, but the Vanguard fund is no-load, whereas the Pimco fund has a 3.75% load: Actual total returns, therefore, need to be adjusted for the load.

As shown in Exhibit 13.1, the broadly diversified intermediate sector experienced losses in 2008 averaging about 4 1/2%, reflecting the fact that all bonds other than Treasuries declined in price during 2008. But average annual total returns for the group were positive for 2009—as shown in Exhibit 13.1, an average gain of almost 13% as investment grade bonds rallied strongly for the entire year. The strong returns of 2009, moreover, elevated average annual total returns for both the 5-year and 10-year periods.

Note also that for investment grade taxable funds, as for munis, the intermediate maturity range represents the sweet spot: Total returns for both the 5-year and 10-year holding periods are almost as high for this maturity range as those of funds with longer maturities (higher for some of the better managed funds in the group) than those of the more volatile longer maturity group (10 years or more, described below).

Note, however, that due to the number of funds in this group, total returns vary much more broadly from fund to fund than you might expect. Once again, funds in the top half of the group performed significantly better, and had more consistent total returns, than those in the lower half. In 2008, a number of the worst performing funds in this group experienced losses above 20%: One catastrophic loss of 84% was due to investments in sub-prime mortgages. Note also that funds that reach for yield exhibit much more volatility: One fund, for example, that showed very high returns in 2009 (+35%) had losses of 15% in 2008.

Long-Term Taxable Funds (10 Years or More)

These are the longest-term funds in the investment grade taxable groups, with average weighted maturities of 10 years or more. Interest rate risk is higher in this grouping than in any of the other "plain vanilla" taxable categories.

Let's first look at the Treasury-only funds. These funds invest primarily in long-term Treasuries.

This is actually a fairly small group of funds. For 2008, long-term Treasury funds had average total returns close to 20%, as shown in Exhibit 13.1. These returns were due primarily to the enormous flight to quality buying that took place during the financial panic of 2008. In 2009, however, as interest rates rose at the long end, this sector experienced losses averaging about 6.5%. But once again, the high total returns of 2009 elevated average annual total returns of these funds for both the 5-year and 10-year holding periods through December 31, 2009.

The two other categories of funds in the long-term group are the corporate A rated funds and the corporate BBB funds. The investment grade, A rated group invests primarily in bonds rated A or higher (in other words, the three highest investment grade categories); whereas the group rated BBB invests in bonds rated just investment grade and higher (in other words, the four highest investment grade categories). Credit quality is somewhat lower in the BBB corporate group, which permits a broader, but possibly somewhat more risky, range of credits.

In 2008, when risk became a four letter word, average annual returns for the Corporate A rated funds were higher than those of the BBB rated group (average losses of close to 6% for the A group compared with average losses of almost 9% for the BBB group). In 2009, when riskier funds experienced the highest returns, corporate bonds rated BBB posted average gains of 21% compared with average gains of about 15% for the A group. The riskier funds had both higher losses in 2008 and higher gains in 2009— in other words, higher volatility. For both the 5-year and the 10-year holding periods, the long-term Treasury group posted the highest average total returns (4.76% for the 5-year and 6.24% for the 10-year) but that was clearly due to the enormous flight to quality buying of 2008.

Summary: "Plain Vanilla" Taxable Investment Bond Funds

One would like to draw some conclusions for these types of funds, but clearly, total returns for 2008 were dominated by the financial crisis of that year, which resulted in enormous flight to quality buying of Treasuries and enormous declines in other sectors of the bond market. In turn total returns for 2009 were dominated by the strong rally in the riskier sectors of the bond market in 2009. Total returns for these two years distorted average annualized returns for longer holding periods.

To some extent, however, the returns of 2008 and 2009 were simply extremes of a general pattern for this sector. Returns of bond funds investing in corporate bonds track the economy and the stock market almost as much as interest rates. One reason is that if an economic downturn is anticipated, the bonds of many corporations are downgraded. As a result, the NAV of bond funds holding a large number of corporate bonds declines. Whenever the economic outlook is poor, or cloudy, a so-called flight to quality occurs. Investors abandon lower quality credits and flock to the security of Treasuries or of higher-quality bonds.

Finally, while there are always trade-offs in bond funds between yield and risk, as was the case for municipal bonds, the "sweet spot" seems to be in the intermediate investment grade category, whose returns are almost as high as those of longer term or riskier funds, with far less volatility. Risk rises to the extent funds invest in bonds with longer maturities; and lower quality credits.

The same caveats apply to long-term taxable bond funds as to long-term, tax-exempt bond funds. Over any short-term holding period, total return is dominated by changes in NAV caused by changes in the level of interest rates, rather than by the income component of the fund. Because of their high potential volatility, long-term taxable funds should be purchased for long holding periods only if you are prepared to live with considerable volatility. Again, unless you are frankly speculating that a decline in interest rates is likely to occur, long-term taxable bond funds should not be purchased for holding periods of one year or less.

Unless you are in a very low tax bracket, taxable bond funds are appropriate investments primarily for tax-sheltered accounts. For money not in tax-sheltered accounts, bear in mind that funds holding Treasuries-only are exempted from state taxes. Whether such a fund would yield more for you than other bond funds (whether taxable or tax-exempt) would vary with your tax bracket and the taxes of the state in which you live.

TREASURY INFLATION PROTECTED SECURITIES FUNDS

As their name suggests, these funds invest primarily (in some cases 100%) in Treasury Inflation Protected Securities (TIPS) (for a discussion of TIPS, see Chapter 5, the section on Inflation-Protected Securities). Whenever a fund invests 100% in TIPS, its credit quality is impeccable. But nonetheless, volatility of these funds has been extremely high, reflecting the volatility of the underlying securities. Exhibit 13.2 shows annual average returns for these funds through December 2009. (Total return is the average annualized compounded total return, based on reinvestment of all dividends and capital gains distributions, if any, plus changes in share price.)

The maturity and duration of TIPS funds averages out to the intermediate range. But if you compare total returns of TIPS Funds to those of the intermediate government sectors, or to those of the Treasury only funds, you will note a totally different pattern of returns. As shown in Exhibit 13.2, total returns for the group averaged out to a loss of approximately 4% in 2008, unlike other bond funds holding Treasuries, whose NAVs soared in 2008. But again unlike other Treasury bond funds, average

EXHIBIT 13.2

Average Annual Total Returns of TIPS Funds for 2008, 2009, and for 5-Year and 10-Year Holding Periods through December 31, 2009 (All Distributions, Dividends, and Capital Gains Are Assumed to Be Reinvested)

	2008 (12/31/2007– 12/31/2008)	2009 (12/31/2008– 12/31/2009)	5 Years (12/31/2004– 12/31/2009)	10 Years (12/31/1999– 12/31/2009)
TIPS Funds	−4.14%	10.75%	3.56%	6.77%

Source: Lipper, a Thomson Reuters Company. Material supplied to the author and reprinted with permission.

total return of TIPS funds in 2009 was a gain of 10.75% (in 2009, longer dated Treasury funds experienced losses, as interest rates rose). The gain in TIPS funds may have been due to fears of inflation, which to date, have proved unfounded.

TIPS funds were introduced around 2000. At the time, there were only a handful of funds, and they remained small. They initially met with little investor enthusiasm as early returns were somewhat disappointing. Then, in 2002, average total returns of these funds soared, to around 16%. This created a lot of excitement: Funds multiplied to well over a hundred, and money poured into the funds.

Since then, total returns of these funds have been extremely variable. Typically, money pours into TIPS funds if consensus opinion is that high inflation looms, or after a period of high total returns for these funds. But monies also flow out of TIPS funds when total returns are poor.

These fund flows point to a fundamental misunderstanding of these instruments. Clearly, in 2003, investors flocked to TIPS funds hoping returns would match those of 2002. But the high 2002 total returns (16%), were due to changes in interest rate levels during the year; as well as to concurrent high demand for TIPS, which generated significant price appreciation for the underlying bonds. These returns were clearly not due to the interest income (around 2.5% to 3%); or to the inflation adjustment, which tracked the rate of inflation (approximately 2.5%).

Given the variability of TIPS returns from year to year, discussions of TIPS funds in the financial press, or on financial Web sites, usually revolve around timing: Is this a good time to invest in TIPS? How likely are they to generate better returns than other sectors of the bond market over the next six months? Unfortunately, few of these articles ever evaluate the accuracy of their crystal ball in the past. In any case, these opinions are beside the point. The main reason to invest in a TIPS fund is inflation protection, not whether the TIPS funds will provide better returns than alternate bond investments over short periods of time.

The variability of total returns of TIPS funds since their inception underlines the fact that these funds should not be regarded as short-term investments. If you look at longer time periods, however, the perspective is quite different. Bear in mind that interest income tracks the inflation adjustment. Therefore, if there is inflation, the price of TIPS bonds will appreciate, reflecting the inflation adjustment. The amount of interest income, which is also adjusted based on the inflation adjustment, would also appreciate. Whether total return from TIPS funds will be higher or lower than that of bond funds investing in conventional Treasury bonds will depend entirely on the rate of inflation.

Is there any advantage to buying TIPS through funds rather than by buying the individual bonds? For reasons that escape me, individual bonds and bond funds are treated in the financial press as interchangeable instruments, and they are not. For starters, if you hold individual TIPS bonds and redeem them when they mature, you will receive, at minimum, no less than the initial face value of the bond; or more likely, the adjusted value of principal. On the other hand, a TIPS fund, like any other "open end" bond fund, has no "maturity" date. That is to say there is no date at which the entire portfolio matures. Given the volatility of the underlying bonds in the portfolio, there is no way to know what its price will be when you want to sell. Finally, the cheapest way to buy TIPS is to buy them at auction, through Treasury Direct. Any fund, even those with low expense ratios, charges those expenses against total return and this obviously reduces total return.

One advantage of funds is that they solve the reinvestment problem. TIPS bond funds distribute interest income, usually on a quarterly basis. They also distribute the inflation adjustment. It is distributed along with interest payments, also on a quarterly basis. But note that while interest income is distributed as it is in any bond fund, the value of the inflation adjustment is deducted from the NAV of the fund. Both types of distributions may be reinvested to buy additional shares. As is the case for individual TIPS bonds, you will be taxed both on the interest income, and on the inflation adjustment. Funds supply a form (1099-DIV) that tells both you and the IRS how much is taxable.

Note that in 2009, for the first time in their history, a number of TIPS funds did not have any distributions for most of the year: The interest income of the bonds in the fund was offset by the "inflation adjustment," which was negative due to actual deflation.

One final remark is in order: Many TIPS funds hold only TIPS bonds. These funds usually include a phrase such as "inflation indexed" or "inflation protected" in the fund name. But in order to generate higher returns, some TIPS funds have added a variety of other investments to their portfolio mix. These include TIPS bonds issued by foreign governments; as well as commodities, high-yield (junk) bonds, or indeed, any asset that the manager thinks will track inflation or add some return. Such funds typically include a phrase such as "real return" or "real income" somewhere in the fund name. So before purchasing any inflation-linked bond fund, the first step would be to find out its investment mix.

If you decide to invest in TIPS through a fund, as a first cut, only invest in a no-load fund with low annual expenses (at the current time, the Vanguard TIPS fund has the lowest annual expenses: 20 basis points). Another option would be to invest in one of the ETF funds that hold only TIPS bonds issued by the U.S. government.

GNMA (AND OTHER MORTGAGE) FUNDS

GNMA fund advertising focuses on two very appealing themes: their high dividend yield (GNMAs typically have yields that track mortgage rates, and that are higher than long-term Treasuries); and the unconditional government backing, which eliminates credit risk. It is therefore a shock to some buyers of GNMA funds to discover that the high credit quality does not eliminate market risk.

Exhibit 13.3 lists average annualized total returns for funds investing in different types of mortgage-backed securities, for 2008, 2009, and for 5-year and 10-year holding periods through December 31, 2009 (Total return is the average annualized compounded total return, based on reinvestment of all dividends and capital gains distributions, if any, plus changes in share price).

Exhibit 13.3 shows total returns of two types of funds investing in mortgage-backed securities: the larger group invests primarily in GNMA securities. A much smaller category of funds is listed by Lipper as "mortgage funds." It appears that these funds do not invest primarily in GNMAs. Some of these hold at least some percentage of their portfolio in bonds derived from subprime mortgages: A number of these funds experienced significant declines in 2008. Hence, the total returns of these two categories are quite different.

EXHIBIT 13.3

Average Annual Total Returns of GNMA (and Other Mortgage-Backed Securities) Bond Funds for 2008, 2009, and for 5-Year and 10-Year Holding Periods through December 31, 2009 (All Distributions, Dividends, and Capital Gains Are Assumed to Be Reinvested)

	2008 (12/31/2007– 12/31/2008)	2009 (12/31/2008– 12/31/2009)	5 Years (12/31/2004– 12/31/2009)	10 Years (12/31/1999– 12/31/2009)
GNMA Funds	5.24%	8.01%	5.07%	5.70%
U.S. Mortgage Funds	−1.61%	9.10%	3.67%	5.02%

Source: Lipper, a Thomson Reuters Company. Material supplied to the author and reprinted with permission.

Again, the categories are those of Lipper. Lipper specifies that GNMA funds invest at least 65% of fund assets in GNMA securities. Mortgage funds invest at least 65% of fund assets in a variety of mortgage-backed securities other than GNMAs. Note again that many funds investing primarily in GNMAs or other mortgage-backed securities do not include the term "GNMA" or any allusion to mortgages in the fund name. Many are called "government" or "government income" or "government-only" funds.

Interest income of funds that invest primarily in GNMA securities is typically about 1/2 of 1% lower than current mortgage rates on 30-year mortgages. As noted above, GNMA funds may hold a variety of securities other than mortgage-backed debt.

Note that average annual returns for both the 5-year and 10-year holding periods have been boosted by the fact that during 2008, funds that invested primarily in GNMA securities generated positive returns whereas most other taxable funds declined in price. Bear in mind that GNMAs have the unconditional backing of the U.S. government, and this guarantee was the key factor in their positive returns both in 2008 and 2009.

Total returns of GNMA funds, however, have had their ups and downs. During the 1980s, GNMA bond funds attracted enormous sums. Indeed, one GNMA fund, with over $14 billion in assets, was both the largest bond fund and one of the largest of all mutual funds at the time. Since then, the appeal of GNMA funds had faded (at least up to 2008) because of a number of disappointing years. As a general rule, when interest rates are stable,

GNMA funds do well because of the (relatively) high dividend yield. In volatile markets, however, total return has often been much less satisfactory. If interest rates rise, the NAV of GNMA funds declines along with that of other bond funds. But if interest rates decline sharply, GNMA bond funds may show poor total returns because of massive prepayments. For most of the 1980s and 1990s, average annual returns of GNMA funds were somewhat below those of intermediate taxable bond funds and well below those of long term corporate bond funds. Returns for the most recent decade look more attractive due to the positive returns of 2008 and 2009.

GNMA funds have a number of advantages compared with individual GNMAs. They require a lower initial investment ($1,000 as compared with $25,000). The size of a fund also results in more predictable cash flows (again compared to individual GNMAs). As a result, GNMA funds mitigate some of the hazards of investing in individual GNMAs. Also, investors in GNMA funds are able to reinvest interest and mortgage prepayments automatically, and at a higher rate than money market yields, which should boost total return over time. Finally, GNMA funds can buy GNMA instruments far more economically than can individuals.

Because GNMA advertising focuses so heavily on yield, some of the more poorly managed funds used to inflate the advertised yield. SEC regulations have made this more difficult. Nonetheless, be aware that total return for GNMA funds (from the best to the worst) varies significantly from fund to fund. The best-performing GNMA funds manage for total return, which means that they may not have the highest advertised yield. Before purchasing a GNMA fund, be sure to check the fund's history and total return compared with other GNMA funds.

If you are considering investing in GNMAs through a fund, be sure to read the chapter on mortgage-backed securities in order to understand the nature of these very complex instruments.

MORE SPECULATIVE FUNDS

These are the bond funds that have the greatest variability of returns, the ones whose total returns are the most volatile and hardest to predict. Risk factors are more complex and less easy to define than for either of the preceding group of funds. This grouping includes bond funds that have had some of the highest total returns at various time periods and also some of the largest losses. Total returns for bond funds in this grouping vary significantly from year to year, and from fund to fund within any one fund category.

There is also a good deal of disagreement concerning the riskiness of some of these funds, particularly for longer holding periods. If you like a lot of "action" and want to speculate, then read on.

"Junk" Bond Funds

The group of "junk" bond funds has had enormous ups and downs. At the end of December 31, 1999, this bond fund sector held over $100 billion in assets. At the time, this was the largest single category among taxable bond funds, holding approximately 40% of all the assets in the taxable sector! As I am writing this, in the spring of 2010, this sector of the bond market still holds a significant amount of assets (around $70 billion); but as a percentage of assets in taxable funds, it has shrunk to well under 10%. The relative attrition of this sector underlines the fact that in spite of enticing high yields, returns to investors have been disappointing.

So-called junk bond funds invest in corporate bonds rated below investment grade. That rating indicates a strong possibility of default. This is the only type of bond fund where the primary source of risk is credit quality. Yields quoted for junk bond funds are always the highest of any domestic bond funds. In the recent past they have sold at a spread to Treasuries ranging from approximately 250 basis points at the low (just prior to the financial panic of 2007–2008) to a unbelievably high 2,000 plus basis points (actual yields well over 25%) toward the end of 2008.

These funds are a perfect illustration of the fact that high yield does not necessarily translate into high total return. Chapter 8 includes a brief history of junk bonds, and there is no need to repeat it here. What is clear is that since their inception, periods of very high returns have alternated with periods of miserable returns—and both parts of the cycle have lasted a long time.

Exhibit 13.4 lists the average annual total return for of high-yield "junk" bond funds for 2008, 2009, and 5 and 10 year holding periods through December 31, 2009. (Total return is the average annualized compounded total return, based on reinvestment of all dividends and capital gains distributions, if any, plus changes in share price.)

Exhibit 13.4 provides a striking example of the volatility of this group: Average aggregate losses in 2008 were almost 26%. But average aggregate gains in 2009 were 46.4%, the highest aggregate gain in this sector for any one year in its entire history. In spite of the outsize gains of 2009, average annual total returns for the 5-year holding period (a gain of 4.36%) and for the 10-year holding periods through December 31, 2009 (a gain of 4.8%)

EXHIBIT 13.4

Average Annual Total Returns of Corporate High Yield ("junk") Bond Funds, for 2008, 2009, and for 5-Year and 10-Year Holding Periods through December 31, 2009 (All Distributions, Dividends, and Capital Gains Are Assumed to Be Reinvested)

	2008 (12/31/2007– 12/31/2008)	2009 (12/31/2008– 12/31/2009)	5 Years (12/31/2004– 12/31/2009)	10 Years (12/31/1999– 12/31/2009)
High Yield (Junk) Corporate Bond Funds	−25.86%	46.41%	4.36%	4.80%

Source: Lipper, a Thomson Reuters Company. Material supplied to the author and reprinted with permission.

were lower than total returns of much less volatile funds such as the intermediate government bond group (average total return of 5.51% for the 10-year holding period, as shown in Exhibit 13.1) or the GNMA funds (average annual total return of 5.7% for the 10-year holding period, as shown in Exhibit 13.3).

Note that if we had shown 5-year and 10-year total returns starting through December 31, 2008, total returns would have been far worse. For the 5-year period from December 31, 2003 to December 31, 2008, the average annualized compounded total return of high-yield funds was a *loss of 1.5%*; the 10-year return was a barely positive 1.2%, *less than you would have earned on a riskless money market fund for that entire period.*

Again, this is a group of funds where returns vary widely from fund to fund. You can expect that any bond fund investing in junk bonds will experience some actual defaults. But because the riskiness of junk bonds varies from somewhat speculative to companies in outright default, bond funds investing in this sector of the market differ from each other in the degree of riskiness they exhibit. The more aggressive funds invest in the riskiest, lowest rated bonds; more conservatively managed high-yield funds invest in the higher reaches of the junk bond market.

In 2008, for example, one junk bond fund posted a loss of 78%; several others posted declines between 35% and 57%. Contrast that with the fact that even in that disastrous year, a number of junk bond funds actually posted gains of between 8% and 10%; while a number of others posted losses of less than 10% (a good performance for 2008).

When junk bonds prosper, aggressive funds tend to have the highest returns. But when returns are poor, aggressive funds experience the most disastrous losses. Erosion of principal also tends to be very high in the more aggressive funds. More conservatively managed funds tend to be somewhat less volatile and somewhat more consistent in their performance. They also tend to have better longer-term performance.

Finally, bear in mind once again that one year of extremely high returns (such as those of 2009) elevates compounded returns for much longer holding periods. In turn, that masks volatility of returns from year to year.

To Buy or Not to Buy?

The main argument in favor of holding junk bonds is that they provide diversification for a large portfolio because returns may not correlate with other sectors of the bond market, such as Treasuries or GNMAs. But if preservation of capital is your goal, and your bond portfolio is small (say under $100,000), then the losses caused by any significant decline may so devastate the portfolio that the losses cannot be recovered for years.

Another argument in favor of junk bonds is that their volatility makes them very good candidates for speculation. But trying to time any market is extremely difficult, and junk bonds are no exception. Clearly, one key to the performance of junk bond funds is the spread of junk to 10-year Treasuries. When the spread is wide, as it was at the end of 2008, even though that coincides with a period when no one wants to own junk, that is the time to buy. It bears repeating, however, that markets can continue to decline for years, and losses can mount, even when the market appears "cheap."

Unfortunately, historical patterns of cash flows in and out of high yield funds show significant inflows after funds have gone up; and outflows after declines—in other words, buying high and selling low—which is a recipe for investment disaster. The message conveyed by these cash flows is that individual investors tend to pile into junk bond funds when spreads to Treasuries are low and risk is high; and panic out after significant losses, when spreads to Treasuries are wide and risk is actually lower.

Nonetheless, if you are tempted to invest in junk bond funds, because of the imperative need to diversify, and the genuine expertise required to analyze individual "junk" bonds, mutual funds represent the most practical way to invest in this sector. The diversification inherent in any bond fund affords some measure of protection against the inevitable defaults. But then, you should investigate carefully the history and the management style of the fund.

Note that, in order to discourage "hot" money from trading in and out of "junk" funds a number of no-load fund groups charge a 1% fee if you redeem shares held for less than one year. During the panic years of the early 1990s, some mutual fund groups adopted the policy of routinely advising potential investors that junk bond funds were speculative, and a number have continued that policy.

In summary:

- If you are investing in bonds for the safe, predictable part of your portfolio, or primarily for income, then you should view junk bond funds as speculative and not worth the risk.
- If you have a large, highly diversified bond portfolio (well in excess of $300,000), and if you can sustain large losses in assets that you will not need for a long period of time, then you may want to consider junk bonds—particularly as a speculation when spreads are wide—but for no more than 20% of your portfolio.
- Because of the imperative need to diversify, and the high degree of expertise that is required to analyze junk bonds, bond funds represent the most practical way for individual investors to invest in junk bonds.
- Be sure to investigate the history and the management style of any junk bond fund before investing any money.

Multi-Sector Funds

The most popular term in the fund name for this group of funds is "strategic," although "multi-sector" also makes a number of appearances. I shall quote Lipper's definition for this group: "Fund seeks current income by allocating assets among different fixed-income securities sectors (no 65% in one sector except for defensive purposes), including U.S. and foreign governments, with a significant portion rated below U.S. investment grade."

In other words, multi-sector funds manage for the highest possible total return, selecting bonds from any group they deem likely to appreciate the most and to have potentially the highest total return over the short term. Managers of these funds are free to select any bond from any sector, and any maturity length from any nationality. Many of these funds invest in securities that are deemed to be well below investment grade (read: rated as junk), not only in the United States but also in emerging markets. A few rely heavily on mathematical, quantitative models. Leveraging techniques (buying or selling futures contracts, writing options) may also be permitted. The hope, of course, is that the freedom given to the managers to invest in high-risk, but potentially high-return securities will enable them to post returns that will be well above average.

EXHIBIT   13.5

Average Annual Total Returns of Multi-Sector Bond
Funds, for 2008, 2009, and for 5-Year and 10-Year
Holding Periods through December 31, 2009
(All Distributions, Dividends, and Capital Gains
Are Assumed to Be Reinvested)

	2008 (12/31/2007– 12/31/2008)	2009 (12/31/2008– 12/31/2009)	5 Years (12/31/2004– 12/31/2009)	10 Years (12/31/1999– 12/31/2009)
Multi-Sector Bond Funds	−14.31%	28.17%	4.64%	5.90%

Source: Lipper, a Thomson Reuters Company. Material supplied to the author and reprinted with permission.

(Total return is the average annualized compounded total return,
based on reinvestment of all dividends and capital gains distributions, if
any, plus changes in share price.)

As Exhibit 13.5 shows, patterns of returns are similar to those of taxable funds other than Treasuries: declines in 2008; and gains in 2009.
Average aggregate losses for the group were lower than those of high current yield ("junk") bond funds (minus 14.3% as opposed to a loss of
almost 26% for the high yield group); but gains in 2009 were also a lot
lower than those of the high yield group: a gain of about 28% compared
with 46% for the high yield group. As noted above for returns of "junk"
bonds, total returns of multi-sector funds for 5-year and 10-year holding
periods, at 4.64% and 5.9% respectively, were either in line with, or just
slightly above those of much less volatile funds such as the intermediate
funds or the GNMA group.

I have listed average annual total returns of this group of funds with
some misgivings. In a sense, the only similarity among these funds is that
their managers are free to follow any direction they feel will give them a
speculative edge. Investment policies are totally different from fund to
fund. As a result, total returns in this group of funds vary significantly from
fund to fund. For example, in 2008, the best performing fund posted a gain
of about 9% whereas the worst performing fund posted a loss of 36%. There
is simply no way to predict how any fund in this sector will perform without analyzing the record and management style of its manager.

It is possible, of course, that some managers will be successful for
more than one year. But unfortunately, how likely is it that you can predict who that manager is going to be? And for how long? I would suggest

avoiding this type of fund unless you have great confidence in a particular fund manager. There are many other more attractive alternatives where risk factors are much more straightforward and total returns far more predictable.

Bond Funds Investing in Foreign Bonds

A very few bond funds investing in foreign-pay bonds were introduced in 1985. Since then, this sector has continued to increase in size and in importance. At the time this is being written, international securities are "hot." One reason is that many pundits are expecting the dollar to decline. Many of these pundits also expect that economies outside the United States are likely to come out of the current recession sooner or more strongly than the United States. I make no predictions about whether either of these forecasts is likely to happen. But what is clear is that you will continue to see suggestions that you increase your allocation to foreign securities, including foreign bonds.

As was discussed in Chapter 10, the international bond market is extraordinarily diverse. It comprises bonds issued in a multitude of currencies, by issuers such as governments, supranational agencies, and corporations, and trading in capital markets worldwide. This, in turn, means that portfolio managers can literally choose from among hundreds of options to create a portfolio of international bonds.

Total return, particularly for international bond funds that invest primarily in foreign pay bonds, is dominated by changes in NAV resulting from changes in the value of the dollar against foreign currencies. Investing in international bonds represents a bet against the dollar. When the dollar weakens, the NAV of foreign bond funds goes up; when the dollar is strong, NAV declines. Because of the dominant role played by currencies, it is not unusual for bonds (and bond funds) to post positive total returns in the foreign currency, and losses in U.S. dollar terms; or the reverse. But bear in mind that changes in currency values are notoriously difficult to predict; and that they can occur suddenly, and dramatically.

The Lipper organization distinguishes between three types of international bond funds:

◆ Global Debt Funds
◆ International Debt Funds
◆ Emerging Market Debt Funds

The two largest categories of international bond funds are the "global" and the "international" categories. Those will be discussed first. Let's start with Lipper's definitions:

+ *Global bond funds* invest in bonds of at least three countries, one of which may be the United States. The bonds may be denominated in U.S. dollars or in foreign currencies.

+ *International bond funds* invest primarily in bonds of foreign issuers, excluding the United States except in periods of market weakness.

In other words, the global category includes U.S. debt in its investment mix. Presumably, this is done in order to lower the volatility of returns to U.S. investors. The International category generally does not include U.S. debt. In other respects, the portfolio make-up of both types of funds, however, allows for great flexibility and few funds are alike. Some funds invest in bonds of many countries. Others are regional, specializing in bonds of developed countries in a particular region such as Europe. Some permit the use of leverage and derivatives. Others do not. As a result, both groups are quite diverse. Note also that for both of these categories, maturities are not specified. Presumably, both invest in intermediate or longer-term bonds. Both the global and the international categories have strong and weak funds.

Exhibit 13.6 shows average annual total returns of both international and global bond funds for 2008, 2009, and for 5-year and 10-year holding

EXHIBIT 13.6

Average Annual Total Returns of Global and International Bond Funds for 2008, 2009, and for 5-Year and 10-Year Holding Periods through December 31, 2009 (All Distributions, Dividends, and Capital Gains Are Assumed to Be Reinvested)

	2008 (12/31/2007– 12/31/2008)	2009 (12/31/2008– 12/31/2009)	5 Years (12/31/2004– 12/31/2009)	10 Years (12/31/1999– 12/31/2009)
Global	−5.09%	15.23%	4.10%	6.18%
International	2.00%	10.84%	3.90%	6.30%

Source: Lipper, a Thomson Reuters Company. Material supplied to the author and reprinted with permission.

periods through December 31, 2009. (Total return is the average annual-ized compounded total return, based on reinvestment of all dividends and capital gains distributions, if any, plus changes in share price.)

It is difficult to generalize about total returns of the Global Funds category compared to those of the International funds. As shown in Exhibit 13.6, the Global Fund category with its U.S. debt component had a worse performance in 2008 (minus 5%) than the international group (plus 2%) for that year. But over the 5-year and 10-year holding periods, average total returns of both groups are similar. Total returns for both groups are a shade higher than those of longer-term U.S. debt funds.

When international funds were first introduced in 1985, the dollar was declining. Subsequently, it continued to decline for three years in a row: Total returns of international bond funds soared. Then the dollar rose, and you guessed it, international funds tanked.

This pattern has continued. When the dollar declines, these funds do well. When the dollar rises, they do poorly.

As we saw in Chapter 10, international bonds are rated by the rating agencies. Perhaps partly for that reason, yields of international bonds tend to be in line with those of U.S. taxable bonds with comparable maturities and credit quality. Moreover, because the financial crisis of 2008 was global, as a group, international bond funds did not provide any shelter.

Once again, showing average annual returns for this group is some-what misleading because as you would expect, total returns vary signifi-cantly from the best-performing to the worst-performing funds. In 2008, for example, the best performing "global" funds posted gains ranging from 8% and 10%; the worst performers posted losses ranging from 20% to 40%. And unfortunately, choosing the fund that has had the best total return over any preceding time period in no way insures that fund will perform equally well into the future.

If you are researching either category, you would want to note one important factor: whether the fund hedges the value of the dollar against the foreign currency. Hedging lowers volatility. But whenever the dollar declines against foreign currencies, hedging also reduces gains. If you are investing in a foreign bond fund primarily as a hedge against a decline in the U.S. dollar, you would want to look for a fund where the manager does not hedge. That would result in a "purer" play against the dollar.

If you use Morningstar to research funds, please note that Morningstar does not differentiate between "international" and "global" categories. All are lumped in one group.

Emerging Markets Bond Funds

This group of funds is more recent than any other category. Few funds had their inception prior to 1995. But this category of funds is likely to increase in size for two reasons. The first is that emerging countries, as a group, need to raise enormous amounts of capital to meet their needs for capital expansion and infrastructure. The second is that these funds have had outsize gains, even dwarfing those of junk bonds.

Lipper's definition of "emerging markets bond funds" is that they invest at least 65% of their assets in debt instruments of "emerging" markets. Emerging market debt is typically rated below investment grade. It is considered highly speculative.

These funds differ from other international bonds primarily because of credit risk. These are the "junk" bonds of the international bond market. Credit ratings of bonds in this group are determined chiefly by the fact that they are issued by and in countries that are poor, and that have "geopolitical" risk—another term for unstable governments and unstable economies. Exhibit 13.7 shows average annual total returns of emerging market bond funds for 2008 and 2009, and for 5-year and 10-year holding periods through December 31, 2009. (Total return is the average annualized compounded total return, based on reinvestment of all dividends and capital gains distributions, if any, plus changes in share price).

As shown in Exhibit 13.7, patterns of returns for 2008 and 2009 look familiar: aggregate average total return for 2008 was a loss of almost 17.5%; and aggregate average annual return for 2009 was a very substantial gain of about 32.5%. But as Exhibit 13.7 also shows, aggregate average annualized

E X H I B I T   13.7

Average Annual Total Returns of Emerging Market Bond Funds for 2008, 2009, and for 5-Year and 10-Year Holding Periods through December 31, 2009 (All Distributions, Dividends, and Capital Gains Are Assumed to be Reinvested)

	2008 (12/31/2007– 12/31/2008)	2009 (12/31/2008– 12/31/2009)	5 Years (12/31/2004– 12/31/2009)	10 Years (12/31/1999– 12/31/2009)
Emerging Market Bond Funds	−17.46%	32.49%	7.23%	11.09%

Source: Lipper, a Thomson Reuters Company. Material supplied to the author and reprinted with permission.

total return for the 10-year period ending December 31, 2009 was approximately 11%, well above that of any other taxable bond fund category. Average annualized total return for the 5-year period ending December 31, 2009 was also the highest of any taxable bond fund group: exceeding 7%.

One would naturally want to know: What caused these superior returns? And is it likely that total returns in this group will continue to be higher than those of any other taxable bond group? A quick look at the history of this sector may help put the returns in perspective.

First, bear in mind that this group of funds is relatively new: Few funds in this category had their inception prior to 1995.

Second, and somewhat coincidentally, 10-year returns through December 31, 2009, have as their starting point the NAVs of the funds immediately after the crash of 1998—which coincided with the crisis that occurred when Russia defaulted on its debt; and total returns of emerging market funds experienced enormous losses.

Nonetheless, returns for the 10-year period between December 31, 1999 and January 2009 were impressive. The remarkable saga of this sector began with the Brady program which was described in Chapter 10. But an equally important factor was the very high interest rates at which these bonds traded initially—well above 20% for the Brady sector. With the success of the Brady program, yields came down but remained relatively high, with spreads to investment-grade debt exceeding 500 or 600 basis points. In addition, as spreads came down, NAVs rose. Note also that where Brady bonds were concerned, the returns were not due to changes in the value of the currency against the dollar; as you will remember from our discussion of Brady bonds in Chapter 10, Brady bonds were issued in U.S. dollars.

Like junk bonds, these bonds have boom and bust periods. During the debt crises of 1997 and 1998, emerging market bond funds experienced dramatic declines: 50% or more in a few months. Declines of some of the issues in the portfolios of these funds were among the worst experienced in any bond funds in any market. The value of Russian bonds, for example, declined to practically zero after the Russian government defaulted on its debt.

But of course, out of spectacular declines often comes opportunity. Bonds of emerging markets were the standouts of 1999.

Between 2001 and 2003, a veritable sea change took place. There was, first of all, a dramatic improvement in credit quality, as the credit rating of bonds of a number of developing countries went from junk to investment grade. At the same time, as interest rates in the United States declined to historic lows, bonds with higher yields and improving credit quality proved to be irresistible to many buyers who previously shunned these markets. Both of these factors eventually resulted in significant capital gains for the sector, but also much lower yields.

This sector did not escape the devastation of 2008. But once again, total returns varied widely from fund to fund. A number of the better performing funds actually had positive returns in 2008, between 8% and 10%. The worst performers had losses in the 20% to 30% range.

As noted in Chapter 10, attitudes toward this group are changing. A number of countries which in the past would have been viewed as very speculative are now regarded as high-growth areas. This includes the "BRIC" countries (Brazil, Russia, India, China); as well as the economies of Latin American countries, particularly those that export commodities. Other countries now viewed more favorably include some of the former Baltic states, as well as some middle European countries (called by some "emerging Europe"). This new outlook emphasizes the growth potential of these countries, rather than their weak capital markets and the geopolitical risks. Increasingly, also, "emerging" market bonds are no longer being viewed as one single market: debt is being judged by the economic status of whatever country is issuing the debt.

Paradoxically, however, the newer, more positive attitudes toward "emerging markets" may cause returns to be more in line with those of better developed countries. One key to future returns in this sector will be the ratings and the yield of the countries involved. If credit ratings improve, and more of these bonds are upgraded, then those yields will be more in line with those of investment quality debt. These bonds would then be priced and trade more in line with other international debt. Currency risk would become the dominant factor in total return.

Note finally that prior to 2005, bond funds of emerging markets have often posted higher total returns than stock funds of emerging markets, partly because of their outsize dividend yields. Perhaps paradoxically, as debt of emerging market countries is upgraded or viewed as less risky, then dividend yields will continue to decline. (Evidence of this was actually seen in Exhibit 10.2—which showed very narrow spreads to Treasuries, and comparatively low yields, on bonds of Mexico and Brazil.) And one of the factors in the past performance of these funds will diminish or disappear.

Finally, it may be that the moniker "emerging market debt" may fade or be used somewhat differently to designate debt of any country that is viewed as facing possible default or restructuring. As this is being written, for example, another debt crisis may be looming as the ability of a number of countries to repay sovereign debt is being questioned. But the governments causing the worry are those of Greece, Portugal, and Spain. There is speculation about whether the debt of these countries will have to be "restructured," following the Brady bond model.

Despite their overall record, and the more generous view of their prospects, any investment in emerging market funds should be viewed as speculative and suitable only for money you can afford to lose. Risks in this market are still poorly understood. If this sector attracts you, investigate a bond fund, but very carefully.

Summary and Conclusion: International and Emerging Market Bond Funds

To sum up, the potential total return of any fund investing in bonds of foreign countries is unpredictable. Risk is high and derives from the inherent unpredictability of currency fluctuations.

Proponents of this sector argue that investing in international bond funds may lower the total risk of a bond portfolio because these bonds do not move in lockstep with U.S. bonds. That, it turns out, is sometimes the case, and sometimes not. (As noted above, it was not the case in 2008.) The argument that makes the most sense to me is that international bonds constitute a hedge against a declining dollar. If you look back, it is true that international bonds have had some of their best years (for U.S. dollar-based investors) when the dollar declined and when other dollar-denominated assets were doing poorly. But also bear in mind that, to be successful, managers have to pick the right foreign currencies. As a result, total returns vary enormously from international fund to international fund.

How Should You Select an International Bond Fund?

Let's assume you want to invest in an international bond fund. What criteria would you use? There is no ready answer. Returns vary significantly from fund to fund and from year to year.

One key factor is a fund's strategy with regard to hedging. But the same strategy has variable results depending on the direction of currency changes. When the dollar declines significantly against other currencies, funds that do not hedge currency risk have higher total returns than funds that did hedge.

In the emerging markets group, portfolio managers have to be astute (or lucky) enough to pick the markets that are going to do well that year. No manager consistently picks winners year after year.

Note finally that fund expenses tend to be very high in this group—typically, between 1 1/2% and 2%. Also, a number of the better-performing funds, based on Morningstar rankings, are loaded funds. If a fund has a 5% load, at current interest rates you are giving up a year's worth of income the first year you invest. Let's do a back-of-the-envelope calculation for a two-year return: Assume that the portfolio earns 10% per year for two years, or a total of 20%. Subtract a 5% load and 3% for expenses. After two years, net return to you: 12% or 6% a year. But even that overstates returns because it does not include taxes on dividends or capital gains.

MISCELLANEOUS FUNDS

Loan Participation Funds

This is a hybrid type of fund that is not, properly speaking, an open-end mutual fund. It is similar in some ways to closed-end funds, although it is a hybrid category belonging in neither group. This remains a small corner of the bond market. The unique characteristic of loan participation funds is that money invested in these funds can only be redeemed one day each quarter.

These funds go under a variety of names, including "prime rate" funds, "floating rate" funds, "income trust," or some combination of terms that includes these phrases. These funds invest in bank loans, and specifically in loans characterized as "subprime," meaning loans that have high yields primarily because they carry a high degree of credit risk. These loans are fairly short term, usually under two years. Interest rates of the funds are reset periodically, based on a spread to a benchmark rate, usually LIBOR (London Interbank Offered Rate). The theory is that interest rates will vary, but invested principal will not decline significantly in value, because maturities are short.

As a result, these funds are marketed as higher-yielding alternatives to money funds. And in fact, articles both on the web and in financial magazines and on the Internet, occasionally characterize these funds as "stars" or as a unique corner of the credit market reserved for savvy investors.

As has been stated many times in this book, higher rates always go hand in hand with some higher degree of risk. These funds are no exception. I have not shown average total returns for this group because it looks to me like a risk not worth taking. Losses in this group were high in 2008, averaging well above 25%. Returns bounced back some in 2009. But in spite of that, for the 10-year holding period ending December 31, 2009, the average annual total return was a shade under 3%, lower than returns of almost any investment grade bond fund, and just a shade above returns of riskless money market funds. (For the 10-year holding period ending December 31, 2008, average annual total return was actually negative, a loss of almost 1%.) But once again, if you want to invest in safe assets, why take the risk of investing in this sector?

Bond Index Funds

Bond index funds are not listed as a separate fund category by either Lipper or Morningstar. Individual bond index funds are included, however, among several different categories, based on their average weighted maturity and on the sector of the bond market in which they are invested. Vanguard, which pioneered stock index funds, also pioneered bond index funds. The concept has spread, however, and many bond fund groups now offer that option.

Like equity index funds, bond index funds are managed passively to mirror a specific benchmark index. All index funds have two advantages: a low expense ratio and low turnover of assets. The anticipation is that, over long holding periods, bond index funds will have higher total returns than most actively managed bond funds, simply by virtue of the fact that they will match the total return of the benchmark, and that expenses for managing the fund will be low.

In a sense, bond index funds are the ultimate plain vanilla funds. Their risk factors are straightforward: They can be summarized as the average weighted maturity of the fund (or its duration) and its credit quality. The oldest of these index funds is also the largest: it is the Vanguard Total Bond Market Index Fund, discussed briefly in the intermediate investment grade section above. This fund tracks the Barclays U.S. Aggregate Index. It has an average weighted maturity of 8.8 years and a duration of five years, which places it in the intermediate sector. But there are now about 90 bond index funds. Vanguard offers the most: approximately 28, followed by Fidelity with 10. But many smaller groups offer one of more index bond funds: American Independence, Columbia, Dreyfus, Nationwide, Schwab, etc. These index funds are managed to match the returns of a variety of indices.

Index funds are an attractive option. The level of risk is easy to predict: simply find out the duration of the fund and position yourself based on your investment horizon: that is, how long you think you will own the fund. Choose a duration close to that number. Choosing a duration close to the amount of time you want to own the fund lowers interest rate risk (see the section on duration). Credit risk should be minimal; and so should NAV erosion.

The concept of indexing, of course, has spread not only to many fund groups, but also, to the ultimate index funds: exchange-traded funds. These will be analyzed in the section dealing with ETFs in Chapter 4.

Zero Coupon Bond Funds

This is a category that was analyzed in the prior edition of this book. As the name indicates, these bond funds invested in zero coupon bonds that would mature on the same date. The name of the fund typically included the term: "target," the target being the date when the zeros would mature. Most of these funds no longer exist. I mention them only because a number of funds now have the term "target" in their name. But those are totally different types of funds. They are so-called life cycle funds that invest primarily in equities and are targeted based on the investor's age.

Some Do's and Don't's for Buying Bond Funds

Before you buy any bond fund, you should have a clear understanding of its objectives and policies. If the language of the objective appears to be full of jargon, or unclear, ask the fund's information people for clarification. If, for example, the objective states that "the fund will buy speculative securities that are well below investment grade," it is important that you understand that this fund will invest in junk bonds. If the objective states that the fund will purchase "high and upper medium quality securities," ask for specific rating information. Be sure that you understand the risk factors described in the objective. The risk factors should be taken seriously, even if recent fund performance has been excellent. Remember, however, that policies are usually defined in broad enough terms to allow fund managers enough latitude to deal with changing market conditions.

If you are investing in bond funds primarily for reliable, steady income, you will want to locate funds that have existed long enough to have gone through both bull markets and bear markets in bonds. Once again, the mantra is to buy a no-load fund with a low expense ratio, no 12b-1 fees, and a track record of conservative management. Look for funds that have not gone down too much during bear markets but have also done reasonably well during bull markets. If that fund ranks in the top quartile (25%) of its category (whether tabulated by Lipper or by Morningstar), you have found a fund that is likely to have a consistent performance over time.

Remember that in choosing any fund, there will be trade-offs. Longer maturities usually result in a higher yield but more volatility. Shorter maturities result in lower volatility but also less income.

The average maturity of a bond fund determines how much share price goes both up and down in response to interest rate changes and interest income. Normally, longer-term funds have higher dividends than shorter-term funds, but price per share goes up and down more. The price per share of shorter-term funds is more stable (goes up and down less), but interest income is lower.

Let's summarize some general principles that should guide the purchase of bond funds:

- Don't buy any fund whose share price fluctuates if you are going to need the money in less than a year; you cannot know at what price you will be able to redeem.

- If you are investing primarily for "income" and safety of principal is important to you, don't buy the longest-term funds or those with the highest stated yields (those will be the riskiest funds). Instead, stick to funds that have intermediate (or shorter) maturities (whether taxable or tax-exempt) and invest in high-quality bonds.

- Where possible, for new money, buy no-load funds, with low expense ratios and no 12b-1 plans.

- Before buying a fund, make sure you know exactly what securities are in it; check the current maturity length, or better still, the current duration.

- Don't invest more than 20% of your bond portfolio in any bond fund that is long-term, international, or junk. Invest in these funds only if you have a large, well-diversified bond or bond fund portfolio (minimum $200,000). It's not necessary to own one of each.

- The more complex the security, the more expertise it requires, then the more appropriate it becomes to buy a fund rather than individual securities. Funds are the most efficient way for individual investors to own international bonds, GNMAs, junk bonds, and corporates.

- Taxable bond funds are appropriate for tax-deferred (or tax-sheltered) monies that you want to place in fixed-income securities. For those purposes, consider high-quality corporate, GNMA, or zero bond funds. For money that is not in tax-deferred or tax-advantaged accounts, do the arithmetic to determine whether taxable or tax-exempt bond funds will result in the highest net-after-tax yield.

SUMMARY

The preceding discussion indicates that over the past 30 years, certain types of bond funds (long-term funds, intermediate funds, municipal funds, junk funds) have had high total returns. During that period, for most years, also, total return has been almost directly related to maturity length. The longest-term funds had higher total returns than intermediate funds; and those in turn had higher total returns than money market funds.

One would naturally want to know: Will longer-term funds continue to have higher total returns than shorter funds? The answer to that question is a qualified yes. Over long holding periods, longer-term funds should continue to have higher total return than shorter-term funds, if for no other reason than that dividend yield is higher. Because of compounding, and because dividends will be reinvested at higher rates, longer-term funds should have higher total returns than shorter-term funds. Over long holding periods, the income portion of bond funds, that is interest income plus interest-on-interest, should dominate total return.

But this scenario is contingent on what happens to interest rates. If rates remain in a relatively narrow range or decline from current levels, the longest-term funds will continue to have higher total returns than

---

The Do-it-Yourself Bond Fund

If you are investing in bonds primarily because you do not want to risk any loss of principal and you want to insure a steady source of income, then the safest way to go is the do-it-yourself route. You can use either Treasuries or munis. For Treasuries, buy any combination of maturities between one and five years that suits your needs. Since Treasuries run no risk of default, you do not need to diversify in order to eliminate credit risk: a one-bond portfolio of U.S. Treasuries runs no risk of default. Buy your Treasuries through TreasuryDirect. Uncle Sam will maintain the account for you at zero annual expense and will not charge any commission. You can also build a totally safe portfolio using municipal bonds. Stick to short maturities (between one and seven years). Buy any combination of AAA bonds, pre-refunded bonds (i.e., premium munis backed by escrowed Treasuries, and therefore even "safer" than AAA), or insured muni bonds or build a ladder. (For a "ladder," see Chapter 15.)

shorter-maturity funds and money funds by a substantial margin. But if rates rise, or if there is great volatility for several years in a row, then total return of long-term bond funds will be highly unpredictable for short holding periods, and may not exceed the total return of shorter or intermediate bond funds. As 2008 has shown, over any short holding period (one or two years), one year of extremely depressed returns can devastate total returns were high for the previous decade.

Finally, the golden decade for bond funds was the 1980s. Total returns were exceptional because the decline in interest rates that occurred in the second half of the 1980s added a large chunk of capital gains to the high interest income generated during that decade. But note that the prior 30 years or so, beginning with the early 1980s, have witnessed a bull market in bonds, which has no historical precedent. Moreover, interest rate volatility for those 30 years is also unprecedented. As we enter the year 2010, the level of interest rates is a lot lower than it was in any of the prior three decades. Consequently, total returns generated by all types of bond funds will be a lot more modest than those of any of the prior three decades. And they are also far less predictable: After all, interest rates are unlikely to decline from current levels. And any sustained increase at the long end would lead, at least initially, to declines in NAVs of long-term bond funds.

Of course, rates could rise from current levels. But if that prospect makes you smile, remember this: A substantial rise in yields from current levels (say 200 to 300 basis points) would translate into a very substantial loss of principal for the longest-term funds (as much as 25% to 30%).

Five-Minute Checklist for Analyzing Bond Funds

Investigating a bond fund need not be overwhelming. Following is a five-minute checklist for analyzing bond funds. Can you do a five-minute analysis of a bond fund that really is meaningful? Well, if you are reading this book, you should have a pretty clear idea of risk factors and land mines you need to be clear about before investing in a bond fund of any variety. These are the steps you can take (in five minutes or less).

◆ Download (or find) a fact sheet on the fund from the fund's Web site or from Morningstar.

- ◆ Estimate volatility by looking at the following:
  - The high and low price for the fund for the past few years.
  - The duration (remember: for every 1% (100 basis points) and increase or decline in interest rates—the fund's NAV will rise or decline by the amount of the duration. If duration is under 5 years, interest rate risk is modest. Under 3 years, interest rate risk is low. Interest rate risk rises significantly with every year above 5 years.
  - The actual returns of the fund for the last few years, either in graph form or in numbers. How much do they vary from year to year?
- ◆ Estimate credit quality, whether you know anything about the bonds in the fund, or not, by looking at the distribution of ratings: If 50% or more of the fund's portfolio is invested in high-quality credits—AAA or AA—or in bonds that have the implicit or explicit guarantee of the U.S. government (for example, Treasuries, or GNMAs, or government agencies), then the fund has high credit quality. If 50% or more of the fund is in lower-quality credits, below investment grade, the fund's credit quality is low. Lower credit quality translates to higher credit risk: the lower the credit quality, the higher the risk; and the higher the potential volatility.
- ◆ Look for answers to a couple more questions:
  - What is the expense ratio? Below 50 basis points? Not bad. Below 25 basis points? Better.
  - Is there any kind of load or 12-B1 fee? Yes, bad. No, good.
  - Check the track record of the fund over a 5-year or 10-year holding period. You want a fund that has had consistent returns, preferably somewhere in the top quarter of its peer group. (You can check this online using either Morningstar or funds.us.reuters.com.)

Believe it or not, that hits all the key points. Many happy returns!

CHAPTER 14

Closed-End Bond Funds, Exchange-Traded Funds, and Unit Investment Trusts

While open-end mutual funds constitute by far the largest and the most familiar part of the fund universe, they are not the only types of funds available. Two alternate types of funds actually antedate open-end funds: closed-end funds and unit investment trusts (UITs). Recently, still another type of fund has come on the scene: exchange-traded funds (ETFs).

All bond funds share certain risks, chief among them, interest rate risk and also credit risk. But each type of bond fund has some unique characteristics. In this chapter, I will focus on those aspects that are unique to each type of fund.

Let's start with closed-end bond funds.

CLOSED-END BOND FUNDS

Closed-end funds (CEFs) constitute a somewhat arcane and specialized corner of the market for funds. CEFs invest both in stocks and in bonds. As of April 2010, there were approximately 600 closed-end bond funds, holding assets worth about $112 billion, a relatively small sum compared to the approximately $4.8 trillion in open-end bond funds. Slightly more than half of all closed-end bond funds invest in municipals. But closed-end bond funds also include taxable bond funds in every sector of that market, including corporates, governments, and international, as well as loan participation funds, which invest primarily in lower-quality floating-rate or variable-rate notes.

Closed-end bond funds share a number of additional characteristics with open-end funds. Both types of bond funds invest in a continually managed bond portfolio. And both types of funds maintain a relatively constant maturity. As a result, there is no date when the entire portfolio is redeemed at par, like an individual bond. Both types of funds also share the risks common to all bonds: namely, interest rate risk and credit risk.

But this is where similarities end. The main attraction of closed-end bond funds is higher yield, which results from the unique structure of CEFs. But in the world of bonds, higher yield always comes at a cost, namely, higher risk. CEFs are no exception. The risk comes in the form of high volatility, derived from a structure that tends to magnify both gains and losses. Let's see why.

NAV and Market Price

One striking difference between closed-end and open-end funds is their share structure. Open-end funds are issued with an unlimited number of shares. When an investor buys shares in an open-end fund, new shares are issued and the added capital allows the fund to buy additional securities. Conversely, if investors sell shares, the fund must sell securities to redeem the shares, and investor sales cause the portfolio to shrink. The net asset value (NAV) of each share is tabulated at the end of each trading day: It is the total market value of the securities in the fund, divided by the number of shares (with a small percentage deducted for expenses).

A CEF, on the other hand, issues a fixed number of shares at its inception. Since the portfolio is managed continuously, the portfolio may change. But the number of shares remains fixed. Unlike open-end funds, after issue a CEF trades on an exchange: it may trade on any one of the three major stock exchanges. (A small number of CEFs are also listed on the Pacific Exchange or in Canada). Shares of CEFs, moreover, are considered stocks. The price of a closed-end bond fund is determined very much like that of any stock: by the demand for that particular stock.

At the end of each day, the market value of the bonds in a CEF is tabulated as it is in an open-end fund, and that market value, divided by the total number of shares, results in a tabulated NAV per share. As a result, the shares of CEFs have two reported values: the NAV of one share and the market price of one share, which can be higher or lower than its NAV.

Because the price of shares of a CEF is determined partly by the demand for those shares, the price of a share can move independently of the value of the bonds in the fund. If demand is high, the share price rises, regardless of what is happening to the underlying value of the bonds in the fund. In fact, at times the price of a closed-end fund and the value of the assets in the fund move in opposite directions. That is, the share price of the fund may be going up while the NAV is actually declining. Or the opposite may take place.

When you look at tables of returns for any CEF (whether a stock or bond CEF), you will see two prices listed. One is *NAV*. For closed-end funds, NAV refers not to the price per share but to the market value of the bonds in the fund. You can also consider the NAV to be equivalent to the liquidation value of the bonds in the fund. The other term you will see listed is *market price*. That is the last price at which a share of the CEF was traded.

If a share is selling for more than the NAV, then the fund is said to be selling at a premium. If its price is lower than its NAV, it is said to be selling at a discount.

Understanding this distinction is critical to understanding how closed-end funds differ from the open-end mutual funds. This distinction is reflected in the way prices of closed-end bond funds are quoted. The format for listings of closed-end bond fund returns looks like the example in Exhibit 14.1.

Reading from left to right, this table tells you the following:

- The name of the fund
- The NAV of the bonds in the portfolio
- The market price at which the shares of the CEF last changed hands (sometimes called "close" or closing price)
- The premium or discount of the market price compared to NAV
- The reported yield of the fund (based on the market price), (for more on yield, see below)

EXHIBIT 14.1

Format for Listing of Closed End Fund Shares

Fund Name	Stock Exchange	NAV	Market Price	Premium/ Discount	12-Month Yield 05/31/10
XYZ	N	3.95	$3.78	−4.5%	10.0
ABC	N	11.84	$12.28	+3.7%	7.0

Since CEFs trade like stocks, you can buy or sell CEFs, or track the price per share of a CEF, in the same manner that you buy, sell, or track any stock. The commission structure is the same as it is for any stock. CEFs trade anywhere that stocks trade, online or offline.

Premiums and Discounts

What, if anything, other than demand (or lack of it) causes shares of a CEF to trade at a discount or at a premium to its net asset value?

Oddly enough, one answer to this question is that there is no clear explanation for this phenomenon. It is just the case that many CEFs seem to generally trade at a discount to NAV, for reasons that are not clear. But note one exception, and that has to do with the market price of shares at issue.

When a CEF is first launched, its shares nominally trade at NAV. But the process for originating shares and bringing a fund to market actually involves hidden fees. What happens typically is that a management company will announce that is it going to be originating the Many Happy Returns Closed-End Bond Fund; that the fund will be structured to buy bonds (say, tax-exempt nationally or for a particular state); and, furthermore, that the fund will be structured so that the yield will exceed, say, 5%. After it has gathered capital, the management company then purchases a portfolio of bonds. But typically, underwriters build in fees of 5% to 8% or so. What that means is that if you buy a closed-end bond fund at issue, approximately 5% to 8% of the NAV represents hidden commissions and underwriter fees: only about 92 cents to 95 cents out of every dollar an investor spends actually buys bonds.

After the fund begins trading, typically, underwriters "support" the price for some period of time, perhaps weeks or perhaps months. But subsequently, many CEFs begin to trade at a discount to NAV.

Demand for shares of CEFs changes continually. For that reason, even though CEFs often trade at a discount to NAV, that discount keeps on changing. If there is a sell-off, the discount widens. If demand rises for a specific sector of the bond market, the discount narrows, or the price of a CEF can even move to a premium to NAV. As we will see below, one key to determining whether shares of CEFs are attractive buys is whether they are trading at a premium or at a discount, and if they are trading at a discount, the size of the discount.

Unfortunately for unsophisticated buyers, the time that your friendly broker is most likely to be aware of a new closed-end bond fund offering is when it first comes to market and when it is therefore quite expensive. So buying a closed-end bond fund at issue is almost never advisable.

Leverage and Yield

The chief attraction of CEFs, particularly those investing in bonds, is higher yield than comparable open-end funds: that is, funds in the same sector of the bond market, with comparable maturities and credit quality. The higher yield is the result of two characteristics of CEFs.

When the price of a CEF trades at a discount, the discount itself results in a higher yield. Why? Simple arithmetic. Suppose you buy a CEF trading at a 10% discount to NAV. When you buy that fund, you are in effect purchasing a dollar's worth of bonds for 90 cents. Further suppose that the portfolio's yield is 5.5%. Buying the portfolio at 90 cents on the dollar boosts yield to 6.1%. You will then receive a higher yield than if you purchased the bonds directly, at their market value.

CEFs, however, boost yield through a second, even more powerful tool: the use of leverage. Approximately 85% of all closed-end bond funds use leverage, and for municipal bond funds, the percentage reaches 95%.

Leverage can best be understood as analogous to the use of margin by individual investors. The strategy relies on borrowing money at short-term rates in order to finance the purchase of longer-term bonds, which typically deliver higher interest. The amount of leverage can vary: A typical percentage is around 30% of the total net assets of the fund. The income per share is boosted by the difference between the cost of borrowing and the higher interest income generated.

Leverage is most effective in boosting yield when the yield curve is steeply upward sloping, and the difference between short-term rates and long-term rates is high. Yield curves are typically quite steep in the municipal bond market. Another key factor is the cost of financing leverage. A best-case scenario occurs when the fund can borrow cheaply to finance leverage and long-term rates are high. This creates a virtuous kind of loop: Reported yields are then significantly higher than for open-end funds. This attracts more investors. As a result, the price of the fund rises.

However, leverage backfires when the yield curve flattens or when the cost of financing leverage increases. This produces a double whammy for leveraged funds. Typically, if the cost of borrowing rises, then the yield of the fund declines. Unhappy investors sell shares. The market price of the CEF then declines.

Just as buying on margin magnifies profits and losses, leverage also magnifies profits and losses. That is the chief reason that the market price of closed-end bond funds is often much more volatile than the market price of ordinary open-end mutual funds.

When market conditions become unfavorable (and this can involve a number of different scenarios—for example, a rise in short-term rates, resulting in increased borrowing costs, or long-term rates rising, causing NAV to fall), then the fund suffers a double or a triple whammy:

- The dividends are cut.
- The NAV declines.
- Investor sales cause the market price of the fund to plummet.

Web sites that publish data about CEFs not only disclose whether a CEF uses leverage or not, they also disclose the percentage of leverage. They may also differentiate between different types of leverage. What is important is the total amount of leverage: if more than one source of leverage is mentioned, just add them up.

"Not Exactly Yield"

Many investors buy CEFs primarily because of their higher reported yields. But as with any bond investment, it is important to understand just what that yield number really tells you about what you are earning in the fund.

The yield that is quoted for CEFs consists of the distributions made by the fund, divided by market price. That is, of course, a current yield. It is not comparable to the yield-to-maturity quoted for individual bonds (since there is no maturity date when the entire portfolio is redeemed at par, and also since the only cash flow included consists of current distributions). It is also not directly comparable to the SEC yield quoted for open-end bond funds, which includes a small change in the value of bonds as they move toward par.

But the yield quoted for CEFs differs from yields reported for other types of funds in other more significant ways. The phrase "not exactly yield" was coined by investment advisor Thomas Herzfeld, whose monthly newsletter specializes in CEFs. He coined the phrase to warn investors that published yield figures may not accurately measure the investment income of CEFs. That is because fund payouts do not consist entirely of interest income. CEFs may make capital gains distributions—generally not more than once a year. Such distributions are taxable as capital gains.

In addition, a number of funds have so-called "managed" payout policies. These dictate that a certain amount will be distributed every month. If income generated by the fund falls short of that amount, these funds actually return a portion of the principal (designated by the funds as "distributions from paid-in capital"). Such distributions are a return of your own money and certainly not income or "yield." Some funds maintain particularly aggressive managed payout policies, in effect, returning more capital than they are earning. Any fund that does that over a sustained period of time in effect is liquidating the fund's capital. Such aggressive payouts are not sustainable and constitute a red flag.

But quote services do not discriminate between the sources of CEF distributions: all are lumped together as income and included in yield quotes. To compound the problem, the high-yield quotes may actually cause demand for the fund to rise, and these funds may actually sell at a high premium to NAV.

Moreover, there is not a standardized formula, such as the SEC yield formula published by open-end mutual funds, that requires funds to calculate yield so that published yields of different closed-end bond funds are directly comparable. Obviously, there is also no figure that can be compared with the yield-to-maturity quoted for individual bonds, since the portfolio has no maturity date and since the yield quote only includes distributions. (Note that at tax time, the fund mails out a detailed description of the sources of distributions to shareholders, for tax purposes.)

Finally, note that reported yields for CEFs are subject to change. The yield may be cut, or it may increase. Dividend increases typically result from lower costs to finance leverage or from a rise in longer term interest rates. Dividend cuts result from a rise in the cost of borrowing to finance leverage, a decline in long-term yields, or older bonds being called if interest rates decline. Quote services usually adjust quotes promptly.

Income Ratios

CEFs are required to calculate and publish one additional income figure, and that is their income ratio. A fund's income ratio is its net investment income (minus expenses) divided by the fund's NAV. The income ratio may differ, and sometimes significantly, from the quoted yield. But because the denominator of the equation is NAV, the income ratio is a more accurate measure than the quoted "yield" of the actual income generated by the fund. Unfortunately, income ratios are published only twice a year, in the annual and semiannual reports, and by the time they are published, they may be obsolete. If, for example, published yield numbers are lower than the income ratio, you should assume that the dividend has been cut, and that the income ratio is obsolete.

Warning: If you are attracted by high quoted yields, you need to be particularly cautious about investing in funds with aggressive managed payout policies. If the income ratio is significantly lower than the distribution yield, then this is a red flag. You need to find out where the bulk of the distribution comes from. A recent newsletter by Herzfeld (May 2010) cited a particularly egregious example: a fund with a 0.79% income ratio, but a greater than 14% "yield." The "distribution" consisted of $0.06 per share from investment income, and $2.09 return of capital, that is, your own money being returned to you. To add insult to injury, that fund was trading at a 44% premium to NAV.

Investors seeking CEFs that generate high income should seek out funds whose income ratios are consistently high compared to quoted distribution yields.

Distributions may occur monthly. But some funds make distributions on a quarterly basis, in order to reduce fund expenses. Reinvesting distributions is also not automatic, as it is with open-end funds. Some CEFs have their own reinvestment programs. But some brokerage firms also have their own programs for reinvesting dividends. If you buy a CEF and intend to hold it and reinvest distributions, then you need to investigate reinvestment options with your broker, or with the CEF.

When Are Closed-End Funds Attractive Buys?

First, make sure that you are buying a CEF trading at a discount to NAV, and preferably at a steep discount to NAV.

Why?

As noted above, if the CEF is trading at a discount to NAV, then you are purchasing the assets of the fund for less than they would cost if you bought them directly in the secondary market. You therefore earn a higher yield than you would if you bought the bond directly.

Also, if a CEF is purchased at a deep discount to NAV, then if the share price rises so that the fund trades at or above the NAV (to a premium, for example), then a sale of the CEF will result in a capital gain. Note that even a narrowing of the discount can boost the market price per share.

Because of their volatility, many investors consider CEFs attractive vehicles for speculation, rather than for income. These investors focus on the possibilities of capturing capital gains.

The opportunity for capital gains derives from the changing size of the discount, as well as from fluctuations in the share price. When discounts narrow, or when the price of the fund moves closer to the value of the assets in the fund (that is, to the NAV), the investor realizes a profit. The ideal trade would involve buying at a wide discount to the value of the assets in the fund (the NAV) and selling when the fund moves to a premium. To realize a profit, however, the fund need only to move to a narrower discount.

This piece of advice, however, is deceptively simple. As noted earlier, leverage magnifies losses, and if market conditions deteriorate, discounts widen resulting in severe losses. Such episodes have occurred whenever interest rates rise significantly, for example, in 1994, in 1999, as well as during the financial panic of 2008.

Professionals who trade CEFs have developed strategies that attempt to take advantage of changes in market price in order to capture capital gains. For example, one leading expert, Thomas Herzfeld, suggests that before you buy any closed-end fund, you track its price for some period of time in order to determine the size of the average discount of the fund. He suggests buying only when the discount is at least 3% wider than the *normal* discount for that fund. That strategy, however, is not foolproof. It is never easy to spot the bottom. During steep declines, the discount can continue to widen, and with it, the price of the fund can continue to decline well below prior lows.

CEFs occasionally become "open ended." When that happens, the price of the fund rises to equal the NAV of the bonds in the portfolio. If the fund was purchased at a discount, that would provide a windfall profit. If, however, it was purchased at a premium (or at issue), that would result in a loss of principal. There is no certain way to predict which funds will become open ended, but it happens occasionally.

Volatility and Total Return

Published total return numbers for closed-end bond funds specify whether returns are based on NAV, or on market price. In either case, total return figures include all distributions and further assume that those are reinvested. The total return figures that show how much an investor actually earned are the market price data.

Because of the extreme volatility of this group of funds, I am not showing multi-year returns. Rather, in Exhibit 14.2, I am showing average total returns for both 2008 and 2009.

Exhibit 14.2 shows returns based both on NAV and on market price. As you might expect, returns shown in Exhibit 14.2 showed wild swings, between significant losses in 2008 and outsize gains in 2009. But this is a group of funds where the averages mask enormous differences in total return from fund to fund. For that reason, Exhibit 14.2 also includes returns of the best-performing funds, as well as those of the worst-performing funds, based both on NAV and on market price. For example, Exhibit 14.2 shows that in the municipal bond sector, the average return in 2008 based on market price was a loss of 22%, whereas return for the best-performing municipal CEF (again based on market price) was a gain of 8%. Total return for the worst-performing municipal CEF was a loss of 48.6%.

E X H I B I T   14.2

Average Total Returns of CEFs for 2008 and 2009, Based on Market Price and NAV (All Distributions Are Assumed to Be Reinvested)*

		AVERAGE		BEST		WORST	
		NAV	Market	NAV	Market	NAV	Market
2	Municipal Bond Funds	−17.7%	−22.1%	+5.4%	+8.25%	−46.9%	−48.6%
0	Taxable Bond Funds	−25.3%	−23.4%	+9.0%	+24.7%	−65.3%	−70.2%
0	Foreign Bond Funds	−19.5%	−22.7%	+6.7%	+7.9%	−38.8%	−43.1%
8	Loan Participation	−46.9%	−43.8%	−38.9%	−35.9%	−58.9%	−55.4%
2	Municipal Bond Fund	29.4%	45.7%	67.3%	92.6%	3.0%	0.56%
0	Taxable Bond Funds	40.6%	50.1%	104.1%	122.7%	−18.5%	−28.1%
0	Foreign Bond Funds	34.6%	51.6%	68.5%	106.2%	1.7%	17.9%
9	Loan Participation	77.1%	84.4%	108.2%	130.6%	58.8%	39.2%

Source: Thomas J. Herzfeld Advisors, Inc. Data reprinted with permission.

* Note that in Exhibit 14.2, in order to simplify a bit, I am using data from Herzfeld Research, which groups closed-end bond funds into four main categories: loan participation funds, taxable bond funds, municipal bond funds, and foreign bond funds. Data reported in many newspapers uses the Lipper categories, which are identical to those for open-end bond funds, and much more numerous. But the format for reporting returns of CEFs follows the conventions displayed above: return reported both for NAV and for market price, premiums or discounts of market price compared to NAV, and yield based on distributions for the prior 12 months.

This is also not just a case of one fund at either end being an outlier: more detailed data shows that in 2008, the seven top-performing municipal CEFs posted modest gains (based on market price) ranging from 0% to 8.25%, whereas the bottom 10 all showed losses in excess of 40%. Note also the significant differences in average total returns based on NAV and those based on market price. This difference exists at the individual fund level as well. For example, in 2008, one of the top-performing municipal CEFs, Nuveen Select Maturity Fund, posted a loss of 3.66% based on NAV but a gain of 6.57% based on market price.

Exhibit 14.2 shows even larger differences in the returns of taxable CEFs: average return for 2008 (based on market price) was a loss of 23.4%. But for the same year, the best-performing fund posted a gain of 24.7%, whereas the worst performer posted a loss of 70%. Finally, as shown in Exhibit 14.2, all CEF groups went from losses in 2008 to gains in 2009: the largest swings were posted in the loan participation group where average losses in 2008 (based on market prices) were close to 44%, but average gains in 2009 were above 84%!

Shockingly, some of the worst performers among municipal CEFs in 2008 included funds from such highly respected groups as Nuveen and Pimco. (A couple of Pimco municipal CEFs actually had to suspend their dividend for a few months.) These CEFs were down close to 50% in 2008, but in 2009 posted extremely sharp gains. In fact, in 2009 several Pimco funds posted gains slightly higher than 50% based on NAV, but well above 70% based on market price.

Finally, one word of caution is in order about municipal CEFs. As I am writing this, in June 2010, yields and returns of municipal CEFs continue to be unusually high. Many municipal CEFs are continuing to benefit from an unusual dynamic that has resulted in a seemingly perfect scenario for boosting yield. As noted above, 95% of municipal CEFs are leveraged. The yield curve in the municipal bond market in 2010 continues to be unusually steep. But more importantly, approximately 57% of muni CEFs still leverage with auction rate municipal securities. Auction rate securities are long-term municipal bonds. Prior to 2008, interest rates on these securities were reset at weekly auctions at short-term rates. As a result, these auction rate securities were considered virtually equivalent to very short-term securities. But that market froze up in 2008 as auctions failed. Under the terms of the sale, issuers are obligated to pay penalty rates in the event the auction fails. The catch is that as this is being written, these penalty rates are continuing to be extremely low, well below 50 basis points annual interest. So issuers able to do so are continuing to pay the penalty rates and continuing to finance leverage at extremely advantageous rates.

For municipal CEFs, this has resulted in a moment in time when the stars line up just right. CEFs investing in municipals have been able to continue to finance leverage at a cost of less than 50 basis points annually, and therefore, to pay out extremely attractive high yields. But this has created a potentially risky situation. If short-term rates rise at some point in the future, as they are bound to do, borrowing costs to finance leverage are bound to climb, setting off a decline spiral.

Volatility of CEFs

As you can infer from the returns shown in Exhibit 14.2, even though many investors purchase CEFs primarily because of their high reported yields, the volatility of these funds means that total returns are extremely variable. Focusing on yield alone misses the big picture. As noted above, the use of leverage magnifies both gains and losses. Changes in market conditions can result in wild price swings. This is often a feast or famine kind of invest-ment. When market conditions change, the market price of CEFs can change suddenly and steeply. A 20% swing in market price during a period of a few months is not uncommon. Steeper declines occurred in 2008, within a period of a few weeks. While both 2008 and 2009 were unusual years, the swings in market price of CEFs during both of those years were not unprecedented. During sustained increases in interest rates, such as those that occurred in 1994 and 1999, many CEFs were crushed.

SUMMARY: CLOSED-END FUNDS

The sales pitch for closed-end bond funds is their higher yield compared to open-end funds or to individual bonds.

The good news is that under favorable market conditions, the funds do deliver higher yield. The cost, however, is higher volatility (due to the use of leverage) and therefore unpredictable total return. If you are a buy-and-hold type of investor, you should purchase CEFs for income only if you are pre-pared to accept considerable fluctuations in the market value of the fund. Also, you should look for funds that have high income ratios compared to their yield, and that tend to be less volatile than others in the same sector.

Note also that published yield figures may not accurately reflect the payout you will receive, since, as noted above, distributions other than interest income include capital gains (taxable at the capital gains rate) and paid-in-capital distributions (your own money being returned to you). Published yield figures supplied by quote services lump all distributions as yield. Finally, under unfavorable market conditions, dividends may be cut.

Advice on when to buy these funds can be summed up very briefly

- Never buy a fund at issue.
- Only buy if the fund is trading at a wide discount to net asset value; that would also be a time when its yield would be particularly attractive.
- One variation of this piece of advice, suggested by Thomas Herzfeld, is to track the discount pattern of a fund, and only buy it if its discount is wider than the normal discount. Sell when the discount narrows significantly.
- Make sure that you understand the payout policies of the CEF and its yield quotes.

QUESTIONS TO ASK BEFORE BUYING A CLOSED-END FUND

Am I buying at issue? If so, what is the underwriting spread?

What is the NAV of the shares?

Is the fund selling at a premium or at a discount?

What is the average discount for this fund?

Does this fund use leverage: If so, how much and what kind?

What is the quoted "yield"? the most recent "income ratio"? Does the fund have "managed payout" policies? If so, how does the payout compare to the income ratio?

What kinds of bonds are in the portfolio? What is their average maturity and credit quality?

SOURCES OF INFORMATION ON CEFS

Data on closed-end bond funds is extremely limited in the daily financial printed media.

Net asset value (NAV) data is available on a weekly basis in *The Wall Street Journal* (Mondays), in the Sunday *New York Times*, and in *Barron's*. But that information is limited to NAV, yield, and whether the fund is trading at a discount or at a premium. It gives you no perspective at all on total return over any longer time period.

Quarterly performance numbers are published in *Barron's*. These figures include historical returns (based on market price) for the quarter and year and for three-, five- and ten-year periods.

These data appear in table form only: There is no analysis of returns, and no comparative analysis of funds.

There is much better data on the Internet.

The most complete Web site is www.cefconnect.com. This was formerly named ETF Connect. This Web site is maintained by Nuveen Investments. It used to cover Exchange-Traded Funds and CEFs, but it now covers only CEFs. In addition to complete performance data, this Web site provides a fund screener. Be aware, however, that some information (for example, management fees) is not updated as often as it should be.

Another useful Web site is the one maintained by the Closed-End Fund Association: www.cefa.com. This site also provides daily NAV and market price information for all CEFs; it also has a fund screener, historical data, and the like.

Both of the preceding Web sites are free. Excellent coverage of CEFs is contained in a newsletter published by Thomas Herzfeld, *The Investor's Guide to Closed-End Funds*. The address of the newsletter is Thomas J. Herzfeld Advisors, Inc., P.O. Box 161465, Miami, FL 33116. The current subscription price is $625 annual. Herzfeld also maintains a free Web site (www.herzfeldresearch.com) that has contact phone numbers for all closed-end funds, price information, and links to numerous Web sites, as well as a free sample newsletter.

If you do not have access to the Internet, the best sources of information on any closed-end fund are the annual or semiannual reports issued by the management companies. Some of the larger issuers of closed-end municipal bond funds are Nuveen Investments, BlackRock Advisors, Pacific Investment Management Co. (PIMCO), and Eaton Vance Management.

EXCHANGE-TRADED FUNDS

Exchange-Traded Funds (ETFs) are the most recent entrants to the world of bond funds, and as I am writing this, they are "hot."

The history of this group is short. Barclays Global Investors (now BlackRock, Inc.) issued four fixed-income exchange-traded funds listed in the United States in July 2002. Although stock ETFs had been trading for a few years, these were the first bond ETFs. Three of these were intended to track Treasury indexes while the fourth tracked a corporate bond index. Initial reception was cool. But starting in 2008, fixed-income ETFs proliferated. As of this writing, there are well over 100 and more are on the way. These funds now invest in every corner of the bond market. Nonetheless, in spite of all the hoopla, at the time this is being written bond ETFs are still a fairly small corner of the bond fund universe, with about $116 billion in assets, compared to the $4.8 trillion in open-end bond funds.

Initially, bond ETFs were designed to track bond indexes. But much more complex structures have emerged, for example, leveraged ETFs and "inverse leveraged" ETFs. (These are defined below.)

Because the history of bond ETFs is so short, generalizations about these funds are a bit hazardous. In this section, I will describe the unique features of ETFs (compared with other types of bond funds). This will be ETFs 101. I will also attempt to dispel some of the misconceptions that have already grown up around these funds. Finally, I will discuss some appropriate uses for ETFs.

Basics of ETFs

Exchange-traded funds are similar to all mutual funds in that they consist of a portfolio of securities; in the case of fixed-income ETFs, a portfolio of bonds. Shares in the ETF represent an ownership interest in that portfolio.

The most unusual aspect of ETFs is the way they are originated and traded. The portfolio of ETFs consists of a basket of securities. All ETFs continuously create new shares, or redeem shares, based on investor demand.

There are two levels on which these baskets of securities trade. Institutional traders (chiefly large broker-dealers) called Authorized Participants (or APs) continuously buy and sell large baskets of securities to "create" or to redeem ETFs. Although these baskets may include hundreds of securities, the securities in ETFs (at least in the stock market) trade virtually instantaneously on electronic trading platforms. These baskets of securities are called "creation units." Only APs are authorized to trade creation units.

In turn, investors buy or sell shares of the ETFs in the secondary market and these shares trade like ordinary stocks on any of the three major stock exchanges. When investors buy shares of an ETF, they are buying a percentage amount of the basic baskets of securities, as they do when they buy shares in any fund. But the supply of ETF shares is elastic as APs create or redeem shares to meet investor demand.

ETFs are priced on three different levels. One share of an ETF has a market price, just like any stock. The market price of an ETF changes continuously throughout the day just like the price of any stock, based on demand. But the bonds in the ETF also have a market value, the Net Asset Value (NAV), which is tabulated at the end of each day. The NAV of an ETF, like that of closed-end funds, may differ from the market price of the ETF. There is also a third value, called the Indicative Optimized Portfolio Value (IOPV). The IOPV is an intra-day estimate of fund NAV: the IOPV (and not the market price) is updated every 15 seconds. The IOPV is an estimate of the changing value of NAV. It is based on the previous day's NAV plus current day changes in the level and direction of interest rates: more specifically, the spreads of bonds in the sector of the ETF versus Treasuries. Because the IOPV is an estimate, it may or may not reflect actual changes in NAV. A number of pricing services use different proprietary formulas to come up with an IOPV. Finally, bear in mind that most bond ETFs track an index. Therefore, returns of an ETF are evaluated based on how closely the returns of the ETF track its index.

APs have the opportunity to earn profits by arbitraging the price differences between the securities in the ETF and the share price of the ETF. For example, if demand for the shares of an ETF is high, the share price of the ETF may be bid up and as a result, may be higher than the value of the underlying portfolio of securities in the ETF. This gives APs the opportunity to purchase the underlying portfolio of securities, create new ETF shares, and sell the ETF shares in the secondary market at a profit. Conversely, if selling pressure is high, and the share price of the ETF is lower than that of the underlying securities, APs can purchase the ETF at a discount, redeem the ETF, and sell the underlying portfolio securities at a profit.

For an individual investor, the creation and redemption process may appear irrelevant. When you buy or sell shares in an ETF, you are buying or selling shares of a fund, as you would for any fund. And since ETFs sell like stocks, the commission paid is the customary commission you would pay to buy or to sell any stock.

What may be confusing to investors is that bond ETFs trade on a stock exchange. But the underlying bonds in the ETF portfolio are bought and sold, like almost all bonds, over the counter. And this is very much a factor in the pricing of ETFs. The liquidity and the cost of buying and selling bonds impacts the cost of "creating" bond ETFs, and as a result it affects the pricing of bond ETFs. Moreover, particularly in the less-liquid sectors of the bond market, such as municipals, junk bonds, and emerging-market bonds, trading a specific list of securities to execute a "creation" or a redemption may require hours. If there is an imbalance between buy and sell orders, or some kind of panic, then that process may take even longer. We will return to this aspect of bond ETFs when we discuss pricing and trading of bond ETFs.

The Basic Structure of Bond ETFs

The basic fixed-income ETF structure is the same as the one developed for stocks. Most ETFs track an index: their composition mirrors that of whatever index they track. Like other index funds, most bond ETFs are passively managed.

The rationale behind this structure is simple. By now, index funds have a long and successful history both in the stock market and in the bond market. Historically, both stock and bond index funds have performed well compared to actively managed funds: returns have been higher than 85% of actively managed funds, partly due to the much lower expense ratios resulting from passive management.

Bond ETFs share the same risks as any other type of bond fund or individual bond, namely, interest rate risk (tied to maturity length) and credit quality risk. But bond ETFs also have many unique characteristics. In no particular order, here are some of the basic characteristics of "plain vanilla" bond ETFs:

- Most bond ETFs track an index. In order to continue to track their index, the portfolio of bond ETFs is rebalanced once a month.
- Because of this rebalancing, bond ETFs have a constant maturity. That constant maturity is far more rigid than that of an open-end fund, where active managers adjust duration somewhat based on anticipated changes in the level of interest rates.
- Because duration is relatively constant, interest rate risk remains constant. It is highest for long term ETFs; and negligible for ETFs with short maturities.

♦ Most bond ETFs pay interest monthly. As with other bond funds, there is no date at which the entire portfolio matures. As a result, none of the yields quoted for ETFs are comparable to the yield-to-maturity quoted for individual bonds. One of the standardized yields quoted for bond ETFs is the 30-day standardized yield; that yield is comparable to the 30-day standardized SEC yield quoted for open-end bond funds.

♦ Because the portfolio of a bond ETF is rebalanced every 30 days, distributions may change somewhat every 30 days. Therefore, yield numbers published for ETFs by services such as Morningstar may not reflect the most recent distributions. More accurate quotes are those listed on provider Web sites.

♦ Expense ratios of bond ETFs are extremely low. They range between 9 and 60 basis points—lower than that of many, but not all, open-end funds. Bond ETFs comprising the most liquid bonds (for example, Treasuries) have the lowest expense ratios. Expense ratios are higher for bond ETFs in less-liquid sectors of the bond market: for example, municipals, junk bonds, and foreign bonds. Exotic ETFs such as "leveraged" ETFs (those are discussed below) have the highest expense ratios, up to 95 basis points.

♦ Commission costs are low compared to those charged by many open-end load funds since commission costs for ETFs are those of stocks. But the costs of investing in ETFs are increased (on a percentage basis) if you have a program of buying small amounts periodically, as you might for example, for a tax-sheltered account such as a 401k. Also, if you reinvest monthly dividends, depending on the broker you use, you may have to pay commissions every month. (Some brokers do not charge commissions for reinvesting monthly interest income. You need to check with your broker.)

♦ Daily listings of bond ETFs in the newspaper are extremely sketchy. Typical listings for bond ETFs look like Exhibit 14.3.

This is the basic information given for any stock. Reading from left to right, the information includes:

♦ The name of the ETF: ISharesiBoxxFd.
♦ Its ticker symbol: LQD.

TABLE 14.3

Typical Listing for a Bond ETF

ETF	Symbol	Closing Price	% Change	YTD %
iSharesiBoxxFd	LQD	107.29	0.49	3

- The price at which the ETF closed the previous day (the market price): 107.29.
- The change in price (in %) compared to the previous day: + 0.49%.
- The market return of the ETF (in %), based on market price.

Note that most newspapers list only the largest ETFs.

This information is too sketchy to provide any perspective on the ETF. See below for data that would be more useful.

Pricing of Bond ETFs: Index Drift and Liquidity

As of this writing, very few bond ETFs have been in existence for more than one or two years. Bond ETFs were much slower to develop than stock ETFs primarily because of the lack of liquidity of many sectors of the bond market.

In order to enhance the liquidity of ETFs, bond ETFs are structured around bonds that are the most liquid bonds in their corner of the bond market, and the most actively traded. This has resulted in a number of guidelines. Many bond ETFs limit holdings to bonds that are part of very large issues and that are at least investment grade. Also, many bond ETFs do not attempt to replicate the index they track. Instead, they use sampling techniques. (This is called optimization.) For example, Barclays iShares S&P National Municipal Bond Fund (MUB), currently the largest municipal-bond ETF, holds 839 bonds as of June 30, 2010, whereas its benchmark index is composed of 7,550 issues.

In the less liquid sectors of the bond market, ETFs attempt to limit holdings to the more liquid bonds in that particular sector. In the less liquid sectors of the bond market, ETFs attempt to limit holdings to the more liquid bonds in that particular sector. In the municipal market, for example, bonds included in an ETF must meet minimum par amount requirements (a minimum of $100 million must be outstanding). Risky credits such as tobacco, health care, airlines, and housing bonds, are excluded.

These requirements mean that credit quality is likely to be concentrated in the higher-quality bonds of this sector.

Theoretically, arbitrage trading on the part of Authorized Participants should keep the market price of fixed income ETFs close to the NAV of its underlying portfolio, and also close to the index tracked by the ETF. But whereas that is the case for some bond ETFs, it is not true of all bond ETFs: many trade at premiums or discounts, some occasionally, but others a good deal of the time.

There are a number of reasons why bond ETFs trade at premiums or at discounts even when the bond market is reasonably stable. Bear in mind that, whereas the shares of an ETF trade on a stock exchange, the bonds that comprise the ETF portfolio are purchased over the counter. The bid/offer spread that bonds trade at is reflected in the market price of ETFs: its impact is particularly high in the less liquid sectors of the bond market, where bid/offer spreads typically range from 150 to 200 basis points. A somewhat simplified explanation is that the AP's cost of trading bonds is incorporated into the market price of bond ETFs. But the NAV of ETFs is calculated based on the bid price (the lower price) of the bonds in the ETF. As a result, in sectors where the bid/offer spread is wide, under most market conditions, bond ETFs can be expected to trade at a premium to the NAV of the bonds in the portfolio. Also bear in mind that an index has no expenses. Therefore, expenses involved in "creating" shares, or in rebalancing the ETF portfolio, are bound to result in "performance drag" compared to the index.

But during periods of high market volatility such as prevailed both during the financial panics of 2008 and in 2009, all spreads widen. APs incur the higher costs when they buy bonds to "create" ETFs, or when they need to sell bonds out of the portfolio to redeem shares.

When the bond market is reasonably stable, actively traded fixed-income ETFs have developed what some professionals call a "liquidity layer," that is, a large number of ETF shares that trade without APs having to create or redeem "creation units." But if the market is volatile, whether due to selling pressure or to high demand, then finding bonds to "create" new ETFs or selling bonds to satisfy the needs of investors trying to sell bond ETFs may be difficult or next to impossible. Again, the most illiquid sectors of the bond market are those most affected. During the panic of 2008, when many individual bonds were simply not trading, many bond ETFs were unable to buy needed bonds, or to find buyers for bonds they needed to sell. As a result, even though bond ETFs continued to trade (and in some cases, they were one of the few bond investments that were trading), the price at which they traded reflected the volatility of their sector of the bond market. If bonds were scarce, then APs had to pay up to buy bonds; if there were no buyers, bonds had to be sold at steep markdowns. In either case, bond ETFs were unable to track their indexes.

As a result, whereas the share price of ETFs in the more-liquid sectors of the bond market tends to stay close to its index, in other sectors the price of ETFs often wanders from the index, and also from NAV. One measure that has been adopted by ETF sponsors is how many days during any given period bond ETFs trade within 50 basis points —that is, one half of 1%—of NAV. Using 50 basis points as a threshold for ETF market pricing versus NAV pricing is somewhat arbitrary, particularly for those sectors of the bond market with wide bid/offer spreads. Remember that the bid/offer spread is incorporated into the cost of "creating" shares. As a result, for very liquid sectors of the bond market, such as Treasuries, where the bid/offer spread is well under 50 basis points, ETFs can be expected to trade within 50 basis points of NAV under most market conditions. For sectors such as high yield bonds where the bid/offer spread is typically 200 basis points, ETFs can be expected to trade more than 50 basis points away from NAV much of the time.

One question I had, therefore, was how conditions of market volatility such as those that prevailed during 2008 and 2009, would impact premiums and discounts of ETFs in different sectors of the bond market. I contacted BlackRock with a list of ETFs they sponsor, asking them if they could supply this information. I was fortunate to obtain from them the data shown in Exhibit 14.4, which shows the largest premiums and discounts reached by a variety of ETFs, both in liquid and in less liquid sectors of the bond market, during both 2008 and 2009.

I was fortunate to obtain the data shown in Exhibit 14.4 from Barclays iShares. This table shows the largest premiums and discounts reached by a number of ETFs during 2008 and 2009.

Note that Exhibit 14.4 also lists the number of days each year that each listed ETF traded within 50 basis points of NAV, as well as the underlying bid/offer spread in that sector of the bond market.

I selected two types of ETFs for this table. The five listed at the top of Exhibit 14.4 (AGG, SHY, TLT, TIP, and LQD) are among the largest of all bond ETFs and also among the most actively traded. The bottom three (HYG, MUB, and EMB) are, if not the largest, among the largest ETFs in their particular sector (junk bonds, municipal bonds, and emerging-market bonds, respectively).

EXHIBIT 14.4

Premiums and Discounts of Selected ETFs during 2008 and 2009

| Fund/Benchmark | Ticker | Premium/Discount - % of NAV | | | | Days within 50 bps of NAV | | Underlying Bid-Offer Spread |
| | | 2008 | | 2009 | | | | |
		Max Prem	Max Disc	Max Prem	Max Disc	2008	2009	
iShares Barclays Aggregate Bond Fund Barclays Capital U.S. Aggregate Index	AGG	2.21	−8.86	3.65	−0.23	164	129	0.750%
iShares Barclays 1–3 Year Treasury Fund Barclays Capital 1–3 Year Treasury Index	SHY	0.29	−0.30	0.17	−0.13	252	252	0.035%
iShares Barclays 20+ Year Treasury Bond Fund Barclays Capital 20+ Year Treasury Index	TLT	1.71	−1.55	0.90	−0.82	234	231	0.200%
iShares Barclays TIPS Fund Barclays Capital U.S. Treasury Inflation Protected Series Index (Series L)	TIP	3.19	−2.65	1.77	0.04	198	196	0.400%
iShares iBoxx$ Investment Grade Corporate Bond Fund Markit iBoxx$ Liquid Investment Grade Index	LQD	4.07	−10.97	4.24	−1.08	53	43	1.500%
iShares iBoxx$ High Yield Corporate Bond Fund Markit iBoxx$ Liquid High Yield Index	HYG	12.71	−8.41	12.76	−3.23	24	19	2.000%
iShares S&P National Municipal Bond Fund S&P National Municipal Bond Index	MUB	4.23	−2.22	3.22	−1.45	136	138	1.500%
iShares JPMorgan USD Emerging Markets Bond Fund JPMorgan USD Emerging Market Bond Index	EMB	11.68	−9.88	13.49	−3.09	17	24	2.000%

Source : Black Rock iShares. Material supplied to the author and reprinted with permission.

A number of facts stand out:

◆ For both 2008 and 2009, the ETFs that remained closest to the NAV of the bonds in the portfolio for most of the year (as indicated by the number of days the ETFs traded within 50 basis points of NAV) were the two Treasury ETFs, SHY, and TLT. These ETFs also have the lowest underlying bid/offer spread.

◆ SHY, the one- to three-year Treasury ETF, traded with the lowest premiums and discounts, well under one-half of 1%.

◆ In spite of the lack of liquidity of the municipal bond market, and a substantial bid/offer spread (1.5%), premiums and discounts of MUB (currently the largest municipal bond ETF) remained well under 5% for both 2008 and 2009.

◆ The other ETFs listed—EMB (emerging-market bond ETF), HYG (junk bond ETF), LQD (investment-grade corporate bonds)—at one point or another experienced either double-digit discounts from NAV or double-digit premiums to NAV during 2008 or during 2009, or during both years. Perhaps surprisingly, the highest discount listed in Exhibit 14.4 was that posted for LQD—close to 11%—in 2008. The highest premium listed in Exhibit 14.4 was posted for EMB, in 2009.

◆ Note also that during both 2008 and 2009 both EMB and HYG traded within 50 bps of NAV fewer than 25 days for the entire year. Somewhat surprisingly, LQD, which trades investment-grade corporate bonds, also traded within 50 BPs of NAV only 53 days in 2008 and 43 days in 2009.

How closely do market returns track either the NAV of the ETFs or their index? This is illustrated in Exhibit 14.5, which shows NAV returns, market returns, and index returns for the ETFs shown in Exhibit 14.4 for both 2008 and 2009.

Exhibit 14.5 shows that market returns for the ETFs shown in Exhibit 14.4 track both NAV and index returns most closely for the ETFs that traded with the lowest discounts and premiums during 2008 and 2009.

◆ Once again, the Treasury ETFs are the closest to tracking their indices, as well as NAV returns.

TABLE 14.5

NAV, Returns, Market Returns, Index Return of
Selected ETFs for 2008 and 2009 and Since
Inception (SI)*

Ticker Symbol		NAV Returns (%)	Market Returns (%)	Index Returns (%)
AGG	2009	5.1	3.1	5.9
	2008	5.9	7.9	5.2
	SI 9/22/2003	5.1	5.2	5.4
SHY	2009	0.5	0.4	0.8
	2008	6.6	6.6	6.7
	SI 7/22/2002	3.3	3.3	3.4
TLT	2009	−21.5	−21.8	−21.4
	2008	33.8	33.9	33.7
	SI 7/22/2002	7.4	7.4	7.4
TIP	2009	11.4	9.0	11.4
	2008	−2.5	−0.6	−2.4
	SI 12/4/2003	5.5	5.5	5.6
LQD	2009	12.1	8.6	12.8
	2008	−0.3	2.3	1.0
	SI 7/22/2002	5.9	5.9	6.2
HYG	2009	40.7	28.5	44.5
	2008	−23.9	−17.1	−23.9
	SI 4/4/2007	3.1	2.8	3.9
MUB	2009	10.6	7.3	12.2
	2008	−0.9	1.1	−2.8
	SI 9/7/2007	4.9	4.9	4.9
EMB	2009	27.7	18.0	28.7
	2008	−11.8	−4.4	−11.7
	SI 12/17/2007	5.9	7.2	7.7

Source: BlackRock iShares. Reprinted with permission.
*Since Inception (SI) Returns are to June 30, 2010 these are average annualized total returns—all distributions are
assumed to be reinvested.

- ◆ Once again, the widest differences between index and NAV
  returns and market returns were posted by HYG and EMB.
  HYG actually performed better than the index in 2008,
  posting a loss of 17% compared to a loss of almost 24% for
  its index, but HYG performed well below its index in 2009,
  posting a gain of 28% compared to a gain of 44% for the index.
  (In all likelihood, the poor showing of 2009 is explained by
  the fact that demand was high for junk bonds. As a result,

APs had to pay high prices to buy the bonds, and this hurt performance.) Differences between market returns and index and NAV returns were less wide for EMB, but still significant.

To summarize, Exhibit 14.4 shows the highest premiums and the highest discounts that were posted by selected ETFs during 2008 and 2009. These were episodic: not constant. Moreover, both 2008 and 2009 were among the most volatile years in the history of the bond market. And as a result, both premiums and discounts may have been abnormally high. But because the ETFs selected for this table are large and fairly heavily traded, these discounts and premiums should be considered representative.

Both Exhibits 14.4 and 14.5 show during over short holding periods (a year or less), or during periods of high market volatility, performance of bond ETFs can be expected to track NAV and index returns only for the most liquid sectors of the bond market. Investors should be cautious about buying bond ETFs selling at a premium, particularly if the premium is high.

But note that Exhibit 14.5 also shows NAV, market and index returns for the same ETFs since inception, and that picture is remarkably different from the one that emerged for either 2008 or 2009. For the much longer periods of time included between the inception dates of the ETFs and June 30, 2010, actual differences between NAV, index, and market returns are much smaller, even for ETFs in the least liquid sectors of the bond market. But note also that differences in inception dates also impacted all returns shown in Exhibit 14.5

ADVANTAGES AND DISADVANTAGES OF BOND ETFs

As noted earlier, within the last year, bond ETFs have proliferated, and more are in the pipeline. The largest amount of assets in ETFs is in the more-liquid sectors of the bond market: Treasuries, TIPS, broad taxable indexes, and investment-grade corporates. But there are now ETFs in high-yield (junk) sectors, municipals, international, and emerging-market bonds.

The first question that arises is whether ETFs are superior investments compared with other types of bond funds.

The structure and composition of ETFs has a number of advantages. The first is transparency. Management companies of ETFs publish the bonds in their portfolio daily. They also publish detailed information about premiums and discounts compared to both NAV and index returns. As I have pointed out in Chapter 11, one of the problems with many of the older open-end bond funds is that it is difficult to know what they own, and consequently, their risk factors are not clear. ETFs disclose their portfolio daily, and also track an index. So there is no guessing. There is one exception to this. The ETFs of some management companies, for example, Vanguard, constitute a share class of open-end mutual funds tracking the same index. Those ETFs do not publish holdings daily.

A second advantage is low cost. But here, the advantage is less clear cut. While the costs of investing in ETFs tend in the aggregate to be lower than those of many open-end bond funds, particularly those with high expense ratios, accurate comparisons of costs have to be based on specific funds. Bear in mind that costs of investing in ETFs include not only the expense ratio, but also commission costs for buying the funds. Investing small sums periodically raises total costs on a percentage basis. Investing in no-load funds with low expense ratios may in the long run be cheaper than investing in ETFs that are their counterparts.

As a point of comparison, Vanguard has open-end funds and ETFs that track the same indexes. One of its screens allows investors to compare exact costs of investing in the ETF or in the open-end fund tracking the same index. Depending on the amount invested and the timing of these investments, sometimes the ETF has the advantage, but sometimes the open-end fund has the advantage.

Note also that many ETFs are passively managed. This lowers management expenses. But this is not a unique feature of ETFs. As noted in Chapter 12, there are passively managed bond index funds with low expense ratios. Also, active managers can sometimes lower risk by protecting against deteriorating credits or by changing the duration of the fund.

One possible advantage of bond ETFs, compared with other types of bond funds, is that many invest in the more-liquid and higher-quality sectors of their corner of the bond market. Yields will be lower, typically, than those of funds investing in lower-quality credits. Over time, however, these ETFs should be less volatile than many of the open-end funds investing in riskier sectors of the market.

Exotic ETFs: Warning, Danger Ahead

In many respects, ETFs were designed to meet the needs of institutional investors. Using ETFs now allows individual investors to use some of the strategies that institutions use.

Whether this is advisable is another matter.

One strategy that ETFs make possible is "shorting." Shorting a stock involves borrowing shares in hopes the price of the stock will go down. The short is successful if the shares in question do decline and can be bought back at a lower price. Shorting can be used either to speculate, or to hedge a position. Prior to the inception of ETFs, it had been difficult, or virtually impossible, to hedge a position in such sectors of the bond market as municipals. Some traders attempted to hedge by using options or futures on Treasuries, but as we saw, Treasuries do not always move in sync with other sectors of the market.

It is now possible to hedge bond fund positions, or to speculate, through the use of ETFs. Suppose, for example, that you have a large portfolio invested in municipal bonds. If you anticipate that interest rates are going to rise, instead of selling bonds out of a core portfolio of individual bonds (or bond funds), you might consider selling short one of the larger municipal bond ETFs. One advantage of that strategy is that your portfolio of bonds would continue to generate income.

But selling short always involves risks. The timing needs to be exquisite. And hedge ratios have to be accurate. I mention the possibility because ETFs make it possible. I do not advocate it, and frankly, describing exact strategies for selling short are beyond the scope of this book.

Selling short, of course, can also be used as a pure speculation; that is, twice as risky as hedging. The risk whenever anything is sold short is that the price of the stock will go up, rather than down. Potential for loss is then open-ended if the price continues to climb. And as noted many times, predicting the direction of interest rates is notoriously difficult.

Another technique made possible by ETFs is buying "on margin." Buying "on margin" means that you borrow money to finance purchases of more securities. The objective is that increases in the price of the stock that is purchased will be larger than the cost of borrowing. The risk is that if the stock declines in price, even temporarily, brokers have the right to liquidate your stock purchases. Again, this is a risky strategy.

Both shorting stocks and buying on margin are risky strategies. But a small number of ETFs that go under the moniker of "leveraged" ETFs and "inverse leveraged" ETFs are risky in and of themselves. Both of these remain a very small corner of the ETF universe. But they are worth mentioning because it appears that their risks are not clearly understood.

Leveraged ETFs (also called short ETFs)—short not in duration but short as in "shorting" strategies—are designed to deliver a performance that is some multiple of the index that they track. For example, a 2x leverage is intended to deliver twice the performance of the index, a 3x, three times the performance of the index, and so on. An inverse ETF is intended to deliver the opposite of whatever index they track. For example, if an index goes up, an inverse index is designed to go down. Inverse leveraged ETFs (also called "ultra short" funds) are designed to deliver twice the inverse or three times the inverse performance of whatever index they track.

All inverse and inverse leveraged bond ETFs use sophisticated and complex strategies involving the use of swaps, futures, and forward contracts. Both leveraged and inverse leveraged ETFs are designed to be used as hedging or speculative tools, and they are intended to be used by experienced traders.

Once again, these types of ETFs were created to meet the needs of institutions. Using these ETFs is extremely dangerous. What makes these ETFs so dangerous is that they are intended to be held for one day only—or even for less than one day. These leveraged ETFs are reset daily. When held for longer periods, their returns diverge significantly from their index. Performance is on steroids, due to the effect of compounded leverage. When they go up, returns are outsize. But when they decline, principal disappears as if in a black hole. Because they are so risky, and so difficult to use, FINRA has issued an alert concerning leveraged and inverse leveraged ETFs. The Web sites of a number of brokers have followed suit and they are listing alerts concerning the extreme risks of these funds.

How Do ETFs Compare with Closed-End Bond Funds?

How do ETFs compare with closed-end funds, with which they share some characteristics?

The main characteristic they share is that both ETFs and closed-end bond funds trade like stocks, on the major stock exchanges. But closed-end bond funds are actively managed. Most ETFs are passively managed and track an index. As a result, the expense ratio of ETFs is far lower than that of closed-end bond funds.

Both types of funds list the market price and the NAV, which is the value of the individual bonds in the portfolio. Both may trade at premiums or discounts to the NAV of the portfolio. But closed-end funds typically trade at discounts, whereas the discounts of ETFs are viewed as being an anomaly. Moreover, significant premiums or discounts to NAV may persist a long time for closed end funds. ETFs can also trade at premiums or discounts, and during periods of market illiquidity, the premiums and discounts (as shown in Exhibit 14.4) may be significant. But arbitrage on the part of APs should bring ETF prices and NAVs closer together. And as shown in Exhibit 14.5, over longer holding periods, excessive premiums or discounts both seem to disappear. Investors in closed-end bond funds view deep discounts as opportunities to capture capital gains. That may also prove to be the case with bond ETFs.

The leverage feature of closed-end funds is also totally different from that of leveraged ETFs. Closed-end bond funds use leverage to boost interest income distributed to shareholders. The leverage feature of leveraged ETFs is intended to deliver a multiple of the total return of the index tracked by the ETF. It is achieved through the use of complex derivatives. Volatility for leveraged ETFs is high and unpredictable. It is far more dangerous.

A very broad generalization is that the structure of closed-end bond funds emphasizes high yield, obtained, as described in the section on closed-end funds, through leverage. ETFs emphasize lower expenses and transparency. Closed-end bond funds sometimes offer attractive opportunities for speculation if their NAV moves to a significant discount. ETFs invested in high-quality, low-duration bonds may in the long run be better investments for core holdings for buy-and-hold, long-term investors.

What Are the Best Uses of Bond ETFs?

Many discussions of ETFs emphasize the ability of investors to quickly gain exposure to highly specialized sectors of the market. And some bond ETFs do provide individual investors with the opportunity to access sectors of the bond market that in the past would have been too difficult, or too expensive to access: for example, foreign pay bonds and foreign currencies.

But the real advantages of ETFs are low cost and transparency. Using bond ETFs should enable investors to build a low-cost bond portfolio whose risks are clear. By buying ETFs with different maturities (or durations), individual investors can build a "laddered" portfolio tailored to their own needs. The most appropriate ETFs for such a portfolio would be high-quality, relatively low-risk ETFs such as low-duration or intermediate, high-quality bond ETFs.

Some Variations Coming down the Pipe

Most of the ETFs currently on the market fit the mold we have discussed. They track an index. Some may be launched to track new indexes: For example, Invesco has announced that it will launch an ETF that will track Build America Bonds. But some ETFs will break new ground.

One example has been announced by BlackRock, which has launched six municipal ETFs that have maturity dates between 2012 and 2017. On the maturity date of the portfolio, the bonds will be redeemed and the cash distributed to shareholders. The intention behind these ETFs is that they will perform more like individual bonds. But note that as the portfolio is rebalanced (as it is, periodically, for all ETFs), the distribution yield may vary as interest rates change. And depending on the price at which you buy, the liquidation value may be somewhat higher, or somewhat lower, than the price you paid. But barring a catastrophic year like 2008, the liquidation price should be within a few percentage points of your purchase price.

No doubt, if this type of ETF, with a targeted maturity date, attracts investor interest, similar funds may be launched in other sectors of the bond market. Moreover, given the rush to launch new ETFs, no doubt, new types of ETFs will make their appearance.

SUMMARY: EXCHANGE-TRADED FUNDS

As of this writing, it looks as if fund groups are competing with one another to launch more and more ETFs. Why they are doing this is somewhat of a mystery. ETFs are low-cost investments, and presumably, for fund groups, they are low-margin products. In other words, fund groups do not make a lot of money on them.

At the moment, according to Morningstar, 85% of all the assets in ETFs are concentrated with three mutual fund groups: BlackRock, State Street, and Vanguard. Vanguard is the only one of these three fund groups that has open-end funds that are counterparts to their ETFs.

It is not clear where this competition is going. As of now, assets in ETFs (and in closed-end funds) represent only a small percentage of assets in traditional bond funds. It is possible that if ETFs are successful, they may succeed in weaning away investors from traditional open-end funds. It is also possible that fees for all types of funds will be lowered through this competition.

The jury is still out, however, on the future of ETFs. First, as noted, many bond ETFs are not tracking either the NAV of their underlying portfolio or their index. Particularly in the less-liquid sectors of the bond market, many ETFs are selling either at premiums or at discounts to NAV and to the index they track a good deal of the time.

Note also that many ETFs were introduced in 2009—a very good year for most sectors of the bond market. A number of municipal bond ETFs launched in 2008 (a spectacularly bad year for most sectors of the bond market) experienced the problems described in this section, namely, prices drifting significantly from their indexes or from the NAV of their underlying portfolio. It remains to be seen how ETFs launched in 2009 will perform in rockier times: if there is a sustained rise in interest rates, for example, or if the market seizes up in illiquid sectors of the bond market such as high-yield bonds.

Finally, while the advantages of ETFs include transparency and low cost, it remains to be seen whether their performance is superior, in the long run, to some of the low expense, no load, conservatively managed open-end bond funds they emulate.

Where to Get Information on ETFs

Some data on ETFs is to be found on most financial Web sites. Morningstar is also launching an ETF Web site, which is sure to contain useful data.

But as of this writing, the best information on ETFs is to be found on the Web sites of the management companies that offer them. Those Web sites provide detailed data on all aspects of their ETF offerings: from portfolio composition, to the index they track, to historical performance. For any bond ETF, these are the basic data you would need in order to evaluate the ETF:

- The index that is tracked
- The market return of the ETF, compared with the return of its index, and the NAV of the portfolio
- Premiums and discounts (or performance data) during periods of bond market volatility
- Number of days the ETF traded within 50 basis points of NAV
- Total assets in the portfolio
- Weighted-average maturity: the average maturity of the bonds in the portfolio based on their percentage holding in the funds, or duration
- Dividend yield: most recent 30-day SEC yield
- Amount of assets in the portfolio
- Expense ratio
- If you intend to trade the portfolio, average daily volume

QUESTIONS TO ASK BEFORE BUYING
A FIXED INCOME ETF:

What index does it track?

Is the underlying portfolio in the more-liquid or in the less-liquid sectors of the bond market? If in the less-liquid sector of the bond market, what is the underlying bid/offer spread in that sector?

Has the market return of the ETF tracked its index in past years?

Is the ETF likely to trade at a premium or at a discount to its index or to NAV?

What is the size of the assets in the portfolio? Is this an actively traded ETF?

UNIT INVESTMENT TRUSTS (UITs)

Unit investment trusts (UITs) represent a third type of bond fund. They are sold through brokers, either by brokerage firms or by banks, and on a commission basis, usually around 5%. UITs have virtually fallen off the radar screen. As of this writing, only a few remain, issued by a very few fund families, for instance, Van Kampen and Nuveen.

When you buy a UIT, you are purchasing a diversified portfolio of securities. But that portfolio is quite different from either an open-end bond fund or a closed-end bond fund. The key characteristic of a UIT is that, once constituted, its portfolio remains unmanaged. With few exceptions, no bonds are added or sold out of the portfolio. Because the portfolio remains unmanaged, its price should rise toward par as the UIT approaches maturity.

The portfolio of a UIT is typically much smaller and much less diversified than that of a bond fund, consisting of perhaps as few as 10 issues. While the portfolio is assigned a maturity date, that date is simply the date when the longest-term bond in the portfolio matures. Each of the bonds in the portfolio may actually mature at a different date, over a span of time that may last as long as 10 years. Each individual issue in the UIT is also subject to call risk. As each bond matures, or is called, the principal is returned to shareholders. Varying percentages of the entire portfolio must then be reinvested as the bonds mature or are called.

There are UITs for most sectors of the bond market: corporates, governments, and municipals—in a variety of maturities, from intermediate to long. Sponsors include Van Kampen, Claymore, and First Trust. But selling a UIT before it matures is somewhat more cumbersome than selling a mutual fund. Particularly during market downturns, UITs can be illiquid (that is, difficult and expensive to sell).

Note also that while a UIT quotes two yields, a current yield and a yield-to-maturity (YTM), the YTM must be calculated with a formula that takes into account the different maturities of the bonds in the UIT. Therefore, once again, the YTM is not comparable to the YTM quoted for individual bonds.

Brokers point to a number of features of UITs as advantages. Income is paid monthly, and since the portfolio does not change, the monthly amount is fixed. Moreover, since UITs are not actively managed, there is no annual management fee. This should theoretically result in a higher yield than for mutual funds with comparable credit ratings and maturities.

These arguments do not appear compelling. The yield advantage may be illusory or based on low credit quality. And the coupon is fixed only until the first bond matures out of the portfolio or is called. Thereafter, as various bonds mature (or are called), the monthly coupon changes. Moreover, the shareholder will have to reinvest returned principal and coupons at an unknown rate.

In addition, the portfolio is not managed. There is no protection of any kind against deteriorating credits. You are purchasing a portfolio of issues, which will not change, and not a manager.

Finally, because each UIT is unique, each portfolio must be scrutinized with some care. Since UITs are advertised on the basis of yield, some UITs play games in order to quote higher current yields. They may, for example, buy high coupon bonds which might be subject to call. Or they may buy bonds with questionable credit ratings. Municipal UITs were widely criticized after the Washington Public Power Supply System (WPPSS) default for stuffing their portfolios with bonds of the project, which ultimately defaulted. This resulted in substantial losses that were passed on directly to shareholders.

The only advantage UITs offer compared to mutual funds is that since the portfolio has a final maturity date, its price rises towards par as the various issues in the fund near maturity. This might make UITs attractive to an investor who does not have sufficient funds to buy a diversified portfolio of individual securities but who wants to know that principal is likely to be returned in full when the fund matures.

SUMMARY: UNIT INVESTMENT TRUSTS

In sum, UITs offer somewhat more diversification than individual bonds but few advantages compared with mutual funds. Because of the high initial commission, they should be considered for purchase only as long-term holdings.

Questions to Ask before Buying A UIT

What securities does the UIT hold?

What is the maturity of the portfolio?

What is the credit quality of the portfolio?

If the portfolio is quoting a relatively high yield, are many of the bonds premium bonds? How likely is it that the bonds will be called?

What is the size of the commission?

To whom could I resell the UIT if I need to sell before the UIT matures?

Do you, the seller, stand ready to buy back the UIT? At what price?

PART FOUR

Management of Bond Portfolios and Asset Allocation

Chapter 15 deals with the management of bond portfolios. It discusses a number of techniques used by professionals in the management of large bond portfolios, which individual investors can easily adapt to their own use: for example, "maturity matching" or building a portfolio "ladder". Other sections review some of the concepts introduced elsewhere in the book such as how to spot undervalued bonds.

Chapter 16 discusses asset allocation: namely, how to divide your money between different asset classes—stocks, bonds, and alternatives such as real estate—over a lifetime of investing. No topic in finance has caused more ink to flow. Many experts agree that the asset allocation decision is the most important investment decision that people make and the key to their financial future. But nonetheless, consensus opinion seems to shift based on whatever the most recent investment climate has been. Chapter 16 discusses how much of your overall portfolio you should put in bonds, in the context of the consensus wisdom and performance of the past two decades.

CHAPTER 15

Management of Bond Portfolios

This chapter discusses

- When will I need the money: "maturity matching"
- Portfolio structures: "ladders" and "barbells".
- Finding attractive buy points
- Swaps
- Managing a bond portfolio for total return

If you invest in bonds, whether by buying individual bonds, or by investing in any type of bond fund, and if you have more than one bond, then you have a portfolio of bonds. The first part of this chapter will discuss a number of strategies that can be used to maximize total returns safely. The second part of the chapter will discuss how much of your portfolio you might want to allocate to investments in bonds.

Any investment in bonds ought to start with a number of questions: What is the ultimate use of the money? Am I saving for a specific need, for example, to fund my son's college education? When will the money be used? Can I afford to lose any part of my investment? Should the money be in taxable or in tax-exempt bonds? Professionals have developed strategies that can be adapted by individual investors in the management of their own portfolios. These are discussed below.

WHEN WILL I NEED THE MONEY?

Assume that you are saving for a specific use (for example, to buy a car). If the money is needed within a fairly short amount of time, say two years or less, then your best option is to confine your choices to securities whose prices do not fluctuate. That limits you to money market funds, CDs, or short-term instruments such as T-Bills, even though, as this is being written, that means in all likelihood that you will earn literally almost nothing or well under 1% a year, annualized.

You might wonder why it is not advisable to buy longer-term bonds with higher yields and enjoy these yields until you need the money. There are two reasons. First, you cannot be certain that you will recover the entire principal when you need it because you do not know where interest rates will be when you want to sell. Also, as explained in Chapter 2, commission costs are particularly high when you want to sell bonds, particularly in the less liquid sectors of the bond market. Brokers will tell you that individual investors get killed by commissions when they sell.

"Maturity Matching," or the "Bullet Portfolio"

However, if the intended use goes out somewhat further in time, say between two and ten years, then you have a different alternative, which professionals call "maturity matching." (This is also called a "bullet" portfolio.) You would buy a security which will mature at the time principal is needed. For individual investors, typical intended uses include saving for a vacation, a car, or a child's college education; in short, any objective where you can anticipate needing a certain amount of money, and you know when the money will be needed.

Buying bonds that will mature at the time the money is needed enables you to go out further along the yield curve and therefore to buy bonds that are higher yielding than the shortest cash equivalents (assuming a normal upward-sloping yield curve). This structure also eliminates the risk that principal will have declined in value if interest rates rise prior to the time that the money is needed.

A bullet portfolio does not dictate which instruments you should choose. If, for example, the money is needed in five years, you might buy a five-year Treasury note, a five-year pre-refunded municipal bond, a five-year bank CD, or a five-year Treasury zero. If rates seem particularly attractive (that is, high), then the zero is an attractive option since it eliminates reinvestment risk.

Another alternative for longer term investors with very large port-folios would be to use what is known as a "weighted maturity" structure. The basic idea behind such a structure is that a variety of maturities are selected. But generally, you would choose a combination of maturities whose duration is close to the expected target date when you would use the money. This protects the bond portfolio against a major erosion of the value of principal. And weighting the maturities enables you to take advantage of attractive buy points in the yield curve. One possibility, for example, would be to overweight the maturity sector that corresponds to the time the money is needed. Or an investor requiring the highest pos-sible level of income might want to overweight both long-term bonds and pre-refunded shorter bonds. Variations of this strategy are discussed below.

PORTFOLIO STRUCTURES

Throughout the book, I have recommended that you stick to intermediate maturities for the greater part of your bond portfolio.

For investors who are buying bonds primarily as a source of steady income or to lower the volatility of their total investment portfolio, the intermediate sector, in the long run, has historically been an excellent choice. But depending on your objectives, there are a variety of strategies that can be used to further customize your choices.

"Ladders"

A very conservative approach to portfolio structure is called "laddering." Laddering involves dividing your money among bonds with different maturities, primarily short to short/intermediate. You might buy, for example, a one-year bond, a three-year bond, and a five-year bond. You would put approximately equal amounts of money in each bond. As each bond matures, you would replace it with a bond equal to the longest maturity in your portfolio, in this case the five-year bond.

This is how your portfolio would evolve:

◆ Initial portfolio: Beginning of year one. You buy a one-year
   bond, a three-year bond, and a five-year bond. Average-
   weighted maturity of the portfolio: three years.

◆ Year two: The one-year bond matures. You replace it with a five-year bond. But your older bonds are now one year closer to maturity. You now have a two-year bond, a four-year bond, and a five-year bond. Average-weighted maturity of the portfolio: three years.

◆ End of year three: Your three-year bond matures. You replace it with a five-year bond. You now have a two-year bond, a three-year bond, and a five-year bond. Average-weighted maturity of the portfolio: three years.

This portfolio structure was initially developed as a disciplined approach to managing large bond portfolios. Laddering has become very popular and has expanded to include ladders of bonds with somewhat longer maturities and somewhat longer average durations than those mentioned in the preceding example. If, for example, you are investing primarily for income, or for longer holding periods, then you would typically choose a ladder with a somewhat longer maturity structure. You might, for example, buy a combination of two-year, three-year, five-year, seven-year, and ten-year maturities. The average maturity of such a portfolio is about half that of the longest maturities. To remain conservative, however, the average maturity of a laddered portfolio should remain at five years or less. If, on the other hand, you are extremely risk averse and if you are mainly concerned with protecting principal against erosion, then you would structure your ladder to have a shorter average-weighted maturity such as the one described initially.

Whatever the average weighted maturity of the ladder turns out to be, the ladder structure has a number of advantages. Replacing maturing bonds regardless of the level of interest rates is similar to "dollar cost averaging" in the stock market: you are buying at different prices, and presumably, unless you are particularly unlucky, you will hit some good buy points. At the same time, laddering protects you against a variety of risks. Keeping the average-weighted maturity of your portfolio short to intermediate protects the principal value of your portfolio against interest-rate risk. So does holding your bonds until they mature since you will then be redeeming at par. Finally, if interest rates go up, you will be investing in maturing bonds at higher rates and you will thereby boost total return.

Given the significant uncertainty about the future direction of interest rates as this is being written, laddering would seem to make a great deal of sense for anyone whose bond portfolio is above $100,000.

Virtually all online broker Web sites now include software that automatically enables you to structure a ladder of bonds according to your specifications. The software calculates the average-weighted maturity and the duration of the portfolio, and lays out its cash flows.

The Barbell Portfolio

This is another variation of "maturity weighting," which is more aggressive than laddering.

A barbell portfolio derives its name from the fact that approximately half of the portfolio is in short-term bonds (under two years) and the other half is in long-term securities (20 to 30 years). This portfolio does not include any intermediate maturities. But the combination of long and short maturities produces a portfolio that has an intermediate average-weighted maturity. Income from this type of portfolio would generally be lower than you would receive if you just bought intermediate maturities.

Institutional investors go to a barbell structure primarily if they think interest rates are about to decline at the long end. If that happens, the longer term bonds appreciate in value. If they have guessed correctly, this gives them the opportunity to boost total return by selling the longer term bonds and "realizing" the capital gains. If they are wrong, at least they would have hedged their bets because the shorter maturities act as a cushion.

Of course, it is always extremely difficult to forecast interest rates. For individual investors, the barbell structure makes the most sense if you want to concentrate your bond portfolio at the long end (for higher yield). Including a chunk of securities at the short end hedges your bets. But you should be aware that this strategy can backfire. Suppose, for example, that short-term rates drop and long-term rates rise. This happens whenever the yield curve becomes steeply upward sloping, with long-term rates rising and short-term rates declining. At such times, a barbell portfolio suffers a double whammy. The principal value of the long-term securities declines. Simultaneously, yields in the short-term sector also decline.

FINDING ATTRACTIVE BUY POINTS

As we know, interest rates go up and down, and occasionally create excellent buying (or selling) opportunities. Below, I will list a number of ways of taking advantage of these opportunities.

Finding Undervalued Bonds Using Yield Spreads

Different sectors of the bond market are not always in sync. At any given period, some sectors of the bond market may be "cheap" compared with other sectors of the bond market. Sectors become cheap for a variety of reasons. A large increase in supply of one sector of the bond market (a large supply of corporate or of municipal bonds, for example) leads to a rise in yields in that sector. Also, periodically, some sectors of the bond market fall into disfavor. Again, that leads to a rise in yields in those sectors. Two examples that come to mind are the periodic collapses in the junk bond market (described in Chapter 8), as well as the steep declines that occurred in all sectors of the bond market other than Treasuries in 2008.

A tool you can use for finding undervalued bonds is the changing size of yield spreads, that is, the difference between yields in a given sector and Treasuries with comparable maturities. Whenever spreads widen significantly between Treasuries and bonds in any sector (that is, when spreads becomes larger), then bonds in that sector may represent attractive buys. The emphasis, of course, is on the term *significantly*. Yield spreads were described and illustrated in Chapter 5. Yield spreads were also discussed in connection with both high yield ("junk") bonds and municipal bonds.

Buying bonds at such a junction gives you the opportunity for two types of gains. First, when spreads widen, yields to Treasuries are higher than normal. Also, if or when spreads move back toward normal, your undervalued bonds go up in price. As described in Chapter 5, some data on spreads is now routinely published in the financial pages of *The Wall Street Journal*, the *Financial Times* and *The New York Times*. Typically, however, determining when to buy is not easy. Markets, including bond markets, tend to overshoot. A sector may appear cheap, and nonetheless keep declining in price. But if you consider yourself a "value" investor for stocks, then you may want to get into the habit of regularly checking yields in sectors of the bond market in which you invest, in order to take advantage of attractive buying opportunities when they occur.

The mother of all such opportunities, of course, occurred toward the middle of December 2008. In fact, it occurred in every sector of the bond market other than the Treasury market.

The one sector where this might have been most readily apparent to individual investors was the unusually wide spread of municipal bonds to that of Treasuries. Ordinarily, the ratio between the yield of municipal bonds to that of Treasuries changes as a result of such factors as proposed changes in the tax laws, or a surge in supply. Prior to the year 2000, any ratio above 85% (that is, yields of munis at about 85% of Treasuries on maturities 10 years or longer) was taken as an indication that for most individuals in higher tax brackets, munis were reasonably attractive compared with Treasuries. A ratio of 90% was usually regarded as a buying opportunity because any investor in a tax bracket above 15% would earn more on the muni on a net-after-tax basis. A ratio of 100% was considered dramatic. Until 2008, ratios had never remained at such a level for more than a couple of weeks.

Partly because of the downgrades of bond insurance firms in 2008, ratios of municipal bonds to Treasuries went above 100% and remained at that level until the fall of 2008. In the fall of 2008, prices of municipal bonds began spiraling downward. In December 2008, ratios of munis to Treasuries reached unprecedented levels: anywhere between 150% to 300% of Treasuries at every point along the yield curve. And even though prices of munis began going up at the beginning of 2009, it took almost a year before ratios of yields of municipals to those of Treasuries went back to levels that would have been considered "normal" prior to 2008.

The totally unprecedented ratios of December 2008 had two distinct causes. The first was the flight-to-quality buying of Treasuries, which caused those yields to plummet. On the other side, indiscriminate selling of munis by hedge funds in dire need of cash and the total disappearance of institutional buyers caused muni yields to rise out of all proportion to the risk of those securities.

If yields of munis are higher than those of Treasuries, say munis yielding 115% of Treasuries, and if the ratio subsequently returns to more usual levels, for example, munis yielding 85% of Treasuries, then, that translates into a decline in yields of munis of approximately 30%. Therefore, prices will rise by a similar amount (30%)—a dramatic possibility for capital gains in what is normally a rather sleepy sector of the bond market. At such time, so called cross-over buyers enter the market. They do so in order to capture the higher yields, but primarily because they anticipate that a return to more usual ratios will result in a steep appreciation in the price of municipal bonds. The unprecedented ratios available in December 2008 when munis were yielding 200% to 300% of Treasuries, at every point along the yield curve, resulted in dramatic gains for those astute enough to purchase municipals at that time, as munis rallied and ratios returned to more normal levels through 2009. But at the time this is being written, ratios between munis and Treasuries have returned to pre-crisis levels.

Information conveyed by yield spreads works two ways, however. While extremely wide spreads may point you toward buying opportunities, narrowing spreads can signal increasing risk. If demand increases in a particular sector, yields fall in that sector. At some point, narrowing spreads become red flags: a warning that bonds in a certain sector have become extremely expensive. Exact timing is never possible; just as stocks can remain significantly overvalued or undervalued for long periods of time, spreads of bonds can remain out of whack for long periods of time, sometimes for years. But any time you see yield spreads at record lows, you can anticipate that at some point, there will be losses.

In the junk bond market, as described in Chapter 8, spreads have become almost a contrary indicator. Before junk bonds became a household word in the 1970s and early 1980s, yield spreads between Treasuries and junk were about 400 basis points. As their popularity increased, yield spreads narrowed to about 200 basis points. The narrowing spread was a signal to alert buyers that the yield of junk bonds was no longer high enough to compensate for their high default risk. Since then, spreads have periodically widened, reaching a new record during the financial crisis of 2008—well above 2,500 basis points (25%). And of course, this was followed by an enormous rally in 2009. As I am writing this, spreads have once more narrowed significantly—not to record levels yet, however.

Even if you do not use spreads as guides for buying or selling bonds, an awareness of spreads gives you a good idea of how attractive—or how risky—any sector of the bond market may be at any given time. The key is to track the spread to Treasuries: a widening spread indicates prices are getting cheaper; a narrowing spread, that prices are rising. But then, so is risk.

Changes in the Shape of the Yield Curve

As explained in Chapter 5, the yield curve is the most basic tool for determining buy points for any particular security. Much of the time, attractive buy points for Treasuries have been in the intermediate sector, somewhere between five and ten years; and slightly longer for munis. These short to intermediate sectors have captured about 80% to 90% of the yield available on long-term bonds, but with far lower volatility.

Occasionally, however, there are anomalies. If you get into the habit of comparing yields, anomalies become readily apparent. Between 1988 and 1989, for example, the Treasury yield curve became steeply inverted. Yields on two-to five-year Treasuries climbed to above 9% for a brief period of time. The muni yield curve failed to invert as steeply.

If, during that period, you had wanted to invest at the short end, and if you had checked the yield curve both of Treasuries and of munis, with the exception of investors in the highest tax brackets, the net-after-tax yield of Treasuries would have been far higher than that of munis. This made two-to-five-year Treasuries doubly attractive: you could buy the safest instruments and realize a higher yield—an unusually attractive opportunity.

Historical Data

Allow me to quote from the first edition of this book

> If you have some basic information concerning historic rates of return, just reading the daily financial press will tell you on a relative basis which sectors appear to provide good value. For example, 30-year Treasuries have seldom yielded above 9% for very long periods (with the notable exception of 1979 to 1982, when they reached up to 15%). A yield above 9% (again for Treasuries) is seldom available for maturities of two years or above.

At the current time, yields of 9% are available only on very low quality credits, if at all. I would probably have to change the preceding statement to: if you see yields on Treasuries rising to 7% or 8%, no matter what the pundits are currently saying, buy! Note that relatively high yields on Treasury zeros are doubly attractive because those yields include reinvestment rates, and they are guaranteed if you hold to maturity. To put that in perspective, remember that the historic rate of return on stocks was about 10% until the current bull market in stocks.

SWAPS

When you swap a bond, you trade a bond for a different bond, rather than for cash proceeds. During the 1970s, swaps used to be an annual ritual for many holders of long-term bonds. These swaps were usually done for the purpose of generating a tax loss. They represented a means of recouping partially the erosion of principal that resulted from annually rising interest rates, or, as some Wall Street wags used to put it, a means of making lemonade out of lemons.

During the 1980s, most holders of long-term bonds had capital gains, rather than capital losses, and for that reason the annual rite of tax selling of bonds diminished significantly. Note also that significantly lower income tax brackets (39% for the top bracket as compared with 70% in the 1970s) reduced the value of tax losses, even when they did exist. But dismal returns in the bond market during 1994 and 1999 revived the popularity of swaps for tax losses.

If after 2010, the market were to enter a period of steadily rising interest rates, swaps may once more become important tools for managing tax liabilities. If tax rates rise for higher net worth individuals, this also would make swaps more valuable.

Note also that there are other reasons for swapping than generating tax losses. Bonds may be swapped

- ♦ To upgrade credit quality (a good time for that is when yield spreads between credit ratings narrow)
- ♦ To increase dividend income (either by extending maturities or by lowering credit quality)
- ♦ To take advantage of anticipated changes in interest rate levels (going shorter or longer along the yield curve)

Any of these swaps might be viewed at different times as improvements of the basic bond portfolio and as a means of increasing total return.

Whatever the purpose of the swap, however, there are good swaps and bad swaps. The chief difficulty in evaluating swaps is that transaction costs are not obvious. Just as when you buy individual bonds, when you swap bonds prices are quoted net and the actual markup remains hidden. (Bear in mind that there are markups on both of the bonds involved in the swap.) On a large trade, for long-term bonds, you should assume that markups will equal perhaps 2% to 3% of the value of principal, that is, $2,000 to $3,000 per $100,000.

There may also be costs to a swap in addition to the commission. To evaluate a swap, you need to compare the total par value of the bonds that are being swapped, the annual coupon interest income, the credit quality of the issues involved, and the maturity of the bonds. Suppose, for example, that you own a $50,000 par value municipal bond, rated AAA, with a 15-year maturity and a 5% coupon. You receive annual dividend income of $2,500. Further suppose that you are offered a swap for this bond. Costs of the swap would include any of the following:

- ♦ You are offered a bond with a lower credit rating (for example, the swap you are offered is a bond rated A+).

- Interest income declines by $300 a year.
- The par value of the potential swap is lower than the par value of the bond you own (say, $47,000 compared with $50,000).
- You are offered a swap which lengthens maturity to 20 years, compared with 15 years for the bond you are swapping.

Any of these represents a cost. To evaluate whether or not to do the swap, you need to compare all of the cash flows of the two bonds; their maturity; and their credit quality.

Another wrinkle to consider when doing a swap is tax considerations. Swaps for generating tax losses are disallowed if they run afoul of the "wash sale" rule. The basic rule is that you cannot buy back the same security that you sell for a tax loss for at least 30 days. But this is a barebones formulation of the wash sale rule. To be certain, consult a tax accountant because wash sale rules can be complex.

Swaps need not be limited to individual bonds; you can also swap bond funds to generate tax losses. The costs of swapping bond funds are easier to determine, particularly if you are using no-load bond funds. You can swap two funds that are similar (for example, sell an intermediate fund, swap into a long-term bond fund, or vice-versa) without significantly altering your position. But because the two funds are not the same, you have not run afoul of the wash sale rule.

If you want to swap bond funds, however, you need to be aware of some additional wrinkles. Because bond funds generate monthly interest income, that can extend the wash sale rule to 60 (not 30) days. Note also that mutual fund groups may restrict the number of annual trades they allow. It may be worth it to you, however, to swap between fund groups if that generates significant tax savings.

MANAGING A BOND PORTFOLIO FOR TOTAL RETURN

As was explained in the sections on bond yields and total return, managing for total return involves taking into account all aspects of a bond's total return, namely, transaction costs, capital gains (or losses), and reinvestment rates. This implies a strategy that minimizes transaction costs, maximizes reinvestment rates, and preserves capital.

The following is a summary of some guidelines that will maximize total return:

- To minimize transaction costs, comparison shop. Buy Treasuries at auction. Buy munis at issue when you can.
- Buy maturities and securities with low markups; that means intermediate maturities and high quality credits. Become an informed investor by checking pricing data on FINRA.org/marketdata, Investinginbonds.com, as appropriate.
- Buy and hold rather than trade. Commission costs are particularly high when you sell.
- As a corollary, if you are investing new money in bond funds, stick to no-loads, with low expense ratios, and no 12b–1 plans. ETFs may also provide excellent choices for investing in funds with low expense ratios and minimal commissions.
- If you are investing in securities other than Treasuries, always check the yield against Treasuries of comparable maturities, and only purchase if the spread to Treasuries is high enough to warrant the additional risk.
- Some securities are bought most economically and efficiently through funds, for example, mortgage-backed bonds, junk bonds, and international bonds.
- If you are buying individual bonds, the longer you extend maturities, the higher the credit quality you should require.
- If you are investing large sums, don't buy smaller lots. It is preferable to buy lots that are at least $25,000. Buying too many small lots raises transaction costs, both when you buy and particularly if you resell.
- If you are investing for the long run, for example, in a tax-deferred account saving for retirement, reinvestment rates are particularly important. This is because over long holding periods, compounding, through interest-on-interest, constitutes the largest part of total return. Boosting reinvestment rates results in higher compounded interest income. To reinvest at higher rates, consider sweeping reinvested interest income into higher-yielding bond funds (for example, intermediate bond funds) rather than into money market funds.
- If you are risk-averse, for most of your bond portfolio, two-to-five-year Treasuries and five-to-ten-year munis will provide the best combination of risk and return.

What Bonds Should I Buy?

Elsewhere in the book, specific uses were suggested for fixed-income instruments as they were analyzed. Obviously, choices will change as interest rate levels change, and as new products come on the market. But Exhibit 15.1 pulls together and summarizes appropriate representative choices for various objectives.

EXHIBIT 15.1

What Should I Invest In?

Cash Equivalents Money market funds (taxable) Money market funds (tax-exempt) T-Bills CDs	*Short-term Uses (1–5 Years)* T-Notes T-Zeros Pre-refunded Munis Munis up to 5 years

Long-Term Uses (>5 Years)
   (For taxable income)
T-bonds intermediate or long munis
	Long-Term Uses (>5 Years)
	   (Tax-deferred accounts)
	Taxable zeros
	Build America Bonds (BABs) or funds
	Intermediate Investment Grade Funds or ETFs
	Long-term bonds: Federal agencies or high-quality corporates
	Long-term or taxable bond funds

High Cash Flow (Current Income) Premium munis GNMA Funds Closed-end bond funds (bought at a discount)	
To Set Up a Retirement "Annuity" I (Savings) bonds zeros—maturing in successive years	*For Call Protection (or to Lock in Yields)* Deep discounts zeros
To Make Interest Rate Bets Zeros	*For Protection Against Inflation* Inflation-indexed Treasuries (TIPS) or I (savings) bonds
For Capital Appreciation (Speculative) Junk bonds (and bond funds) Emerging markets bonds (and bond funds)	*To Fund a Child's College Education* I and EE (savings) bonds Muni zeros
	To Hedge Against a Falling Dollar International bonds (or bond funds) Currency ETFs

CHAPTER 16

Portfolio Allocation

This chapter discusses

◆ Asset allocation
◆ The case for bonds revisited
◆ The current environment and the bond market
◆ What percentage of your portfolio should you keep in bonds?
◆ Conclusion

PORTFOLIO ALLOCATION

This is the third edition of this book. Each of the prior two editions appeared at a time when attitudes toward both stocks and bonds were very different from the present.

The first edition was published in 1990. At that time, the great bull market in stocks that began in 1982 was still young. But the decade of the 1980s had been a turbulent one for stocks partly due to the stock market crash of 1987. That decade was equally turbulent for bonds. At the beginning of the 1980s, interest rates on the 10-year Treasury were still rising, until they reached a peak of almost 16% in 1982. That rise devastated bond market returns up until that date. But in 1982, a gradual decline in rates began. At the end of the 1980s, bond market returns were stellar (returns on long-term government debt averaged close to 13% for the entire decade, according to Ibbotson Associates). These high returns were due to the very high interest rates of that decade, and to the decline in rates which added a chunk of capital gains to interest income.

The second edition of this book was written in 1999. Some of you may remember 1999 as a year of miserable returns in the bond market. Interest rates climbed relentlessly for the entire year. As a result, all sectors of the bond market experienced significant losses; and to add insult to injury, 1999 was a banner year in the stock market. In fact, 1999 was the year that the Dow first crossed the 10,000 mark. Stocks were in the seventeenth year of an enormous bull market run. Average annual returns had reached 18% to 20% each year since the great bull market began in 1982. The stock market crash of 1987 was viewed in retrospect as the last great buying opportunity. Pundits were proclaiming the dawn of a new era. In fact, consensus wisdom was that individual investors ought to put 100% of their portfolios in stocks. The bond market was regarded as a place for dead money.

Fast forward to 2009. The past decade has seen two devastating bear markets in stocks: the first in 2000, and the second in 2008—each one with losses that at their peak reached around 50% of broad indices such as the S&P 500 or the Dow Jones Industrial Average.. Certain indices fared worse (for example, the NASDAQ reached a peak of 5,400 in 2000; its most recent high in 2010 was around 2,500). In spite of the enormous rally that took place in stocks in 2009, for the 10 years between December 31, 1999, and December 31, 2009, an index based on the S&P 500 was actually negative (–2.72% average annual return) for that entire decade. For the same decade, the bond market has generated significantly higher returns than the stock market based on almost any benchmark you might choose. For example, an index based on the Barclays capital U.S. aggregate index (tracked, as noted in Chapter 12, by a number of bond index funds) has generated average annual returns of 6.33%. (Cumulative returns make the contrast even more stark: the cumulative return of the Barclays U.S. aggregate bond is 87.59%, that of the S&P 500 is a loss of 24.1%.)

As this is being written, attitudes toward stocks and bonds have made a 360-degree turn compared to 10 years earlier. For the past year or so, more money has been going into bond funds than into stock funds, and by unprecedented margins—virtually 10 times as much money is going into bond funds as into stock funds. (No, that is not a misprint.) Moreover, this flood of money going into bond funds has occurred at the same time as a very significant rally in the stock market.

Clearly, the pendulum has swung dramatically in favor of the bond market. Should it have?

As usual, the future remains cloudy. Financial history shows only that returns vary significantly from decade to decade. In fact, if the past three decades have demonstrated anything it is that predictions based on current consensus wisdom, or immediate past performance, are hazardous, as a wag is reputed to have said, particularly for the future.

Could returns in the bond market continue to exceed those of the stock market? The simple answer is: it could happen. But the more important answer is that no one knows. And the corollary to that is that the previous decade has shown how dangerous it is to base investment decisions on anyone's crystal ball.

ASSET ALLOCATION

One pillar of investing wisdom is that asset allocation (that is, what percentage of your portfolio to invest among different asset classes such as stocks, bonds, etc.) in large part determines investment returns. To what extent should the asset allocation decision change as markets gyrate?

Framing the question as I just did almost makes the answer obvious. The first edition of this book described a very simple plan for asset allocation: 60% stocks (mainly index funds) and 40% bonds (mainly Treasuries, two to five years). For older investors, or more risk-averse investors, my suggestion was to reverse ratios: put 60% in bonds and 40% in stock index funds. The rationale for that allocation could not have been simpler. On the bond side, two- to five-year Treasuries have zero credit risk, and only modest interest-rate risk. And if purchased through TreasuryDirect, this is a zero-cost portfolio. On the stock side, broad-based index funds were even then performing better than 80% to 85% of actively managed equity funds. (For more affluent investors, my suggestion was that intermediate high quality munis could be substituted for some of the Treasury portfolio with a modest increase in risk.)

I saw no reason to change that allocation in 1999. Even though bonds were definitely out of favor when I revised this book in 1999, I disagreed with the new-era pundits. I felt that an all stock portfolio was too unpredictable and that bonds continued to have a place in the portfolios of most investors. The basic issue, as I saw it, was summed up in the following sentence (and this is a quote from the prior edition):

> The issue is simply this: how much are you willing to bet on the belief that all of past financial history no longer applies? More importantly, if the new era pundits are wrong, how would the volatility of stock market returns affect your standard of living?

The relevant question as this is being written is once again whether the devastating stock market declines of 2001 and 2008 require a change in asset allocation strategies.

As an aftermath to the devastating declines of 2008, new attitudes toward asset allocation are appearing, along with new buzzwords. Among some financial advisers, emphasis has switched from aggressive stock strategies to preservation of capital. A parallel concern is the search for "absolute return" strategies. These are strategies designed to produce positive returns no matter what the markets are doing. Managers pursuing such a strategy will tell you that beating a benchmark is a meaningless goal: if the market declines by 50%, will you be happy because your assets declined by only 30%? The goal of absolute return strategies is first of all to preserve capital; but in second place, to generate positive returns in all investment environments.

Unfortunately, many of these absolute return strategies are based on the use of elaborate quantitative models, with names like "market neutral" or "long short." I claim no expertise in any of these, but frankly, I am suspicious of so-called sophisticated strategies. Ask yourself how these "sophisticated" strategies would have performed throughout the decade. On the other hand, at the very least, the bond component of the asset allocation model suggested above would have dramatically mitigated the stock market declines of the decade between 1999 and 2009.

THE CASE FOR BONDS REVISITED

Clearly, the flood of money going into bonds in 2009 and 2010 has reflected the search for a safe harbor. Given the given the extreme volatility of the stock market between 2000 and 2010, and the new emphasis on preservation of capital, the case for bonds seems almost obvious. Nonetheless, it needs to be placed in context.

The general case for bonds has not changed. First of all, bonds provide a steady income stream. Dividend yields on stocks remain exceptionally low by historical standards: somewhere between 1.5% and 2%.

Second, bonds, and the cash flows they generate enable you to get through periods of subpar returns in the stock market. If you have a portfolio predominantly invested in equities, and if you need cash during a period of poor stock market returns, you have no other recourse than to sell stocks at a loss. Even worse, if you have to sell stocks during or right after a stock market crash such as the one that occurred in 2008, your portfolio will be devastated.

More importantly, the returns of bonds and stocks are not correlated. There have been long stretches in the United States (the 1930s, for example) when bonds had higher returns than stocks. Think of a portfolio of umbrellas and straw hats. Each has a season, but they are different seasons. A more recent and more striking example is the decade between 2000 and 2009, when, as noted above, returns on bonds exceeded those of stocks. This historical evidence demonstrates that even though total returns in both the stock and the bond markets are unpredictable, investing in bonds as well as in stocks lowers the volatility and the total risk of a portfolio of financial assets.

THE CURRENT ENVIRONMENT AND THE BOND MARKET

That said, it seems unwise to overstate the case in favor of bonds.

First, as has been abundantly documented in this book, for investors seeking safety in the bond market it is critical to bear in mind that all sectors of the bond market are not equally safe. The devastating losses that hit most sectors of the bond market in 2008 are a powerful reminder that few corners of the bond market are truly safe. By now, it should be clear what the least risky sectors are: cash equivalents such as T-Bills and money market funds, very short Treasuries, and very short high-quality municipal bonds. For somewhat higher income, but still low risk, you can invest in short to intermediate Treasuries (no longer than seven years) or very high-quality bonds or bond funds with short to intermediate maturities (maturities under seven or eight years, or durations under four years).

You can, of course, find higher yielding bond investments. But then you need to remember that risk rises along with yield. Longer maturities of even the highest quality bonds such as Treasuries are subject to interest rate risk. As an example, the total return of the ishares Barclays 20+ Treasury Bond Fund (TLT), a good proxy for the total return of long-term Treasuries, was a loss of 21.5% for 2009. And lower quality credits are subject to a variety of risks described throughout the book. Crashes of bonds such as "junk" bonds or "emerging market" bonds or even "sovereign" debt periodically devastate portfolios invested in these sectors.

Moreover, as this is being written, returns in the safest corners of the fixed-income market are at record lows: 0 to 25 basis points for Fed Funds and the discount rate, six-month T-Bills at less than 25 basis points, and even the two-year Treasury note at less than 1%. Furthermore, these rates appear unlikely to rise significantly from current levels for the near term. (Bear in mind that the very high returns experienced on bond funds in 2009 were due primarily to huge gains in NAV as longer-term bonds or riskier credits reversed the catastrophic declines of 2008.)

There is every likelihood that the Federal Reserve will raise short-term rates, both on Fed Funds and on the discount rate, sometime within one or two years. At that point, other relatively short-term rates (one year, two year, perhaps five years) will also rise. This will be good news for investors in T-Bills, money market funds, and short-term certificates of deposit, but there is no certainty longer-term rates will also rise. As noted elsewhere in the book, between 2004 and 2006 the Federal Reserve raised short-term rates seven different times, but long-term rates actually declined. Moreover, a rise in long-term rates, if it were to occur, would mean declines in outstanding long-term bonds and bond funds—and consequently, mediocre to poor returns for investments in long-term bonds or bond funds.

In short, investors in the safest corners of the bond market are in a very low return environment, potentially for a few years. The outlook for riskier bonds (either weaker credits or longer-term bonds) is highly uncertain. The economy will determine both the direction of interest rates and the total return of bonds with weaker credit.

Some pundits are arguing that this will "force" investors to invest in riskier, but potentially higher return, sectors of both the stock and bond markets. But if the past 10 years have shown anything, it is that higher risk does not necessarily translate into higher returns. For the last 10 years, higher risk has often translated into higher losses.

So what is a poor investor to do?

Again, there are no cookie cutter answers. If you are retired, or close to retirement, then capital preservation becomes paramount. Even though my suggestions, to stick to high quality, short to intermediate bonds and bond funds, will result in low but safe returns, I see no alternative.

For younger investors who need to invest for growth, then the answers are different. First, bear in mind that nothing lasts forever. But the other lesson of the past 10 years is that one of the primary goals of investing should, first of all, be a variation of the Hippocratic oath: First, do no harm. Capital preservation is always paramount. In the world of investing, that means that the first rule of investing is not to suffer devastating losses. (The second rule of investing is not to forget the first.)

Capital preservation means two things. It means, first of all, avoiding significant losses. As was pointed out in Chapter 3, it takes a 100% gain to recover from a 50% loss. If you try to work through the consequences of such a loss, what that means is that if you earn an average of 10% a year, it takes 10 years of 10% returns to recover from a 50% loss. And at the end of the 10 years, you have not increased your net worth.

You are simply back where you started. But on the other hand, if you avoid significant losses, compounding will do the rest: please revisit Chapter 4 if that does not make sense.

Another key to capital preservation is avoiding extreme volatility. Volatility is two sided. No one complains about volatility when assets are going up. But downside volatility is painful and frightening. Many investors overestimate their tolerance for losses. It is all too common for investors to panic and sell out after significant losses only to buy back after the market has turned around. This is a recipe for selling low and buying high—in other words, it is a recipe for investment failure. But flow-of-funds analysis of money going in and out of mutual funds show that this is typical investor behavior.

Furthermore, even though tolerance for losses is usually discussed as a psychological trait, it has a more down-to-earth meaning. If you are on a tight budget, losses can mean you can't afford to pay your mortgage or buy groceries.

To sum up, despite the low returns currently available in the safest sectors of the bond market, if you cannot afford to lose any money, then you should continue to invest in extremely safe sectors of the bond market: perhaps laddering two-, five-, and ten-year Treasuries to increase yield a bit; or among munis, investing in high quality credits no more than 10 years in length; or short to intermediate high-quality bond funds. The argument that investors must invest in riskier bonds because returns are too low in safe bonds does not make sense from the point of view of capital preservation.

What Percentage of Your Portfolio Should You Keep in Bonds?

Nevertheless, emphasis on capital preservation does not eliminate the need for growth for most investors. How much of your portfolio should you keep in bonds? Again, this question does not have a one-size-fits-all answer. Rather, the answer to that question varies with your age, the size of your portfolio, and your tolerance for risk.

For most investors, a properly selected bond portfolio can constitute a core portfolio of safe assets. But particularly for younger investors, a more up-to-date version of the portfolio sketched above continues to makes sense: 40% in bonds, and the remainder in assets such as stocks or alternative investments for growth.

In earlier editions of this book, I suggested that the growth portion of the portfolio should be in broadly diversified stock index funds. Exchange-traded funds (ETFs) have expanded that choice enormously. ETFs now provide an extremely broad array of index funds not only for the U.S. market, but also for international markets, including not only stocks, but also commodities, foreign currencies, real estate, and many kinds of derivatives. It has become simple to invest in many types of assets that used to be too arcane, too obscure, and too expensive to be accessed by individual investors. In the two prior editions of this book, I limited suggestions about growth assets to stocks, and specifically to index funds. These suggestions may now seem somewhat timid and obsolete. And clearly, for investors who have both the time and the interest to research alternatives, it makes sense to include some of these newer possibilities as part of their growth portfolio.

But I would urge investors to resist the temptation to put together a scattershot portfolio of assets that you don't understand. Take the trouble to understand the products. If you have limited time, or if you are not interested in spending a lot of time on finances, then stick to products that are straightforward and that you do understand. And bear in mind that there is a huge difference in risk between broadly diversified index funds and many ETFs which track extremely narrow and specialized benchmarks.

I do not have the expertise to evaluate the incredible variety of choices available at the current time—nor would I attempt to. But in my own life, I have made it a rule to invest only in assets that are uncomplicated and whose risks are fairly straightforward. And that rule has served me well. I continue to believe that the most important question to ask before making any significant investment decision is not, "How much do I think I can earn from this particular investment?" but rather, "What happens if I am wrong?" and, "How would a loss affect my standard of living?"

Does that mean that you are condemned to low returns? This type of investing will not lead to world-beating returns. Over time, however, it should result in a solid nest egg. The fabled investor, Warren Buffett, is reputed to have advocated never following strategies that you cannot explain on the back of an envelope. I would follow that advice.

For older investors, or retirees, the situation is more difficult. For high net-worth retirees, an all-bond portfolio, primarily invested in Treasuries and high-quality municipals, may actually provide both adequate income and capital preservation. But for retirees who cannot afford a loss, investing in the safest corners of the bond market may also be the best strategy.

In the current low-return bond environment, less affluent retirees on fixed incomes are in a difficult place. Investing in the safer sectors of the bond market may not generate sufficient income. Nevertheless, the less you can afford to lose, the more conservative you need to be in your choice of investments in either the stock or the bond market.

CONCLUSION

I began thinking about revisions for the third edition of this book in the spring of 2009. This was still very close to the financial crisis that began in September 2008. During the financial crisis all sectors of the bond market, other than Treasuries, had suffered losses, many of them devastating. Frankly, I thought the bond market had changed forever. I thought I would be writing about a totally changed bond market.

I was proved wrong during 2009. Virtually all sectors of the bond market that suffered significant losses recovered. Particularly surprising to me were the record gains in riskier sectors of the bond market, particularly high yield debt. But recoveries were also significant in investment-grade corporate bonds and municipals.

But still, the scars, or the shadow, of the financial panic of 2008 continue to overhang the bond market. The financial panic is the reason that interest rates on short Treasury debt remain at record low levels: less than 1% on the two-year Treasury, and somewhere between 10 basis points and 25 basis points (one-fourth of 1%) for Treasury bills that mature in three months or less. The financial panic also manifests itself in the recurrent bouts of flight-to-quality buying of Treasuries. Indeed, one might say that the financial panic will not be truly over until and unless Treasury rates, at least at the short end, rise above 1% and stay there.

Other significant issues remain that will continue to affect the level and the direction of interest rates. In the United States those issues include the seemingly intractable problems of Fannie Mae and Freddie Mac, still under "conservatorship" by the U.S. government, and what will happen to all interest rates when and if the Federal Reserve sells off the over $1 trillion of "toxic" debt purchased from banks and other financial institutions.

Moreover, the recession induced by the financial panic has also resulted in extremely strained finances of states and other municipal issuers of debt, which are certain to be much in the news in the near future. And as this is being written, debt problems of sovereign governments (Greece, Spain, Italy, and possibly even Great Britain) are the stories dominating the news of both the debt and the stock markets in the United States and abroad. This is almost a repeat of the start of the financial panic of 2008: looming potential defaults threaten the banking system of a number of countries.

To sum up, there is no shortage of problems in both the stock and the bond markets, and the legacy of the financial panic is still with us, as is the recession that started at that time. Nonetheless, it bears repeating that the safer sectors of the bond market came through the panic and its aftermath in good shape.

This is the third time I am writing a conclusion to this book. One common thread has run through all three conclusions: each preceding period saw significant volatility. And each time, the crystal ball was extremely cloudy. At the moment, while it seems relatively certain that interest rates at the very short end will rise within one or two years, the future level of interest rates for longer maturities is very much in doubt. Interest rates could rise, or they could remain relatively close to current levels for many years, as they have in Japan, for example.

One thing is certain. For the last two decades, interest rate levels have been changing more within a few months than they did within a period of several years prior to 1979. If someone were to ask me what the bond market will do, my answer would be to paraphrase a famous statement about the stock market: it will fluctuate. Because of the inherent unpredictability of interest rates, if you are investing in bonds primarily for safe and predictable income, I continue to believe that the best course is to stay away from both the longest and the shortest instruments, and to stick to relatively straightforward high-quality securities.

Whatever happens, my hope is that the information contained in this book will help you to put together a portfolio of bonds that meets both your financial objectives and your tolerance for risk.

So once again, many happy returns.

Teaneck, New Jersey
August 2010

INDEX

ABOUT THE AUTHOR

Annette Thau, Ph.D., is a former municipal bond analyst for the Chase Manhattan Bank and a visiting scholar at the Columbia University Graduate School of Business. She has written over 20 articles about the bond market for the *AAII Journal* and lectured to groups nationwide. In November 2009, she was a featured speaker at the national meeting of the American Association of Individual Investors.

Annette Thau earned a Ph.D. (in French literature) from Columbia University and taught French at the college level for several years. Her first book was a study of the poetry of Max Jacob, a friend and collaborator of Picasso and Apollinaire. She was elected to Phi Beta Kappa and she has received numerous awards including a Woodrow Wilson Fellowship, a National Endowment for the Humanities Fellowship, and University Fellowships from Columbia University.

Annette Thau wrote *The Bond Book* in order to fill a need for a book that would explain bonds and the bond market in clear language that could be understood by any individual investor. Sales of prior editions suggest that it met that need. This third edition was written in order to bring *The Bond Book* up to date.